European Merger Control

Badia Fiesolana – Firenze

European University Institute

1982

Walter de Gruyter · Berlin · New York

European Merger Control

Legal and Economic Analyses
on Multinational Enterprises
Volume I

Edited by
Klaus J. Hopt

1982

Walter de Gruyter · Berlin · New York

Library of Congress Cataloging in Publication Data

Main entry under title:
Legal and economic analyses on multinational enterprises.
At head of title: European University Institute.
Vol. 2, English and French, with summaries for each item in the other language, has also parallel title: Analyses légales et économiques sur les entreprises multinationales.
Includes indexes.
Contents: v. l. European merger control --
v. 2. Groups of companies in European laws.
1. International business enterprises -- Law and legislation -- Europe -- Addresses, essays, lectures.
2. Antitrust law -- Europe -- Addresses, essays, lectures.
3. International business enterprises -- Europe -- Addresses, essays, lectures. I. Hopt, Klaus J., 1940-. II. European University Institute. III. Title: Analyses légales et économiques sur les entreprises multinationales.
Law
ISBN 3-11-008703-0 (v. 1)   346.4'07   81-19615
ISBN 3-11-008704-9 (v. 2)   344.067   AACR2

CIP-Kurztitelaufnahme der Deutschen Bibliothek

Legal and economic analyses on multinational enterprises /
ed. by Klaus J. Hopt. [Europ. Univ. Inst.]. – Berlin ; New York :
de Gruyter
   Teilw. mit Parallelt.: Analyses légales et économiques sur les
   entreprises multinationales

NE: Hopt, Klaus J. [Hrsg.]; Istituto Universitario e Europeo
<Firenze>; PT

Vol. 1. → European merger control

European merger control / ed. by Klaus J. Hopt. [Europ.
Univ. Inst.]. – Berlin ; New York : de Gruyter, 1982.
   (Legal and economic analyses on multinational enterprises ;
   Vol. 1)
   ISBN 3-11-008703-0

NE: Hopt, Klaus J. [Hrsg.]; Istituto Universitario e Europeo
<Firenze>

Dust Cover Design: Rudolf Hübler, Berlin. – Printing: Georg Wagner, Nördlingen. – Binding: Verlagsbuchbinderei Dieter Mikolai, Berlin.
Printed in Germany

Foreword

The emerging law of multinational enterprises has been one of the major concerns in international business law over the last two decades. The phenomenon of the multinational enterprise is of course much older. Its origins can be traced to the big merchant companies of the 17th century or even to the merchant banks of the Italian Renaissance and of Southern Germany, such as the Fugger whose markets extended all over Europe and whose commercial interests reached beyond Europe to the New World. Yet, despite this long tradition, multinational enterprises in their modern form and especially with their present size and economic power are mainly a phenomenon of the period after 1950. The political attention given to multinational enterprises in Europe and the specific problems created by them both for home countries and host countries are highlighted by the catch phrase "le défi américain" which was coined by Servan-Schreiber in 1967. In the meantime, the United Nations, ECOSOC, UNCTAD, ILO, OECD, the Commission of the European Communities, the European Parliament and the Council of Europe, as well as most national states, for example France, Great Britain, Germany and the U.S.A., have tried to cope with these problems by countless hearings, reports and resolutions. Since March 1975 a special United Nations Commission on Transnational Corporations has been active. The Commission, which was created by ECOSOC, has established a Centre on Transnational Corporations in New York and is playing an important role in the preparation of the United Nations' Code on Transnational Corporations. In Europe, the OECD has succeeded in codifying and implementing guidelines for multinational enterprises and for home countries and host countries. These guidelines have just been revised in 1979. They have had a net impact on the behaviour of multinational enterprises, at least in specific cases, even though technically speaking they lack the binding force of law. The EEC on the other hand seems to rely more on legal instruments and on the harmonization of the laws of its member States. The harmonization of European company laws is a good example not only of the difficulties of any harmonization process which needs much patience, but also of the steadiness of these activities of the Commission of the European Communities and of their final results.

In parallel to these political developments the literature on multinational enterprises has grown at a breathtaking speed. Law and economics have been two of the more important sectors of this scientific development. The sheer number of books and articles in the field is such as to fill multi-volume bibliographies. The work of collection and enumeration surpasses the forces of the traditional one-man researcher in the humanities and has been taken over by such institutions as the OECD, the Centre on Transnational Corporations in New York, and specialized centers affiliated to business itself. The legal problems involved have long since gone beyond the traditional conflict of laws problems, such as the question of recognition of a foreign enterprise or the intricate problems of the applicable law. The elbow-room which the multinational enterprises enjoy, due to their activities in various countries with different legal and economic systems, is such as to affect a great number of areas of the law, for example antitrust law, corporate law, banking law, labour law, tax law, commercial law, currency law etc. While the multinational enterprises insist on being treated like national enterprises and on not being discriminated against by specific laws and regulations, the national states, both home states and host states, fear that multinational enterprises can evade the national laws more or less easily, since the force of the law ends at the state's frontier while the very essence of the multinational enterprises is their cross-frontier activities and their transnational organization.

After the many efforts of politics, law and economics at the national and the international level, it seems time to sum up the experience to date, and on this basis to concentrate on some more specific problems in the field. This was done by the participants in a *Colloquium on "Multinational Corporations in European Corporate and Antitrust Laws"* which I organized as Chairman of the Law Department at the European University Institute in *Florence,* Italy, from *28-31 May 1980.* Two problem areas in particular have attracted growing theoretical and practical interest in Europe, both of the nation states and the international organizations, as well as of the multinational enterprises themselves: the treatment of the multinational enterprise in antitrust law and, specifically, in the different merger control systems; and the emerging European laws on enterprise groups.

The acute problems involved in the first area – *European merger control* – stem from a basic conflict of interests. Modern business, and especially the multinational enterprises, want and need elbow-room for expansion and mergers. On the other hand, since the 1960's the naïve belief in the superiority of big business has faded away. Today in more and more European countries the public interest is conceived differently. In many cases, it is argued, economic performance may be achieved as well or even better by smaller or medium-sized enterprises, and efficient markets may be impaired by too much economic concentration and unreasonable enterprise mergers. One of the most far-reaching merger control systems in Europe is the *German* one, even though it does not rival the strictness of the merger control practised in the United States. *Great Britain* has also long since established its particular merger control system and continues improving and strengthening it. *France* introduced formal merger control in 1977, but there were many indirect ways of control long before. Other countries have not yet followed this trend – the *Dutch* Rules relating to mergers are not antitrust-oriented – but nevertheless in several of them economic concentration and its dangers are widely discussed, as for example in *Switzerland.* On the *European Economic Community* level, up to now the only general merger control measure is that which exists under Article 86 of the EEC Treaty. While this control has become famous through the European Court of Justice's *Continental Can* case, it is a mere abuse control and it is hardly able to cope with the problem of economic and enterprise concentration in a more general and systematic way, with a long term perspective of the European markets. A proposal for a Council Regulation on the control of concentrations between undertakings was made by the Commission in 1973. But even though there is the example of a full-fledged European merger control scheme under the European Coal and Steel Treaty, the member States are still debating on the proposal of the Commission. Meanwhile the Commission tries to exercise a certain control under the existing law, especially whenever joint ventures are involved. The multinational enterprises which tend to be in expansive markets and to be active in expansion and mergers are especially affected by these discussions and developments.

The second major problem area concerns the law of enterprise groups: *groups of companies in European laws*. The actuality and importance of this topic is reflected in the efforts of the Commission of the *European Communities* to have EEC directives concerning group accounts and a substantive law of groups adopted. Unlike *Germany* which already in 1965 introduced legislation on groups in its Stock Corporation Act, other European countries do not yet have codified laws of groups ("Konzernrecht"). But in practice, shareholders, creditors and enterprises are everywhere faced with similar problems and important court decisions have paved the way for dealing with at least some of these problems, as the experience in *France* and in *Great Britain* shows. A unique example of coping efficiently with these problems is given by *Belgium* where the *Commission bancaire* has taken over the role of an arbitrator respected by all sides of the economic community. In other countries still, for example *Sweden*, the trade unions seem to have played an important role in the field. But there are also countries such as *Switzerland* where, despite certain discussions by lawyers and politicians, there is still a basically uninhibited trust in the majority decision and its reasonableness and fairness for all those involved: majority, minority, individual shareholders and creditors. Shareholder and creditor protection is, of course, the core of the law of enterprise groups, but the problems of enterprise groups and specifically of multinational enterprises reach well beyond the interests of shareholders and creditors. They cannot be understood without taking into consideration the role played by banks, by labour and by taxation vis-à-vis such groups.

It is true that traditionally the control of enterprise merger and the law of enterprise groups have been discussed more or less separately. There are certain academic and other reasons for this which are pointed out in some of the contributions. Yet from the viewpoint of the enterprise the strict separation does not really make sense. For it is obvious that the restrictions of merger control and the requirements of the law on the affiliation of enterprises are part of the same difficult entrepreneurial decision: how to develop a multinational corporation or group. But also in the theory of corporate and antitrust law it is more and more apparent that both problem areas overlap and influence each other, as shown for example by the concepts of "enterprise" and of "merger" in both laws, or by the relevance of a relationship of control between two or more enterprises in both laws alike.

The leading idea in organizing the colloquium and in editing the reports was, beyond the choice of the topic, to achieve the right mixture of the participants, viewpoints and contributions. There would have been little challenge in holding yet another conference on the general problems of multinational enterprises or to add just another book to the many which already exist on this subject. Instead, concrete problems in the field are taken up from different angles. This is guaranteed by a triple mixture: First, of course, it would be hardly adequate to treat the problems of multinational enterprises and groups just from the viewpoint of one or two jurisdictions; a multinational phenomenon such as the multinational enterprise is bound to provoke a multinational, and by no means uniform, response. The choice of countries represented was, therefore, partly based on the respective contributions made by each to the problems involved, partly a practical compromise: they are Great Britain, France, Germany, Belgium, Switzerland and the Scandinavian countries. Of course the European Communities are not left out. It would have been challenging to include also the United States; but because of financial and technical problems this had to be postponed to another time. Second, not only academics were asked to present their theories and viewpoints. What counts in this field is the law in action. Therefore at the colloquium reports and oral contributions were presented by the general counsel of a multinational corporation; by an attorney at law and tax consultant dealing in private practice with the problems of multinational corporations; by several members of important commissions and regulatory agencies in the field; and by a judge in the antitrust division of the German *Bundesgerichtshof*. Finally, if business law is a means of influencing enterprise behaviour in order to further and to protect, for example, economic performance, competition, minority rights and creditors' claims, then it is dangerous to stick only to legal theories or legal precedents. It seems important also to know and to appreciate what other disciplines than law, especially economics, can contribute. Therefore the colloquium was and the publication is, if I may say so, a multinational joint venture between theory and practice in law and economics.

For the convenience of the readers, especially those in legal practice and in business and within the multinational enterprises themselves, it has been decided after thorough deliberation to split the publication into two volumes: *Volume I* deals with *European Merger Control; Volume II* treats *Groups of Companies in European Laws*. While both volumes have a common origin and belong together, it is perfectly possible to buy and to use just one of them according to each user's professional specialization or personal choice. This relative independence of both volumes is also shown in the fact that Volume I is only in English, while Volume II gathers contributions in English and in French. Each volume has its separate annex covering the necessary legal materials and giving a concise report about the discussion on the reports.

I thank here all those colleagues and friends who participated in the conference and who by their contributions and experience made it a memorable and fruitful undertaking. I also would like to mention and thank Brigitte Schwab, Nadine Magaud and especially Monica Seccombe for their great help in editing.

Florence/Italy   April 1981
Tübingen/Germany   Klaus J. Hopt

Table of Contents (Volume I)

Chapter I: Economic Considerations

John H. Dunning, B. Sc. (Econ.), Ph. D., Professor and Head of Department of Economics, University of Reading, England

Roger G. Opie, C. B. E., M. A., M. Phil., Fellow and Tutor in Economics, Member of the Monopolies and Mergers Commission, New College, University of Oxford, England

Chapter II: Merger Control Systems in European Countries

Valentine Korah, LL. M., Ph. D., Reader, Faculty of Laws, University College London, England

Klaus J. Hopt, Dr. iur., Dr. phil., M. C. J., Professor of Law, University of Tübingen, Germany, and European University Institute at Florence, Italy

Claude Champaud, Professor of Law and Honorary President of the University of Rennes, France

Walter R. Schluep, Dr. iur., Professor of Law, President of the Swiss Cartel Commission, University of Zurich, Switzerland

Chapter III: Merger Control in the European Communities

Alexis Jacquemin, Professor and Director of the Center of Interdisciplinary Research of Law and Economics, Catholic University of Louvain, Belgium

Paul M. Schmitt, Head of the General Competition Policy Division in the Directorate General for Competition, Commission of the European Communities, Brussels, Belgium

Annex I: Discussion Report

Joseph H. H. Weiler, Assistant, European University Institute at Florence, Italy

Annex II: Relevant Legal Provisions

Table of Contents / Table des Matières (Volume II)

Klaus J. Hopt, Dr. iur., Dr. phil., M. C. J., Professor of Law, University of Tübingen, Germany and European University Institute at Florence, Italy

Chapter/Chapitre I:
Horizontal Groups and Joint Ventures: the Practical Experience
Les groupes de sociétés horizontaux et les filiales communes dans l'expérience pratique

Wilhelm F. Bayer, Dr. iur., Attorney at Law and General Counsel, Enka AG, Wuppertal, Germany

Chapter/Chapitre II:
Groups of Companies in Major European Laws
Les groupes de sociétés dans les droits européens

Herbert Wiedemann, Dr. iur., Professor of Law and President of the University of Cologne, Germany

Roger Houin, Professeur de droit, Doyen honoraire, Ancien Conseiller d'Etat, Université de Droit, d'Economie et de Sciences Sociales de Paris II, France

Pierre Van Ommeslaghe, Avocat à la Cour de Cassation et Professeur de droit, Université Libre de Bruxelles, Belgique

Chapter/Chapitre III:
Groups of Companies in the Law of the European Communities
Les groupes de sociétés dans le droit des Communautés Européennes

Chapter/Chapitre IV:
Multinational Groups of Companies: Banks, Labour, Taxes
Les groupes de sociétés multinationaux: Banques, Travail, Fisc

Chapter I

Economic Considerations

Multinational Enterprises in the 1970's: An Economist's Overview of Trends, Theories and Policies

JOHN H. DUNNING
Reading

I. The Changing Pattern of Activities by Multinational Enterprises (MNEs)

A. The Main Features of MNEs in the 1970's

The main features of international direct investment and MNEs[1] in the 1970's may be conveniently summarised under six headings.

1. The Growth of International Direct Investment and Foreign Production

According to the UN Centre on Transnational Corporations, the value of the accumulated foreign direct investment stake of developed countries in 1978 was $ 369.3 billion, $ 255.2 billion greater than that in 1967, the first date at which the data set out in Table 1 were first compiled. The average per annum rate of growth in money terms has remained remarkably consistent between 11.0% and 13.0% between 1967 and 1978;[2] however, accelerated inflation and shifting exchange relationships suggest that, in real terms, the rate of growth has slowed down quite considerably since 1973 — particularly when compared to that achieved in the mid-1960's.

At the end of the 1970's, the world direct investment stock of MNEs from DAC countries[3] was about the same or a slightly higher proportion of the gross national product (gnp) of these countries as in 1967 — viz. 7.0%[4] — but, due mainly to the above average rise in oil prices, world trade and foreign production kept more or less in pace with each other. According to *Who Owns Whom* (1978), in 1976 there were nearly 11,000 MNEs which operated 82,000 foreign affiliates. This is a 20% increase over an earlier estimate by the EEC Commission for 1973 and mainly reflects the entry of Japan and some less developed countries onto the multinational scene.[5]

2. The Geographical Origin of International Direct Investment

As Table 1 reveals, there has been a considerable diversification of the countries generating foreign direct investment since 1967. Indeed, in retrospect, the US dominance as a source country in the two decades following the Second World War may be seen as the first stage in the evolution of the modern MNE.[6] From a

Table 1

Stock of Direct Investment Abroad of Development Market Economies
(by Major Country of Origin) 1967-1978

Country of Origin	Billions of dollars end of							
	1967	1971	1975	1978	1967	1971	1975	1978
United States	56.6	82.8	124.1	168.1	49.6	49.3	47.2	45.5
United Kingdom	17.5	23.7	30.4	41.1	15.3	14.1	11.6	11.1
Germany[a]	3.0	7.3	16.0	31.8	2.6	4.3	6.1	8.6
Japan[b]	1.5	4.4	15.9	26.8	1.3	2.6	6.0	7.3
Switzerland	5.0	9.5	17.6	24.6	4.4	5.7	6.7	6.7
Netherlands	11.0	13.8	19.0	23.7	9.6	8.2	7.2	6.4
France	6.0	7.3	11.1	14.9	5.3	4.3	4.2	4.0
Canada	3.7	6.5	10.4	13.6	3.2	3.9	4.0	3.7
Sweden	1.7	2.4	4.4	6.0	1.5	1.4	1.7	1.6
Belgium-Luxembourg	2.0	2.4	3.6	5.4	1.8	1.4	1.4	1.5
Italy	2.1	3.0	3.3	3.3	1.8	1.8	1.3	0.9
Total above	110.1	163.1	255.8	359.3	96.5	97.0	97.3	97.3
All other (estimate)[c]	4.0	5.0	7.2	10.0	3.5	3.0	2.7	2.7
Grand Total	114.1	168.1	263.0	369.3	100.0	100.0	100.0	100.0

[a] Federal Republic of Germany.
[b] Fiscal year beginning 1 April of the year indicated on the basis of cumulative annual flows of direct investment as reported to the International Monetary Fund.
[c] Includes Austria, Denmark, Norway, Finland, Portugal, Spain, Australia, New Zealand and South Africa. For 1978: data not available for Denmark and South Africa.

share of around three-fifths of the accumulated foreign direct investment stake of market economies in 1960 and 49.6% in 1967, that of the US had shrunk to 45.5% by 1978. The proportionate fall in the UK's participation has been even more dramatic, viz. from around 17% in 1960 and 15.3% in 1967 to 11.1% in 1978. By contrast, between 1967 and 1978, Germany increased the value of its foreign direct investment stake by over ten times, while Japan increased its stake by eighteen times; their combined share rose from 3.9% in 1967 to 15.9% in 1978. Not revealed in Table 1 is the small but rapidly growing outward direct investment from some industrialising countries. Data from the Harvard Business School put the number of foreign affiliates of MNEs from developing countries at 1,100 in June 1979. Brazil, India, the Republic of Korea and Hong Kong are among the contries which are expected to increase their share of outward direct investment in the 1980's.[7]

Data from the Fortune list of leading industrial companies depict even more clearly the growing significance of non-US companies. In 1962 292 (60.5%) of the world's largest 483 industrial companies were American; 51 (10.6%) British; 91 (18.8%) other European; 29 (6.0%) Japanese and 3 (0.6%) were from developing countries. The corresponding figures for 1977 were: US 240 (49.7%); UK 40 (8.3%); other European 104 (21.2%);[8] Japanese 64 (13.3%) and developing countries 18 (3.7%) (Dunning and Pearce 1981). In all major industries except aerospace, the number of US companies in the world's top 12 enterprises fell between 1959 and 1976 (Franko 1978).

3. The Geographical Distribution of Foreign Direct Investment

There are no comparable published statistics to those set out in Table 1 for the geographical distribution of the foreign direct investment stake, but data available from the leading outward and inward investors suggest that during the 1970's, there was a shift of interest of US and European MNEs away from developing to developed countries — and, in the later 1970's, to Eastern Europe. In 1975, the developed (mainly OECD) countries were host to more than three-quarters of the foreign affiliates of MNEs[9] and of the foreign capital invested in them. Ten years earlier, the developing countries accounted for about 30% of such investment: in the intervening period, nationalisation and expropriation of assets of, or voluntary divestment by, foreign affiliates in the resource-based sectors, and the gradual indigenisation of some of the less technology intensive manufacturing sectors has slowed down the growth of new investment in developing countries; this has only been partially compensated by the acceleration of all kinds of Japanese investment and offshore or export platform investment by North American and European MNEs, especially in the newly industrialising developing countries (NICs) in South East Asia. Like investment in natural resources, the motive for this kind of foreign investment is to take advantage of the availability of a particular endowment — in this case labour — and to produce goods which are subsequently exported to industrialised countries.

Of the developed countries, Canada, the US, the UK and West Germany continue to be the leading host countries to the affiliates of foreign MNEs; in the late 1970's, they accounted for nearly two-thirds of foreign direct investment in developed countries and nearly one-half of all foreign direct investment. In the 1970's, the growth of inward direct investment was fastest in the United States[10] and West Germany and slowest in Canada. More generally, due inter alia to the convergence of living standards and technological capabilities among OECD member countries and a significant realignment of exchange rates, outward and inward direct investment flows among developed countries in the late 1970's were rather more balanced than they had been ten years previously.[11]

4. The Industrial Distribution of Foreign Direct Investment

MNEs have always tended to be most concentrated in capital and/or technology intensive industries and in the manufacture of mass production income-elastic branded consumer goods. However, the 1970's have seen a higher proportion of foreign direct investment being directed to four main branches of manufacturing industry, viz. (1) the secondary processing of raw materials or foodstuffs, e. g. petrochemicals, copper refining, aluminium fabricating, food canning, etc. — particularly in the resource rich developing countries, e. g. the Middle East, parts of Africa and the Caribbean; (2) the medium or high technology import substituting industries, e. g. basic chemicals, pharmaceuticals, machinery and rubber tyres; (3) export platform labour intensive industries, e. g. consumer electronics, textiles and clothing, leather goods; and (4) mass production, income-elastic consumer goods, subject to economies of scale and the benefits of horizontal integration which enable MNEs to specialise their production of particular products in certain locations and to trade these across national boundaries, e. g. domestic electrical appliances, agricultural equipment, cars.

As these sectors have become more important, others, and especially the less technology intensive industries, have attracted proportionately less investment, except that in the case of the fastest growing outward investor, i. e. Japan, they have attracted a considerably higher than the average share (Dunning 1979).

In the 1970's, international direct investment has also grown very rapidly in many service sectors, e. g. banking, insurance, management consultancy, shipping, tourism, while in most primary industries, and particularly basic minerals, it has dwindled. For example, in 1968, 37.4% of the US direct investment stake was in petroleum and mining ventures; in 1978, the corresponding proportion was 23.9%. By contrast, between 1973 and 1978, the investment stake of US finance and insurance MNEs rose from 9.4% to 14.3%.

5. The Extent of Multinationality of the Leading MNEs

One of the most noticeable features of the 1970's has been the growth in the *degree* of multinationality of the world's largest enterprises. It is estimated that, in 1977, about 27% of the total production of the 866 largest industrial enterprises was produced outside their national boundaries (Dunning and Pearce 1981). Another source (UN 1978) suggests that, of the 422 billion-dollar industrial corporations in 1976, 12% derived 51% or more of their sales from their foreign affiliates, and 36% more than 26% of their sales from this source. Some 64% of some 403 of the largest firms in 1977 asserted that, over the previous five years, the ratio of their foreign to domestic production had increased; and only 11% that it had fallen. About the same proportion expected that, by 1982, they would further increase their degree of multinationality (Dunning and Pearce 1981).

Data on the number of foreign affiliates associated with MNEs tell the same story, although it is worth recalling that four-fifths of MNEs have affiliates in 5 or fewer countries. At the other end of the spectrum, at least 400 MNEs operated in 20 or more countries in 1978. It is these enterprises which expanded among the fastest in the 1970's, by horizontally or vertically integrating their international activities. Especially within the EEC, LAFTA and between the export processing zones and industrialised countries, the amount of process and product rationalisation among the individual operating units of the MNE has substantially increased. This is shown inter alia by the rising proportion of the exports of the parent companies of the MNEs despatched to their own affiliates, which in 1977 averaged 33% among all MNEs, but was as high as 61% in the case of MNEs whose foreign production ratio was over 52½% (Dunning and Pearce 1981). As this latter ratio increases, so MNEs tend to view their foreign activities as part of a regional or global strategy, and plan the disposition of their physical and financial resources to take advantage of differences in the markets, factor endowments and Government policies between countries. This has been particularly noticeable in the high technology industries, which may explain why MNEs in these sectors, e. g. IBM, have been among the most reluctant to relinquish a 100% equity participation in their affiliates.

6. The Rise in Joint Ventures and Non-Equity Arrangements

Parallel with the trend just described has been another towards greater local equity participation in the foreign affiliates of MNEs and towards the international transfer of technology and management skills, via the contractual (viz. externalised) rather than the direct investment (viz. internalised) route. Quite apart from any enforced divestment by MNEs, the most recent generation of foreign direct investors – typified by those from Japan and less developed countries – have opted for majority or minority, rather than 100% equity participation.[12] Many US and European MNEs have also voluntarily sold off part of their shareholdings; but in those sectors where the degree of multinationality has most noticeably increased, the trend has, if anything, been in the opposite direction. As the foreign production of Japanese MNEs increases in the 1980's, it will be interesting to see whether their current policy, which favours joint ventures, is replaced by a movement towards at least a majority of equity capital stake. It is also worth observing that as some developing countries are encouraging the indigenisation of foreign owned enterprises, so Eastern European countries (and, most latterly of all, mainland China) are opening their borders to foreign direct investment. Apart from in Japan, the 100% owned affiliate in developed countries is still generally accepted, although in Canada and Australia, where the participation of foreign owned firms is well above average, the clear preference is for a substantial local involvement in foreign affiliates.

The growth in non-equity arrangements in the 1970's has been so spectacular that some commentators (Malgrem, 1978; Rose 1977) have expressed the view that the multinationals are "at bay" or "in retreat". Gabriel (1977) puts forward a more cautious viewpoint, when he argues that although the role of the MNE as a dominant supplier of equity capital may well have peaked, it still is by far and away the most significant reservoir of advanced technology, managerial talent, marketing skills and organisational capacity; and that, however the package of resources which direct investment comprises is unbundled, the more important ingredients will continue to be supplied by the same source.

Much, of course, depends on the kind of resources being transferred; certainly the channels of finance capital, standardised technology, and mainstream managerial, financial and marketing capabilities are widening all the time, but whenever anything out of the ordinary is required or the above ingredients need to be packaged into a tightly organised and integrated system, the peculiar strengths of the MNE qua MNE remain largely unimpaired. Yet, even here, in some cases, quite complicated organisational or managerial systems may be transferred – and profitably transferred – by companies with a minimal amount of equity participation; the hotel industry is an excellent case in point (UN 1981). This has led some observers on the MNE (e. g., Mikesell 1979; UN 1978) to be less concerned with the issue of the costs and benefits of equity as opposed to non-equity involvement of MNEs, and more with the *terms* of any contracts concluded between themselves and local producers (or host Governments).

B. Conclusion: The Trends of the 1970's

The evolution of MNEs in the 1970's has proceeded from being a mainly US and European phenomenon to being a genuine international phenomenon, with the decade ending with the emergence of MNEs from several developing countries, and with inflows and outflows of direct investment from developed countries becoming more evenly balanced. The geographical distribution of MNE activity has shifted towards the US, Europe and South East Asia and the Middle East, and away from the rest of the Americas, Africa and Australasia. The industrial composition of foreign direct investment of US and European MNEs has become more oriented towards the advanced technology industries and skill intensive service activities (e. g. banking, consultancy) or those supplying high income services (e. g. tourism); the major exception being the growing interest in "defensive" investment in the labour intensive sectors (e. g. textiles) in the NICs.

Japanese and developing country investment has been more concentrated in the medium skill and mature technology sectors. In some cases, e. g. Korean investment in Middle Eastern constructional projects, the foreign investment package includes unskilled and semi-skilled labour (Heenan and Keegan 1979). Whereas, to take advantage of horizontal and vertical international specialisation, many of the faster growing large and diversified MNEs have increased their centralisation of decision taking and their intra-group transactions, others have divested themselves of part of their equity involvement; at the same time, a new generation of medium size and smaller MNEs — particularly from the periphery developed economies e. g. Canada and Sweden and from India and South East Asia — have increasingly preferred the joint venture to the fully owned subsidiary. As the sources of capital and technology have become more diffused and more host Governments seek to rid themselves of the foreign control of decision taking, so, in many sectors of economic activity, the package of resources transferred through direct investment has been "unbundled". By contrast in Eastern Europe, however, the trend is towards new forms of "bundling", which involve at least a minority foreign stakeholding.

II. New Thinking on the Theory of MNE Activity: Towards an Eclectic Approach

A. Early Theories

The developments just described have necessitated some re-appraisal of the economic theories of foreign direct investment and MNEs which, in the 1950's and 1960's, were put forward to explain a largely US phenomenon. Early attempts to explain the multinationalisation of firms by drawing on international capital theory were soon abandoned for two main reasons. First, foreign direct investment involves the transfer of other resources than finance capital and it is the expected return on these, rather than on the capital per se, which prompts enterprises to produce outside their national boundaries. Second, in the case of direct investment, resources are transferred *within the same firm*, rather than *externally* between two independent parties: in consequence, de jure control is still retained over their usage. Furthermore, in some cases, without this control (which is often necessary to capture the economies of synergy) resources which are transferred may not be transferred, and thus the production capabilities of the recipient firm are different from what they would otherwise be. This is the essential difference between *portfolio* and *direct* investment.

B. Industrial Organisation Theory versus Location Theory

If international capital theory could not explain the growth of MNE activity, what could? By the mid 1960's two main approaches led the stage, viz. the "why" or "how it is possible" approach, based on industrial organisation theory; and the "where" approach based upon location theory.

1. The Industrial Organisation Theory Approach

This theory concentrated on identifying the characteristics of MNEs which gave them a net competitive advantage over other firms which might supply the same foreign markets. Though the gist of this idea was contained in the studies of Southard (1931) and Dunning (1958), it was left to Hymer, in a seminal doctoral thesis (Hymer 1960), to refine and formalise it into a separate theory of foreign direct investment. Based on an internationalisation of Joe Bain's notion of barriers to entry, Hymer asserted that foreign direct investment presupposed that investing firms possessed assets (e.g., technology, access to markets, managerial capacity) that other firms did not, and that these advantages could be sustained over time, because of competitive barriers. The identification and evaluation of these advantages commanded much of the attention of economists in the 1960's and early 1970's.

2. The Location Theory

This second approach tried to answer the question "Why do firms produce in one country rather than in another?" The pioneering work of Frank Southard on *American Industry in Europe* (1931) followed this approach as did the authors of most of the early country case studies published between 1953 and 1970. In most cases, the influences of location were extracted from field study data, and, occasionally, ranked in significance.[13] Later, as more complete statistics became available, statistical analysis was used to identify the main factors leading to US direct investment in Europe and Canada.

3. Theoretical Shortcomings and the Development of the Product Cycle Theory

For the most part, these two approaches evolved independently of each other, and for this, if for no other reason, neither was wholly satisfactory. The industrial organisation approach did not explain *where* competitive advantages were exploited; location theory could not explain *why* foreign owned firms could outcompete domestic firms on their own territory. Neither approach grappled with the dynamics of foreign direct investment. In this respect, the work of Raymond Vernon and his colleagues on the product cycle theory (Vernon 1966; Wells 1970) was of pioneering significance, partly because it treated trade and investment as part of the same process of exploiting foreign markets, and partly because it explained how the process varied over time. To the questions "why" and "where", Vernon added "when" to the theory of foreign direct investment. But even the Vernon theory was initially put forward to explain the growth of US manufacturing investment abroad, and in the 1960's at least, relied exclusively on data about US corporate activity.[14]

C. Theoretical Advances in the 1970's

Advances in the theories of international production in the 1970's have taken five main directions.

1. Extensions of Industrial Organisation Approach

There have been numerous extensions of this approach. These have focused on identifying and evaluating which of the advantages are most likely to explain patterns of the foreign manufacturing activities of US based MNEs.[15] Of the competitive (sometimes called firm or ownership specific) advantages which seem best to explain such investment, superior management technology and innovatory capacity and product differentiation consistently appear to have the best explanatory power. Limited testing has been done on the industrial structure of foreign direct investment by other countries.[16]

2. Extensions of Financial Theories

There has been a resurgence of interest on some of the *financial* aspects of the foreign activities of firms.[17] There have been a series of strands, but most fall into one of two groups: first, those which emphasise the imperfections of capital markets and foreign exchange, e. g. Aliber (1970), (which inter alia explain why enterprises of one nationality may value assets denominated in a foreign currency differently from firms of another nationality); and, second, those which extend portfolio theory to explain the industrial and geographical distribution of foreign activities and take account of risk diversification and the stability of earnings. Here the work of Lessard (1979) and Rugman (1979) is especially illuminating.

3. Extension of Theory of the Firm

There has been a new theoretical advance in seeking an explanation for international production as an extension to the theory of the firm. This reflects a switch in attention from the act of foreign direct investment per se — which is now recognised as a particular *form* of involvement by firms outside their national boundaries — to the *institution* making the investment. Here, the MNE is essentially treated as a special case of a large diversified firm. Using the principles first expounded by Coase (1937) and Penrose (1958), but more recently developed and extended by Arrow (1971), Alchian and Demsetz (1972) and Williamson (1975), in their analysis of information markets and the economics of vertical integration, economists such as McManus (1972), Buckley and Casson (1976) and Magee (1977) have sought to explain the propensity of firms to engage in foreign direct investment, in terms of the failure of the market (as an economic institution) to efficiently transact the exchange of assets, goods and information between independent sellers and buyers. Such failure may show itself inter alia in high negotiation and transaction costs, particularly in the intermediate product markets; supply instabilities; the protection of proprietary rights; the absence of future markets; and the inability of the selling firm to extract the maximum price of the product or asset being sold, either because of buyer ignorance or uncertainty, e. g. in the case of a patent, or because the full benefit of a particular asset depends on it being used jointly with other assets, which only the selling firm possesses. The higher these costs, relative to those of internalised decision taking (Buckley and Casson 1976), the more an enterprise is likely to wish to supervise its foreign investments.

This approach helps to explain *by which route* a firm chooses to exploit any advantages it possesses over its foreign competitors (although the route itself may sometimes affect these advantages), a question largely ignored in the early literature on international direct investment. The problem of choosing between the alternative ways of servicing a foreign market was first taken up systematically by Hirsch (1976), who identified the conditions under which a firm might exploit its ownership specific advantages through exports or foreign direct investment. More recently, this theme has been extended by Lall (1980), Buckley and Davies (1979) and Giddy and Rugman (1979), who have also addressed themselves to the principles of choice between foreign direct investment and licensing, and between exports and licensing.

4. Development of an Eclectic Approach

It was, however, the dissatisfaction with these partial explanations of international direct investment and their failure to integrate investment with trade or portfolio resource transfer theory that led economists to favour a more eclectic approach to the subject. This fourth line of development draws upon and integrates the three strands of economic theory just described. Its principle paradigm is that a firm will engage in foreign direct investment if each of three conditions are satisfied:

(a) It possesses net ownership advantages vis-à-vis firms of other nationalities in serving particular markets. These ownership specific advantages largely take the form of the possession of intangible assets, which, at least for a period of time, are the exclusive right of the firm possessing them.
(b) Assuming condition (a) is satisfied, it must be more beneficial to the enterprise possessing these advantages to use them itself rather than to lease them to foreign firms to use, i.e. for it to *internalise* its advantages through an extension of its own activities rather than *externalise* them through market transactions with independent firms.
(c) Assuming conditions (a) and (b) are satisfied, it must be beneficial for the

enterprise to utilise these advantages in conjunction with at least *some* factor inputs (including natural resources) outside its home country; otherwise foreign markets would be served entirely by exports and domestic markets by domestic production.

The matrix below illustrates the options of servicing a market, which is related to the presence or absence of these three conditions. The eclectic theory suggests that a country's propensity to engage in foreign direct investment, or to be invested in by foreign companies depends entirely on the extent and form of the ownership advantages of its enterprises, whether or not these are internalised within these enterprises, and how far the enterprises find it beneficial to exploit them in a foreign rather than a domestic location. It asserts that most kinds of activities by MNEs irrespective of their country or origin or involvement, can be explained in this way, although the nature and significance of these advantages will differ according to *country industry* or *firm* specific characteristics. Table 3 encapsulates the main features of this approach and illustrates the kinds of activities in which MNEs tend to play a dominant role.

Table 2
Market Servicing – The Options

		Advantages		
		Ownership	Internalisation	(Foreign) Location
Route of Serving Market	Foreign Direct Investment	Yes	Yes	Yes
	Exports	Yes	Yes	No
	Portfolio Re-source Transfers	Yes	No	No

5. A Macro-Economic Approach

The fifth theoretical development of the 1970's is that typified by the work of Kojima (1978) who prefers a macro-economic approach to explaining international direct investment. Making use of the received theory of international trade, Kojima explains the propensity of countries to engage in international investment, in terms of (a) their comparative advantage of particular resource endowments and (b) the market structure in which their enterprises operate. He argues, for example, that while post-war Japanese foreign direct investment has been primarily directed to exploiting resources in which Japan has a comparative disadvantage, thus releasing capacity in the home country to produce goods which require resources in which she has a comparative advantage, US foreign direct investment has been directed to those sectors in which the home country has a comparative advantage and the host countries a comparative disadvantage. Kojima puts this "anti-trade" type investment down to the defensive competitive strategy of large US MNEs operating within a oligopolistic market environment.

Table 3

Types of International Production: Some Determining Factors

Types of International Production	Ownership Advantages (The "why" of MNE activity)	Location Advantages (The "where" of production)	Internalisation Advantages (The "how" of involvement)	Illustration of types of activity which favour MNEs
1. Resource based	Capital, technology, access to markets	Possession of resources	To ensure stability of oil supply at right price. Control of markets	Oil, copper, tin, zinc, bauxite, bananas, pineapples, cocoa, tea
2. Import substituting manufacturing	Capital, technology, management and organisational skills; surplus research and development and other capacity, economies of scale, trade marks	Material & labour costs, markets, government policy (e.g. with respect to barrier to imports, investment incentives etc.)	Wish to exploit technology advantages, high transaction or information costs, buyer uncertainty, etc.	Computers, pharmaceuticals, motor vehicles, cigarettes
3. Rationalised specialisation (a) of products (b) of processes	As above, but also access to markets	(a) Economies of product specialisation and concentration (b) Low labour costs, incentives to local production by host governments	(a) As 2, plus gains from interdependent activities (b) The economies of vertical integration	(a) Motor vehicles, electrical appliances, agricultural machinery (b) Consumer electronics, textiles & clothing, cameras, etc.
4. Trade & distribution	Products to distribute	Local markets. Need to be near customers. After sales servicing, etc.	Need to ensure sales outlets & to protect company's name	A variety of goods – particularly those requiring close consumer contact
5. Ancillary services	Access to markets (in the case of other foreign investors)	Markets	Broadly as for 2/4	Insurance; banking & consultancy services
6. Miscellaneous	Variety – but include geographical diversification (e.g. airlines and hotels)	Markets	Various (see above)	Various kinds (a) Portfolio investment properties (b) Where spatial linkages essential e.g. airlines & hotels

Although this argument is somewhat simplistic and not entirely borne out by the facts, Kojima has directed the attention of economists to some important resource allocative problems associated with foreign direct investment. His approach can be reinterpreted in terms of the eclectic theory in as much as he is arguing that for countries to make the best use of their human and physical resources, they should seek to encourage inward direct investment in those sectors which use location specific (i. e. immobile) endowments in which they have a (comparative) advantage, and which use ownership specific (and largely mobile) endowments in which their own enterprises have a (comparative) disadvantage; and to encourage outward direct investment in those sectors in which they require resources in which their enterprises have a (comparative) ownership advantage but need to be combined with other (immobile) resources in which they are (comparatively) disadvantaged. One suspects that in the 1980's more attention is being given to the structural implications of *both* inward and outward investment than in the past.

D. Applications of the Eclectic Theory of International Production

Space does not allow us to spell out in any details the way in which the eclectic theory of international production helps to explain the changes in MNE activities set out in Section II of this paper. But one or two illustrations may be in order.

1. Industrial Composition of Foreign Direct Investment

The different industrial composition of the foreign direct investment by US, European and Japanese MNEs may be explained by differences in the structure of resource endowments, markets and Government intervention of the home countries, which both generate different types of ownership specific advantages (e. g. US in labour-saving, the Europeans in material-saving industries and the Japanese in energy-saving activities) and different location specific endowments (which may also influence the extent to which the ownership advantages are exploited by exports or foreign direct investment).

2. The Trend towards Joint Ventures and Non-Equity Foreign Involvement

This reflects a reduced need of MNEs to *internalise* the transfer of resources, and/or the increased role of Governments, e. g. in State trading in mineral and commodity markets, and/or an improvement in the market as a resource co-ordinator and allocator. On the other hand, the movement towards more centralised control by MNEs (especially the larger MNEs in the high technology industries), suggests that the advantages of internalisation (and particularly those to do with the economies of systematisation) (Kojima 1978) are favouring the growth of institutional rather than market integration.

3. The Emergence of Outward Direct Investment by Developing Countries

This development suggests that enterprises from these countries are now generating their own ownership specific advantages, which are best exploited outside their home countries. The fact, however, that most of these investments take the form of joint ventures points to the fact that, by themselves, these ownership advantages are not sufficient to capture foreign markets and that they need to be complemented by other advantages, e. g. in marketing, in dealing with Governments of the host countries or in joint possession with local firms or other MNEs.

4. The Growth of Export Platform Type Investment

This expansion is associated with the vertical integration of different processes of production by MNEs, again to take advantage of differential resource endowments and the economies of synergy. Like product specialisation, it flourishes in the absence of trade barriers, and in recent years has been stimulated by the establishment of export processing zones. Just as much import substitution investment was (and is) induced by Governments placing obstacles to trade (in pursuance of import substituting policies) so the expansion of rationalised production by MNEs rests on the free movement of goods *and* substantial internalising advantages within MNEs.

E. A Summary of the Developments of the 1970's

The eclectic theory of international production provides a framework both for understanding the extent and pattern of activities by MNEs in the late 1970's and the main changes which have taken place in the past decade. As the economic and technological hegemony of the US has declined, so the ownership advantages of, first, European and, second, Japanese firms have risen. This, coupled with a realignment of exchange rates (noticeably the devaluation of the dollar and revaluation of mark and yen) together with an increase in both market and institutional integration, has encouraged a continual growth in international direct investment. At the same time, due to the widening of sources of finance, capital, technolgy and management skills, and the actions taken by some Governments to reduce the extent of foreign participation in their economies, (at least over key sectors of their economies), the rate of growth of MNE (qua MNE) activity has decelerated from its peak in the late 1960's. While innovations in product, production and managerial technology, and improvements in international transport and communication facilities have continued to push out territorial boundaries of enterprises, the forces of economic nationalism and autarchy have had the reverse effects, and in some countries – particularly resource rich developing countries – foreign direct investment now plays a less decisive role than it once did. On the other hand, new and often very complex forms of MNE involvement have been opening up (UN 1978) and it seems that as fast as one door closes against MNEs another opens up. We have already alluded to the expansion of MNEs in the service sectors, notably in banking and in Eastern European tourism; we should also note the growth of State owned MNEs, especially from some developing countries.

III. Reactions and Policies Towards MNEs: from Confrontation to Uneasy Alliance

A. Changing Policies Towards MNE

The 1970's began with a rising tide of hostility of many nation states towards MNEs, which culminated with the ITT affair in Chile in 1973, and the setting up, by the UN, of a high level study group to investigate the role of MNEs in the economic development. At the recommendation of this Group a permanent Commission Centre on Transnational Corporations (TNCs, the UN nomenclature for MNEs) was set up in 1974, the purpose of which was to study and monitor the activities of TNCs and to advise Governments in their policy measures towards them. Two years later the OECD produced a set of guidelines setting out the kind of behaviour they expected (or did not expect) from MNEs.

Yet only 15-20 years earlier, MNEs (or foreign firms, as they were then simply known) had been almost unreservedly welcomed by host developed and developing countries alike. Europe, recovering from the Second World War, and many developing countries seeking the speediest way to promote their economic growth, saw in foreign direct investment not only all the necessary ingredients for prosperity, but the only way to obtain these ingredients. The fact that within a few years foreign direct investment was being criticised as much as it had earlier been praised is to be variously explained: the dissatisfaction partly reflected a failure on the part of host countries to appreciate the nature of foreign direct investment, and, in particular, its generally uneven impact on economic development; partly it arose because of the fact that, in some countries, and/or in key sectors, activities of foreign companies soon came to play a dominant role; partly because of the high profits earned and repatriated by the MNEs, especially in the resource based sectors; partly because of a much less significant impact of their activities on employment, or less local value added, than had been hoped; and partly because of the movement of many countries towards political independence and Government economic intervention.

In the 1960's, unilateral policy first centred on minimising the economic rent which might be extracted by foreign investors. Next attention was channelled towards curbing the alleged distorting resource allocative effects of MNEs, e. g. the inappropriate transfers of technology and/or control over the use made of the technology; unacceptable employment practices; undesirable product promotion; control of export outlets; transfer price manipulation; tied sourcing and so on. By the use of policy instruments, e.g. to do with entry, performance, and exit criteria, foreign affiliates were encouraged to perform in a way consistent with national economic and development goals. While such policies met with some success — particularly those implemented by strong industrialised nations which had good bargaining power vis-à-vis MNEs — there were many instances where the economic power and flexibility of MNEs were too much for host Governments, which had either to accept the terms of the MNEs or risk losing their presence altogether. And accepting the terms often meant that control over decisions on resource allocation was transferred to the MNE parent company, which often took such decisions to promote global strategy rather than with the best interests of each and every affiliate in mind.

It was the "control" aspect of foreign direct investment — especially as it affected the transfer of technology and the export markets served by affiliates, and the extent to which local linkages were formed — that became uppermost in the minds of most nations as the trend towards economic nationalism increased in the late 60's and early 70's. In particular, it was felt that MNEs were simply perpetuating the existing international economic order and division of labour, whereby high level activities, including most research and development activities, were undertaken in home countries, while lower level activities — often in a truncated form — were decentralised to domestic or foreign satellites. Since barriers to entry often inhibited indigenous firms from effectively competing with MNEs, many smaller host countries found it difficult to promote their long term comparative advantage. Even some of the larger advanced industrialised countries, e.g. the UK, were forced to rationalise their industries to compete with US giants. Japan, as is well known, pursued a different strategy by largely outlawing foreign direct investment, until her indigenous technological capacity was strong enough to absorb it without being dominated by it.

B. Conditioning Factors for the Government-MNE Relationship in the 1980's

While the search for economic autonomy and political sovereignty still goes on unabated and while criticisms of MNEs continue to abound, my reading of the situation in 1980 is that the environmental climate facing MNEs is more relaxed than it was 7-8 years ago and that Governments are taking a more positive reasoned and discriminatory approach to their impact on economic development. There are several reasons for this quite significant change of heart.

First, with notable exceptions, like Iran, and some African countries, there has been a general move of Governments in the 1970's towards more conservatism and less radicalism in both economic and political policies, and a greater recognition that, whether they like it or not, most nations are economically interdependent on each other.

Second, since the oil crisis of 1973, the rate of world economic growth has slowed down, and countries have become more acutely aware of the need to gain the kind of resources which MNEs are especially well equipped to provide.

Third, not only have the sources of technology, management and finance widened, but competition among MNEs has tended to increase. This has assisted countries in their bargaining power vis-à-vis individual MNEs.

Fourth, both home and host Governments have become better educated both on the costs and benefits of foreign direct investment and on negotiating tactics with MNEs. Moreover, most are now technically much better equipped to deal with abuses arising from their activities than they were a decade ago.[18] In general, they have a less emotive and more constructive approach to MNEs.

Fifth, many developing countries — particularly those in South East Asia and

Latin America – have made remarkable economic strides in the 70's,[19] as witnessed by a marked improvement in their educational and technological infrastructures and the competitiveness of their enterprises in world markets. It is now recognised that, in most sectors, MNEs and local firms both have unique advantages, which as much complement, as substitute for, each other and that each has a role to play in the development process.

Sixth, as we have seen, the new generation of MNEs have generally learned from the mistakes of their predecessors and are adapting their modes of involvement and behavioural patterns to the needs of host Governments, e.g. by engaging in joint ventures, by integrating themselves into the local economy and by delegating as much decision taking as possible.

Seventh, there has been some disillusionment among Governments about the benefits of the contractual arrangements *in place of* foreign direct investment. Often the costs of control and high economic rent seem almost as great while the foreign company bears little or none of the risk of an equity investor; again the hotel industry is a good case in point. The result is that many Governments are encouraging minority foreign participation to ensure that MNEs have a positive stake in their economies and have something to lose if the venture does not succeed.

Eighth, international action, both in the form of recommendations by bodies such as the UN and OECD, harmonisation of policies by regional associations, e.g. EEC, LAFTA, and the Andean group, have most certainly influenced the behaviour of MNEs. At the very least, (as shown, for example, by the publicising of companies breaching the OECD guidelines or Article 86 of the Rome Treaty) they are more aware that their actions may lead to unpleasant results, while new investors know what is expected of them; but, perhaps more important, a framework of "case law" (in the loosest sense of the term) is being built up which, while it gives MNEs some sense of stability and Governments some sense that they are in control, also leaves MNEs in no doubt that stricter measures could be implemented.

For all these reasons and others – not least the learning process of both MNEs and Governments about each others' objectives, options and negotiating tactics, and a recognition that each has something to contribute to the others' goals – I believe the 1980's augur considerably better for a more conciliatory and mutually rewarding relationship between MNEs and host countries than the 1970's. The rules of the game and lines for negotiation have now been quite firmly drawn; in most cases, the parties know what to expect from each other and, although changes of leadership of both Governments and MNEs may modifiy – and even drastically change – attitudes and policies, and individual MNEs may still be arraigned for particular actions perceived to be against the public interest, I would not expect any wholesale return to the kind of confrontation which marked the beginning of the 1970's.

IV. Some Thoughts on the Future of MNEs

Looking a little into the rest of the 1980's and beyond, any judgement about the likely future of MNEs will rest largely on one's expectations about the world economic and political scenario.[20] If one believes the world will steer a course towards economic nationalism and autarchy, then clearly the role of the MNE is likely to decrease. If one considers that nations will move towards more economic interdependence, then MNEs will continue to occupy a major position on the world stage. However, most commentators agree that the trend towards the geographical diversification of MNEs will continue and that their participation will differ according to the part of the world one is considering. The consensus seems to be that, within the OECD area, they will continue to play a major role, albeit within a framework of more circumscribed policies or guidelines than in the past. In developing countries — which can by no means be considered as a homogeneous group — much will depend on the political complexion and developmental stage, economic characteristics and goals of individual host countries. It does, however, seem likely that in key sectors the contribution of MNEs as direct investors will be less decisive than in the past, even though they may continue to be important suppliers of technology and management. Many new forms of involvement, with the participation of consortia of MNEs, Governments, international agencies, banks and local institutions seem likely to arise. One might also expect to see more countervailing power to MNEs in the form of State-owned corporations and the gradual indigenisation of sectors in which the ownership advantages of MNEs are eroded over time. At the same time, as new industries develop in which MNEs have a comparative advantage, their participation may increase.

Looking at the future in terms of the eclectic theory of international production, the question is how far enterprises of one nationality will continue to generate ownership specific advantages which give them an edge over those of another in servicing particular markets; how far conditions (especially market conditions) favour the internalisation of these advantages; and how far location specific endowments, including Government attitudes to trade and investment, will be sufficiently distinctive between countries to affect the balance between foreign production and exports.

Again, answers to these questions are not primarily to do with MNEs as such. For example, the first will depend on such variables as the pace of innovations (itself affected inter alia by patent laws and regulations), the economics of production and marketing and the extent to which Governments continue to allow large firms to gain economies of systematisation, even though some of the results may not always be in the public interest. Regarding the second, if one believes that as countries develop markets become less imperfect and the costs of supervising foreign investment are reduced, then one might believe that some of the advantages of the internalised route of resource transference will disappear and be replaced by more licensing, management contracts, technical service agreements, franchises, turnkey operations; here the crucial question is whether market improvement outpaces the market deterioration in other directions, including the action of Governments. On the final question, one might very well see less incentive for certain types of investment as, e. g., some costs become equalised across national boundaries (e. g. labour); on the other hand, it is worth noting that within the EEC, where costs are among the highest in the world, intra-industry foreign direct investment is increasing all the time. What may happen is that, just as Ricardian type trade[21] has been partially replaced by technology gap and monopolistic competitive trade of an intra-industry kind, so later international investment will increasingly follow the same pattern, with vertically integrated investment giving way to horizontal investment, based on differences in consumer tastes and specialised technology gaps. Here again much will rest on the extent to which home Governments continue to permit the growth of conglomerate companies. Our own reading of the situation suggests that the 1980's might be more the decade of the medium-large MNEs than that of the really giant companies.

The main theme of the above paragraphs can be summarized as follows:[22]

In retrospect, the two decades up to 1975 may be regarded as the maturation of one phase in the evolution of international resource transmission. This phase began at the turn of the 20th century, remained inactive in the inter-war years, and blossomed after the second world war in conditions which were ideally suited to the extension of activities of firms across national boundaries, through the medium of equity investment. This particular phase followed a much longer era which dated back to the Industrial Revolution and even before. But it differed from the period which followed it in three fundamental ways. First, the resources used were transmitted separately and independently of each other; there was no single organisation packaging them together and arranging for their joint shipment. Second, the resources, or the right to their use, were exchanged between independent parties at arms length prices. Thirdly, the exchange was accompanied by a change in the ownership of the use of resources, i.e. the seller transferred control of the allocation of resources to the buyer.

After a period of almost unrestrained growth of MNEs, the wheel is now turning full circle regarding the way resources are internationally transmitted. But this is not to say that the MNE is in retreat. For every door which closes another opens up. The forms of contractual involvement and the nature of resources provided by MNEs in the last quarter of the 20th century will be very different from those of the 19th century. Resources may be packaged together in various ways, and many different institutions may be involved in particular projects. In addition, although I expect the environment for international investment to improve rather than deteriorate over the next decade or more, the activities of MNEs and other foreign firms are bound to be circumscribed by guidelines, codes, regulations and laws, many of these backed by international consensus. But, hopefully, in exchange for these constraints on behaviour, there will be a greater awareness of governments of their responsibilities to MNEs and a greater perception of their needs, and this may show itself in a more stable environment in which such business may operate. Within these constraints, and if governments take advantage of half the opportunities to make proper use of MNEs, the future for such companies offers both scope and promise.

Notes

[1] Throughout the paper we shall adopt the 'threshold' definition of MNEs, i.e., MNEs are enterprises which engage in foreign direct investment. International (or foreign) production is defined as production financed by foreign direct investment.

[2] For example the value of the stock of US foreign direct investment rose by 2½ times both between 1958 and 1968 and 1968 and 1978. However, the rate of the world inflation in the latter period was more than twice as high as in the former period.

[3] Members of the Development Assistance Committee of the OECD. For further details *see* OECD (1979).

[4] Using a 2:1 output/investment ratio would suggest that the output of these same MNEs as a % of the gnp of DAC countries was around 14%. (UN 1978).

[5] At the same time the growth of new US MNEs has slowed down. For example, the number of new US affiliates entering into the networks of 180 US based MNEs in the period 1973/8 was only 60% of those entering in the period 1967-1972.

[6] Which, in many respects, parallels the UK's domination of international trade in the first part of the 19th century.

[7] For a recent study of third-world MNEs, *see* Kumar (1980).

[8] Excluding Anglo-Dutch and Anglo-Italian companies.

[9] 61,000 of the 82,000 affiliates.

[10] By the end of 1980 it is estimated that the US will replace Canada as the leading inward investor.

[11] For example, the outward/inward investment ratio has fallen in the case of the US and UK, and risen in the case of Germany, Japan, Australia and Canada.

[12] In 1975, 44% of Japanese foreign investments involved a minority Japanese equity participation compared with 8% of Japanese multinationals. Of the subsidiaries set up by all MNEs in developing countries between 1961 and 1975, 25.3% were 100% owned compared with 41.1% of those subsidiaries set up before 1961. In contrast, however, all major Japanese trading companies operate through 100% owned foreign subsidiaries.

[13] For further details *see* Dunning (1973).

[14] For Vernon's later view on the value of the product cycle theory as an explanation of other types of foreign investment and of non-US investment *see* Vernon (1979).

[15] For the most recent, and one of the most detailed studies (with respect to US participation in Canadian industry), *see* Owen (1979).

[16] Geroski (1976) has done some work on explaining UK foreign investment, Juhl (1979) in explaining German investment and Swedenborg (1980) in explaining Swedish investment in these terms.

[17] Described inter alia in Dunning (1973) and Stevens (1974).

[18] In this respect, the Centre on Transnational Corporations has performed a useful role, especially in developing countries, by setting up workshops and training seminars, and providing consultants and support staff to help countries evaluate alternative modalities of technology transfer and prepare for negotiations with TNCs.

[19] *See*, for example, World Bank (1979).

[20] For an excellent discussion of the future of MNEs, viewed from a US perspective, *see* Hawkins and Walter (1979).

[21] E.g. a country exports manufactured goods and imports raw materials and foodstuffs.

[22] Dunning (1978) at 3,10.

References

Alchian A. and Demsetz H. (1972): "Production Information Costs and Economic Organisation," *American Economic Review* 62 (1972): 777-795

Aliber R. I. (1970): "A Theory of Foreign Direct Investment," in KINDLEBERGER C. P. (ed.), THE INTERNATIONAL CORPORATION (Cambridge, Mass., MIT Press, 1970).

Arrow K. J. (1971): ESSAYS IN THE THEORY OF RISK-BEARING (Chicago, Markham Publishing Co., 1971).

Buckley P. and Casson M. (1976): THE FUTURE OF THE MULTINATIONAL ENTERPRISE (London, Macmillan, 1976).

Buckley P. and Davies H. (1979): "The Place of Licensing in the Theory and Practice of Foreign Operations," University of Reading Discussion Papers in International Investment and Business Studies No. 47 (November 1979).

Coase R. (1937): "The Nature of the Firm," *Economica* (New Series) 4 (1937): 387-405.

Dunning J. H. (1958): AMERICAN INVESTMENT IN BRITISH MANUFACTURING INDUSTRY (London, Allen and Unwin, 1958).

Dunning J. H. (1973): "The Determinants of International Production," *Oxford Economic Papers* 25 (1973): 289-336.

Dunning, J. H. (1978): "Multinational Business and the Challenge of the 1980s," *Multinational Business* 1 (1978): 3-10.

Dunning J. H. (1979): "Explaining Changes in International Production: in Defence of the Eclectic Theory," *Oxford Bulletin of Economics and Statistics* 41 (1979): 269-295.

Dunning J. H. and Pearce R. D. (1981): THE WORLD'S LARGEST INDUSTRIAL COMPANIES 1962-1978 (Farnborough, Hampshire, Gower Press, 1980).

Franko L. (1978): "Multinationals: the End of US Dominance," *Harvard Business Review* 56 (1978): 93-101.

Gabriel P. P. (1977): "Management of Public Interests by the Multinational Corporation," *Journal of World Trade Law* 11 (1972): 15-36.

Geroski P. (1976): "An Industry Characteristics Analysis of UK Direct Investment," Warwick Economic Research Papers No. 85 (1976).

Giddy I. and Rugman A. (1979): "A Model of Foreign Direct Investment Trade and Licensing" (Unpublished Paper, 1979).

Hawkins R. and Walter I. (1979): "Multinational Corporations: Current Trends and Future Prospects," New York University Graduate School of Business Administration 79-110 (November 1979).

Heenan D. A. and Keegan W. J. (1979): "The Rise of Third World Multinationals," *Harvard Business Review* 57 (1979): 101-109.

Hirsch S. (1976): "An International Trade and Investment Theory of the Firm," *Oxford Economic Papers* 28 (1976): 258-270.

Hymer S. (1960 (1976)): THE INTERNATIONAL OPERATIONS OF NATIONAL FIRMS: A STUDY IN FOREIGN DIRECT INVESTMENT (Cambridge, Mass., MIT Press, 1960).

Juhl P. (1979): "On the Sectoral Patterns of West German Manufacturing Investment in Less Developed Countries: the Impact of Firm Size, Factor Intensities and Protection," *Weltwirtschaftliches Archiv* 3 (1979): 508-521.

Kojima K. (1978): DIRECT FOREIGN INVESTMENT (London, Croome Helm, 1978).

Kumar K. (ed.) (1980): MULTINATIONALS FROM DEVELOPING COUNTRIES (Cambridge, Mass., MIT Press, 1980).

Lall S. (1980): "Monopolistic Advantages and Foreign Involvement by US Manufacturing Industry," *Oxford Economic Papers* 32 (1980): 102-122.

Lessard D. (1979): "Transfer Prices, Taxes and Financial Markets," in HAWKINS R. G. (ed.), THE ECONOMIC EFFECTS OF MULTINATIONAL CORPORATIONS (Greenwich, Conn., JAI Press, 1979).

Magee S. (1977): "Information and the Multinational Enterprise: An Appropriability Theory of Direct Foreign Investment," in BHAGWATI J. N. (ed.), THE NEW INTERNATIONAL ECONOMIC ORDER (Cambridge, Mass., MIT Press, 1977).

Malmgren H. (1978): "Multinational Business and the Decline of Overseas Investment," *Multinational Business* 1 (1978): 10-17.

McManus J. F. (1972): "The Theory of the Multinational Firm," in: G. PAQUET (ed.), THE MULTINATIONAL FIRM AND THE NATION STATE (Toronto, Collier Mac-Millan, 1972).

Mikesell R. (1979): NEW PATTERNS OF MNE INVOLVEMENT IN THE MINERAL PROCESSING INDUSTRIES (London, British North American Committee, 1979).

OECD (1979): INVESTMENT PATTERNS IN DEVELOPING COUNTRIES (Paris, OECD, 1979).

Owen R. F. (1979): "Inter-industry Determinants of Foreign Direct Investment: A Perspective Emphasising the Canadian Experience," Working Papers in International Economics, Princeton University (May 1979).

Penrose E. (1958): THE THEORY OF THE GROWTH OF THE FIRM (Oxford, Basil Blackwell, 1958).

Rose S. (1977): "Multinationals in Retreat" *Fortune* 96 (August 1977): 111.

Rugman A. (1979): INTERNATIONAL DIVERSIFICATION AND THE MULTINATIONAL ENTERPRISE (Lexington, Lexington Books, 1979).

Southard F. (1931): AMERICAN INDUSTRY IN EUROPE (New York, Houghton Mifflin, 1931).

Stevens G. V. (1974): "The Determinants of Investment," in DUNNING J. H. (ed.), ECONOMIC ANALYSIS AND THE MULTINATIONAL ENTERPRISE (London, Allen and Unwin, 1974).

Swedenborg B. (1980): THE MULTINATIONAL OPERATIONS OF SWEDISH FIRMS: AN ANALYSIS OF DETERMINANTS AND EFFECTS (Stockholm, Industrial Institute for Economic and Social Research, 1980).

United Nations (1978): TRANSNATIONAL CORPORATIONS IN WORLD DEVELOPMENT: A RE-EXAMINATION, UK Economic and Social Council, E. 78 II A5 (1978).

United Nations (1981): TRANSNATIONAL CORPORATIONS AND INTERNATIONAL TOURISM (to be published by the UN Centre on Transnational Corporations, New York, 1981).

Vernon R. (1966): "International Investment and International Trade in the Product Cycle," *Quarterly Journal of Economics* 80 (1966): 190-207.

Vernon R. (1979): "The Product Cycle Hypothesis in a New International Environment," *Oxford Bulletin of Economics and Statistics* 41 (1979): 255-267.

Wells L. (1970): THE PRODUCT LIFE CYCLE AND INTERNATIONAL TRADE (Cambridge, Mass., Harvard University Press, 1970).

Who Owns Whom (1978): WHO OWNS WHOM (London, A. Roskill & Co., 1978).

Williamson O. (1975): MARKETS AND HIERARCHIES (New York, Free Press, 1975).

World Bank (1979): WORLD DEVELOPMENT REPORT (Washington, World Bank, 1979).

Summary

This paper has three aims: first, to review the most significant trends in the foreign activities of multinational enterprises in the 1970's; second, to report on the major thrusts in the thinking of economists about the determinants of these activities; and, third, to take note of the more important changes in attitudes of Governments and international fora towards multinational enterprises. The first part of the paper treats the main features of international direct investment and multinational enterprises, such as the growth, the geographical origin and the geographical and industrial distribution of foreign direct investment, the extent of multinationality of leading multinational enterprises and the rise in joint ventures and non-equity arrangements. The second part deals with the economic theory of multinational enterprises' activities. The general trend is a movement away from the mere application of the industrial organization theory or international location theory towards a number of eclectic combinations of these theories, together with the financial theory, the theory of the firm, the macro-economic theory etc. This eclectic explanation of international production helps to evaluate the above-mentioned features of and changes in multinational enterprises' activities. As the third part of the paper demonstrates, reactions and policies towards multinational enterprises have tended to develop from the initial stance of confrontation to a more detached position of the states and multinational enterprises towards each other. There are several reasons for the evolution of this different relationship: Insight into the interdependence of the nations is certainly growing; the oil crisis has made states more aware of the services multinational enterprises are especially well equipped to provide; the development of international action, for example by the UN, the OECD or the EEC, also plays an important role. As to the future of multinational enterprises and their relationship with the states, most rests, of course, on the world economic and political future. But much will depend also on the extent to which home Governments will continue to permit the growth of conglomerate companies or will forbid further growth by merger control laws or other means. There is some evidence that the 1980's might be more the decade of the medium-large multinational enterprises than that of the really giant companies.

Merger Policy in the United Kingdom

ROGER G. OPIE[*]
Oxford

I. Determining Factors for a Merger Policy

A. Lack of Any Real Competition Policy in the U. K. Prior to 1965

The monitoring, let alone the control, of mergers has not been a high priority during the history of competition policy in the U. K. That it did become so in 1965 was the result of a number of accidents.

The enabling legislation was the Monopolies and Mergers Act 1965, later consolidated into the Fair Trading Act 1973. Until 1965, mergers (or acquisitions or take-overs – the distinctions are not relevant here) could be investigated only ex post and if the merger created a statutory "monopoly situation", i. e. a market share of not less than 33¹/3%. Such a power was too cumbersome ever to be used. Nor was it ever used. Indeed, an adverse judgment by the Monopolies Commission would have embarrassed any British Government since no Government has so far been willing to divest enterprises (except of course in the public sector).

B. Factors Leading to the Adoption of the Monopolies and Mergers Act 1965

The factors leading to the passage of the 1965 Act can be separated:

1. The Return of a Labour Government in 1964

It might be thought that the 1964 election which returned a Labour Government for the first time since 1951 was significant. I believe not. A Conservative Government would have introduced legislation with similar intent and outcome, even if not identical detail. Competition policy is, in any case, not an area of party-political contention in the U. K.

2. Governmental Impotence to Control a Highly Controversial Take-Over

More important by far was the discovery that Whitehall was powerless to influence the outcome of the (contested) take-over bid by *I.C.I.* for *Courtaulds*, a very large vertical merger by the largest U. K. chemical manufacturer with one of its major customers, itself a very large synthetic fibres manufacturer.

---

[*] The Author is a Member of the Monopolies and Mergers Commission. The views expressed here are purely personal and commit no-one but himself.

3. Fear that Mergers might be used as a Means of Avoiding the Restrictive Trade Practices Act 1956

Whitehall was concerned that a consequence of the Restrictive Trade Practices Act of 1956, which virtually outlawed restrictive agreements, may have been to encourage firms to merge instead. This is not to suggest that all mergers are as wicked as most restrictive trade practices — but simply that there was no machinery for judgment.

4. Rising Concentration and its Controversial Evaluation

a) As an examination of Tables 1-2 shows, even by the mid-1960's concentration at the "firm" level in U. K. industry was already high and rising.

Table 1

Share of the Hundred Largest Enterprises in Manufacturing Net Output, U. K. 1909-72

Year	Share %
1909	16[a]
1924	22[a]
1935	24
1949	22
1953	27
1958	32
1963	37[b]
1968	41
1970	39
1971	40
1972	41

Source: For 1909-1970, S. J. PRAIS, THE EVOLUTION OF GIANT FIRMS IN BRITAIN, p. 4 (Cambridge University Press, London, 1976). Thereafter, compiled by the Author.
[a] Approximate figures.
[b] Includes steel companies; reduced to 36½ per cent approximately if steel companies are excluded.

The majority of mergers were (and still are) horizontal, and this automatically produces an increase in the level of firm concentration at the industry level as is shown by Tables 3 and 4.

On the other hand, in contrast with the position today, vertical mergers and the increasingly popular diversification or conglomerate mergers, which cause such increase at the economy level, especially perhaps in an economy which has grown as slowly as that of the U. K., were, as Table 5 shows, relatively few.[1] Mergers are made easier by the existence of a highly developed capital market in the U. K. (and in the U. S.) and there seemed a correlation between merger

---

[1] *See,* generally, S. J. PRAIS, THE EVOLUTION OF GIANT FIRMS IN BRITAIN: A STUDY OF THE GROWTH OF CONCENTRATION IN MANUFACTURING INDUSTRY IN BRITAIN, 1909-1970 (Cambridge University Press, London, 1976).

Table 2
Share of 100 Largest Manufacturing Establishments[a] in Net Output
and Employment, 1930-68

	Percentages Share in	
	Net output	Employment
1930	10.8[b]	8.2[b]
1935	11.2	8.4
1948	9.0	9.5
1951	9.4	9.3
1954	10.1	9.6
1958	10.5[c]	9.9
1963	11.1	10.1
1968	10.8	9.2

Source: S. J. PRAIS, THE EVOLUTION OF GIANT FIRMS IN BRITAIN p. 46 (Cambridge University Press, London, 1976). .
[a] On a ranking by employment in each establishment (distributions ranked by size of net output per establishment are not published in the Census).
[b] Approximate figures. The published size-distribution was based on returns, with an average of 1.17 establishments per return. The largest 85 (= 100/1.17) returns were taken here.
[c] Share in sales (net output not available for this year).

Table 3
Contribution of Mergers to Growth of Concentration

Period	1958-63	1954-65	1958-67	1957-69	1969-73	1958-70
Percentage of Change in Concentration attributable to Mergers	33	43	62	116[a]	95	50

Source: A REVIEW OF MONOPOLIES AND MERGERS POLICY (Cmnd. 7198, H.M.S.O., 1978).
[a] i. e. concentration would have fallen in absence of mergers.

Table 4
Monopolies Created or Strengthened by Proposed Mergers 1965-77

Market Share %	25-50	51-80	81-100	Not given	Total
Number	164	108	54	47	373
Percentage	44	29	14	13	100

Source: ANNUAL REPORT OF THE DIRECTOR GENERAL OF FAIR TRADING FOR 1978 (H.M.S.O., London, 1978).

Table 5A

Percentage of Proposed Mergers by Value of Acquired Assets Considered by the Mergers Panel 1965–77 Classified by Type of Integration[a]

Type of Integration	1965[b]	1966	1967	1968	1969	1970	1971	1972	1973	1974	1975	1976	1977	1978
Horizontal	84	85	92	91	91	78	66	40	76	65	77	66	57	53
Vertical	9	8	4	2	0	0	4	10	2	2	4	7	11	13
Conglomerate	7	7	4	7	9	22	30	50	22	33	19	27	32	34
Total value £ millions (100 per cent)	1,125	998	2,273	8,499	3,714	2,596	1,687	3,588	4,878	7,621	5,786	4,123	4,676	11,999

Source: Annual Report of the Director General of the Office of Fair Trading for 1979 (H.M.S.O., London, 1979).
[a] The allocation of mergers to the three categories involves an element of judgement and this should be kept in mind when interpreting these figures.
[b] part-year

Table 5B

Percentage of Proposed Mergers by Value of Acquired Assets Considered by the Mergers Panel 1965–77 Classified by Statutory Criteria

Statutory Criterion	1965[a]	1966	1967	1968	1969	1970	1971	1972	1973	1974	1975	1976	1977	1978	1965–78
Value of Assets	83	62	55	87	91	98	75	87	92	96	98	91	97	90	90
Market Share[b]	3	4	2	1	2	1	2	1	1	0	0	1	1	5	2
Both Criteria	14	34	43	12	7	1	23	12	7	4	2	8	2	5	8
Total Value £ millions (100 per cent)	1,125	998	2,273	8,499	3,714	2,596	1,687	3,588	4,878	7,621	5,786	4,123	4,675	11,999	63,564

Source: Annual Report of the Director General of the Office of Fair Trading for 1979 (H.M.S.O., London 1979)
[a] part-year
[b] one-third up to November 1973; one-quarter thereafter.

booms and equity booms. In addition, the U. K. tends to follow U. S. fashions in most things within a short time-lag. The "urge to merge", or even "merger-mania" became the trendy thing for business-men in the U. K. soon after its boom in the U. S. A.

b) While there was growing doubt among academic investigators that mergers were successful even in achieving the private benefits of higher profits, lower costs and so on[2] (a view which is supported by the statistics set out in Table 6), it was nevertheless a fashionable view of the 1960's (in the U. K. at least) that "bigger is better." Economies of scale were thought to be king. It was argued by many observers, officials and Ministers that British industry had got into a vicious circle of low productivity levels and growth, poor international competitiveness, defeat in export markets and high import penetration, squeezed sales and profits, low investment and hence low productivity. One breakout might be through mergers which would create size and hence the opportunity of economies of scale, albeit at the expense of rising concentration.

Table 6
Post-Merger Profitability

Year after Merger	Per Cent of Firms with lower Profits
0	34
1	54
2	52
3	53
4	66
5	67
6	52
7	62

Source: G. MEEKS, DISAPPOINTING MARRIAGE: A STUDY OF THE GAINS FROM MERGER (Cambridge University Press, London, 1977).

Even the dangers of rising concentration were perhaps overstressed, it was argued, because the increasing openness of the U. K. domestic market, and later our entry into full membership of the E. E. C., meant that concentration of *output* could rise while concentration of the market could drastically fall.

C. Active Competition Policy Since 1965

1. The Positive and Negative Aspects: Encouraging Beneficial Mergers and Discouraging Potentially Detrimental Mergers

As a result of the combination of all these factors the need was felt for a positive policy to encourage mergers where market forces alone were too feeble to

---

[2] *See,* for a general consideration of these factors, G. MEEKS, DISAPPOINTING MARRIAGE: A STUDY OF THE GAINS FROM MERGER (Cambridge University Press London, 1977).

produce them, in parallel with another policy to monitor merger proposals which market forces did throw up. Institutions also grew up in parallel — publicly-financed quasi-merchant banks like the Industrial Reorganisation Corporation and later the National Enterprise Board on the one side, and the enlarged and renamed Monopolies and Mergers Commission on the other.

a) Ironically, the positive arm of the policy has been from the outset enmeshed in party-political controversy. On the change of government from Labour to Conservative in 1970, the Industrial Reorganisation Corporation was wound up, only to be reborn within a few years to be used actively both in rescue operations (such as of British Leyland) and in more active support of corporations too small to appeal to the Stock Exchange but wishing to expand by merging.

b) The negative, monitoring side of the policy has never been the object of party-political controversy — any more than has the policy of monitoring monopolies or restrictive trade practices. But if it is not contentious, how can it be thought to have been successful? Does it matter a row of beans? A respectable case can be made out on each side of the argument. I believe (naturally) that it has been useful, but could be made much more so.

2. Reconciling the Public and the Private Interest

One controversial point made most often by Counsel for one (or both) of the would-be merging enterprises concerns the role of the respective owners, viz. the shareholders of the enterprises. It is argued that unless there is the prospect of the creation or intensification of a "monopoly situation", the public and the private interest coincide. In that case, the shareholders alone should judge whether they want to accept the offer of Company A for their holdings in Company B. If they do, that is enough, it is argued. This proposition clearly is relevant only in so-called conglomerate or diversification mergers where concentration is negligible or zero at the industry level, and possibly also at the economy level.[3]

II. The Control of Mergers under the Fair Trading Act 1973: Problems of Practice and Procedure[4]

A. The Procedure for Examining Proposed or Actual Mergers

The procedure to be followed is now contained in Part V of the Fair Trading Act 1973 (FTA 1973), (consolidating the Monopolies and Merger Act 1965).[5]

---

[3] This point was argued at length in the case of *Rank Xerox Ltd.* and *de la Rue Ltd.* (1969) H. C. P. 298.

[4] Only the practical and procedural aspects of U.K. merger control will be considered in this chapter. For a substantive analysis of the U.K. position, reference should be made to V. Korah, *Control of Mergers in the U.K. on Grounds of Competition: Legislation, Practice and Experience, infra* this Volume pp. 45 *et seq.*

[5] The relevant sections of the FTA 1973 (sec. 57-77 and sec. 84) are annexed. *See* Annex II *infra*, pp. 231 et seq. Reference should also be made to the Competition Act 1980, which will not be discussed here, but is discussed in Korah, *supra* note 4 at pp. 67 *et seq.*

1. Distinction between "Newspaper" and "Other" Mergers

The Act draws a sharp distinction between "newspaper mergers" (defined in Sec. 57) and "other mergers" (defined in Sec. 63), the former being regulated by the special provisions of sec. 57-62 and the latter by the general provisions of sec. 63-77. This difference in the treatment accorded the two types of merger in the Act reflects the great concern in the U. K. about the increasing concentration of ownership (and ultimately of control) of the press and its possible dangers to freedom of expression and diversity of opinion. Purely economic considerations of the efficient use of resources are not decisive in this field — there are more important things than economics. Thus the provisions governing newspaper mergers provide for a generally stricter control than the provisions governing other mergers, eliminating much of the discretionary element, e.g. in the Secretary of State's power of referring mergers to the Monopolies and Mergers Commission, and providing more effective enforcement measures.

2. Referals of Mergers to the Monopolies and Mergers Commision

a) In the case of "other" mergers, the power and the responsibility to refer a proposed merger for investigation by the Monopolies and Merger Commission lies within the discretion of the Secretary of State for Trade alone[6] (although the advice and recommendation of the Director General of the Office of Fair Trading is often sought).

b) In the case of newspaper mergers, unlike "other" mergers, the Secretary of State has no discretion in making a reference[7] except for a de minimis provision,[8] and where the newspaper taken-over would otherwise cease publication.[9]

3. Notification of Mergers

a) In so-called "other mergers" the parties have no responsibility to notify the Secretary of State of a proposed or actual merger. Instead, it is the duty of the Director General (Sec. 76 (a)) "to take all such steps as are reasonably practicable for keeping himself informed about actual or prospective arrangements or transactions which may constitute or result in the creation of merger situations qualifying for investigation" and to make recommendations to the Secretary of State concerning possible action.[10] This laxity seems to me pointless although there is no reason to believe that the Director General will "miss" any mergers of any significance. In any case, a merger can be referred at any time within 6 months of its consummation:[11] the danger to the parties of such a reference at an inconveniently late stage in their negotiations is no doubt great enough to deter any attempt at secrecy.

b) On the other hand, in the case of newspaper mergers, the parties to the

---

[6] Sec. 64 FTA 1973.
[7] Sec. 58 (2) FTA 1973.
[8] Sec. 58 (4) and 59 (2) FTA 1973.
[9] Sec. 58 (3) and 59 (2) FTA 1973.
[10] Sec. 76 (b) FTA 1973.
[11] Sec. 64 (4) FTA 1973.

proposed merger are responsible for alerting the Secretary of State to the proposal and can be fined for failing to notify.[12] A recent case[13] uncovered such a failure to notify an earlier merger involving one of the parties, but no action was taken by the Department of Trade.

c) Voluntary notification has been an increasing phenomenon in recent years, the parties to mergers frequently approaching the Office of Fair Trading informally for guidance on the "acceptability" of their proposed merger,[14] prompted, no doubt, by a desire to avoid the consequences of an ex post facto annulment.

B. The Role of the Director General of the Office of Fair Trading: "Watchdog" Function and Duty to Make Recommendations

As we have seen above,[15] the Director General is charged with the duty of keeping himself informed on the "merger situation". This is no more than a first step, however, since it is also the Director General's responsibility "to make recommendations to the Secretary of State as to any action under . . . this Act [the FTA 1973] which in the opinion of the Director it would be expedient for the Secretary of State to take . . ." (Section 76 (b)).

1. The Procedure for Making Recommendations: Making Use of the Expertise of the Mergers Panel

The Director General makes recommendations after a merger proposal has been vetted by a Mergers Panel. Members of this Panel include his own lawyers, economists and accountants, and also the secretary ex officio (and possibly some staff) of the Monopolies and Mergers Commission, and some civil servants from the relevant Department (or Departments) in Whitehall. Only a proportion of mergers are considered at all.

I suspect that discussions within the Panel are rarely unanimously in favour of recommending a reference to the Monopolies and Mergers Commission. No outsider knows, of course. What we do know is that such recommendations are relatively rare, and a more than possible explanation of this is that the various factions on the Panel are more successful at opposing than promoting. Certainly, in recent years, the failure of Ministers to refer certain merger proposals for examination has roused more puzzled, even cynical, comment than has any excessive zeal.

2. The Time Element

A decision on whether to recommend a reference is usually made within three or four weeks. It may sometimes happen that undertakings on future behaviour are sought by the Department from the parties, or are offered, as a condition for

---

[12] Sec. 58 (1) and 62 FTA 1973.

[13] *West Somerset Free Press Ltd.* and *British United Press Ltd.* (1980).

[14] *See* Table 7, *infra* p. 33, where the 1970-78 statistics *inter alia* on applications to the Office of Fair Trading for guidance are set out.

[15] *Supra* § II.A.3.a.

Table 7

Merger Panel Activity

Year	No. of Mergers	Mergers Considered by Panel		Guidance
		No.	%	%
1970	899	80	9	18
1971	961	110	10	21
1972	1311	114	9	16
1973	1313	134	10	16
1974	570	141	25	13
1975	388	160	41	21
1976	402	163	41	20
1977	521	194	37	8
1978		229		

Source: ANNUAL REPORTS OF THE DIRECTOR GENERAL OF THE OFFICE OF FAIR TRADING FOR 1978 AND 1979 (H.M.S.O., London, 1978-9).

Table 8

Mergers Referred to Monopolies and Mergers Commission (1965-1978)

Category	No.	No. Abandoned without Report	No. Found to be Against Public Interest	No. Found not to be Against Public Interest
Horizontal	26	6	9	9
Vertical	3	–	1	2
Conglomerate	15	9	3	3
Total	43	15	13	14[a]

Source: ANNUAL REPORT OF THE DIRECTOR GENERAL OF THE OFFICE OF FAIR TRADING FOR 1978 (H.M.S.O., London, 1978).

[a] 1 outstanding

allowing the merger to proceed. To an outsider this seems commendably swift, although I imagine that the parties, if the merger is an agreed one, chafe at the delay. By contrast, if a take-over is an unwelcome and hence contested one (e.g. *Beechams Ltd.* and *Glaxo Ltd.*),[16] the target firm will probably use the time (certainly Glaxo did) to try to persuade the Secretary of State to refer the take-over for investigation.

Sometimes, a merger is proposed on condition that it is not referred. The parties have argued that they were unwilling to wait for the six months that the Commission is allowed (but sometimes does not need) in order to complete the investigation. This has always seemed to me to suggest that the proposal was scarcely serious. It is true, of course, that relative share prices may shift a lot on

[16] (1972) H. C. P. 341.

the Stock Exchange during the enquiry, but the public benefits of a quick snap purchase seem to me to be unimportant compared with the need to weigh up the "pros and cons" of an irreversible switch of ownership.

3. The Effect of a Recommendation

If the Panel does decide to recommend a reference, it is likely but not certain that the Secretary of State will concur. On three occasions so far (out of some 900 merger proposals in 5 years) the Secretary of State of the day has declined, once after being overruled in the Cabinet. The Director General was not amused. The reason (or at least the excuse) given in public was "wider considerations" such as a worsening of regional unemployment if the merger was not allowed. This is somewhat unsatisfactory, if only because regional unemployment is one of the dimensions of the "Public Interest" (see Sec. 84 of the Fair Trading Act) which the Monopolies and Mergers Commission is bound to consider in its own recommendations.

C. The Monopolies and Mergers Commission

1. Procedure

Once a merger has been referred, the procedures of the Monopolies and Mergers Commission are standard.[17]

a) The first step is a hearing before a Monopolies and Mergers Commission Panel. The parties are invited to appear separately, with or without counsel (in earlier days often without, but nowadays always with), before a panel of Commission members. The panel is chaired by the Chairman of the Commission in all enquiries except the smallest ones, e. g. some of the small but non-discretionary newspaper mergers. The panel itself varies in number from about five to as many as ten members. It is essential that the panel should include, and be seen by the parties and the public to include, the widest possible range of backgrounds, experience, expertise, political and regional sympathies, without any conflict of interest such as might prejudice or condition one's judgment. It is common therefore to mount a panel containing at least a professional accountant, a trade unionist, an economist, an active and possibly also a retired business manager, and a lawyer; and, in the case of an important merger, to double up on one or more of these professions.

b) The Commission's staff assigned to an enquiry will number as many as eight or ten, including the Secretary of the Commission, an assistant secretary, economists, accountants and industrial advisers.

c) A basic characteristic of the proceedings is that they are open and all interests are represented. The Commission puts notices in the national press, and the relevant specialist press, inviting comment and argument from suppliers, customers, competitors, local authorities, the trade unions and the "general public". Separate hearings are held with the parties as early as they can arrange

---

[17] *See* generally A. SUTHERLAND, THE MONOPOLIES COMMISSION IN ACTION (Cambridge University Press, London, 1969).

and with anyone else who asks; and a second (or more) hearing will be given to the parties after the Panel has heard all other representations in order to discuss the public interest issues that have arisen and seem to the Commission to be important and relevant.

d) The Panel will also hold numerous internal meetings with the Commission staff, to consider the conclusions and to vet the draft factual chapters of the report. These latter only are sent to the party concerned and the facts checked and the draft (if possible) agreed.

e) As to time limits, it is rare for this procedure to exceed the six months allowed for such enquiries (an extra three months was allowed for *Lonrho/ Suits/House of Fraser*[18]).

2. The Function of the Monopolies and Mergers Commission

The Act only allows the Commission to decide whether the merger is or is not against the public interest. It is not asked to decide whether, let alone how much or in what ways, the merger is in the public interest. Of course, the judgment is sometimes very much a balancing act — "this argument tells against the merger, that one for it" — and the balance may be tilted by asking for and receiving undertakings from the parties on, e. g., redundancies, pension arrangements or export targets. When and if we find against a merger, it is because we find detriment to the public interest but no (persuasive) remedies for that detriment.

3. Preventing a Merger: Formal and Informal Methods

If a merger is to be prevented, the Commission needs to produce at least a two-thirds majority of the panel members against the merger. Any division at all is very rare. In the case of the Clearing Banks merger[19] a majority of only 6 to 4 against the merger of Barclays and Lloyds was enough to allow the (then) President of the Board of Trade to "persuade" the two managements not to proceed (although Barclays was allowed to acquire the much smaller Martins). This reflects more the influence of the monetary authorities over the rather tame English financial institutions than the acceptance of the Monopolies and Mergers Commission's recommendations. It may also have reflected one of the potential benefits of a prolonged, objective analysis of the private costs and benefits of a particular merger proposal. For example, the Commission investigated the proposed merger of *Unilever* and *Allied Breweries*[20] and did not recommend against it. So lukewarm was the report, however, that the merger proposal lapsed and, within a short time, the Chairmen of both companies resigned. In other words, the investigation, the questions asked, the answers probed, the attitudes struck and the time taken are all valuable in possibly cooling the passionate ardour of potential marriage partners, and converting a hot-headed proposal into a sensible separation before the marriage ceremony takes place. No-one loses by

[18] (1979). H. C. P.
[19] *Barclays, Lloyds and Martins* (1968) H. C. P. 310.
[20] (1969) H. C. P. 297.

such a process, although the "engagement period" does of course impose both financial and real-resource costs on the companies concerned. In my view, it would be cheap at twice the price.

III. Evaluating Mergers: Economic and Legal Considerations

A. Efficiency Considerations

Mergers are, of course, much concerned with efficiency.[21] One can distinguish between three types of efficiency: static, dynamic and managerial efficiency.

1. Static Efficiency

This is a matter of minimum efficient scale (or economics of scale), or economies of rationalisation (i. e. one-off gains). In the three Banks merger[22] both rationalisation and scale offered economies – although the Commission doubted whether they would in fact be realised. Indeed we thought that if the economies were so great as were claimed, the two groups of clearing banks not included in the merger would be driven into each other's arms in order to survive. That outcome would be highly undesirable.

2. Dynamic Efficiency

This is concerned with inventiveness, aggressive, adventurous and successful research and development, and with innovations. The *Beechams, Boots and Glaxo* merger[23] was found to be against the Public Interest largely on the grounds that profits and finance were ample to maintain three separate centres of research and to fund the risks of the necessary development. To merge either Boots or Beechams with Glaxo would result in the loss of the benefits of inspired intuition and differences of judgment.

3. Managerial Efficiency

Both the above dimensions of efficiency are most closely connected with horizontal mergers, although there are some examples in vertical ones. Managerial efficiency is likely to be most important in conglomerate or diversification mergers – indeed what else matters? The Monopolies and Mergers Commission turned down *Rank/de la Rue*[24] largely because we judged the managerial styles were wholly incompatible, and we thought none too highly of the bidder's managerial prowess in any case. To add still more divisions to the unwieldy Rank structure would, we felt, endanger two companies, whereas each, we thought, had good prospects on its own.

By contrast, we thought compatibility was possible in the *British Match/Wilkinson Sword* merger.[25] One company was cash-rich, and in a static, even

---

[21] Only the efficiency aspects of the policy will be considered here. For a discussion of the competition aspects *see* Korah, *supra* note 4 at pp. 45 *et seq*.

[22] Cf. *supra* note 19.

[23] Cf. *supra* note 16.

[24] Cf. *supra* note 3.

[25] (1973) Cmnd 5442.

declining, market; the other had technical prowess, good growth prospects, but great difficulties in raising external finance — to adapt the phrase on Keynes' famous wedding invitation, it was a marriage not of "beauty and brains" but "money and brains".

B. Balancing the Pros and Cons

Such considerations matter most where there is need for some balance to the possible detriments arising from greater size or greater concentration. Often, there are neither efficiency benefits nor monopoly dangers. The balance of the legislation forbids us to reject such a proposal — people should then be allowed to do what they want to do. Hence, we could see no great gains nor great disadvantages in the *Unilever/Allied Breweries* merger,[26] and were bound to let it through (although it was not in fact consummated).

IV. Basic Dilemmas of Merger Policy

A. The Problem of Forecasting

1. The Choice Between Two Possible Futures

The Monopolies and Mergers Commission is required to compare and contrast two forecasts — the future performance of the two companies if they remain separate, and the future of a merged company. In horizontal or vertical mergers, which promise (or threaten) much (and irreversible) integration, these alternative futures are likely to be very different — if they were not, what would be the purpose of the merger?

2. Forecasts not Open to Proof

But if the merger is contested, each side is flying blind. If it is agreed, it is hard to test the propositions they put forward. In either case, few of the claims are quantifiable and fewer still are quantified. Indeed, to many entrepreneurs, quantification is in itself an alien and irrelevant procedure — if you know in your heart you are right, what have mere numbers to do with anything?

3. Enterpreneurial Forecasting by a State Body?

The fact that the decision to be taken must be guided by instinct raises a problem for the whole procedure of Monopolies and Mergers Commission investigation. Can middle-class members of the Establishment (and who else is likely to be appointed, or even proposed, as a member of the Commission?) really ever judge the prospects of pure entrepreneurship? I realise that our task, and duty, is to judge the consequences for the public as well as, or rather than, for the private interest — but it is not easy. All I can say is, in spite of our varied backgrounds, experiences and prejudices, we are usually unanimous. But are we sometimes unanimously wrong? I expect so, but how can we learn by experience? How can

[26] Cf. *supra* note 20.

we ever discover what would have happened if we had decided otherwise? We can proceed only on general principle (I hardly dare say "in the light of theory") and each case is extremely particular. Precedent may help, but not much.

The element of "entrepreneurship" is no doubt reduced by two forces: a) the prevalence of horizontal or vertical mergers compared with (pure) conglomerate mergers — and the fact that managers are not "whiz-kid entrepreneurs". The latter are more likely to pursue the conglomerate (but not the diversification) direction of merger — and there, each case is certainly different. And, b) the lawyers have taken over. One result is, no doubt, that we now face a better class of proposal, but equally a smoother presentation. No longer is a proposal merely frivolous or fashionable. As the Director General has written, the consultation procedure and the threat of a full investigation have "reduced the number of ill-thought-out proposals". Have they merely smoothed out the abrasive, entrepreneurial proposals? Are we suffering from "anti-trust overkill"?

B. Problems Arising from the Economic Complexity of Mergers

1. Disclosure and the Legitimate Interests of Business Secrecy

We face a problem in relation to other monitoring bodies. In the U.K., the Stock Exchange Take-over Panel is concerned to ensure fairness for shareholders. One consequence is that, in a takeover involving companies A, B and C, no one company may reveal to another any facts it does not reveal to all. In a recent case (*Beechams, Boots, Glaxo*),[27] Glaxo rejected the advances of Beechams but embraced Boots. When asked about the future, Beechams could legitimately reply "wait and see", and Boots were also forced to move into the dark. Neither could learn the true state of Glaxo's operations or prospects. Our questions about the future were not well answered — how could they be?

2. The Limits of a "Negative" Role

The Monopolies and Mergers Commission is sometimes convinced that a merger of A and B is in itself unobjectionable, except for the hunch that a merger of A with an, as yet, unknown C would be better. Does that alone make the merger A/B operate against the public interest? Is the answer for the Commission to operate more closely with a (public) merger-marriage-bureau? But what do we do if there is no such bureau?

3. Difficulty in Determining "Who Controls What"

Sometimes, it is not certain that a merger is in prospect! The question is not "who owns whom?" but "who controls what?" How much of the equity does one have to own in order to control? If I own 51% of the equity and you own 49%, I control. If no-one else owns more than 1% each, how little do I need to own in order to control — 10%? 20%? Certainly much less than 51%. Is control, like beauty, in the eye of the (be)holder? The Fair Trading Act tries to cover this position through Sec. 65 (4) (a) and (b), but the issue of "who controls

---

[27] Cf. *supra* note 16.

what?" depends on motive, the dispersion of ownership, the accident of proxy votes at annual and special general meetings. A "merger" is not always a simple affair.[28]

C. Problems Created by Conflicts in Different Public Interests: Merger Control v. Full Employment

There is an underlying absurdity in competition policy and, within it, merger policy. Each is an aspect of applied welfare economics, of how to allocate resources in the most efficient way. But suppose that the economy cannot even find use for the resources it has. What is the point in saving resources if they have no alternative use except to stand in the dole queue? Is increased unemployment which results from a merger a good thing (because it allows a potential growth of output somewhere else) or a bad thing (because those resources are now simply and openly wasted)? Is competition policy a necessity in a fully-employed economy, and a luxury in contemporary Western Europe? Such issues become even more agonising when a merger (which perhaps increases market power) is the alternative to bankruptcy and closure. Where does the public interest then lie?

V. Suggestions for Reform

A. Abolition of Discretion to Refer in All Cases of Mergers Involving "Large" Companies

The present legislation catches mergers which create or strengthen a "monopoly position" (25% of the relevant market) or which involve more than £ 15 million assets. Both are necessary, to catch both the "step-by-small-step-to-monopoly-merger" as well as the conglomerate/diversification merger. But whether a merger proposal is investigated is discretionary. I would urge that any merger involving a "large" company should automatically be referred for investigation. "How large is large?" is an amusing question, but Civil Servants can doubtless produce an answer acceptable to the House of Commons. This would not imply that any and every such merger was against the public interest (in which case it would be simpler to prohibit them) but simply that they should without exception be vetted.

B. Shifting the Onus of Proof

A more important and general reform would be to shift the "onus of proof". At present the legislation is supposedly neutral. The Monopolies and Mergers Commission can only prevent a merger found to be against the public interest. Should the parties to mergers, at least of large companies, be required to satisfy the Commission that the merger is positively in the public interest? I think so.

---

[28] See *Lonrho/Suits/House of Fraser, supra,* note 18.

VI. Overall Evaluation on the Basis of the U. K. Experience

The concept of "competition" is largely a structural one — "competitiveness" is one of behaviour. Mere numbers are, if not irrelevant, at most incidental to a judgment of future conduct. The real issues are: Are there economies to be gained from size? Even so, will they be pursued, let alone gained, from the present management? Why were they not already gained from competitive prowess? A reasonably sceptical attitude by outsiders has resulted in only nine out of twenty-six horizontal mergers (Table 7) passing the investigation. And even those mergers might not have been treated as "acceptable" if the onus had been on the parties to prove a positive case in the Public Interest.

"Efficiency" is both a "static" and a "dynamic" concept. We are here concerned with research and development, innovative behaviour, new products and new techniques, all of which are the outcome of a balance of resources (finance and manpower), desire, need, compulsion, competitive pressures, room for manoeuvre, rate of growth of the industry and of the economy, the state of "business confidence". Each case is therefore very much a matter of 'ad hoc' judgment.

But does the real threat not arise from the facility which an active equity market, viz. the City of London and the Stock Exchange, offers to effect changes of ownership with no certain private gains (Table 5) and even less certain public gains?

It is of course clear that "merger policy" in the U. K. has failed to halt the increase in concentration (Tables 1, 2 and 3) but that begs the question of whether concentration and hence "diminished numerical competition" have reduced, or affected, or enhanced competitiveness.

Everything in this field, as in so much else, is coloured by the slow rate of growth of the U. K. economy since the War relative to the rest of the industrialised world outside the U. S. (although not, of course, relative to its own historic rate of growth). To what extent this "failure" has been due to structural problems, or behavioural ones, or failures of policy is a question of (many) judgments.

Summary

An active merger policy in the U. K. dates only from 1965. It began as a reaction to waves of mergers, (perhaps made easier in the U. K. than in other advanced industrial countries by the operation of the Stock Exchange in the City) and to the ever-rising degree of industrial concentration.

The policy takes a broadly neutral view of the effects of mergers on the public interest. This latter is defined in terms of promoting effective competition, increasing efficiency and productivity, strengthening the balance of payments and improving the regional balance of employment. Some mergers may achieve one or more of these goals, but in addition may increase the degree of concentration in a particular market by an unacceptable margin.

Mergers which involve more than £15 million of assets or create or strengthen a market share of more than 25 per cent, are vetted by the Mergers Panel of the Office of Fair Trading. In a very small proportion (some 2 to 3 per cent) of cases, on a recommendation from the Office of Fair Trading and a reference from the Secretary of State for Trade, the proposal is investigated in depth and at length by the Monopolies and Mergers Commission.

The Commission is allowed and required by the Fair Trading Act of 1973 only to pronounce whether in its view the proposed merger "operates or may be expected to operate against the public interest."

Of the three per cent of merger proposals referred, one per cent is dropped by the parties concerned, one per cent is found to be against the public interest, and one per cent is found not to be so. With so few cases referred, and with each case necessarily treated on its merits, it is difficult, if not impossible, to discover a "philosophy" of merger policy in the U. K.

Such philosophy as there is, is established behind closed doors at the Office of Fair Trading and the Department of Trade. It is clear, however, that in spite of 15 years (so far) of surveillance, the degree of concentration in British industry has continued to rise, as has the pace of diversification and conglomeration. The "market" is of course more open as the ratio of imports in most sectors rises, and entry barriers to imports are removed.

Furthermore, scepticism about the public benefits of merging is increasing, linked loosely with growing disenchantment about even the expected "private" benefits (in the form of raised profits) of such irreversible shifts in ownership. It seems likely that, in time, policy on mergers will be stiffened, ultimately moving perhaps to automatic reference of really large mergers, and to a shift of the "onus of proof" of public benefit (rather than absence of public detriment) to the merging parties.

Chapter II

Merger Control Systems in European Countries

Control of Mergers in the U.K. on Grounds of Competition: Legislation, Practice and Experience

VALENTINE KORAH
London

I. Development and Main Features of the U.K. Merger Control System

A. The Background to the Adoption of The Current System

Since 1957[1] price fixing and many other anticompetitive agreements have been controlled very strictly in the United Kingdom, and it is possible that this has led to mergers in industries that were already concentrated.[2] In the early 1960's there was some concern that mergers might be anticompetitive and also that the management of the bidding company might not be able to use the resources of the target company efficiently. Power was therefore taken in the *Monopolies and Mergers Act 1965* (now the *Fair Trading Act 1973*, Part V)[3] for ministers to refer a merger or prospective merger to the Monopolies Commission (now Monopolies and Mergers Commission) for an investigation into whether the merger might be expected to operate against the public interest. The policy was bipartisan, the Labour Government largely implementing a White Paper[4] published by the previous Conservative Government, although the legislation finally adopted in fact went further than the recommendations of the White Paper.[5]

B. The Principal Characteristics of the System

1. Wide Definition of Merger, But No Duty to Notify
The definition of a merger[6] in terms of enterprises coming under common control is very broad indeed, but as there is no duty on the citizen to do

[1] With the introduction of the Restrictive Trade Practices Act 1956.
[2] For further discussion on this point and some statistical data, *see* R. Opie, *Merger Policy in the U.K., supra* this volume, pp. 25 *et seq.* particularly Tables 1-3 at pp. 26-27.
[3] The relevant provisions of the Fair Trading Act 1973 are annexed. *See infra* Annex II pp. 231 *et seq.*
[4] Cmnd 2299 (H.M.S.O., London, 1964).
[5] The Conservatives had expressed concern about "monopolising" or horizontal mergers; the statute also covered mergers where substantial assets were involved.
[6] See *infra* § II.B.1. pp. 50 *et seq.*

anything, even to notify, this causes no hardship provided that ministers receive and follow sensible advice from officials.

2. Reference by the Secretary of State

The Secretary of State[7] may refer a merger to the Commission, but has no duty to do so,[8] and where, for instance, a marriage constitutes a merger, he would be unlikely to do so, unless control of substantial assets were likely to change.

3. The Role of the Office of Fair Trading

The Office of Fair Trading looks at mergers voluntarily notified to it or published in the commercial press. It then advises the Minister whether each should be referred. This process is carried out within the secretariat of the Office of Fair Trading and is not open to public scrutiny. There is a Mergers Panel consisting of certain named officials from the Commission, the Ministry of Agriculture and Fisheries, the Department of Employment, and of the Environment, and the Treasury; an economist and sometimes a lawyer from the Office of Fair Trading. Others (e. g. representatives from the Bank of England, or the government department most closely concerned) join the Panel ad hoc. On occasion the Minister has refused to accept the advice given to him — one notable instance, widely reported, was the merger between *Manbré and Tate & Lyle* in 1976,[9] which resulted in only two sugar refiners being left in the U.K. — the British Sugar Corporation, which refines sugar beet; and the merging firms, which refine imported cane. It is said that the Minister was concerned that the merger would result in the loss of 600 jobs.

4. References to the Monopolies and Mergers Commission

About 2-3% of the mergers that qualify for reference are actually referred to the Commission. Although there is no duty under the Fair Trading Act to notify mergers in advance, the Takeover Code promulgated by the City Panel on Takeovers and Mergers requires that public share offers be made subject to the condition that the merger be not referred. The Office of Fair Trading is normally informed. Usually it can clear a merger within two or three weeks, but some difficult decisions may take four or five weeks. The Office gives high priority to such decisions. If a merger is referred, it may well be announced that it will not take place and, on a suitable undertaking being given, the reference is then withdrawn. If the merger is referred, and the Commission does not condemn it, a

---

[7] Several important Ministers bear this title, and in theory any one of these can exercise all the powers of the Secretary of State. In practice, however, those relating to competition policy are currently (1981) exercised by Mr. John Biffen, a Secretary of State at the Department of Trade.

[8] Newspaper mergers are subject to special regulation and the Secretary of State may be under a duty to refer where a newspaper merger is concerned. See § II.A. *infra* pp. 49 *et seq.*

[9] *See*, e. g., A. Cairncross, J. Kay and A. Silbertson, *The Regeneration of Manufacturing Industry,* (1977) MIDLAND BANK REVIEW 9, 17, (Autumn 1977).

further offer may be made for the shares, although often relative share prices may make the merger no longer attractive.[10]

5. The Public Interest Test

The test of public interest is quite open ended: the Commission is required to take into account all matters which it thinks may be relevant, including the matters contained in a list.[11] The list is not important, since the Commission is required to consider everything, mentioned or not, that it considers relevant. Habitually the Commission starts by analysing the effects of competition, but it also considers efficiency, and any effects on the balance of payments and on unemployment.

C. Contrasting Appraisals of Economic Concentration and Mergers

When the legislation was first implemented, most politicians seemed to favour most mergers on the ground that larger firms are needed to compete in world markets, although there was some concern about "monopolizing" mergers. Then and since, several economists have doubted the desirability of many of the mergers to which very large firms have been party and suggested that the onus should be altered, so that very large firms would have to show that mergers were likely to promote the public interest by making economies of scale possible or otherwise.[12]

Recently the Labour Government set up an inter-departmental working party under Mr. Liesner, which produced a consultative document: *A Review of Monopolies and Mergers Policy*.[13] It concluded that

3.46. The economic evidence points to a continuing high level of concentration in Britain which probably exceeds that in the economies of many of our international competitors. This, together with the possible effects of further increases in concentration, gives cause for concern although, as we have seen, high concentration does not necessarily imply an absence of competition and in some cases it may bring about benefits in the form of greater efficiency. Thus there is no strong case for abandoning the traditional UK pragmatic approach to competition policy of treating each case on its merits.

3.47. Nevertheless, in the light of the accumulated evidence and experience several aspects of competition policy need further attention. Mergers are an important source of greater concentration yet several academic investigations have suggested that roughly half of those

[10] As, *e. g.*, in the case of *Unilever/Allied Breweries* (1969) H.C.P. 297.
[11] S. 84 (1) Fair Trading Act 1973. *See* § II.D. *infra* pp. 57 *et seq.*
[12] S. Brittan, *An Excess of "Pragmatism"*, O.E.C.D. International Conference on Monopolies, Mergers and Restrictive Practices, 54 (1969); A. Sutherland, *The Management of Mergers Policy*, in A. CAIRNCROSS, ed., THE MANAGED ECONOMY 106, 130-4 (Blackwells, Oxford 1970); A. Cairncross, J. A. Kay and A. Silberston, *op. cit. supra* n. 9 at 9, 17. See also G. NEWBOULD, MANAGEMENT AND MERGER ACTIVITY (Gutshead, Doncaster, 1970) and G. MEEKS, DISAPPOINTING MARRIAGE: A STUDY OF THE GAINS FROM MERGER (Cambridge University Press, London 1977) whose researches show the inefficiencies resulting from many mergers; and M. D. Utton, *British Merger Policy* in K. D. GEORGE & C. JOLL, eds., COMPETITION POLICY IN THE U.K. AND THE E.E.C. 105-111 (Cambridge University Press, London 1975).
[13] Cmnd 7198 (H.M.S.O., London, 1978).

examined have an unfavourable effect on profits. There would therefore seem to be a strong case for a more careful appraisal of mergers. Furthermore, some sectors of the economy are now dominated by a few very large firms and these may give rise to worries about economic power. Finally, certain practices of dominant firms are directly aimed at restricting competition and are unlikely to benefit consumers. These forms of behaviour are often unsuited to investigation case-by-case and might be dealt with on some more general basis.

Nevertheless, the Working Party[14] did not favour a complete reversal of the presumption, as that would require virtually all mergers to be referred to the Commission, leading to delay and rigidity in the process of merger control. Nor was it prepared to make such a recommendation even for certain types of mergers, such as of very large companies, or those leading to a very large market share, since it thought that, with a reversed onus, the Office would have to recommend reference of virtually all the mergers falling within the limits of mergers presumed to be against the public interest, as it would not have time to consider possible justifications. The Commission, with up to six months for an investigation might, however, condemn very few. The Working Party, therefore, recommended (at para. 1.14) that mergers policy should be shifted to a more neutral position by the Government making a statement of the new policy, backed up by issuing non-statutory guidelines to the Mergers Panel to ensure that all mergers which could have a significant effect on competition or economic power would be critically assessed. At the same time, the existing legislation should be amended so that the Commission be required to report upon each reference whether the merger might be expected to prevent, restrict or distort competition significantly or to have other adverse effects on the public interest, and if so, to assess the benefits to be expected from the merger and the likelihood of their being achieved; and, finally, to balance the benefits and detriments and recommend action. It also suggested (at para. 5.21) that the list of public interest considerations, at least on merger references, should include:
(a) desirability of minimising the detriments of reduced competition and increased concentration; and
(b) the desirability of restructuring to improve the international competitiveness of British industry.

The Conservatives did not make these amendments with the others made in the Competition Act 1980, although, during the debates in Parliament, several references were made by Conservative spokesmen to a further Bill to be prepared on competition policy. This now seems less likely, at any rate for mergers. The Government will instead try to remove the tax disincentives for merged and other firms to sell part of their assets and return the proceeds to shareholders.[15]

---

[14] *Id.* Paras. 5.13-5.17.
[15] On July 1st, 1980, however, the Secretary of State announced that he had decided against new legislation on mergers for the time being. He expected the authorities to view mergers primarily for their effects on competition, though he did not expect the number of references to increase greatly. Presumably fewer conglomerate mergers will be referred to make way for horizontal and vertical ones.

II. The Legislative Framework

A. Newspaper Mergers

The transfer of a newspaper or newspaper assets[16] is treated separately from other kinds of mergers. Newspapers are usually sold at less than the cost of their production, and supported by advertising revenue. When circulation drops, such revenue can decline dramatically and several well-known newspapers have disappeared or been transferred to groups owning other papers. There have been fears that some political views, especially on the left, may find no paper to represent them. Consequently, since 1965 the transfer of a newspaper to a newspaper proprietor whose newspapers after the transfer will have an average circulation per day of publication of half a million or more copies, has been illegal and void, unless the Secretary of State has consented (Fair Trading Act 1973, S. 58 (1)). Normally, consent may be given only after the Commission has considered the transfer (S. 58 (2)), although there are provisions for failing and very small papers. Rather surprisingly, the definition of newspaper is limited to a daily, Sunday or local newspaper circulating wholly or mainly in the U.K. (S. 57 (1)). One might have expected that the independence of weeklies, such as the *New Statesman, New Society* or the *Economist*, would also have been protected. The sanctions, unlike those for other anti-competitive practices, are imprisonment for up to two years and/or a fine (S. 62).

Newspaper transfers are normally considered mainly by "additional" members of the Commission, who cannot sit on other matters. There have been some references of newspaper transfers, chiefly of strings of local papers. The Commission has found it difficult to condemn any of them, even though it has expressed concern about the trend.[17] The Commission, in assessing the public

---

[16] For a fuller description, *see* V. Korah, *Legal Regulation of Corporate Mergers in the United Kingdom*, 5 TEXAS INTERNATIONAL LAW FORUM 71, 85-89 (1969).

[17] E. g., in its report on *Surrey Advertiser Newspaper Holdings Ltd. and the Guardian and Manchester Evening News Ltd.* of 25 May 1979, H.C.P. 100, at para. 8.5 it said:

> Like the Royal Commission [on the Press], we are anxious about the tendency towards wider local newspaper monopolies, and had the intending purchaser been a newspaper group with interests in an area adjacent to the district served by the SA group, we should have regarded this as a matter for some concern. But in the present case the combined effects of the Scott Trust, the range of assurances given and the obvious commercial interests of GMEN all sustain our confidence that under new ownership the SA group of newspapers will continue to serve the interests of readers, advertisers and others in the areas in which they circulate . . .

It also considered the possibility of the SA papers subsidising the Guardian:

> We note that the Royal Commission on the Press judged that, despite the arguments of principle against cross-subsidisation, in the particular case of the Guardian there was no preferable alternative to an assured subsidy, since otherwise it might have closed long ago.

interest in a newspaper merger, is required to take into account any matter it considers relevant and in particular, "the need for the accurate presentation of news and free expression of opinion" (S. 59 (3)).

B. "Other Mergers"

1. Definition of "Other Mergers"

The concept of *"merger"* is wide: it covers the acquisition of shares, or assets, and other means of obtaining common control over two businesses.

S. 64 (1) A merger reference may be made to the Commission by the Secretary of State where it appears to him that it is or may be the fact that two or more enterprises, of which one at least was carried on in the United Kingdom or by or under the control of a body corporate incorporated in the United Kingdom, have, [within the previous six months], ceased to be distinct enterprises, and . . .

a) Two or More Enterprises

"Enterprise" means the activities or part of the activities, of a business (S. 63 (2)), so the acquisition of a single division or subsidiary of a conglomerate may be caught. A joint venture of existing activities may be subject to control as a merger as well as under the Restrictive Trade Practices legislation.

b) Cease to be Distinct: Common Control

According to S. 65 (1), enterprises cease to be distinct when they are brought under common ownership or control, or one of them ceases to be carried on at all, in consequence of any arrangements or transaction entered into to prevent competition between undertakings.

The notion of "common control" is elaborated in the rest of S. 65:

(2) For the purposes of the preceding subsection enterprises shall (without prejudice to the generality of the words "common control" in that subsection) be regarded as being under common control if they are –
(a) enterprises of interconnected bodies corporate, or
(b) enterprises carried on by two or more bodies corporate of which one and the same person or group of persons has control, or
(c) an enterprise carried on by a body corporate and an enterprise carried on by a person or group of persons having control of that body corporate.
(3) A person or group of persons able, directly or indirectly, to control or materially to influence the policy of a body corporate, or the policy of any person in carrying on an enterprise, but without having a controlling interest in that body corporate or in that enterprise, may for the purposes of subsections (1) and (2) of this section be treated as having control of it.
(4) For the purposes of subsection (1) (a) of this section, in so far as it relates to bringing two or more enterprises under common control, a person or group of persons may be treated as bringing an enterprise under his or their control if –
(a) being already able to control or materially to influence the policy of the person carrying on the enterprise, that person or group of persons acquires a controlling interest in the enterprise or, in the case of an enterprise carried on by a body corporate, acquires a controlling interest in that body corporate, or
(b) being already able materially to influence the policy of the person carrying on the enterprise, that person or group of persons becomes able to control that policy.

"*Interconnected bodies corporate*" is the concept used in the Companies Act 1948 to define a corporate group for the purpose of publishing consolidated accounts. One company is a subsidiary of another if the other, which I shall call P, owns at least half of its equity share capital or has power to appoint or dismiss a majority of its board of directors. All companies of which the parent or subsidiary company, or the latter's subsidiary and so on *ad infinitum*, has such control are interconnected.

Diagram 1
Interconnected Bodies Corporate

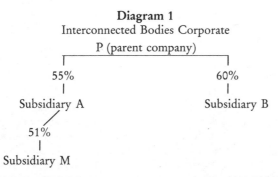

In the diagram, Subsidiary M is inter-connected with Subsidiary B, even though P's indirect shareholding in M is less than 50%. It is likely that P has fairly comprehensive control over M, although outside shareholders of M or A may be able to block special resolutions.

It is clear that "*a controlling interest*" is almost the same as being inter-connected bodies corporate.[18] In *N.F.U. Trust/F.M.G.* (1975),[19] at para. 215, the Commission said that

A person . . . has a controlling interest in a company if and only if his shareholding is such that he . . . can at a general meeting of the company outvote the aggregate of all other shareholders. His . . . shareholding must therefore exceed 50%.

It therefore rejected the argument that with 40% of the shares before the further acquisition, the Trust already had a "controlling interest" and that the acquisition of the balance did not constitute a merger capable of reference. This test has the advantage of precision.

"*Ability to control policy*" does not depend on any simply applied test. The Commission thinks in terms of one company having enough votes in another to be likely in practice to be able to secure in a shareholder's general meeting that enough of its nominees be elected to enable it to control the policy of that other company. This may depend on the concentration of the remaining shares. In *Eurocanadian/F.W./M.L.* (1976)[20] the Commission considered the disposition of

[18] Technically the concepts should be kept separate. The person acquiring a controlling interest might be an individual and so outside the definition of inter-connected bodies corporate. More than 50% of the shares might be required in general meeting, etc.
[19] (1975) H.C.P. 441.
[20] (1976) H.C.P. 639.

the voting shares and likely loyalties of the various shareholders and said at para.
380:

> In view of this situation, the absence of other large holdings of F.W. shares and the large
> proportion of these shares held by nominees, we consider that a holding of just under 30%
> would enable E.C.S. to get a sufficient number of its representatives elected to the Board to
> control the policy of F.W. . . . . A further merger situation qualifying for reference is thus
> created.[21]

"Ability materially to influence policy" is also an imprecise concept. From the
Commission's reports so far it is not clear whether it regards "ability materially
to influence" as stemming from power to block in a general meeting or on the
Board of Directors, or both.

In the case of *"creeping mergers"* where one company acquires a few more
shares each year in the target company, there are various points within six
months of which a merger reference can be made: when the acquirer obtains
either the ability materially to influence policy; or the ability to control policy;
or a controlling interest. At first sight one would think that this gives adequate
powers to intervene. The difficulty for the minister and those advising him,
however, lies in the imprecision of the first two concepts. They must decide
whether the acquisition of shares during the previous six months, and the
changes in other shareholdings have resulted in one of these thresholds being
exceeded.[22] The first exercise of control or ability to influence is not within the
definition, only the transaction leading to the ability to do so.

c) Associated Persons

In relation to both newspaper transfers and other mergers, the concept of control
is supplemented by provisions related to associated persons (S. 77). Associated
persons are treated as a single person, so if I control company A and you control
company B, a marriage between my Uncle and your Aunt might bring the
companies under common control and thus create a merger situation qualifying
for reference. No such reference has been made. Nor has a reference been made
where power materially to influence policy has been obtained by becoming a
large customer or supplier. All the situations referred have been caused by a
change in shareholdings.

---

[21] For further examples of ability both to control and materially to influence policy *see*
J. F. Pickering, *Implementation of British Competition Policy on Mergers*, 1 EUROPEAN
COMPETITION LAW REVIEW 177 (1980).

[22] There is no such difficulty for newspaper transfers, where the threshold is 25%. For a
more detailed analysis of the legislation *see* V. Korah, Chapter 5.2.4 in D. GIJLSTRA & F.
MURPHY, eds., COMPETITION LAW OF WESTERN EUROPE AND THE UNITED STATES (Kluwer,
Metzner, Rothman, 1976) (looseleaf). Acquisitions between the same parties over two
years may be treated as occurring on the date of the last (S. 66 (1)). A course of conduct
consisting of a series of mergers may conceivably be investigated as an anti-competitive
practice, under the Mergers provisions of the Competition Act 1980. See *infra* § IV p.
67.

d) Connection with the U.K.

Note that only one of the enterprises ceasing to be distinct need have any connection with the U.K. When a reference is made, attention is paid to which activities and which foreign subsidiaries should be included. But should the Italian subsidiary of a U.K. company acquire an interest in another Italian company, the Commission would be concerned only with the United Kingdom public interest – the effects in the United Kingdom economy.

2. Mergers That Qualify For Investigation

Not all situations where enterprises cease to be distinct qualify for reference. There must either be horizontal aspects, or the total assets of the target company must satisfy certain statutory limits.

a) Value of Assets

The total assets employed in or appropriated to the target company or activity must be valued in its books of account at £ *15 million* [23] or more (Sec. 64 (1) (b) FTA). Where one of the enterprises remains under the same ownership or control, the assets of the others are aggregated. Where all change hands, as where the merger is achieved through a holding company, then one excludes assets of the enterprise with the greatest assets and aggregates the assets of the others (S. 67).

b) Specific Part of Supply of Goods or Services

The horizontal test in Section 64 (1) (a) is more complex. As a result of the merger, one firm must supply or acquire at least *one quarter of the goods or services specified* in the reference either in the United Kingdom or a substantial part of it. This test may be important: sometimes, quite small companies may hold a key position in the supply of components, and if one is acquired by its competitor, the industry may become concentrated, even though its assets do not exceed £ 15 million as written down in its books. Vertical mergers, however, are caught only by the assets test. Foreclosing practices after the merger might result in less competition and an increased market share, but it is thought that it is only direct results of the merger that are relevant.

3. Notification

a) No Duty to Notify

There is no duty to notify mergers coming within these definitions. Indeed, until the reference products are specified, one cannot be sure whether a merger qualifies for reference under the second test.

b) Pre-notification in Practice

Most substantial mergers are nevertheless *pre-notified* to the Office of Fair Trading, and I have heard of no case where confidential information of this sort

---

[23] The figure of £ 5 million in S. 64 of the Fair Trading Act 1973 was raised to £ 15 million by the Mergers Reference (Increase in Value of Assets) Order 1980, S. I. No. 373, which came into force on April 10th 1980.

has leaked. Where the Office could not reasonably have known of the merger, a reference may be made by the Minister any time within 6 months of the date on which the Office of Fair Trading should have learnt of the merger and businessmen usually delay the merger until it is clear that it will not be referred. After an adverse report, the Minister has power to order divestiture if that would be the appropriate remedy for the mischief found by the Commission, and few would want to go through the trouble of making and digesting an acquisition, only to be ordered to dispose of some factories to those who might compete.

C. The Reference to the Monopolies and Mergers Commission and Its Consequences

1. The Role of the Office of Fair Trading in Preparing a Ministerial Reference

Although references are mady by the minister, the preparatory work is done by the Office of Fair Trading, which has staff experienced in competition policy.

a) Procedures of the Office of Fair Trading

These procedures are set out in its Mergers Guide,[24] Chapter II. As soon as it hears of a proposed merger, without waiting for a formal bid, it approaches the financial advisers of the companies concerned, or the companies themselves, in order to establish the main facts. If the merger seems to qualify for reference, it seeks an early meeting with the parties. If a takeover is contested, parties are seen separately; where it is agreed, they are usually seen together. The Office may approach customers, suppliers and competitors of the parties, as well as trade associations and trade union representatives, and is ready to receive comments from anyone likely to be affected.

b) The Recommendation to Refer

A paper is then prepared for the Mergers Panel.[25] Simpler cases are dealt with on the basis of this paper, without a formal meeting of the Panel, but members may always ask for a meeting. A submission including a recommendation is then sent by the Director General,[26] or his Deputy, to the Secretary of State if a reference is recommended, or the matter is likely to be contentious. This outlines the proposal, assesses the questions of public interest, records the view of the Panel and makes a recommendation as to whether a reference should or should not be made. It also recommends a period within which the Commission should be asked to submit a report. This submission is not sent to the Commission.

[24] The Office of Fair Trading produced a new edition of MERGERS: A GUIDE TO THE PROCEDURES UNDER THE FAIR TRADING ACT 1973 in 1978 (H.M.S.O., London, 1978).

[25] This is a non-statutory body, normally chaired by the Deputy Director General of Fair Trading. For a description of its membership see supra § I.B.3, p. 46. See also, R. Opie, Merger Policy in the United Kingdom, § II.B.1. Supra this volume at p. 32.

[26] The Director General of Fair Trading is independent of Government and responsible for implementing much of the competition policy. In the field of merger control, however, his functions are confined mainly to advising the Secretary of State. His secretariat is known as "the Office of Fair Trading".

c) Publication of References

The Secretary of State, if he makes a reference, must publish it, but he does not normally give any reasons, although the unanimity of the press speculation may indicate a "non-attributable" briefing. The decision whether to refer is normally published, except when confidential guidance is sought from the Office of Fair Trading. In the latter case, any confidential guidance communicated to the parties will be qualified. At that stage the Office is unable to question outsiders and is unlikely to come to a firm view.

d) Criteria for Making Recommendations

Not unnaturally, the Office in deciding whether to recommend a reference looks to the same sorts of matters as the Commission. Will a horizontal merger lead to a firm unconstrained by much competition? Would one of the firms be likely to survive without the merger? Do the products made by the parties actually compete or are they complementary, although in the same industrial classification? In relation to vertical mergers, it is concerned to see whether the integrated firm might cease to deal with outsiders, when it could deal within the group, even if it would be more efficient to deal with outsiders. Surprisingly, it seems concerned about discrimination in favour of companies within the group, but that reflects the practice of the Commission.[27] On the other hand, vertical mergers may lead to cost savings and a better appreciation of customers' needs.

British monopoly policy has always been concerned with both allocative and "X" efficiency − competition is desired not in itself, but where it is likely to lead to more efficient firms expanding, and resources being allocated to sectors producing what customers want to buy, or where particular resources will be better used. The Office, in advising the minister, may also be concerned if it thinks that the balance of payments might suffer significantly, or that the merger might lead to unemployment, particularly in development areas. Thus although conglomerate mergers may not raise problems of competition being restricted significantly in the short term, they are nevertheless also scrutinised and sometimes referred. Mergers that will lead to asset stripping may result in a better use of the resources of the target company, but they will be scrutinised to see that the interests of customers and employees are not likely to be ignored.

2. The Role of the Monopolies and Mergers Commission

a) The Function of the Commission

Most references are made before the merger actually takes place, but the Commission is required to assume that it has been consummated.[28] Usually it is asked whether the merger operates or may be expected to operate against the public interest, but it may be asked to limit its consideration of the public interest to such elements in or possible consequences of the merger as may be specified

---

[27] *See* for example, *infra* § III.A.2., especially at n. 42.
[28] It therefore ignores the possibility that it may not take place. *See Smith Brothers Ltd. and Bisgood/Bishop & Co. Ltd.* (1978) H.C.P. 242.

(S. 69 (4)). This might be appropriate if, for example, a largely conglomerate merger had ancillary horizontal or vertical aspects and the minister wanted the Commission's opinion about a limited remedy such as the divestiture of one activity, or he might want to obtain power to monitor exclusionary practices.[29] The terms of reference enable the Commission to condemn a merger only if it is satisfied that it may be expected to operate against the public interest. Unless so satisfied, the Commission cannot condemn it. The legislation was originally prepared in 1965, when politicians thought that mergers were normally highly desirable. Indeed, at that time, there was an Industrial Reorganisation Corporation whose task was to encourage mergers likely to lead to the rationalisation of British industry. It is only recently that politicians have become seriously concerned about the undesirable effects of non-monopolising mergers. Few mergers have been condemned, about half of those on which a report has been published.

b) The Composition of the Commission

The Commission may have up to 25 members, mostly working part time. It has always been considered that the fact that members have other activities helps them to assess the public interest without tending to judge their success by the number of condemnations. The Chairman works full time and, as merger investigations must be conducted at speed, he normally takes the chair. The whole Commission rarely meets — it operates in groups, usually of five or seven members and any group is sure to include an economist and probably a trade unionist. The Chairman has always been an eminent lawyer, so for mergers enquiries there is usually a lawyer.

c) Time Element

A time limit must be set for the investigation, and this may not exceed six months: three to four months are not unusual. This period may be extended by up to a further three months only for special reasons (S. 70). The Secretary of State has power to make an interim order under Section 74, restraining the firms from doing anything inconsistent with control over the merger.[30] Normally these days he invites the Director General of Fair Trading to seek an undertaking from the parties not to take action which might prejudice the investigation.

d) Publication of Reports

The Commission's Report must be laid before Parliament and published as a House of Commons Paper, or published as a Command Paper when Parliament is not sitting.

---

[29] Under the Competition Act 1980 these may now be investigated irrespective of the Merger, but there has been no experience yet of operation of the Act. *See, infra* § IV.

[30] There is some doubt whether such interim orders are valid, and since the City Code ensures that public offers are made conditional on no reference being made to the Commission, there is rarely much need for making an order.

3. Order-making Power of the Secretary of State

Where the Commission has concluded that a merger may be expected to operate against the public interest, the Secretary of State has power to make an order exercising any of the powers listed in the eighth Schedule to the Fair Trading Act. This includes an order providing for the division of any business by the sale of any part of the undertaking, as well as an order to prohibit or restrict an acquisition. Normally, these days, the merger is stopped in its tracks during the Commission's investigation so as to comply with the City Code, so an interim order forbidding the acquisition, or allowing it only if certain activities are hived off may not be necessary. There has *never* been *any need to make an order* after a merger report: since the power is there, firms have always discontinued the merger after an adverse report.

Were there any need to take action, the Office of Fair Trading would negotiate undertakings with the firms concerned, as it does after an adverse report by the Commission on a monopoly reference. These are not enforceable by law, but where the Commission has condemned a merger or some aspects of it, a Ministerial order could be made on the basis of the original report were an undertaking to be broken. Such orders operate only from the time they are made, but the possibility of a divestiture order being made makes it silly to ignore a condemnation by the Commission.[31]

4. The Practical Impact of References

Since merger references are now running at about 2% of those qualifying for reference, the *Minister's* decision whether to refer is far more important to the economy than are the reports of the Commission. The latter are the visible tip of the iceberg, but affect few acquisitions. Of course, advisers take into account the reasons given by the Commission for condemning a merger or not, but with so few references, it is not thought that the legislation deters mergers except when either the Office of Fair Trading or the Minister indicates that a reference is likely. Since the advice whether to refer is given to a Minister, it must also take account of political decisions, such as the statement by Mr. Nott mentioned above.[32]

D. Criteria Used for Judging Mergers: The Public Interest Test

The criteria of the public interest are open ended and, as I said earlier, the list is merely illustrative.

84.(1) In determining for any purposes to which this section applies whether any particular matter operates, or may be expected to operate, against the public interest, the Commission shall take into account all matters which appear to them in the particular

---

[31] Contrast the position where an assurance is given to the Commission and, consequently, the Commission does not condemn the Merger. (*See infra* n. 42 and accompanying text.) For this reason, it is no longer the practice of the Commission to accept an assurance and to clear the merger in consequence.

[32] *Supra* n. 15.

circumstances to be relevant and, among other things, shall have regard to the desirability —

(a) of maintaining and promoting effective competition between persons supplying goods and services in the United Kingdom;

(b) of promoting the interests of consumers, purchasers and other users of goods and services in the United Kingdom in respect of the prices charged for them and in respect of their quality and the variety of goods and services supplied;

(c) of promoting, through competition, the reduction of costs and the development and use of new techniques and new products, and of facilitating the entry of new competitors into existing markets;

(d) of maintaining and promoting the balanced distribution of industry and employment in the United Kingdom;

(e) of maintaining and promoting competitive activity in markets outside the United Kingdom on the part of producers of goods, and of suppliers of goods and services, in the United Kingdom.

The list of particular matters to be considered was altered in 1973, but probably represents the matters that were in fact being considered under the old monopolies legislation. There was no list for mergers referred under the Act of 1965.[33] The desire for competition is more clearly expressed than under the 1948 list, but a balanced distribution of industry and employment in the U.K. would seem to lead in a contrary direction. No weighting is given to the various matters to be considered. Where a merger has substantial horizontal or vertical elements, the Commission naturally considers first to what competitive restraints the merging firms will still be subject and, for this purpose, may consider actual or potential competition from products other than those specified in the reference.[34]

III. Practice and Experience

To give some idea of the width of the Commission's investigation I shall describe a few reports as a whole and then try to make some more general comments based on several reports. There were several commentaries on the early reports,[35]

---

[33] See the Restrictive Trade Practices Act 1956 and the Monopolies and Mergers Act 1965.

[34] Not that this has been its invariable practice. In a very early report, *Ross/Associated Fisheries* (1966) H.C.P. 42 (criticised by T. S. Ellis, III, *A Survey of Government Control of Mergers in the U.K.*, 22 NORTHERN IRELAND LEGAL QUARTERLY 251, and 459 at 460 (1971)), the Commission confined its consideration exclusively to white fish landed at the Humber Ports. Contrast the approach adopted in *BICC/Pyrotenax infra* § III.A.2. esp. at pp. 61 *et seq.*

[35] *See, e. g.,* C. K. Rowley, *Mergers and Public Policy in Great Britain*, 11 JOURNAL OF LAW AND ECONOMICS 75-132 (1968); A. SUTHERLAND, THE MONOPOLIES COMMISSION IN ACTION (Cambridge University Press, London 1969); V. Korah, *op. cit. supra* n. 16; T. S. Ellis III, *op. cit. supra* n. 34; M. D. Utton, *op. cit. supra* n. 12; J. F. PICKERING, INDUSTRIAL STRUCTURE AND MARKET CONDUCT, Chapter 8 (Martin Robertson, Oxford 1974).

but little[36] thereafter. Competition is not the object sought by the Commission, but a means for stimulating efficiency, and mergers substantially restricting competition have not always been condemned, when they were expected to lead to other benefits to the public.

A. Two Leading Cases

1. H. Weidmann AG/B.S. W. Whiteley Ltd.[37]

This report conveniently indicates the wide range of aspects considered by the Commission. The reference was based on the horizontal test: it was alleged that the merger would result in a single firm supplying one third of (i) electrical insulating pressboard; and (ii) goods made therefrom. There were problems both in deciding that there was a merger qualifying for reference and in assessing the public interest. Weidmann was a Swiss company holding nearly 10% of the shares in Whiteley and was intending to raise this holding to 33.4% by acquiring Whiteley shares owned by three other Swiss companies. There had never been any agreement among the Swiss holders that they would nominate Weidmann to represent them or exercise their voting rights, so the Commission concluded that at the time of the proposed acquisition Weidmann was not able, directly or indirectly, to control or materially influence the policy of Whiteley (para. 85). It also added that a 33.4% shareholding would result in Weidmann and Whiteley ceasing to be distinct. The object of the transaction was to give Weidmann a significant influence on Whiteley's management and the Commission had no doubt that this would enable Weidmann materially to influence its policy.

In 1974 Whiteley supplied 79% and Weidmann 9% of electrical insulating pressboard, while Whiteley supplied 42% and Weidmann 43% of the goods made therefrom that were supplied in the United Kingdom. The 25% test was therefore well satisfied, so the merger qualified for investigation. At this jurisdictional stage, there was no need to analyse the market — over a quarter of both kinds of products specified in the reference were supplied by the parties. The market is habitually analysed only when considering the public interest.

The Commission found that although it was intended that the two companies would retain their commercial identities, the control of Whiteley by Weidmann would materially reduce competition between them. When discussing the public interest, the Commission did not take account of the fact that Weidmann would have only a minority shareholding. It observed that there were few suppliers of any reference goods and even fewer of pre-compressed board and goods made therefrom. Consequently, the merger would make it possible for prices to be raised to a level higher than were Whiteley to remain independent. The Commission did consider potential competition from the subsidiary of a

---

[36] J. F. Pickering, *op. cit. supra* n. 21; V. Korah, *op. cit. supra* n. 22; D. Barounos and W. Allan, Chapter 9 in J. O. VON KALINOWSKI, ed., WORLD LAW OF COMPETITION, UNIT B: WESTERN EUROPE, VOLUME 4: UNITED KINGDOM, (Bender, New York, 1978) (loose-leaf).

[37] Cmnd 6208 (H.M.S.O., London, 1975).

Swedish supplier of transformers, and from existing suppliers who might extend their volume and range. Nevertheless it recognised that barriers to entry were high: capital costs of a production unit are high and the minimum efficient scale is large in relation to the limited world market. It is the relationship between minimum efficient size and the available market that is noted by the Commission, not just the cost of investment. Only the former would deter almost all firms from entering a profitable market and so enable the existing suppliers to exploit dominance. There was already some excess capacity, likely to be increased were the Swedish company to build plant, and a new entrant would have to satisfy the exacting quality standards of buyers.

Of course, were Weidmann to take undue advantage of its enhanced market power, users might modify the design of their products, so as to reduce their requirements of pre-compressed board. Alternatives were available though the cost would be high. This is an example of the Commission, unlike the Community authorities, looking to competition from substitutes assumed to be outside the relevant market — one of the lessons that might be learned from the U.K. experience. Moreover there are only a few makers of power transformers in the U.K. and they might be able to exercise some countervailing power, provided they could use substitutes or encourage competing suppliers, actual or potential.

Despite these constraints, the Commission concluded that Weidmann would be likely to raise prices for reference goods to some extent, and this would have an adverse effect on the interests of makers of transformers and other users of reference goods.

The Commission was also concerned that Weidmann might discontinue some Whiteley lines that it no longer produced; but it was satisfied by Weidmann's assurance that it would not discontinue any lines without taking the advice of users, and that it intended to continue production of any line for which there was an evident commercial demand. It would not be in Weidmann's interest to discontinue such lines.

The next issue considered was whether Weidmann would transfer the production of the most profitable lines from Whiteley's plant at Poole to its own plant at Rapperswil, to the detriment of British employment and balance of payments. Strangely, the Commission did not point to the interests of the other shareholders, but pointed out that it would be unremunerative to divert production and profits to Switzerland. Indeed, it thought that the merger would lead in the long run to greater production at Poole, which is well placed for meeting the requirements of United Kingdom users, since labour is more readily available there. Moreover the £ was then undervalued in comparison with the Swiss franc. Against the loss of competition, the Commission could therefore balance the favourable effects on the level and range of activities at Poole. This reasoning affected its conclusions on both the balance of payments and the level of employment.

It did not think that research and development would be greatly affected by the merger, and had no objection to Weidmann considering which plant was best capable of developing each product on its merits. It was not satisfied that the buying power of the two companies would enable them to buy their raw materials more cheaply.

It had difficulty in comparing the relative efficiency of the two firms in the short time available for its investigations. Moreover, any results would be expressed in different currencies which made comparison difficult. Nevertheless, it did conclude that Weidmann was more efficient, largely in generating internal funds for development.

It had, therefore, to balance the detriment to the public caused by higher prices against the favourable effects on efficiency, a higher level of production and employment at the Whiteley plant at Poole and the benefits to the United Kingdom balance of payments. It concluded that the desirable effects might be expected to outweigh the undesirable ones.

This attempt to balance unquantified, and unquantifiable, probable effects is typical of the United Kingdom approach. The Commission has grasped the difficulty of trying to balance reductions in competition against efficiency.[38] Its task was made more difficult by the five-month time limit placed on a body of part-timers. One may wonder whether such a task is possible for any body. There is little time for the Commission to carry out or order independent studies, so it must be dependent on the statements of the parties to the merger, their suppliers, customers, competitors, unions of their workers and Government Departments. The outsiders may see causes for concern, but are unlikely to be in a position to evaluate them. Most of the mergers condemned by the Commission have been contested, so the target company was able and willing to give adverse evidence to the Commission. In the case of uncontested mergers the lack of a prosecutor familiar with the industry creates a real difficulty that must be faced by any enforcement body.

2. BICC/Pyrotenax[39]

This merger, too, was not condemned despite very substantial horizontal and vertical connection between the firms, in this case because of balance of payments considerations. The merger qualified for investigation on the ground that each firm supplied some 45% of the mineral insulated cable (m.i.c.) market in the U.K., the remaining 10% being produced by Glynwed. It took place because I.C.I. decided to sell its 17.3% shareholding in Pyrotenax to whoever would give a satisfactory price, in fact BICC.[40] Once Pyrotenax's main competitor had become a substantial shareholder, Pyrotenax had little choice but to acquiesce in the offer made for the remaining shares.

---

[38] Contrast O. E. Williamson, *Economies as an Antitrust Defense: The Welfare Trade-offs*, 58 (1) AMERICAN ECONOMIC REVIEW 18-36 (1968).

[39] (1969) H.C.P. 490. For criticism of this report see A. SUTHERLAND, *op..cit. supra* n. 35; V. Korah, *op. cit. supra* n. 16; T. S. Ellis, *op. cit. supra* n. 34.

[40] One would have thought that this acquisition could have been prevented, on the ground that BICC acquired the ability materially to influence Pyrotenax's policy. At that date, however, no partial mergers had been referred, and 17% is rather lower than the shareholdings where such an ability has been found. I do not know whether the other shareholdings were concentrated.

What was the relevant market in which to judge the merger: m.i.c., of which the firms supplied 90%; or heat resistant cables, of which they supplied just over one-third? Some witnesses described m.i.c. as essential for certain uses, and some tenders specified its use, but it was hardly used in Germany or the United States, which seemed to show that it was not technically essential, nor was it prescribed by any government regulations. The Commission therefore accepted the parties' statement that it was regarded as essential only as a result of vigorous promotion. The Commission accepted that competition from alternative cable systems set a ceiling to m.i.c. prices, but it was not a uniform ceiling: for some uses, substitutes could be bought at lower differentials than for others; in some situations, m.i.c. enjoyed such advantages that the market was to some extent differentiated. Unlike the American and EEC authorities, the Commission did not decide what was the relevant market and let that determine its decision on competition: it was concerned about the supply of m.i.c., but gave considerable weight to competition from other kinds of cable. It seems to the writer that this approach is far better than letting the decision depend on the arbitrary definition of the relevant market, when the market has no clear boundaries.

The Commission then considered the constraints of competition that had existed between the parties before the mergers. Originally, Pyrotenax had been the only supplier of m.i.c., but BICC entered the market. Shortly before that, Pyrotenax dropped its list prices in anticipation of the competition to be expected on the expiration of its patents. Since BICC entered, the list prices of the parties had remained similar, but there was such competition in secret discounts that Pyrotenax's price structure had become somewhat irrational. Resale prices were not maintained, and the benefits of this competition were passed on through distributors to those who bought indirectly. The parties claimed that it was the price of other cables that constrained their pricing, but the Commission pointed out that m.i.c. prices had risen less fast than others, and that the firms also competed in service and technical development.

The Commission concluded that, although not creating a watertight monopoly, the merger would have undesirable consequences: within the limit allowed by other cable systems, constraints on pricing, service and other matters would disappear, and the potentialities of m.i.c. might not be fully exploited. The Commission placed little weight on the assurance by BICC that the Pyrotenax operation would remain an operating division separate from BICC's existing one. It had not been suggested that they would compete in price. A safeguard against the possibility of m.i.c. not being adequately exploited was its profitability — some 30% on capital employed in 1965-66. Glynwed's existence, however, would be almost the only safeguard against the reaping of monopoly profits — but its chances of survival were dubious. The desire of customers to have two sources might lead to an increase in the demand for Glynwed's output, and it had spare capacity. The Commission looked at the barriers to entry: plant that would cost at least £ 1 million[41] and difficulties to be overcome at the early stages of

---

[41] In this report, it did not state whether this would produce too big a plant for the available demand, but the fact that Glynwed had more capacity than it could use seems

manufacture, despite the expiry of patents. It considered the barriers high, although the profits were also high, which had attracted Glynwed to the cable industry in which, as a newcomer to the industry, it might have had greater difficulty than another cable maker. The Commission concluded that meanwhile the possibility of entry was not strong enough to constrain BICC greatly. The various safeguards mentioned in this paragraph were not sufficient to prevent detriments to the public ensuing from the merger. The Commission was not concerned that some customers would lose the benefit of particularly large discounts, provided average prices did not rise as a result of the merger; but it was not satisfied that they would not increase.

The Commission dealt rather unsatisfactorily with BICC's supply to electrical contractors and other cable manufacturers who competed with it. They feared that BICC might subsidise its other activities by charging its own divisions a lower price for m.i.c. than it charged outsiders. How are competitors or the public interest affected by such internal "prices"? BICC should be concerned with its profits overall, not those of each division. If it were to charge the same "price" for m.i.c., it could predate equally effectively by cutting the charges for its other activities. The Commission, however, accepted and seemed happy with an assurance that BICC would not discriminate in favour of its own divisions.[42] It was on firmer ground when it stated that its competitors downstream received some protection from the existence of cable wholesalers.

One of the most dubious parts of the report was the acceptance of assurances to protect various kinds of firms. Some of the assurances which have been accepted seem to be meaningless, and others positively harmful. In any event, if the Commission fails to condemn a merger because of assurances given to it, there is no power for anyone to enforce them, except by making a monopoly reference. Recently such assurances have not been taken by the Commission. The first assurance was that BICC would supply other cable makers on prices and terms making it commercially practicable for them to participate in sales of m.i.c. This seems to be a formula for a cartel. All buyers would get comparable prices and not face competition at the buying level save from purchasers from Glynwed. The second assurance was that it would not give better terms to its own electrical company. But I have argued that this is meaningless: if BICC were to charge as much for m.i.c. to its own division, it could take the profits in the m.i.c. division instead of the electrical contracting one. Thirdly, BICC promised not to charge low prices for m.i.c. to win orders for other kinds of cable; and, fourthly, not to offer *uneconomic* terms for m.i.c. to drive competitors out of the m.i.c. market. But why should it have done so? It agreed to publish its prices and discounts, which must have made it easy for Glynwed just to undercut it. Finally it agreed that at the Government's request it would offer to grant patent

---

to indicate that it would. The later *Weidmann/Whiteley* report (*supra* n. 37) was better argued in this respect.

[42] The Commission has been concerned by such discrimination in favour of subsidiaries and divisions in other reports, *e. g.*, *Cellulose Fibres* (1968) H.C.P. 130.

licences[43] on "reasonable terms", but the methods of assessing these were not stated.

Having tried to take the sting to BICC's customers out of the merger, the Commission looked to the benefits. It was sceptical about cost savings, save for copper tubes. BICC had a purpose built and underused plant for producing these at a cost far lower than the price being paid by Pyrotenax. So this was a real saving, though the Commission observed that it might have been achieved by other means. The merger was saved, however, by the export argument. Pyrotenax had developed sales in the United Kingdom rapidly, but lacked the resources for intensive promotion in more than a few overseas markets. BICC had ample resources and considerable experience in exporting and intended to devote some of the savings accruing from the merger to promotion overseas.

The conclusion was that although the benefits were not important enough to cause the public interest to suffer were the merger not to go ahead, they were important enough to prevent the merger from being expected to operate against the public interest.

In most ways this report was a model: the market analysis was good, and it was clear that the merger was likely to reduce price competition between the firms; but the vertical effects were less well analysed, and remedies suggested were useless or unnecessary. The benefits likely to result from the merger seemed slight, apart from the availability to Pyrotenax of BICC's copper tubes, and that might have been obtained by Pyrotenax building a plant or buying from BICC. Surely a firm as profitable as Pyrotenax could have borrowed to promote profitable exports, or mounted joint ventures with BICC or other cable makers for overseas promotion, which would have been a less anti-competitive solution. The only explanation that I can understand for the failure to condemn the merger may not be true, but it is possible that since the merger had been consummated during the Commission's enquiry, BICC had seen Pyrotenax's discount structure, which would make it difficult for Pyrotenax to continue independently.[44]

B. Horizontal Mergers

The Commission has sometimes been stricter towards horizontal mergers: In *Barclays Bank, Lloyds Bank and Martins Bank*,[45] it did condemn the merger of two of the big five clearing banks (Barclays Bank — Lloyds Bank) as well as that of these two plus one smaller clearing bank (Martins).

In *UDS/Montague Burton*,[46] it was even stricter in condemning the merger of two firms making mens' ready-made suits at the cheaper end of the market. They supplied 45% of those costing (in 1967) less than £ 20 and 35% of ready-made

---

[43] At the time of the report, BICC did not enjoy patent protection for m.i.c. but might have developed something later.

[44] Nowadays, owing to the provisions of the City Code, it is habitual for a public offer to be withdrawn during the investigation.

[45] (1968) H.C.P. 310.

[46] Cmnd 3397 (H.M.S.O., London, 1967).

suits generally, a far smaller market share than BICC's after the merger, and barriers to entry were low. In both the Three Banks and the UDS/Burton reports the Commission was impressed by evidence that each of the parties had looked to the other as its main competitor before the merger and in both cases it thought that the merger would reduce competitive pressures.

In *G.K.N./Birfield*,[47] a merger bringing together the only two makers of propeller shafts and the only maker of constant velocity joints[48] and having other significant horizontal effects was allowed because of the countervailing power of the vehicle manufacturers who were their customers.

Charter Consolidated Investments/Sadia[49] brought together two firms, one supplying a third of the electric water heaters with one water outlet, and the other rather over a third. Yet the Commission thought this would have no effect on competition as the third supplier was an I.C.I. subsidiary, enjoying financial strength and charging less for its electric water heaters. Moreover, in places where gas was already used, gas heaters were a close substitute. Entry barriers to electric heaters were low.

In *Dentsply International/A.D.I.*[50] the acquisition of an English firm by an American firm which was a potential competitor, though currently making only complementary goods, was positively welcomed, on grounds of efficiency, although competition was not strong.[51]

In *BP/Century Oil Group*,[52] BP was prevented from acquiring a small specialised maker of lubricants on the ground that it might affect Century's development of refining capacity, lead to a risk of diminished price competition and of customer orientated research and eliminate the independence of the largest independent specialist producer of lubricants in the United Kingdom.

C. Vertical Mergers

The Commission's first merger investigation, *B.M.C./Pressed Steel*,[53] involved the acquisition by one of its principal customers of the only remaining independent producer of motor vehicle bodies in the United Kingdom. B.M.C. was then one of the five large British vehicle manufacturers, though it has since been merged into British Leyland. Rootes, Jaguar and Rover were then independent manufacturers largely dependent on Pressed Steel for their car bodies. Rolls Royce and Standard also obtained some bodies from it. The Commission accepted that some cost savings and other benefits would probably result from the merger, although not to the extent claimed. Moreover, it was

---

[47] (1967) H.C.P. 3186.
[48] These are fairly remote substitutes, one component being needed for front wheel drive and the other for rear wheel drive.
[49] (1974) H.C.P. 345.
[50] (1975) H.C.P. 394.
[51] In fact, however, the merger did not take place.
[52] Cmnd 6827 (H.M.S.O., London, 1977).
[53] (1966) H.C.P. 46.

concerned that in the long term Pressed Steel's future might be precarious. One of its other customers might start to make its own bodies, or might take it over. It was also concerned by the possibility of a foreign bid, and would prefer any acquisition to be made by a British company, which would be less likely to have interests abroad with which its policies would have to fit to the possible detriment of British customers. Normally, the Commission shows no bias against foreign acquisitions, and it positively welcomed acquisitions by Weidmann and Dentsply. The fact that the bidder was British was only one reason for not condemning the merger, and the Commission accepted an undertaking that, if required, Pressed Steel would continue to perform the same services as in the past under contracts to be negotiated on terms shown to be fair and reasonable. Of course, there would be great difficulty in showing whether the terms were fair or reasonable. Comparisons with the prices charged to B.M.C. would be meaningless, in that it might be prepared to take high profits in the body making division or subsidiary, at the expense of its assembling operation, if it wished to charge high prices to outsiders.

The bids of both *Beecham* and *Boots* for *Glaxo* [54] were condemned because each would have eliminated one of the few centres of decision making covering research and development in the British owned pharmaceutical industry – an objection to the horizontal aspects of the merger. The Commission, however, dismissed fears that the acquisition of Glaxo's wholesaling subsidiary, Vestric, would enable Boots, which had interests in manufacturing and a strong chain of retail stores, to discriminate against other manufacturers and retailers. The Commission was impressed by the reflection that it would be in Boots' interest to develop Vestric's trade with independent retailers, and not sensible to charge them more than its own retail outlets and so antagonise them. It also dismissed fears that Boots might promote retail sales of Boots Glaxo products at the expense of competing products of other manufacturers. The latter had access to alternative channels of wholesale distribution so it would not be commercially sensible for Boots to discriminate.

The Commission did condemn the proposed merger between *Pilkington*, the only maker in the United Kingdom of lens blanks, and *U.K.O.*, the only United Kingdom maker of lenses. [55] It considered that it was less likely that the British opthalmic glass industry would remain internationally competitive if U.K.O. ceased to be an independent company in a position to exert pressure on Pilkington. Once acquired, U.K.O.'s threat to go elsewhere would cease to be credible.

D. Conclusion: The Importance Given to Competition in the Cases

As I have said before, the Commission has not taken a doctrinaire view about the desirability of competition, or the undesirability of mergers that might foreclose other firms; often it pays a vertically integrated firm to deal with outsiders. It has

[54] (1972) H.C.P. 341.
[55] (1977) H.C.P. 267.

looked at competitive pressures coming from products other than those specified in the reference. Mr. Sutherland[56] was very concerned that in both monopoly and merger investigations, the Commission was being inconsistent, but it is difficult to judge when everything is relevant, and outsiders have not seen the underlying evidence.

IV. Mergers under the Competition Act 1980

I shall not deal fully with the possibility of investigating mergers under the Competition Act 1980.[57] The Director General of Fair Trading,[58] not the Secretary of State, has been given power to investigate anti-competitive practices engaged in by any person. He is then required to publish a report (a) specifying the person or persons concerned and the goods or services in question; and (b) stating, with reasons, whether he considers that it is appropriate for him to make a reference under section 5.

If he considers that a reference to the Monopolies and Mergers Commission is appropriate, he has a short period (from 4-8 weeks after publication of his report, which the Secretary of State may extend to 12) in which he may negotiate undertakings, and if none is accepted within the time limits, he has power to refer the practice to the Commission.

An *anti-competitive practice* is defined in Section 2(1):

> a person engages in an anti-competitive practice if, in the course of business, that person pursues a course of conduct which, of itself or when taken together with a course of conduct pursued by persons associated with him, has or intended to have or is likely to have the effect of restricting, distorting or preventing competition in connection with the production, supply or acquisition of goods in the United Kingdom or any part of it or the supply or securing of services in the United Kingdom or any part of it.

When a single firm, with a significant market share, buys up one small competitor or customer after the other, each merger might be capable of reference under the Fair Trading Act, if the bidding company already fulfils the one quarter test. The public interest would, however, be confined to the particular merger[59] which, on its own, might be quite insignificant. Where three or four firms each supply about 15% of the market, and one or more of them starts buying small competitors, customers or suppliers, a merger would not even qualify for reference, unless the £ 15 million threshold were exceeded by a single acquisition. In these circumstances, an investigation might be made by the Director General under the Competition Act into the course of conduct of one

---

[56] See A. SUTHERLAND, *op. cit. supra* n. 35.

[57] The provisions are briefly analysed in V. Korah, *supra* n. 22, Chapters 1.13 and 5.11-5.11.6; and *The United Kingdom Competition Act 1980*, 11 INTERNATIONAL REVIEW OF INDUSTRIAL PROPERTY AND COPYRIGHT LAW 460-471 (1980).

[58] For a brief description of his Office see *supra* n. 26.

[59] This may cover successive acquisitions within two years between the same parties (Fair Trading Act 1973, S. 61 (1)), but not successive acquisitions from other parties. *See* the concern of the Commission over a trend of mergers quoted at n. 17, *supra*.

or more of the oligopolists, and if the series of acquisitions reduced the chances of competitive behaviour in the industry, the matter could be referred to the Commission as an anti-competitive practice. Were it to make an adverse finding on the public interest, then an order could be made restraining further acquisitions, but not ordering the firm to hive off some of the firms already bought, or their assets.[60]

This possibility might constrain the oligopolist investigated by the Director to give a voluntary undertaking, not only after an adverse report by the Commission, but also at the earlier stages, e.g., when the Director made a report finding the acquisitions to be anti-competitive, and so avoid the trouble and expense of a Commission enquiry. Before starting a statutory investigation, it appears that the Director General intends to make an informal approach to the firms suspected of adopting anti-competitive practices, and at that stage also, the firms might be prepared to agree to acquire no more competitors, customers and suppliers, if that would satisfy the Director sufficiently to avoid an investigation being made.

Apart from mentioning the possibility of use being made of the Competition Act, it does not yet seem to be worth while pursuing the matter. Few mergers will be part of a course of conduct, in which case they can be controlled only under the Fair Trading Act. A series of acquisitions by a single firm, however, might amount to "a course of conduct" subject to a simpler investigation by the Director. If he reports that it is anti-competitive then the Commission could consider the public interest in relation to a series of mergers and not only to one, which on its own might be insiginificant. There has been no experience under the Competition Act. The part relating to anti-competitive practices is to come into force on August 12, 1980.[61]

V. Evaluation of the System: General Questions under the Fair Trading Act

The main issue of policy remains whether the Fair Trading Act is too lenient, with the Commission having to be satisfied from a short investigation that the merger may be expected to operate against the public interest before it can be stopped. It has to judge what will happen on the alternative hypothesis that the merger is or is not carried out, and compare the results. So it is hardly surprising that it seldom is satisfied of the adverse effect overall. Between 1965, when mergers were first controlled, and July 1980, out of about 2,000 qualifying

---

[60] Competition Act 1980, S. 10 (2) (b).
[61] *See* The Competition Act 1980 (Commencement No. 2) Order 1980, S. I. 1980, No. 978. *See also*, the Anti-Competitive Practices (Exclusions) Order 1980, S. I. 1980, No. 979; and the Competition (Notices) Regulations 1980, S. I. 1980, No. 980. The only report made by the Director General of Fair Trading by Easter 1981 found anti-competitive the practice of refusing to supply retail chains likely to operate on low margins. The practice has been referred to the Commission.

54

mergers (other than newspaper transfers) were referred to the Commission – some 2.7%. Since late 1972, the proportion referred has increased slightly to about 3% of those qualifying. The parties to some mergers that were not referred gave assurances to ministers, *e.g.*, not to discriminate in price or supply, to consult government and trade unions about possible redundancies. Some of these were too vague to be policed and they were unenforceable anyway, in the absence of an adverse report by the Commission. Such assurances are never taken now. Of the mergers referred by mid-1980, 20 mergers were held not contrary to the public interest (though some were not positively approved), 18 were condemned and 17 proposals were abandoned.[62] Of course, the impact of the legislation may be greater than is disclosed from the statistics – some mergers may not be taking place because of fears that they would be referred and condemned; but with such a low percentage being referred, the risk may be low. There may be some notified to the Office of Fair Trading in confidence, where the Office indicated its probable intention to refer were the merger to be announced, that have been abrogated.

The Commission has tried to adopt a cost-benefit approach, balancing the detriments, such as increased market power against other benefits. In a short investigation, however, it has seldom been possible to forecast the future and quantify either benefits or detriments, at any rate in the published reports. Its success is difficult to assess – there have been few studies of how mergers have turned out, and there can be fewer of how the firms would have fared had the merger not taken place.[63] The power to control mergers in the United Kingdom is considerable, but it is rarely used and may have made little impact on our economy.

It is doubtful whether the merger powers will be very successful in breaking up established oligopolies. Divestiture is considered a penal remedy and would cause considerable disturbance. In its report on Parallel Pricing,[64] however, the Commission did recommend that the desirability of preventing oligopolies from developing should be borne in mind when deciding whether a merger should be referred, and this is taken into account by the Office of Fair Trading. The number of references made, however, seems to indicate that this advice has not been followed. Probably, it would not result in many adverse reports, given the onus of proof in favour of the merger.

[62] Figures are taken from the statement of the Secretary of State of July 1st, 1980. *See* n. 15 *supra.*

[63] J. F. Pickering, The Causes and Consequences of Abandoned Mergers, U.M.I.S.T. Occasional Paper No. 7906 f.

[64] Cmnd 5330 (H.M.S.O., London, 1973).

Summary

Mergers have been subject to control in the United Kingdom since 1965. A Minister may refer certain actual or proposed mergers to the Monopolies and Mergers Commission for its view whether the merger may be expected to operate contrary to the public interest. The advice he receives from officials remains confidential and in practice under 3% of those qualifying for reference have been referred to the Commission, so British mergers policy remains secret, save in so far as it has been explained in fairly broad terms by Ministers or officials.

The definition of a merger, in terms of common ownership or control, is very broad indeed, though actual references have been confined to occasions on which shareholdings have been altered. The Commission has condemned few mergers, since to do so it must be satisfied that the merger under consideration may be expected to operate against the public interest. It is required to take into account everything that it considers relevant, and in particular a list of matters. Its main concerns have been with competition and efficiency, but it does also devote paragraphs of the public interest chapter of its reports to such matters as increased unemployment and the balance of payments, although its conclusions on such matters usually follow from the finding on efficiency. In assessing effects on competition, the Commission has not felt compelled to define the relevant market: rather it considers the competitive pressures that will continue to constrain the merged companies, both from firms supplying similar products and from substitutes. It also considers barriers to entry and expansion, including the possibility of certain kinds of firms being able to enter the market should the merged firm attempt to reap monopoly profits.

A civil service Committee has recommended that the criteria applied by the Commission should be more neutral, but legislation would be required to implement this, and the Secretary of State announced on July 1st 1980 that no legislation is currently contemplated in the merger field.

The British legislation is far reaching but, since it merely empowers the Government to make a reference and few are made, it may not have had very significant effects on the British economy.

Merger Control in Germany:
Philosophies, Experiences, Reforms

Tübingen/Florence

I. Philosophies of Merger Control in the Context of the German Economy

A. Some Facts about Economic Concentration in Germany

1. Sensitivity to the Problem

Long before the introduction of merger control in Germany in 1973 there had been increasing concern about the growing economic concentration. This phenomenon not only was subjected to extensive study in German postwar economics,[1] but also led to several official inquiries, such as the Governmental Concentration Inquiry of 1964, the inquiries published by the Federal Cartel Office, and recently the inquiries by the Monopolies Commission in its main biennial reports of 1973/1975, 1976/1977 and 1978/1979.[2] Some of the observations made by the latter, even though open to different interpretations and conclusions,[3] serve to highlight the German situation.

2. Concentration Ratios

Concentration in a given branch of industry can be measured by determining the share of the turnover in that industry which the largest legally independent enterprises have. If we adopt this test, in 1977, on the average, the three largest enterprises in a branch were found to combine more than one quarter of the total

---

[1] See, e. g., H. ARNDT, ed., DIE KONZENTRATION DER WIRTSCHAFT (Berlin, 2d ed., 1971); H. O. LENEL, URSACHEN DER KONZENTRATION (Tübingen, 2d ed., 1968); E. HOPPMANN, FUSIONSKONTROLLE (Tübingen, 1972); E. KAUFER, KONZENTRATION UND FUSIONSKON-TROLLE (Tübingen, 1977).

[2] KONZENTRATIONSENQUÊTE, BUNDESTAGS-DRUCKSACHE [hereinafter BTDrs] IV/2320 (1964); Bericht des Bundeskartellamtes über seine Tätigkeit im Jahre 1968 [Federal Cartel Office, Annual Report, 1968] BTDrs V/4236 p. 31-32 (1969); 1972, BTDrs 7/986 p. 40-42 (1973); 1973, 7/2250, p. 35-37 (1974). MONOPOLKOMMISSION: HAUPTGUTACHTEN 1973/1975 [Monopolies Commission, Main Report 1973/1975] (Baden-Baden, 2d ed., 1977); HAUPTGUTACHTEN 1976/1977 (Baden-Baden, 1978); HAUPTGUTACHTEN 1978/1979, BTDrs 8/4404 (1980). See also OECD, CONCENTRATION AND COMPETITION POLICY, p. 27 et seq. (1979).

[3] For a methodological critique of the different studies see, for example, KAUFER Supra note 1, at p. 14 et seq.

turnover; the six largest more than one third; and the ten largest more than 40%. Concentration ratios of course vary considerably among industry branches (3.5% of the total turnover held by the three largest in wood-processing industry; 81.3% in aircraft building). Variations are even more marked among the more narrowly drawn enterprise classes[4] (from 5% up to 99% in 1975). Between 1960 and 1973, concentration ratios concerning the ten largest enterprises went up in 24 out of 30 industry branches and went down in only 6 branches. Between 1975 and 1977 in 11 out of 33 industry branches the number of enterprises in the branch increased, and in 22 it decreased. Within the industries the differences in size of the enterprises have in general widened since 1963, especially between the top-ranking enterprises and the rest. In contrast, within the top-ranking enterprises the distances have been continuously shrinking.

a) Concentration in the Top 100 Enterprises

If one focuses specifically on the concentration of the top-ranking enterprises, it turns out that the contribution made by the 100 largest enterprises to the German economy went up from 21.7% of the total turnover in 1972 to 24.6% in 1974, while slightly decreasing thereafter until 1978 (24.2%). There is a marked tendency of the largest enterprises to grow more quickly than the rest. In 1978 the 100 largest enterprises held around 5,700 participations in other domestic enterprises. The largest single German enterprise, the VEBA AG, alone held 440 direct or indirect participations. Of the participations of the top 100 enterprises, 332 were in joint ventures involving at least two out of these top 100. The corresponding figure in 1976 was 284 joint ventures. In 1978, again the VEBA AG alone had 151 joint ventures, involving 46 out of these 100. Many of the top 100 have interlocking directorates with at least one other enterprise out of the 100: 82 enterprises are connected at the supervisory board level (i. e. by at least one common member in these organs), 40 by having a member of their managing organ in the supervisory board of the other enterprise – these figures being based on the data of 90 of the top 100 only, no figures being available for the remaining ten. In nearly every second completed merger notified to the Federal Cartel Office from 1973 to the end of 1975, the acquired enterprise was a small- or medium-sized enterprise (with annual turnover of no more than 50 million DM); and more than one-half of these small- and medium-sized enterprises were acquired by one out of the 100 largest enterprises. In 1978/79 enterprises belonging to the top 100 were directly or indirectly involved in 496 enterprise mergers, i. e. 42.8% of all mergers notified under the law. The additional turnover acquired by these 496 mergers was around 40,000 million DM (as compared with 29,000 million DM in 1976/77).

b) Particular Concentration Problems (Banking, Energy, Newspapers etc.)

In some branches of the German economy economic concentration acquires a specific dimension because of the economic or political impact of the branch. This is especially true for banks. It must be remembered that under the system of

---

[4] These branches and classes are not the same concept as the relevant market. *See infra* § II, C. 1.

all-purpose banking not only are German private banks the major source of credit and finance for the enterprises (the capital markets not playing such an important role), but also they have important holdings in industry, and exercise the so-called depository voting rights of their clients in other corporations and, for these and other reasons, send bank representatives into the supervisory boards of most major corporations. This is support for the thesis that German banks have for a long time played a pivotal role in industry and in industry concentration.[5] Other areas of concern are the energy supply industries (oil, gas, coal, atomic energy). Even after the introduction of merger control, some of the most important and controversial mergers were carried out in these industries, and this with the specific permission of the Ministry of Economics. As it will be seen later, the public enterprises in these and other industries are said to get special treatment from the state-owner. Finally newspaper mergers present a special danger due to their effect on information dissemination and opinion-formation in a democracy. For example, in relation to newspapers which are primarily sold over the counter rather than by subscription, the three largest newspapers combine 80% of the total output. Concentration ratios based on turnover here seem less indicative than elsewhere, since most newspapers have local or regional markets.

B. Philosophies of Merger Control

1. Distinct Evaluation of Cartels and Mergers

In the original draft of the German Law against Restraints of Competition of 1955 strict provisions of merger control were envisaged, at that time still based on the classic concept of perfect competition and to a certain extent influenced by the American example. But when it came to passing the Act in 1957, the Parliament was not yet ready to accept merger control. It was pointed out that the tendency towards optimal plant size was economically desirable and it was feared that merger control could possibly hinder the full development of this tendency.[6] This corresponded to a broad economic discussion on the optimal

---

[5] For a historical analysis, *see* K. J. Hopt, *Functions of the Supervisory Board in the Bank-Industry Relationship*, in N. Horn & J. Kocka, eds., Law and the Formation of the Big Enterprises in the 19th and Early 20th Centuries, p. 227-242 (with English summary) (Göttingen, 1979). For a discussion of the German banking system, *see* H. E. Büschgen, *The Universal Banking System in the Federal Republic of Germany*, 2 Journal of Comparative Corporate Law and Securities Regulation, 1-27 (1979); and U. Immenga, *Participatory Investments by Banks: A Structural Problem of the Universal Banking System in Germany*, *ibidem* p. 29-48. As to the reform discussion on bank participations in non-banking enterprises, *see now* Bericht der Studienkommission "Grundsatzfragen der Kreditwirtschaft" [Report of the commission to study basic problems of the banking industry] (set up by the Federal Minister of Finance, p. 74 *et seq.*, 257 *et seq.* (Bonn, 1979).

[6] *Schriftlicher Bericht des Ausschusses für Wirtschaftspolitik über den Entwurf eines Gesetzes gegen Wettbewerbsbeschränkungen* [Report of the Committee for Economic Policy of the Bundestag], BTDrs II/3644 p. 27 (to § 18) (1957). *Cf.* § 18 of the Original Draft of 1955, BTDrs II/1158 (1955).

size of enterprises and optimal forms of markets. For example, it was argued that oligopolies, if not consisting of too few enterprises, are generally more efficient and desirable than polypolies since enterprises should have at least some market oversight in order to react competitively.

2. Critical Reappraisal of Mergers

During the 1960's this philosophy was eroded more and more. While the Federal Cartel Office concentrated under the 1957 Act on restraints of competition, both by cartels and vertical restraints, and also started very carefully to tackle the problem of abuses of monopoly power, concentration continued at a faster rate than before. Indeed, to a certain extent cartels and mergers are interchangeable means of reducing cumbersome competition. If only one means is barred by law, this is but an inducement for enterprises to concentrate more on the other, especially if intermediate forms of concentration, such as joint ventures, remain unaffected by the cartel prohibition. Increased observation and understanding of concentration, together with a change in government and in the general public perception of industry, finally led to the introduction of merger control in 1973.[7] The underlying philosophy starts with the premise that while mergers remain necessary in certain cases as a means of furthering economic and technical progress, many mergers are not justified by that aim. Therefore, the key problem in competition policy today is no longer cartels, but concentration. Economic concentration needs control, both for economic and for socio-political reasons.[8] Economically, undue concentration, by restraining competition, reduces the market impetus to higher performance and economic and technical progress. The myth of the big enterprise and its superior performance has vanished,[9] since there is evidence that it was often small- and medium-sized firms which initiated technical progress. Socio-politically, undue economic power endangers the free market economy and, ultimately, political democracy. It is quite important to keep this double basis for German merger control in mind since it goes together with a definite trend in modern German antitrust law: economic theories on competition and on markets are taken into consideration, but they are not allowed to become decisive in the legal reasoning and for the final outcome of a merger control case.

3. Particular Evaluation of Newspaper Mergers

This general philosophy of merger control needs adaptation in the case of newspaper mergers. There, non-economic goals prevail and an especially strict treatment of press mergers is necessary. The Legislator realized this in 1976,

---

[7] For the text of the Law, see Annex II. 1.a., infra at pp. 213 et seq.

[8] Cf. the Draft of the Second Antitrust Law Reform Act of 1973 (Entwurf eines Zweiten Gesetzes zur Änderung des Gesetzes gegen Wettbewerbsbeschränkungen), BTDrs VI/2520 (1971) = BTDrs 7/76 p. 16 (1973).

[9] For a recent reappraisal of the realities of merger in general, see, e. g., W. F. Bayer, Horizontal Groups and Joint Ventures in Europe: Concepts and Reality, in K. Hopt, ed., GROUPS OF COMPANIES IN EUROPEAN LAWS (Volume II of LEGAL AND ECONOMIC ANALYSES ON MULTINATIONAL ENTERPRISES) (Berlin, New York, 1981).

lowering the intervention threshold twenty times as compared with normal mergers. The philosophy is that by maintaining economic competition within the press the spectrum of opinions may best be furthered. This spectrum of opinions, which is primarily articulated in regional and local markets and especially by medium-sized and small press enterprises,[10] is essential for the free formation of public opinion. Yet press merger control is also founded on the same basic convictions as control of enterprise mergers in general. Consequently the focus is on maintaining competitive market structures, and the single press enterprise is not kept alive artificially if it is not able to compete on the market.[11] The latest case before the Federal Cartel Office concerns the envisaged merger between *Springer AG* and *Burda*, both of which have a turnover of more than 1,000 million DM and are leading competitors on the market for TV and radio program reviews.

C. Merger Control and Multinational Corporations[12]

1. Discussion in Germany

In Germany, discussion on multinational corporations was too broad and dealt with too many issues to allow more than a superficial treatment of the merger problem. The economists, political scientists and others who took part in this discussion usually were not familiar with the intricacies of antitrust law. On the other hand, the main stream discussion on merger control has been kept within the framework of economic and industrial policy and of antitrust law reform. This may be in part due to the traditional aversion of antitrust legislation to consider international restraints of competition unless they have an effect on the domestic market. Even more important may be the insight that most of the

---

[10] *Cf.* the Draft of the Third Antitrust Law Reform Act of 1976 (*Entwurf eines Dritten Gesetzes zur Änderung des Gesetzes gegen Wettbewerbsbeschränkungen*) BTDrs 7/2954 p. 5 (1974). For a general discussion of the press concentration, *see* E. J. MESTMÄCKER, MEDIENKONZENTRATION UND MEINUNGSVIELFALT (Baden-Baden, 1978); W. MÖSCHEL, PRESSEKONZENTRATION UND WETTBEWERBSGESETZ (Tübingen, 1978). *See now*, the decisions: Bundesgerichtshof, 18 December, 1979, "Springer/Elbe Wochenblatt", 76 BGHZ 55 = WuW/E BGH 1685; Kammergericht, 24. October, 1979, "Zeitungsmarkt München", WuW/E OLG 2228; Bundeskartellamt, 9 January, 1981, "Gruner + Jahr/Zeit", WuW/E BKartA 1863.

[11] Bundeskartellamt [Federal Cartel Office], 6 July, 1978, "Kaufzeitungen", WuW/E BKartA 1733 at 1741.

[12] At the same time as the increases in the concentration ratios noted *supra* § I.A.2. were occuring in German industry, there was also an increase in German foreign direct investment. For a general overview of the European situation (including Germany) in this respect over the last two decades *see* J. Dunning, *Multinational Enterprises in the 1970's: An Economist's Overview of Trends, Theories and Policies, supra* this volume, at pp. 3 *et seq.* and especially Table I.

problems of multinational corporations are but the problems of economic power which theoretically can arise as well with strictly national corporations.[13]

2. Competitiveness Abroad

On a second look, however, the issue of multinational corporations certainly did come up in the merger control discussion, even though under industrial policy concepts and in antitrust terms. The main link was, of course, the concern about the competitiveness of German industry abroad. A German national merger control system, it was argued, is incompatible with economic integration in the EEC. The German Government until 1967 justified its inactivity in the matter by pointing to the necessity of merger control on the European level. Only from 1967 onwards did the Governmental position as to this argument begin to change.[14] And indeed, if a system of European merger control cannot be reached because of the unwillingness of certain Member States, the others cannot be expected to wait and see the structure of their national markets steadily worsening as a result of accumulation of economic power through concentration. This is especially true in view of the fact that it is nearly impossible on practical and political grounds to dissolve an enterprise once a merger has been consolidated, even if the law were to provide for such a possibility. This does not mean that the transnational perspective is lost from sight in the German merger control system. While the competition of foreign enterprises on the German market is necessarily considered when the market domination of the German enterprise in question is examined, the Law of 1973 expressly provides that the Minister of Economics in deciding about a merger shall also consider the ability of the participating enterprises to compete in markets outside Germany.[15] Actually, if one relates the German "hit list" of the 100 largest enterprises in 1976 to the overall European position, one finds the first German enterprise at place 6 and the 100th at place 240. In 1978 the corresponding ranks on a world-wide scale were 18 and around 700. In 1978 the largest German enterprise (VEBA AG) had but 22.8% (1976: 22.3%) of the turnover of the largest enterprise on a world-wide scale (1978: General Motors; 1976: Exxon).[16]

---

[13] Cf. K. J. Hopt, *Recht und Geschäftsmoral multinationaler Unternehmen*, in J. GERN-HUBER, ed., TRADITION UND FORTSCHRITT IM RECHT, FESTSCHRIFT ZUM 500JÄHRIGEN BESTE-HEN DER TÜBINGER JURISTENFAKULTÄT, p. 279, at 288 *et seq.* (Tübingen, 1977).

[14] *See Bericht des Bundeskartellamtes über seine Tätigkeit im Jahre 1967*, BTDrs V/2841 p. 3 (1968); and for 1968, *supra* note 2, at p. 3.

[15] Sec. 24 III No. 1. GWB (= Law Against Restraints of Competition); Unterrichtung des Ausschusses für Wirtschaft zu dem von den Fraktionen der SPD, FDP eingebrach-ten Entwurf eines Zweiten Gesetzes zur Änderung des Gesetzes gegen Wettbewerbs-beschränkungen, BTDrs 7/765 p. 7 *et seq.* (1973). [Committee for Economics of the Bundestag]. *Cf. also* the lengthy discussion in the annotation to the Draft of the Second Antitrust Law Reform Act, *supra* note 8, p. 16 *et seq.*

[16] In the meantime due to the oil price boom and the structural problems of the automobile industry, Exxon is now by far the largest enterprise. While by 1978 the difference in turnover between General Motors and Exxon was very small, by 1981 Exxon's turnover reached nearly double that of General Motors, which fell to fourth

3. International Reach of Law

In the meantime, the international perspective has been intensified. More weight has been given not to the international-competitiveness argument, but rather to a broader international application of German antitrust law.[17] This is hardly surprising since there is a clearly increasing trend of mergers with links to or from abroad. In 1980 this was true for 45% of all notified merger cases (1979: 38%).[18] The *Bundesgerichtshof* in its *"organic pigments"* decision of May 1979[19] held that also mergers concluded abroad must be notified to the Federal Cartel Office, if they have an impact on the domestic market. This by itself is not noteworthy. But the Court held that the impact was substantial enough in a case in which the merger was concluded between an American vendor, an enterprise with only 0.23% of the German market, and the American "great-grand-daughter" of a German enterprise with only 3.5% of the German market (0.14% and 4.4% respectively one year earlier). It was held sufficient that the merging foreign enterprises satisfied the size requirements which under the Law determine whether German enterprises must notify the agreement and that one of the merging enterprises transferred its qualified know-how to the other and retreated from the German market. To be sure, legally the decision stays within the territoriality principle and concerns only notification, not actual control of mergers. But practically its consequences are that all big foreign enterprises (with 10,000 workers or a 500 million DM turnover) doing business in Germany must notify their mergers abroad. In September 1980 the Federal Cartel Office forbade for the first time a merger between two foreign enterprises.[20] *Bayer*

place after Exxon, Royal Dutch/Shell and Mobil Oil. FAZ No. 168, 24. 7. 1981, p. 10.

[17] Cf. Federal Cartel Office, Memorandum on "Inlandsauswirkungen im Sinne des § 98 Abs. 2 GWB bei Unternehmenszusammenschlüssen", Annex II.1.c., *infra* at pp. 230-231, taken from *Bericht des Bundeskartellamtes über seine Tätigkeit im Jahr 1975*, BTDrS 7/5390 p. 45.

[18] *Bericht des Bundeskartellamtes über seine Tätigkeit in den Jahren 1979/1980*, BTDrS 9/565 p. III (1981).

[19] Bundesgerichtshof, 29 May, 1979, "Organische Pigmente", 74 BGHZ 322 = WuW/E BGH 1613; *cf.* Kammergericht, 5 April, 1978, "Organische Pigmente" WuW/E OLG 1993 = 1979 AG 158. The decision has been criticized in the legal literature, *see, for example*, C. Klawitter, in WuW/E BGH 1616. But it has been praised by the Monopolies Commission, HAUPTGUTACHTEN 1978/1979, *supra* note 2, at No. 545 *et seq.* See also K. M. MEESEN, VÖLKERRECHTLICHE GRUNDSÄTZE DES INTERNATIONALEN KARTELL-RECHTS (Baden-Baden, 1975); K. M. Meesen, *Zusammenschlußkontrolle in auslandsbe-zogenen Sachverhalten*, 143 ZHR 273 at 286 *et seq.* (1979); H. C. Kersten, *Zur Anwendbarkeit des GWB auf ausländische Unternehmenszusammenschlüsse mit Inlandswirkungen*, 1979 WuW 721; K. Autenrieth, *Die Anzeigepflicht beim Zusam-menschluß ausländischer Unternehmen*, 1980 RIW/AWD 820; R. Belke and W. D. Braun, *German Merger Control: A European Approach to Anticompetitive Takeovers*, 1 NORTHWESTERN JOURNAL OF INTERNATIONAL LAW & BUSINESS 371, at 398 *et seq.* (1979); H. Roth, *Die Fusionskontrolle internationaler Unternehmenszusammen-schlüsse*, 45 Rabels Z 501 (1981).

[20] Federal Cartel Office, 23 September, 1980, "Bayer France/Firestone France", WuW/E

France S.A., an indirect 100% subsidiary of the German Bayer AG, planned to acquire most of the assets of *Firestone France*, a subsidiary of the American Firestone Tire & Rubber Co. The Federal Cartel Office argued that Bayer AG has a position of domination on the synthetical rubber and tire markets (*in toto* 39.5%) and that this position would be strengthened, first, by the projected merger by 0.8% and 0.4% of the two markets respectively; second, and more important, by the disappearance of a potential competitor; third, by the acquisition of new production capacity, patents and licenses. The prohibiting decree has been disaffirmed by the *Kammergericht*, but only on formal grounds (lack of sufficient service and hearing of the parent corporation, Firestone USA).[21] There is already a second case, the projected merger of *Philip Morris Inc.* and *Rothman's International Ltd.*, both leading cigarette producers with subsidiaries in Germany.[22] Other cases are expected to follow which could lead Germany into substantial international conflicts,[23] which so far have been known in the international community mainly from the U.S. and have led to retaliatory laws in several countries. This tendency of reaching out over the borders is confirmed in other contexts. For example, the traditional neglect of restraints of competition by German enterprises abroad begins to give place to more active intervention. Since 1980, the Federal Minister of Economics may also prohibit export cartels having no impact on the German market, if they affect considerably prevailing interests of German foreign economic policy. The Legislator meant this as promotion of free world trade, but made clear that the competitiveness of German industry abroad must not be lost from sight.[24]

D. Merger Control and the Law of Enterprise Groups

Originally the Law of Enterprise Groups of 1965 and of Merger Control of 1973 were in domains quite apart from each other. The Law of Enterprise Groups defends the legitimate interests of creditors and outside shareholders of corporations which are members of a group and tries to achieve these aims by corporate law devices. Merger control law instead aims at keeping market structures competitive and entrusts this task to state agencies. However, today it is more and more acknowledged that there are not only important overlapping areas, such as the concept of merger, but that the Law of Enterprise Groups must be

BKartA 1837 = BAnz No. 181, 27. 9. 1980; *cf.* C. T. Ebenroth and K. Autenrieth, *Die Fusionskontrolle beim Zusammenschluß ausländischer Unternehmen unter indirekter Beteiligung eines inländischen Unternehmens*, 1981 BB 16.

[21] Kammergericht, 26 November, 1980, "Synthetischer Kautschuk I", WuW/E OLG 2411 and "Synthetischer Kautschuk II", WuW/E OLG 2419, with annotation by K. Markert, *Fusionskontrolle bei Zusammenschlüssen im Ausland*, 1981 RIW 403.

[22] W. Gehrmann, DIE ZEIT No. 20, 8 May, 1981, p. 19.

[23] Seen correctly by Kammergericht, "Synthetischer Kautschuk II", *supra* note 21, at 2420 *et seq.*

[24] Sec. 12 II No. 2 GWB as of 1980. *Cf.* Draft of the Fourth Antitrust Law Reform Act of 1980 (*Entwurf eines Vierten Gesetzes zur Änderung des Gesetzes gegen Wettbewerbsbeschränkungen*), BTDrs 8/2136 p. 18 (1978). For the latest factual information on German export cartels *cf.* Minister of Economics, Daily Informations (BMWI-TAGESNACHRICHTEN) No. 8090, 12. 6. 1981, p. 1-6.

interpreted in the spirit of antitrust law.[25] Therefore major decisions concerning the Law of Enterprise Groups – such as the famous *"VEBA-AG"* decision of the Bundesgerichtshof of October 1977 which applied the Law to public enterprises of the Federal Republic[26] – may very well have an immediate impact on merger control and antitrust law.

II. Merger Control in Germany: Legal Structure and Practical Experience

A. Survey of the Legal Structure[27]

1. Substantive Merger Control Law

If we look first at substantive merger control law as distinguished from procedure, three fundamental problems, common to every merger control system, appear: When are mergers sufficiently relevant to merit legal scrutiny (minimum threshold or "take-up" criteria)? Under what conditions are mergers subject to legal prohibition (intervention point or "no-go" criteria)? What defenses are available in order to have an illegal merger exceptionally declared legal (overall justification or "let-off" criteria)?

a) Minimum Threshold Criteria
Under German law mergers are taken up for legal scrutiny if two conditions are fulfilled. One seems obvious: there must be a merger. But the corporate lawyer

---

[25] *See, e. g.* V. EMMERICH & J. SONNENSCHEIN, KONZERNRECHT, p. 9, (Munich, 2d ed., 1977).

[26] Bundesgerichtshof, 13 October, 1977, "VEBA/Gelsenberg", 69 BGHZ 334, with critical annotation by W. Zöllner, 1978 AG 40; B. Kropff, *Zur Anwendung des Rechtes der verbundenen Unternehmen auf den Bund*, 144 ZHR 74 (1980). *Cf.* also Bundesgerichtshof, "WAZ", *infra* note 31.

[27] Sec. 23, 24, 24a, 24b GWB. For a short memorandum by the Federal Cartel Office on merger control issued for the information of the enterprises concerned *see* 1981 WuW 183-187, reprinted Annex II.1.b. infra, at pp. 224 *et seq.* For regular reports on the practice *see* the annual reports of the Federal Cartel Office, *supra* note 2, e. g. for 1978, BTDrs 8/2980 (1979). For a critical evaluation, *see* the reports of the Monopolies Commission, *supra* note 2. The case law is reported, for example, in WIRTSCHAFT UND WETTBEWERB, ENTSCHEIDUNGSSAMMLUNG ZUM KARTELLRECHT (WuW/E). For practitioners' commentaries, *see, e. g.*, KLEINMANN & BECHTOLD, KOMMENTAR ZUR FUSIONSKONTROLLE (Heidelberg, 1977), and the general antitrust law commentaries by KAUFMANN, RAUTMANN et al. (FRANKFURTER KOMMENTAR) since 1958; MÜLLER-HENNEBERG, SCHWARTZ, eds. (GEMEINSCHAFTSKOMMENTAR) (3d ed., since 1972) (merger control still to be commented); LANGEN, NIEDERLEITHINGER, SCHMIDT, (5th ed., 1977); MÜLLER, GIESSLER, SCHOLZ, (3d ed., 1978); WESTRICK, LOEWENHEIM, (4th ed., since 1977). For a students' introduction *see* V. EMMERICH, KARTELLRECHT (Munich, 3d ed., 1979); *see also* the series of case reviews by the same author, 1978 AG 85 *et seq.;* 1979 AG 6 *et seq;* 1980 AG 205 and 240. For a very good survey in English *see* J. F. Baur, *The Control of Mergers Between Large, Financially Strong Firms in West Germany*, 1980 ZEITSCHRIFT FÜR DIE GESAMTE STAATSWISSENSCHAFT 136.

must beware. Unlike corporate law, merger control law does not define merger on the basis of disappearing corporate entities, but rather on the basis of decision-making and control. Details will be examined later. The second take-up criterion is minimum size. Mergers are not considered to be dangerous if the combined turnover of the participating enterprises is less than 500 million DM or, as a general rule, if an independent enterprise with no more than 50 million DM turnover merges into another enterprise. Cases of press concentration are taken up at much smaller sizes due to their specific dangers as seen above (25 million DM combined turnover, no minimum size of single turnover).

b) Intervention Criteria

While these figures are nothing more than a somewhat arbitrarily drawn minimum threshold, the actual merger control takes place only if it is to be expected that the merger will create or strengthen a position of market domination. In this case the Federal Cartel Office will step in and prohibit the merger. Two cases of market domination must be distinguished: First, an enterprise is in a dominant position if, as a seller or buyer of a particular type of goods or commercial services, it has no competitors. The same is true if the enterprise (or, in the case of an oligopoly, each of the oligopolists) is not subject to any substantial competition. In this first case the focus is obviously on the market share of a single enterprise. Second, even without such a major market share, an enterprise is treated as dominating the market if it has a superior market position in relation to its competitors (or, in the case of an oligopoly, if the enterprises together have such a market position and there is no substantial competition between them). There are various indicators for superior market power: besides the market share, for example, the financial strength of the enterprise, its access to supply and sales markets, its corporate ties to other enterprises and legal or factual barriers to market access by other enterprises. For each of the two above cases there are lengthy legal presumptions facilitating proof for the Federal Cartel Office (market share of a single enterprise of one third, combined market shares of three enterprises of 50%, combined market shares of five enterprises of two thirds).

c) Justification Criteria

It this "no-go" criterion of market domination in one of the two forms is fulfilled, the merger will be prohibited – but subject to two possible justifications. Firstly, the enterprises may prove that the merger will also lead to improvements of competitive conditions and that such improvements outweigh the detrimental effects of the market domination. Secondly, the merger can be let off if the restraint on competition is balanced by the overall economic advantages of the merger or if the merger is justified by an overriding public interest. As mentioned above the ability of the participating enterprises to compete in markets outside Germany shall also be considered in this context.

2. Procedure

Merger control can only be understood in relation to its procedure, even though under German legal tradition attention focuses probably more on substantive law.

a) Notification to and Prohibition by the Federal Cartel Office
Proceedings start with the Federal Cartel Office in Berlin. This agency has broad inquiry rights (and corresponding duties of confidentiality) and is under the direction of the Minister of Economics. As a general rule the Federal Cartel Office gets to know of the merger through notification. It is true that notification of a proposed merger is obligatory only in exceptional cases, for example if two merging enterprises have an annual turnover of 1,000 million DM each or, since 1980, if one has an annual turnover of 2,000 million DM. But voluntary notification is in the enterprises' own interest, since then the Federal Cartel Office may prohibit the proposed merger only within four months of the date of notification. Where no notification is given either before or after completion of the merger, there are no time limits for intervention. It is obvious that enterprises cannot afford this risk.

b) Application to the Federal Minister of Economics for Exemption
If the Federal Cartel Office has prohibited the merger, the enterprise may apply within one month to the Federal Minister of Economics for exemption on the grounds of overriding economic or public interest. Thus German merger control law clearly distinguishes between two procedural parts and, correspondingly, two levels of evaluation of the merger. Before the Federal Cartel Office only competition and the balance of the pros and cons for competitive conditions are at stake. This evaluation is a legal one and subject to full legal review by the courts. Before the Minister public interest in general is at stake and must be balanced against the restraint of competition. This evaluation is a political one and almost completely exempt from legal review. Only in the extreme case in which the restraint of competition is such as to jeopardize the system of the market economy is the political discretion of the Minister curtailed by law.

c) Review by the Courts
Usually in the interim between these two procedural parts the case will be tried before the courts. This is possible since the one month deadline for applying to the Minister of Economics begins to run only when the prohibition decree of the Federal Cartel Office has become final. There are only two court instances, the Court of Appeals in Berlin *(Kammergericht)* and the *Bundesgerichtshof* in Karlsruhe. The delay built in by this whole procedure is in itself hostile to mergers. For example, in the *"motor-car clutch"* case,[28] the British group Guest, Keen & Nettlefolds Ltd. (GKN) had already notified its proposed merger with the German Sachs AG (controlling Fichtel & Sachs AG) as early as 1975. GKN lost before the Federal Cartel Office, won before the *Kammergericht* and lost again before the *Bundesgerichtshof* in February 1978. By that time GKN and Sachs had made other plans. GKN still applied for permission to the Minister of Economics, but withdrew its application at the end of May 1978.

---

[28] Bundeskartellamt, 12 May, 1976, WuW/E BKartA 1625; Kammergericht, 1 December, 1976, WuW/E OLG 1745; Bundesgerichtshof, 21 February, 1978, "Kfz-Kupplungen", 71 BGHZ 102 = WuW/E BGH 1501.

d) Consultative Role of the Monopolies Commission

The German Monopolies Commission, with five members and a small staff, is not directly involved in these proceedings. Its task is consultative. Every two years it reports on the development of enterprise concentration. It further gives opinions concerning pending cases, either at its own initiative or at the request of the Minister of Economics.[29] Since 1980 the Minister of Economics is bound to make such a request if the proceeding reaches its second stage before him.

3. Postmerger Notification

This procedure has been part of German antitrust law since 1957. Originally it substituted for politically unfeasible merger control, but it has been maintained even after 1973. While premerger notification is generally voluntary and is part of the merger control system, postmerger notification is obligatory and is legally, even though not practically, separate from merger control in its strict sense. Postmerger notification requirements exist in two cases: first, if as a result of the merger a market share of 20% ist reached or increased, or if one of the participating enterprises holds at least 20% of another market; second, if the participating enterprises had together in the previous year at least 10,000 employees or a 500 million DM turnover. Since these figures are rather high, one may wonder at first sight why German industry considered postmerger notification cumbersome and even damaging.[30] But in fact postmerger notification is very far-reaching, since the labour force and turnover of all members of a group must be computed as soon as any member of the group (either dominating or dependent within the meaning of the Law of Enterprise Groups) participates in the merger. The Bundesgerichtshof in its 1979 "WAZ" decision[31] has extended the requirements even further. In the case of a merger involving a dependent enterprise, the name of the enterprise dominating the group must also be mentioned in the notification, and this and other details concerning the group are subject to publication in the Federal Bulletin. Also a private shareholder is subject to the notification and publication requirements as an enterprise, if, in addition to a major shareholding, he has economic interests outside the corporation which may be an incentive for him to influence his corporation in restraint of competition. This is already the case if he has substantial holdings in

---

[29] Besides its main reports, *see supra* note 2, the Monopolies Commission up to now has given 9 so-called special reports, (Sondergutachten): (1) Missbrauchsaufsicht über marktbeherrschende Unternehmen, 1975; (2) Veba/Gelsenberg, 1975; (3) Kaiser Aluminium/Preussag, 1975; (4) Babcock/Artos, 1976; (5) Karstadt/Neckermann, 1976; (6) Thyssen/Hueller Hille, 1977; (7) Missbräuche der Nachfragemacht, 1977; (8) BP/VEBA, 1979. (9) Die Rolle der Deutschen Bundespost im Fernmeldewesen, 1981.

[30] Cf. Frankfurter Kommentar, *supra* note 27, at § 23, Tz. 20-23.

[31] Bundesgerichtshof, 8 May, 1979, "Westdeutsche Allgemeine Zeitungsverlagsgesellschaft", 74 BGHZ 359 = WuW/E BGH 1608. *Cf.* the controversial evaluation of this decision by F. J. Säcker, *Mehrmütterklausel und Gemeinschaftsunternehmen*, 1980 NJW 801; and E. Steindorff, *Gemeinschaftsunternehmen mit zwei paritätisch beteiligten Gesellschaften*, 1980 NJW 1921.

several enterprises which lead to market-oriented planning. The court even applied the postmerger notification requirement to two private shareholders who had a 50% holding each and led the corporation under a common enterprise policy. Under the so-called *"Flick"*-provision of the law, private majority shareholders of one enterprise acquiring 25% of the shares in another enterprise are irrefutably deemed to be enterprises within the meaning of the antitrust law.

4. Merger as an Abuse of Monopoly Power

Finally in German law, as well as under Article 86 of the EEC Treaty, a merger may be prohibited if it can be considered as an abuse of monopoly power. While this possibility has been stressed by some authors,[32] the Federal Cartel Office and prevailing legal literature have been more hesitant. Still a market-dominating enterprise which ruins a remaining competitor and forces him to accept a merger could be considered to commit an abuse of its market power.[33] But it is open to controversy whether in German law the exclusion by merger of the last functioning competition is such an abuse as it is in EEC law. In any case an abuse control system cannot be used for full scale merger control in default of the substantive and procedural safeguards of merger control so far described.

B. The Broad Concept of Merger in Antitrust Law

Merger in the strict corporate sense is the union of two or more corporations one of which continues in existence, while the other is swallowed. This corporate law definition is too narrow for merger control purposes since the consequences for competition on the market may be the same if an enterprise directly or indirectly adds resources of another enterprise to its own. Therefore, merger control law defines merger autonomously, distinguishing serveral forms.

1. Acquisition of Assets

In one form merger can consist in the acquisition of the assets of another enterprise, wholly or to a significant extent. Whether this is done by means of merger in the corporate law sense or in any other form, is irrelevant. In practice everything depends, of course, on what is considered to be a significant part of the assets of the selling enterprise. Case law goes very far. The *Bundesgerichtshof* in its 1975 *cement processing plant* decision[34] added a qualitative meaning to the

---

[32] In this sense, see e. g., E. J. MESTMÄCKER, DER MISSBRAUCH MARKTBEHERRSCHENDER STELLUNGEN IM DEUTSCHEN, ITALIENISCHEN UND EUROPÄISCHEN RECHT, p. 13 et seq. (Karlsruhe, 1969); V. Emmerich, 1978 AG 150, at 153. See also, incidentally, Bundeskartellamt, 18 January, 1978, "Springer-Elbe Wochenblatt", WuW/E BKartA 1700, at 1705 = 1979 AG 20, at 23. For European Law, see European Court of Justice, 21 February, 1973, Case 6/72 "Continental Can", 1973 EUROPEAN COURT REPORTS 215, at 244 et seq.; P. M. Schmitt, *Multinational Corporations and Merger Control in Community Antitrust Law*, *infra* this volume, at pp. 174 et seq.

[33] *Cf.* Kammergericht, 12 January, 1976, "Weichschaum", WuW/E OLG 1637, at 1638, but leaving the question open.

[34] Bundesgerichtshof, 20 November, 1975, "Zementmahlanlage", 65 BGHZ 269 at 272 et seq. = WuW/E BGH 1377.

quantitative one. Even an insignificant part of assets of a large vendor may in fact be significant on the market. Thus a separate plant or other operative economic units with independent importance, for example for production or sales, may be significant. In *Pfaff/Industriewerke Karlsruhe*[35] the *Kammergericht* considered as significant a complete sewing machine program including the necessary machines, trademarks and know-how. The program amounted to only 0.5% of the assets of the vendor, but accounted for a turnover of 9 million DM and a market share of 3.2%. While these cases have been criticised strongly in part of the legal literature,[36] the tendency is clear. The courts refuse to consider the legal concept of merger as an important threshold in taking up cases of enterprise concentration.

2. Acquisition of Shares

A merger can also consist in the acquisition of shares of another enterprise, if as a result the acquiring enterprise holds 25% or more of the voting capital of the other enterprise. This may seem modest, but actually goes very far indeed since again the shareholdings of all members of a group will be computed. For example when *Iran* in its famous transaction acquired 25.01% of the *Krupp GmbH Essen*, this implied also a merger between Krupp and Deutsche Babcock AG in which Iran held 33.92%. Since Krupp through its subsidiary Walther & Cie. AG had an important influence on EVT GmbH, it further implied an indirect merger between EVT and Deutsche Babcock, the two main competitors in the big steam generator and the cooling tower markets with a combined market share of 80%.[37] It is obvious that industry tries to find an escape route by staying formally under 25%. For example *AEG-Telefunken AG* acquired only 20% of the Italian *Zanussi s.p.A.*, but with a contractual provision to have the rights of a 25% shareholder including a fourth of the seats in the administrative board of Zanussi.[38] But the Federal Cartel Office now holds this to be a fraud on the law and this has also just been affirmed by the 1980 Reform Act.[39] Another case is the *Metro/Kaufhof* merger in which both Metro and the Swiss Bank Corporation (Schweizerische Bankgesellschaft) each acquired 24% of the shares of Kaufhof and the Bank got an option for an additional 2.3%. While the Federal Cartel Office held this to be a merger, the *Kammergericht* failed to find proof of an at least 25% acquisition.[40] The latest possibility tried out is found in the pending

---

[35] Kammergericht, 21 September, 1977, "Kettenstichnähmaschinen", WuW/E OLG 1908, but remanded for further market inquiries under sec. 23 No. 1 GWB, Bundesgerichtshof, 13 March, 1979, 74 BGHZ 172 = WuW/E BGH 1570.

[36] For example KLEINMANN, BECHTOLD, *supra* note 27, at § 23, Tz 47 *et seq.*; F. Rittner, *Erweiterte Anzeigepflicht bei Unternehmenszusammenschluß*, 1976 NJW 546.

[37] *Bericht des Bundeskartellamtes über seine Tätigkeit im Jahre 1977*, BTDrs 8/1925, p. 52 (1978).

[38] *Cf.* Federal Cartel Office, Annual Report 1973, *supra* note 2, at p. 70 *et seq.* At that time the Office still gave in.

[39] For example Federal Cartel Office, Annual Report 1978, *supra* note 27, at p. 94. *See now*, Sec. 23 II No. 2, sentences 4 and 5 as of 1980.

[40] "*Das Kartellamt verliert vor dem Kammergericht*", FAZ No. 135, 13. 6. 1981, p. 11;

case of *Ullstein (Springer) / Haupt & Koska,* a case of a contractual separation
between capital and votes; the merger would thus result in a 25% participation of
the shares, but not of the voting capital.[41]

3. Other Forms of Merger

In practice enterprise mergers consist in most cases in the acquisition of shares or
(less frequently) in the acquisition of assets. Remaining loopholes are closed by
three other forms of merger within the meaning of the law. These are the
combination of enterprises in a group under uniform direction (a so-called
concern); interlocking directorates of at least half the board; and, by a final
catch-all clause, any direct or indirect control relationship between two enterprises. Very exceptionally a merger is deemed not to exist under the so-called
banking clause. Accordingly, a bank, in connection with the formation or capital
increase of an enterprise or otherwise within the scope of its business activities,
may acquire shares of another enterprise for the purpose of resale in the market,
but the bank may not exercise the voting rights relating to these shares and the
resale must take place within one year. Under this clause the *Deutsche Bank* in
1974/1975 acquired the Flick holding of 29% in *Daimler-Benz* in order to
prevent its purchase by Iran.[42] All this shows that the concept of merger despite
all its legal niceties has been watered down so much as not to be decisive for the
outcome of a merger control case. The keystone criterion instead is market
domination. But before turning to this a short remark must be made on groups
and joint ventures.

4. Groups and Joint Ventures

As to groups of enterprises, a standard antitrust problem in German as well as in
European law has been whether agreements between members of the group may
be treated as illegal restraints of competition. Usually the answer is negative since
the members of the group form one economic unit. But an exception is proposed
for the case of a subsidiary which may determine its market behaviour freely
without directives from its parent.[43] A quickly growing minority opinion goes
further and refuses to acknowledge any kind of concentration privilege.[44] A
similar problem arises for mergers within a group. Here the law is stricter.
Mergers within a group, or between enterprises which have merged already

"Metro: Wir sind sicher keine bequemen Konkurrenten", FAZ No. 137, 16. 6. 1981,
p. 17. Cf. now *"Kartellamt stellt Metro-Verfahren ein"* FAZ No. 193, 22. 8. 1981,
p. 9.

[41] Cf. *"Das Kapital hat keine Stimme"*, FAZ No. 148, 1. 7. 1981, p. 13; *"Springer verliert
vor dem Kammergericht"*, FAZ No. 151, 4. 7. 1981; p. 11.

[42] As to such bank participations *cf.* K. J. Hopt, Der Kapitalanlegerschutz im Recht
der Banken, p. 204 (Munich, 1975). See also *supra* note 5.

[43] *Bericht des Bundeskartellamtes über seine Tätigkeit im Jahre 1961,* BTDrs IV/378, p. 61
(1962); and for 1969, BTDrs VI/950, p. 57 *et seq.* (1970). For European Law *see e. g.,*
European Court of Justice, 31 October, 1974, 1974, Case 15/74, "Centrafarm/Sterling
Drug", 1974 European Court Reports II 1147, at 1167.

[44] E. J. Mestmäcker, Europäisches Wettbewerbsrecht, p. 405 *et seq.,* 409 (Munich,
1974); V. Emmerich, *supra* note 19, p. 48 (with further references).

(within the meaning of merger control law), clearly are not exempt from subsequent merger control unless there is no substantial strengthening of the already existing ties between or among the group members.

Today attention, both in theory and practice, is much more on joint ventures. They have gained enormous importance in modern business, certainly also for multinational corporations.[45] For example out of 1,237 mergers notified to the Federal Cartel Office in 1979 and 1980 there were 288 joint venture cases.[46] Their evaluation is one of the most controversial problems in today's antitrust and merger control law. This is so because joint ventures combine elements both of a cartel and of a merger. Quite aptly they have been called "the chameleons of competition law" or even "modern day open marriages". Under German merger control law, if at least two parent enterprises, simultaneously or successively, acquire holdings in a common subsidiary of 25% or more each, a merger is deemed to exist not only between each parent and the joint venture, but also between the parents themselves in respect of the markets in which the joint venture is active. This is because of the so-called group effect of such a joint venture on the competitive behaviour of parents.[47] In contrast, a joint venture by five parent companies with 20% each would not be subject to merger control. The hotly debated issue is whether in this case, and more generally in all cases of joint ventures, the creation and the operation of the joint venture may still be treated as an illegal restraint of competition. Traditional legal opinion tries to distinguish between joint ventures with a cooperation character and others with a concentration character.[48] But now there is a growing tendency to apply both, cartel prohibition and merger control,[49] as in the European practice under Article

---

[45] See E. J. Mestmäcker, *Gemeinschaftsunternehmen im deutschen und europäischen Konzern- und Kartellrecht*, in E. J. Mestmäcker, D. T. Donaldson, J.-B. Blaise, Gemeinschaftsunternehmen (Joint venture – filiale commune) im Konzern- und Kartellrecht, p. 9 (Frankfurt, 1979).

[46] Federal Cartel Office, Annual Report 1979 and 1980, *supra* note 18, p. 19 *et seq*.

[47] Sec. 23 II No. 2 sentence 3 GWB. But this relates only to the merger being deemed to exist. Whether by such a merger a position of market domination of the two parent corporations of the joint venture will be created or strengthend (sec. 24 I), has still to be examined in each single case. Bundesgerichtshof, 12 February, 1980, "Bituminöses Mischgut", WuW/E BGH 1763, taking once more an intermediate position between the Federal Cartel Office and the Kammergericht.

[48] For example, Federal Cartel Office, Annual Report 1978, *supra* note 27, at p. 23 *et seq.*; U. Huber, *Gemeinschaftsunternehmen im deutschen Wettbewerbsrecht*, in U. Huber & B Bürner, eds., Gemeinschaftsunternehmen im deutschen und europäischen Wettbe-werbsrecht, p. 1, at 65 *et seq.* (Cologne, 1978); similarly W. Harms, *Fusionskontrolle: Praxis, Novellierungspläne und kritische Würdigung*, in Schwerpunkte des Kartell-rechts 1976/77, FIW, p. 43, at 51 *et seq.* (Cologne, 1978). W. Harms and H.-G. König, *Gemeinschaftsunternehmen 1977-79*, in Schwerpunkte des Kartellrechts 1978/79, FIW, 121 (Cologne, 1980); R. Bechtold, *Zur Fusionskontrolle über Gemeinschaftsun-ternehmen*, 1980 BB 344.

[49] *Cf.* with variations, Monopolies Commission, Main Report, 1976/1977, *supra* note 2, No. 447 *et seq.*; Main Report 1978/1979, *supra* note 2, No. 530 *et seq.*; Mestmäcker, *supra* note 35, at p. 30 *et seq.*; W. Gansweid, Gemeinsame Tochtergesellschaften im

65 of the ECSC Treaty and Article 85 of the EEC Treaty. If one follows this line of reasoning, most joint ventures will have to be treated as cartels or else restraints of competition. Only in those rare cases in which the parent enterprises were not actual or potential competitors, or in which the parent enterprises were once and for all to retreat from the market in which the joint venture operates, would mere merger control apply. Partisans of this theory argue that under German law, as well as under Article 85 (3) of the EEC Treaty, there is ample opportunity for having restrictive agreements exempted. But industry worries, and indeed competition mavericks already proclaim that irrespective of merger control practically all joint ventures of big enterprises are to be treated as restraints of competition. This controversy is an interesting illustration of the stands of different German bodies and authors towards antitrust generally and of how the process of opinion making in antitrust law functions today in Germany.

C. The Creation or Strengthening of Market Domination

1. The Substantial Competition Test

The keystone of every merger control system is the choice of the legal criterion which will be used to determine whether mergers as a general rule are illegal. In German law this decision depends on whether it is to be expected that the merger will create or strengthen a position of market domination. As seen in the survey, (*supra* § II.A.1.b) an enterprise is considered to have a dominant position if it is not subject to any substantial competition. The question whether such substantial competition exists can be answered only in respect of a specific market. Therefore all the well-known antitrust problems of defining the relevant market also arise in this context. Since these are not problems specific to merger control, a few words must suffice here. Product market, geographic market and sometimes the temporal market are distinguished in German antitrust law. Product markets are not broken down according to industry branches and classes as is the case for measuring concentration ratios. Rather the functional interchangeability of different products for the user and the cross-elasticity of their prices are decisive. As a matter of practice, the Federal Cartel Office and the courts have gone very far in breaking down separate markets, as for example was done for small groups of pharmaceutical products (depending on the actual medical prescription practices) in the *"Vitamin B-12" (Merck OHG)* case or for tranquillizers in the *"Valium" (Hoffmann-La Roche)* case.[50] The consequences

---

DEUTSCHEN KONZERN- UND WETTBEWERBSRECHT, p. 207 *et seq.* (Baden-Baden, 1976). *Cf.* also Bundesgerichtshof, *supra* note 47, and Federal Cartel Office, Annual Report 1979 and 1980, *supra* note 18, p. 19 *et seq.*, 25 *et seq.* As to European law, *cf.*, recently, P. Ulmer, *Gemeinschaftsunternehmen im EG-Kartellrecht*, 1979 WuW 433.

[50] Bundesgerichtshof, 3 July, 1976, "Vitamin-B-12", 67 BGHZ 104, at 113 *et seq.* = WuW/E BGH 1435; Bundesgerichtshof, 16 December, 1976, "Valium I", 68 BGHZ 23, at 27 *et seq.* = WuW/E BGH 1445, and 12 February, 1980, "Valium II", 76 BGHZ 142 = WuW/E BGH 1678; all cases were monopoly cases, not merger control cases. For further examples from case law, *see* KLEINMANN & BECHTOLD *supra* note 27, at § 22 Rz. 37.

are obvious: the narrower a product market, the fewer the enterprises on this market and the bigger their market shares. The market share is the single most important criterion for evaluating the existence of substantial competition. As has already been mentioned, there is a presumption of market domination in the case of a market share of one third, but this is just a guideline for the order of magnitude which the Legislator considered relevant. The final decision can be made only by taking into consideration the various competition factors such as price, quality, the influence of potential competition, and other elements. This final decision is not quantitative, let alone mathematical, but is the result of an overall evaluation.

2. The Superior Market Position Test and Its Application in the Fichtel & Sachs Case

Experience has shown that the Federal Cartel Office has great difficulties in proving the lack of substantial competition on a market. In cases where substantial price competition does not exist, the enterprises point, for example, to the existence of substantial competition in quality etc. Therefore today the practical emphasis has shifted to a second alternative for defining market domination which was introduced by the reform of 1973. The relevant point here is to establish that an enterprise has a superior market position in relation to its competitors. This test backs away from considering the market share and the competitive behaviour on the market, and rather concentrates on the market structure and the resources of the enterprises. It is quite obvious that the real market power, say, of a conglomerate enterprise is underrated by looking only at its absolute share of a specific market. For example, a conglomerate which is also active on the supply or the sales markets may be able to pay less or to earn more than its competitor which has the same share of the product market but is confined to this market. Similarly a financially strong conglomerate may be able to resist longer than such a competitor in case of a market depression by temporarily shifting resources from one market to another (deep pocket doctrine). The problem of the superior-market-position test, therefore, is to choose and to evaluate the indicators of the existence of such a position. The law itself helps with examples which are not conclusive however: relative market shares, financial strength, access to supply and sales markets, corporate ties to other enterprises, legal or factual barriers to market access by other enterprises. If due to these or similar market characteristics and enterprise resources the enterprise has superior elbow-room in determining its market behaviour, it is market-dominating under this second test.

The difficulties which still remain under the superior market position test are best shown in the *"motor-car clutch"* case,[51] the first merger control case to reach the *Bundesgerichtshof*. The British company Guest, Keen & Nettlefolds Ltd. (GKN), a huge conglomerate with 297 subsidiaries all over the world, intended to take over nearly 75% of the share capital of the German Sachs AG. The Sachs

---

[51] See, supra note 28; E. Steindorff, *Zur Verstärkung einer marktbeherrschenden Stellung nach der GKN/Sachs Entscheidung des BGH*, 1978 ZGR 778.

AG, a holding company without any turnover of its own, controlled *Fichtel &*
Sachs (F & S) and through the latter 15 other enterprises. F & S held 78 and
79.5% in two separate automobile industry supply markets (motor-car clutch
plates and disks). Yet GKN and F & S were not competitors, but were active in
different markets. The case was highly controversial with different outcomes in
the various instances. Two main issues appeared: market domination and its
strengthening by the projected merger.

The issue of market domination was the less controversial. Since despite the
large market shares it might have been difficult to prove lack of substantial
competition, the Federal Cartel Office immediately turned to the superior
market position test. In addition to the large absolute market shares of F & S
there were other indicators. F & S had only one competitor who was of practical
relevance, and, in terms of market shares, this competitor was out-numbered by
F & S by four to one. Furthermore, the high market shares of F & S had been
relatively constant over a number of years, and at the time in question there was
no tendency to decline. F & S had a very high know-how and an excellent
reputation with the German automobile industry for the quality of its products
obtained in long-standing business relations. According to branch estimates a
new-comer to the markets would need considerable financial means which, as far
as economies of scale alone were concerned, would have amounted to at least 60
to 65 million DM. The Federal Cartel Office and the Courts correctly held that
these indicators were sufficient to establish the existence of the superior market
position of F & S.

On the second issue, in sharp contrast, the Federal Cartel Office, the
Kammergericht and the *Bundesgerichtshof* split in a way which some consider
significant for the specific approach adopted by each of these bodies. The Federal
Cartel Office took little pains in finding that the proposed merger of F & S with
the huge GKN group would strengthen the already existing market domination
of F & S. The Office just added the turnover and cash flow of GKN to those of
F & S and found an increase of between five- and sixfold. This by itself, it
argued, would strengthen the deterrents to potential competitors entering the
market. The *Kammergericht,* on the contrary, was extremly cautious in dealing
with the factual barriers to market access by other enterprises and asked for
concrete proof of increased financial strength and of its imminent use and effect
on the relevant markets. The *Bundesgerichtshof,* as the last resort, took its own
intermediate position: The mere fact that the merger increases the financial
strength of an enterprise is not sufficient to justify the conclusion that potential
competitors are thus more easily deterred and market domination is strengthened. But in each single case the present and probable future effects of the merger
on the market and its competitiveness must be explored. On the other hand, the
requirement of concrete proof of an imminent effect is too short-term a view.
Even if no such imminent effects can be found, still a prognosis must be made as
to what the future development of competition on the market will be, assuming
that probable changes in competitive conditions will shortly occur. Under these
standards of evaluation the *Bundesgerichtshof* found that even though the
market share of F & S remained the same, the merger would have imminent

effects on the actual and potential competitors of F & S. When deciding about price competition or market entry the latter must and will take into consideration the fact that a highly conglomerated big enterprise such as GKN will subordinate its newly acquired subsidiary to the overall business policy of the group. In this context special weight must be given to the fact that the merger was not a mere financial participation, but a so-called market extension merger, 40% of the complete turnover of GKN consisting in supplies to automobile industry.

It is not surprising that the "motor-car clutch" case is considered to be the leading case in merger control even though in the meantime there have been further cases.[52] The *Bundesgerichtshof*, in my opinion, took a very fortunate view, discarding grave misdevelopments in merger control law. The opinion of the Federal Cartel Office could have led in practice to an absolute prohibition on mergers of big enterprises, not only in cases of horizontal, but also of vertical and conglomerate mergers. Such per se prohibitions may be a serious alternative for future merger control policy, but this is clearly not the present state of German

---

[52] Especially Bundesgerichtshof, 12 December, 1978, "Erdgas Schwaben", 73 BGHZ 65 = WuW/E BGH 1533. The court held that the creation of a joint venture between an electricity supply enterprise and a gas supply enterprise in which the former was to have only 1/3 of the holdings, could lead to the strengthening of the dominant market position of the electricity supply enterprise. However, although under the merger provisions parent companies holding more than 25% each of a joint venture are deemed to have merged, the parents are not per se deemed to be an economic unit and no longer competitors, as the Federal Cartel Office had tried to argue (once again in Annual Report 1979 and 1980, *supra* note 18, p. 24 *et seq.*, invoking the practice of the EC Commission: "WANO/Schwarzpulver"), and as the Monopolies Commission maintains in its sharp critique of the decision (Main Report 1978/1979, *supra* note 2, No. 529); as to the superior market position test in general, *see, ibidem*, No. 495 *et seq.* – *Cf.* now Bundesgerichtshof, 12 February, 1980, *supra* note 47, concerning joint ventures; Bundesgerichtshof, 24 June, 1980, "Mannesmann/Brueninghaus", 77 BGHZ 279 = WuW/E BGH 1711. If the merger leads to a superior market position, a financially strong large enterprise involved in the merger may be presumed to make use of this position in the market. The latest decision of the Bundesgerichtshof is 2 December, 1980, "Klöckner/Becorit", *infra* note 69. – In the case of horizontal mergers, a strengthening of a dominant market position has been seen in the gain of a very small additional market share, *e. g.* Kammergericht, 15 March, 1978, "Zement-mahlanlage II", (Hansa-Zement (Alsen-Breitenburg)/Klöckner), WuW/E OLG 1989 = 1979 AG 17 (4.3%), affirmed Bundesgerichtshof, 23 October, 1979, WuW/E BGH 1655; Kammergericht, 1st November, 1978, "Springer/Elbe Wochenblatt", WuW/E OLG 2109 at 2112, affirmed Bundesgerichtshof, 18 December, 1979, WuW/E BGH 1685 at 1692. (1.3%). – The existence of a superior market position may already be accepted in cases involving as little as a 10% to 20% market share, if the enterprise has outstanding resources. E. Niederleithinger, *Praxis der Fusionskontrolle 1977/78*, in SCHWERPUNKTE DES KARTELLRECHTS 1977/78, FIW, p. 31 (Cologne, 1979). As to the concept of the relevant market also under the superior market position test *see* J. F. Baur, *Der relevante Markt – eine durchaus notwendige Figur des Rechts der Zusammenschlußkontrolle*, in FESTSCHRIFT FÜR KUMMER 293 (Bern, 1980).

law. On the other hand, the narrow interpretation given by the *Kammergericht* presented the danger of thoroughly disabling the superior market position test by imposing too strict requirements of proof. Merger control would, strangely enough, have become more difficult the bigger and the more autonomous the merging enterprises were already before the merger — certainly for conglomerate mergers, but possibly also for horizontal mergers. The *Bundesgerichtshof* corrected this position and opened a new chapter of merger law concerning conglomerate enterprises.

3. The Oligopoly Problem

Market domination by two or more oligopolists has been one of the most difficult problems in the field of monopoly power and legal control of its abuses. This cannot be treated here. But the definition of market dominating oligopolists is valid also for merger control. Accordingly two conditions must be fulfilled. First, the two or more oligopolists together must be market dominating. This is to be established applying the same two tests of lack of substantial competition or superior market position. As seen above, the superior market position test is less difficult to satisfy. The real difficulty lies with the second condition: In addition to market domination by the oligopolists together, there must not be substantial competition among the oligopolists themselves. Members of the Federal Cartel Office have maintained that this is nearly impossible to prove.[53] As a consequence merger control of oligopolists has hardly been exercised. The Monopolies Commission has criticised this practice of inactivity strongly. Yet the reform plans to abolish this second condition for merger control purposes were not successful. The 1980 reform brought only some rebuttable presumptions together with a change of the burden of proof. It is possible, however, that the 1978 *"Valium"* decision of the *Kammergericht* which was rendered on remand by the *Bundesgerichtshof* starts a new phase. The *Kammergericht* held that lack of substantial competition between the oligopolists themselves already exists if there is no substantial price competition. It is not enough that there is still substantial competition in quality, service and advertisement.[54]

---

[53] *Cf.* Monopolies Commission, Main Report 1976/1977, *supra* note 2, No. 419 *et seq.* and 428 *et seq.*

[54] Kammergericht, 24 August, 1978, "Valium", WuW/E OLG 2053, at 2058 *et seq.;* (left open by Bundesgerichtshof, 12 February, 1980, "Valium II", 76 BGHZ 142 = WuW/E BGH 1678 at 1682). *Cf. supra* note 50, and now Bundeskartellamt, 30 March, 1979, "Tonolli/Metallgesellschaft", 1979 AG 228. But according to the courts this is only true for sec. 22 II GWB (oligopolies), not for sec. 22 I No. 1 GWB (substantive competition test). The latest, rather restrictive, decisions are, Kammergericht, 16 January, 1980, "Tonolli/Metallgesellschaft", WuW/E OLG 2234, and 24 January, 1979 "Makadamwerke Schwaben/Teerbau" 1980 AG 189, (both cases are pending before the Bundesgerichtshof). *See* now also Federal Cartel Office, 28 October 1980, "Texaco/Zerssen", WuW/E BKartA 1840 (oligopoly asserted to exist between 16 mineral oil enterprises on the market for light oil for heating).

D. Possible Justification of Merger by Public Interest

1. Improvements In Competitive Conditions: Evaluation by Federal Cartel Office

If the merger can be expected to create or strengthen market domination, it must be prohibited by the Federal Cartel Office, unless the merger will also result in improvements in competitive conditions and such improvements outweigh the detrimental effects of the market domination. It is important to remember that the German legislator in order to have full transparency of the decision-making process took pains to separate clearly the evaluation of competition and of public interest more generally. Only evaluation of competition is up to the Federal Cartel Office. In practice, however, both are not so easily separable and the Federal Cartel Office has been criticised for having overstepped its competence thereby giving in to public pressures and rendering merger control inefficient. The two major points of interest in this instance are the reorganization mergers and mergers in oligopolistic markets.

In a reorganization merger a failing company is taken over by another sound enterprise. The pros are strongly emphasized by the participating enterprises, by labour and sometimes by public bodies such as cities, regions and Länder. If the merger is not allowed, the failing company will have to go out of business. Resources will be destroyed. Jobs will disappear. Plants will be dismantled with consequent loss of industry for the city and the region. The cons have repeatedly been underlined by the Monopolies Commission.[55] The main problem is that very often the only available candidate for taking over the failing company is the market leader. It has the best possibilities to integrate the failing company, to bear the risk involved and to pay the highest purchase price to the owners. Under the Law the Federal Cartel Office cannot take into consideration such unwelcome effects as the loss of jobs or the disadvantages for cities and regions, but is confined to weighing the pros and cons of the merger for the competitive conditions on the market. Overall competition on the market will be improved, for example, if the merger results in keeping alive an especially competitive-minded enterprise or in avoiding that all participating enterprises will leave the market. The same may be true even if as a result of the merger the merging enterprises would become the second largest unit in the market, provided that but for this merger the market leader alone, who has already an overwhelming market position, would win the market share of the failed company. On the other hand, there are no sufficient improvements if but for this merger the market share of the failed company would probably not be won by the market leader alone, but by the various competitors on the market.[56] Today, as a general

---

[55] Monopolies Commission, Main Report 1973/1975, *supra* note 2, No. 933 *et seq.*; Main Report 1976/1977, *supra* note 2, No. 437 *et seq.*, *cf.* 478 *et seq.*; Special Reports 5, 6 "Karstadt/Neckermann", "Thyssen/Hüller Hille", *supra* note 29; W. Möschel, *Die Sanierungsfusion im Recht der Zusammenschlußkontrolle*, in M. Lutter, W. Stimpel & H. Wiedemann Festschrift für Robert Fischer, p. 487 (Berlin, 1979).

[56] *Cf.* Kammergericht, 1 November, 1978, "Springer/Elbe Wochenblatt", WuW/E OLG 2109, at 2113.

rule, a reorganization merger of a failing company with the market leader will not be permitted by the Federal Cartel Office unless the enterprises can prove that exceptionally there will be such decisive improvements on other markets as to outweigh the disadvantages of market domination in the market concerned.[57] This has been confirmed by the *Kammergericht*, in its 1978 *"Springer/Elbe Wochenblatt"* decision,[58] relating to the press market. Following that decision, the positive result of maintaining the existing variety of publications and of public opinions cannot be taken into consideration by the Federal Cartel Office.

The other major problem of justification lying within the competence of the Federal Cartel Office turns up in oligopoly situations. The Federal Cartel Office in several cases has permitted a merger on the grounds that it resulted in lowering the distance between the market leader and the merging enterprises. The idea was that this rendered the oligopoly more symmetrical and could improve competition with the market leader. This reasoning is questionable since then the market share or the market position of the market leader could easily become a target towards which the remaining oligopolists in the market will legally orientate their merger plans.[59] If such catch-up mergers were to be more generally allowed, merger control would fail where it is most urgently needed, namely in the markets which already have the highest concentrations.

Exceptionally, the Federal Cartel Office will not forbid the merger if the enterprise promises to behave in such a way that the overall effect of the merger leads to a positive balance. This practice has been severely criticized in the legal literature for being inefficient and dangerous, but it is accepted by the courts.[60] The practice started in 1975 and has so for been applied in over 10 cases, most recently in the *Feldmühle AG/Kopparfors A/B* case and the *PWA Papierwerke Waldhof-Aschaffenburg AG/Svenska Cellulosa A/B* case. In both cases the enterprises had promised to ensure, by means of a subsidiary in which their competitors would participate, that every competitor would be able to obtain the raw materials of which he might have need.[61]

2. Overall Economic Advantages or Overriding Public Interest: Evaluation by Federal Minister of Economics

If the case is lost before the Federal Cartel Office, the enterprises can try a second line of defense. The Federal Minister of Economics must permit the merger if the restraint of competition is balanced by the overall economic

---

[57] *Bericht des Bundeskartellamtes über seine Tätigkeit im Jahre 1976*, BTDrs 8/704 p. 23 (1977).

[58] See *supra* note 56.

[59] Monopolies Commission, Main Report 1976/1977, *supra* note 2, No. 428 *et seq.*

[60] *Cf.* M. Wolter, *Die Zusagenpraxis des Bundeskartellamtes*, 1979 WuW 213 with further references; C. Traumann, *Die zusammenschlußrechtliche Zusage*, 1981 DB 976.

[61] *Cf.* P. Krause *"Die geduldeten Fusionen; zur Zusagepraxis des Kartellamtes"*, FAZ No. 61, 13. 4. 1981, p. 13. See also C. Windbichler, *Informal Practices to Avoid Merger Control Litigation in the U. S. and West Germany: A Comparison*, 25 ANTITRUST BULL. 619 (1980).

advantages of the merger *or* if the merger is justified by an overriding public interest; competitiveness outside Germany is also to be considered. Insofar as the restraint of competition by the merger is concerned, the decision of the Federal Cartel Office is binding. Even though the Minister must respect general principles of law (such as existence and proof of the overriding interests, suitability of the merger for these interests, lack of less far-reaching alternatives), he is basically making a free political decision.[62] Up to now, the Minister has been seized only in very few cases. Usually the enterprises first go to court. While in a single case the Minister refused permission,[63] in several others permission was granted:[64] first in the giant *VEBA/Gelsenberg* merger in 1974, on grounds of long-term energy supply for Germany, the enterprises being only medium sized on a world scale even after the merger; then in the *Babcock/Artos* merger in 1976, on grounds of preserving jobs in economically weak regions (the market of certain textile refinery machines being a very small one); in the *Rheinstahl Thyssen/Hüller Hille* merger in 1977, with permission only in part, on the grounds of saving a failing company and maintaining the special know-how of the enterprise's team which was important for German exports; and finally, in the famous *VEBA/BP* merger transaction in 1979, again on the grounds of long-term energy supply for Germany.

These cases of merger permission by the Minister of Economics are very few in number, but very important in size and weight. The Monopolies Commission usually pleaded against permitting the mergers. A short report of the *VEBA/BP* case[65] may give an idea of the problems involved. The two main participating enterprises were VEBA, a 43.7% subsidiary of the Federal German Republic and ranked numer one in Germany as far as turnover is concerned; and the Deutsche BP AG, a 100% subsidiary of The British Petroleum Company Ltd. and ranked number 20 on the German turnover list. The projected merger consisted in the sale by VEBA of Gelsenberg AG and of important holdings in mineral oil processing and natural gas, among them a 25% participation in the Ruhrgas AG, which is a joint venture of large German enterprises, the largest importer of natural gas and ranked numer 41 on the German turnover list. Consideration for the sale was 800 million DM and a long-term contract on the supply of raw oil at market prices until the year 2000. The Federal Cartel Office prohibited the merger because the superior market position of Ruhrgas would be strengthened by the financial resources of BP and by the disappearance of BP as a serious

---

[62] Kammergericht, 7 February, 1978, "Thyssen/Hüller", WuW/E OLG 1937 (*See also* at 1921).

[63] Federal Minister of Economics, 26 June, 1975, "VAW/Kaiser", WuW/E BWM 149.

[64] Federal Minister of Economics, 1 February, 1974, "VEBA/Gelsenberg", WuW/E BWM 147; 17 October, 1976, "Babcock/Artos", WuW/E BWM 155; 1 August, 1977, "Rheinstahl Thyssen/Hüller Hille", WuW/E BWM 159; *cf.* Monopolies Commission, Special Reports 2, 4, 6, *supra* note 29.

[65] Federal Cartel Office, 27 September, 1978, WuW/E BKartA 1719; Monopolies Commission, Special Report 8, *supra* note 29, 1979; Federal Minister of Economics, 5 March, 1979, "VEBA/BP", WuW/E BWM 165. *Cf.* EEC Commission, Press Release, 2 March, 1979, JP (79) 41, 1979 WuW 311 *et seq.* (under Art. 85 EEC Treaty).

potential competitor on the gas market. The Monopolies Commission somewhat differently underlined the general dangers for substitutive competition between mineral oil and natural gas, since as a consequence of a 25% holding of BP in Ruhrgas, the majority in Ruhrgas would no longer be with the coal and steel industry, but with the mineral oil companies. The Monopolies Commission, therefore, proposed to refuse permission, but made clear that there were no objections to BP acquiring interests in Ruhrgas up to 9%. The Minister of Economics, the last resort, granted permission, but with several restrictions which aimed at preventing BP and the other mineral oil companies from getting a majority influence in Ruhrgas. If necessary at a later stage BP would be obliged to reduce its 25% holding in Ruhrgas to 9%. The public interest in long-term energy supply, the access to international natural gas supply markets and the participation in international technology were considered decisive, while the job preservation argument did not convince. The Minister argued that in the case of reorganizations within a group it is up to the group to find solutions for the ensuing loss of jobs and that as a general rule mergers may be able to preserve jobs in the short run, but not in the long run due to the rationalization effects of the merger.[66] As far as the Monopoly Commission's opinion was concerned, the Minister of Economics in a clear dig warned against the dangers of underevaluating the public interest just because big enterprise is involved in a merger.

III. The Antitrust Law Reform Act 1980 and the Future Outlook

A. Efficiency or Inefficiency of Merger Control in Germany

At the beginning it was pointed out that measuring and evaluating economic concentration in Germany is neither easy nor undisputed. It is even far more difficult to measure and evaluate the performance of merger control. While it would be interesting to know to what degree economic concentration has proceeded since the introduction of merger control in 1973 up to now, conclusions drawn from such figures would be misleading, since German merger control is not directed against economic concentration as such, but rather against certain aspects of external growth while leaving internal growth untouched. If we look at the number of mergers which were notified, and the number of those which were actually prohibited, the results do not seem impressive. Up to the end of May 1981, 3,575 mergers were notified (either before or after their completion), but in only 35 cases did the Federal Cartel Office prohibit the merger. As of June 1981 only 12 of these prohibitive decrees have been finalized.[67] Four of them have been disapproved of by the Minister of Economics, who granted them his permission. Two prohibitory decrees have

---

[66] *Idem* at 173. See *also* the factual inquiries of the Monopolies Commission which back up this view, Main Report 1976/1977, *supra* note 2, No. 452 *et seq.*

[67] Federal Cartel Office, Statistics presented to the Working Group on Antitrust Law at its meeting in Berlin in October 1979; Monopolies Commission, Main Report 1978/1979, *supra* note 2, No. 461.

finally been annulled by the courts, while other cases are still pending. In 61 cases since the introduction of merger control, merger plans have been given up by the enterprises concerned without decrees, after notification to and opposition by the Federal Cartel Office.[68] This seems no record of which to be proud. On the other side, performance is not truly reflected in prohibitive decrees. It is a fact that German enterprises, especially the larger ones, are well aware of the difficulties and the burdens of merger control and do evaluate the risk involved long before concluding a merger. The real effects of merger control, therefore, may very well lie in its very existence as a "fleet-in-being". Expert opinion concerning the efficiency of merger control is split, and quite often is also biased. A fair judgement would have to be very careful and would have to distinguish between horizontal mergers on the one side and vertical and conglomerate mergers on the other, and possibly also between private and public enterprise (VEBA transactions) and eventually even between branches.

B. Exemptions for Small Enterprises Reconsidered

In March 1980 the Legislator passed the Fourth Antitrust Law Reform Act, the second reform of merger control since 1973. After a fierce battle of opinions and pressures a politically very difficult compromise was found which can be expected to last for a while and makes it futile to recapitulate the different proposals and positions.[69] Besides closing some of the gaps relating to (premerger and postmerger) notification and procedure, the reform concentrates on two major issues: Minimum threshold and market domination. When introducing merger control the German legislator had exempted enterprises with no more than a 50 million DM turnover. The idea was not just one of irrelevancy, but also of welcome long-term effects on competition. Small entrepreneurs should be attracted to enter a market by the possibility of selling out and of merging at a good price if after some years they could not survive. But experience showed a completely opposite development. The exemption was used by big enterprise to buy up systematically small and medium-sized enterprises without facing merger control. Up until the end of 1975 alone 42.2% of all mergers notified after completion were exempted due to this clause. Even more problematic, the largest enterprises turned out to be the most active acquirers, with 84.7% of all these exempted cases concerning acquiring enterprises with a turnover of more than 1,000 million DM.[70] This is an excellent example of how careful one has to be in the field of merger control with judgements on impact or efficiency of laws and regulations. It may easily be that well-meant legal measures have unforeseen side effects or that they even turn out to be outright counterproductive. It is but of small comfort to lawyers that prognosis is not always easier for economists, as is

---

[68] Federal Cartel Office, *supra* note 18 at p. 16 *et seq.*
[69] A good survey can be found in the records of the Hearings by the Committee on Economics of the German Parliament, 12 and 14 March 1979. *Cf. also* briefly D. Wolf, *Fortentwicklung der Fusionskontrolle*, 1980 WuW 462.
[70] Monopolies Commission, Main Report 1973/1975, *supra* note 2, No. 925 *et seq.*

shown in this very instance. The new compromise solution abolishes the 50 million DM exemption in respect of those mergers in which the acquiring enterprise has at least a 1,000 million DM turnover and the acquired enterprise at least a four million DM turnover. Radical proposals to cut out the exemption completely have been rejected.

C. On the Way to per se Prohibitions for the Largest Enterprises

The largest enterprises were also the object of the second major reform issue. The legal presumptions which already existed (market share of a single enterprise of one third; combined market shares of three enterprises of 50%; combined market shares of five enterprises of two thirds) had proved helpful, but not sufficient. Therefore, a complicated additional set of legal presumptions has been introduced. The creation or strengthening of market domination is now also presumed in the following cases.[71] First, where an enterprise with a 2,000 million DM turnover intrudes into a market in which small and medium enterprises prevail with a two-thirds share of the market and the participating enterprises together have a market share of at least 5%. These so-called foothold mergers of the largest enterprises tend to initiate a wave of concentration in these markets since they attract other big enterprises and discourage the smaller ones from staying independent. Second, where an enterprise with a 2,000 million DM turnover merges with an enterprise which has a dominant position in one or more markets in which overall turnover is 150 million DM or over. Here the intention is to prevent big conglomerates from accumulating market dominating positions. Third, where the participating enterprises together have a 12,000 million DM turnover and at least two of them have a 1,000 million DM turnover each. An exception is made for joint ventures on markets with an overall turnover of less than 750 million DM. These so-called marriages of elephants influence the concentration climate in the country because of their mere size. Finally, in certain cases oligopolists are deemed to be market dominating unless they prove that substantial competition among them is to be expected also after the merger. This possibility for rebuttal was a last minute victory against the Government's proposal which would have done away with the possibility of rebuttal at all and thus could have really meant an important change in merger control of oligopolists. The overall impression is a mixed one. On the one side, there is certainly a growing concern about sheer size and the merger activity of the largest enterprise. Far-reaching proposals for per se prohibitions have been made. Even deconcentration by dissolution has been studied and just been recommended in a reform proposal by the Monopolies Commission, despite the

---

[71] As to these presumptions *see* now Bundesgerichtshof, 2 December, 1980, "Klöckner/Becorit", 79 BGHZ 62 = WuW/E BGH 1749 with annotation K. Autenrieth, *Mehr Rechtssicherheit bei der Fusionskontrolle*, 1981 DB 1025. The law suit has now been mooted by a compromise before the Kammergericht, *"Kartellstreit beendet"*, FAZ No. 149, 2 July 1981, p. 11.

fact that the Reform Act 1980 had been enacted only two months before.[72] On
the other hand, the very complexity of these four new presumptions (which
actually are much more complicated than shown here) indicates that there is no
willingness to make mere size an offence and to come up openly with per se
merger prohibitions against the largest enterprises. The latest statement of the Ministry of Economics (on the occasion of the presentation of the 1979 and 1980 activity report of the Federal Cartel Office to the public in June 1981) denies any
short-term plans of generally introducing the instrument of deconcentration and
other legislative reforms of the Cartel law.[73] Furthermore, the deteriorating
economic climate in Germany has had its impact also on the Federal Cartel
Office. In such times, it is necessary, according to the President of the Federal
Cartel Office, to concentrate merger control on the most relevant cases.[74]

D. German and European Merger Control: Uneasy Partnership?

It is common knowledge that little progress has been made with the plans for
introducing preventive merger control in the EEC. The Commission proposal
for a merger control regulation first made in 1973 is still pending in the
Council.[75] There is strong resistance, especially, but not only, from Italy.
Retroactive merger control under Art. 86 of the EEC Treaty, as developed by the
European Court of Justice in its famous *"Continental Can"* decision, is for
many reasons not an adequate substitute, even though the EEC Commission has
succeeded in preventing several major mergers (for example *Saint Gobain/BSN*,
merger plans in the sugar production industry, etc.) without formal decrees or
court proceedings.[76] . Therefore, the problem of the relationship and possible
conflicts between German and European merger control has up to now been
more theoretical than practical. The problem did come up as a side issue in the
"GKN/Sachs" case. The *Bundesgerichtshof* accepted the *Kammergericht's* view
that both the European and the German control of mergers had their own areas

---

[72] Monopolies Commission, Main Report 1978/1979, *supra* note 2, No. 764, 662 *et seq.*;
W. MÜSCHEL, ENTFLECHTUNGEN IM RECHT DER WETTBEWERBSBESCHRÄNKUNGEN (Tübin-
gen, 1979). R. SCHOLZ, ENTFLECHTUNG UND VERFASSUNG (1981). By June 1981 the Federal
Cartel Office had issued its first dissolution order ("Springer/Elbe Wochenblatt", *cf.*
also *supra* note 52): Yet this was a dissolution of a merger which was contested by the
Federal Cartel Office from the very beginning and after long proceedings before the
Bundesgerichtshof had turned out to be illegal. Dissolution in such cases is already
possible under the present law. Another dissolution case is "Thyssen Industrie AG
(formerly Rheinstahl) / Hüller Hille". *Cf.* Federal Cartel Office, Annual Report 1979
and 1980, *supra* note 18, p. 21 *et seq.; see* also C. Klawitter, *Nochmals: Die Auflösung
von Unternehmenszusammenschlüssen im Fusionskontrollverfahren,* 1981 WuW 245.
[73] *Cf. "Das Kartellamt will seine Politik nicht lockern",* FAZ No. 147, 30. 6. 1981,
p. 11.
[74] *"Kartte: Nur noch wesentliche Fälle",* FAZ No. 113, 16. 5. 1981, p. 13.
[75] EEC Commission, 11 October, 1979, Answer on Written Request No. 225/79 by Mr.
Schyns, 1980 WuW 124. For a detailed discussion *see* P. Schmitt, *supra* note 32, *infra* this
volume at pp. 182 *et seq.*
[76] *Cf.* W. Schlieder, DIE ZEIT No. 16, 10. 4. 1981, p. 22.

and aims and may function independently from each other. The German merger control authorities must not step back just because the merger also marginally involves coal and steel and has been permitted by the Commission under Art. 66 of the ECSC Treaty.[77] This view has been strongly criticised. Indeed, at least under a system of a full-fledged European merger control, in which permission for a merger may result from a deliberate industrial policy, it is hardly conceivable that national merger control measures could prevent the merger. From this it quickly becomes obvious that it is difficult to reach a compromise on European merger control, not only for those Member States which have no such control system at all, or have just "a fig-leaf system", but to a certain degree also for those which conceive merger control to be a means of protection against too much economic and perhaps political power. Yet despite all these difficulties a European merger control is necessary as the markets are no longer just national, but more and more international and European. Legal and practical solutions can be found for the co-existence of German and European merger control — if the latter were only really wanted.[78]

[77] See supra note 28, 71 BGHZ 102 at 107 et seq. with critical annotation by C. Hootz, 1978 BB 825; see also K. Markert, 1978 BB 678.
[78] The latest strong and convincing plea for European merger control has come from the Monopolies Commission in June 1980 in its Main Report 1978/79, supra note 2, No. 632-661.

Summary

This article deals with merger control in the Federal Republic of Germany, its underlying philosophies, experiences since 1973, and the reforms enacted in 1980.

In a brief first part the background for understanding the German system is given, presenting some legal facts and statistics about economic concentration in Germany. The reaction to high and still growing economic concentration and the changing philosophies concerning "big business" are described. The somewhat naïve belief in the myth of size has more and more given way to a realistic appreciation of the actual performance of enterprises of different sizes. The specific relevance of merger control for multinational enterprises is shown by the far-reaching case-law since 1979.

In the second, main, part the legal structure of and the practical experience with merger control in Germany are discussed in detail. After a short survey of the legal structure, both of the substantive law and the procedural law, the three main problems of German merger control are analysed. First, the broad concept of merger for antitrust purposes is explained point by point (for example, acquisition of assets, acquisition of shares, interlocking directorates, etc.). The special difficulties created by groups of enterprises and joint ventures are discussed. The second problem is the choice of the criterion to be used to determine whether a merger is, as a general rule, illegal: in Germany the criterion is the creation or strengthening of market domination, to be ascertained by applying one of two alternative tests: the substantial competition test or the superior market position test. The application of these tests in case law is shown. One of the most difficult problems, which is not yet solved, is market domination by two or more oligopolists. The third main problem is the possible justification of the merger on grounds of public interest. German law has established a specific two-step examination and procedure. Justification by improvements in competitive conditions is evaluated by the Federal Cartel Office, while it is up to the Federal Minister of Economics to decide about justification on the basis of overall economic advantages or overriding public interests. This is illustrated by the 1979 VEBA-BP case.

In the third part of the article, the Antitrust Law Reform Act of 1980 and possible future developments are discussed, such as the tendency towards per se prohibitions of mergers of the largest enterprises. Finally, the problems of co-existence between the full-fledged German merger control system and the future European system are raised.

Merger Control in France:
Direct and Indirect Ways of Control

CLAUDE CHAMPAUD
Rennes

I. Introduction

1977 marks a turning point in French antitrust law. On the 19 July 1977 a Law introducing a new system for the "control of concentration" was adopted, whereas previously there had been a refusal for many years to supplement the regime for the control of concerted practices and abuse of dominant positions by adopting the two measures that usually go with it (control of concentration and a law of groups). Taken together, these three measures respresent the classic triptych of the means by which the legal systems of industrialized countries with market economies endeavour to limit the exercise of economic power to the extent necessary to safeguard economic freedom and competition.

The particular circumstances in which the Law of 19 July 1977 was adopted will be mentioned later, at the start of the section devoted to a study of the Law. These circumstances account for the Law's omissions and imperfections. However, before embarking on a commentary on the legislation, it appears appropriate, on the one hand, to give a succinct, and therefore imperfect, account of the economic data relating to concentration in France today; and on the other hand, to describe the attitudes of the public and of the legislative and executive powers towards this phenomenon. These are the two corner-stones that make it possible to understand the way in which problems relating to the control of concentration in France present themselves and are solved today.

A. Economic Concentration in France

1. Economic Data versus Legal Definitions

The presentation of economic data is not a pure question of fact. It is conditioned by the definitions which are given to the phenomena under observation. When is there economic concentration? What sorts of concentration are involved? Should, for example, the concentration of agricultural undertakings be included? It appears not; but is this reply based on sound theoretical reasons?

Problems concerning the concentration of undertakings and the definition of this notion are not new. The present author himself considered them almost twenty years ago[1] and it does not appear that substantial progress in juridical

---

[1] C. CHAMPAUD, LE POUVOIR DE CONCENTRATION DE LA SOCIETE PAR ACTIONS (Paris, 1962).

science has been made since then. The term "concentration" is used interchange-
ably to describe both various kinds of operations which reflect the internal
growth of firms and operations of external growth resulting from absorption,
acquisition of control, formation of subsidiaries, creation of groups, etc.
Concentration is looked at merely in terms of the growth of an economic entity
in question, without also measuring to see if there has been a corresponding
reduction, maintenance or increase in the number of competing entities in the
market concerned. In this connection, it should be noted that the Law of 19 July
1977 has not attempted to give a legal definition of what constitutes a
concentration operation. We will come back later to consider the wide, vague
and factual concept of concentration contained in Section 4 of the Law. At the
moment, it is enough to note that the Law covers "any legal act or operation, in
whatever form . . ." As in the field of concerted practices, the Law refuses to lay
down a legal definition, or any criteria of recognition other than those of a
pragmatic or economic nature. Concentration is a legal fact, in the same way as is
"possession", as opposed to the strict legal concept of "ownership".

The lawyer, therefore, has to turn to the economist if he is to understand the
substance of the legal categories that he is studying. This task is not, however, a
simple one because the notion of horizontal and vertical mergers, and homogenous and heterogenous mergers, do not correspond to the legal structures with
which lawyers are familiar. The term "merger" is specific for the lawyer, but is
used by the economist in such a wide sense that it becomes meaningless. On the
other hand, economists become more precise when they measure the concentration, or more exactly the rate of concentration, which exists in a market or when
they try to assess the impact which a given rate can have on the actual
competitive behaviour of undertakings. This is, in fact, the real heart of the
problem of the control of concentration.

2. Degrees of Concentration and Competition Policy

In view of the fact that there is no single ideal model for competition, and that
oligopolistic competition can be sharper and more productive than atomistic
competition, economists hesitate to affirm a univocal connection between the
rate of concentration and the liveliness of competition. They admit, however,
that in overall terms a high rate of concentration favours policies which are
deliberately parallel or which closely resemble each other in the field of prices
and production targets, and consequently that a high degree of concentration is a
potentially anti-competitive factor.[2]

This explains why economists tend to concentrate on the indices of concentration and on defining the threshold above which rates of concentration involve
a real or serious risk of anti-competitiveness rather than on drawing up the kind
of typology which is so favoured by lawyers. However, where the question is
not one of description but of control, the economist's approach can prove
adequate for the lawyer. In view of this, the Law of 19 July 1977 made no
attempt to provide a legal definition of concentration, but rather tried to

---

[2] See, OECD, CONCENTRATION ET POLITIQUE DE CONCURRENCE at p. 14 (Paris, 1974).

establish the thresholds beyond which economic dangers are presumed to arise.

The rate of concentration is calculated by measuring the proportion of the quantifiable part of a variable given factor (e. g. turnover, number of employees, cash flow) which can be attributed to the three of four (or more) economic entities which head the list of undertakings which operate on the basis of such a factor. Generally, turnover is taken as the reference base. If, for example, the three leading undertakings in a given sector account respectively for 30%, 20% and 10% of the turnover in that sector, the rate of concentration will be 60%. In reality, this brief resumé gives only a very approximate and imperfect explanation of the methods employed, which are, in fact, very diversified. Depending on the country, preference is given to the Herfindahl-Hirschman index, which is expressed in terms of an impressive mathematical formula, or to the Gini coefficient, inspired by the Lorenz curve. Practice has shown that these methods are equally valuable provided that the same reference base is used throughout and, above all, that the basic numerical data is available. It is more efficient, however, to effect a cross-check of all the various methods in order to get closer to the true situation.

The Law of 19 July 1977 has introduced into French law for the first time a quantitative system based on "rates of concentration", making them into a legal criterion. The use of this method is nowadays common in economic law. Examples can be found in the laws concerning the control of monopolistic undertakings, or of enterprises occupying a dominant position, in Austria, Germany, Ireland, Japan, Norway, and the United Kingdom. In the field of mergers (in the broad sense) the same approach can be found in the laws of Germany, Ireland, Japan, New Zealand, the United Kingdom and the United States, and also, but to a lesser extent, in the laws of other countries, and of course, now also in French law. Finally, this type of quantitative criterion can also be encountered in EEC law and in Austrian law.

One criticism can be made of economists' studies: in general, they only deal with concentration in industrial sectors, leaving out sectors concerned with agriculture and the provision of services. This point will not be developed at greater length here, to avoid making this report too long, but in view of the fact that such a restriction can be considered as falsifying any discussion from the legal point of view and, especially from the competitive point of view, attention should be drawn to this common truncation and its effects limited. This will be done by devoting the second part of this paper to the indirect control of concentration, focussing mainly on non-industrial sectors.

3. Some Statistics on Concentration in France

So as not to become enmeshed in interminable preliminary remarks, no account will be given of the comparative advantages and disadvantages of the concentration of undertakings. This would be of marginal utility and purely digressive because the 1977 Law, like other French legislation, leaves it to expert bodies to weigh up the advantages and disadvantages, and to draw up an *economic balance sheet,* before pronouncing on the lawfulness of a case of concentration. On the other hand, it appears indispensable to give some idea of the evolution of the concentrationist phenomenon in France.

The only studies which are available are based on figures which are five to ten years old, and this time lapse means that the information is only of relative value. In 1969, in only six sectors out of 48 (12.5%) was there a concentration rate (C. R.) in excess of 60%. Eight sectors had a C. R. of more than 50%. The substantial majority of sectors (32 out of 48) had a C. R. of less than 30%.[3] Another approach to the same problem[4] gives slightly higher concentration rates, but in overall terms ten years ago French industry was still concentrated to only a small extent. A study of more recent figures (1973) confirms this picture, while clearly showing up the difference which exists between certain highly monopolistic sectors (e. g. energy, overland transport equipment) and others which are quasi-atomistic (e. g. the agricultural food industry, and unfinished products).[5] The slow rate of growth of concentration in France can be appreciated from the fact that the average concentration rate for all French industry increased from 20.1% in 1961 to only 22.1% in 1969. It can also be noted that the most concentrated sectors are those in which there are undertakings which are nationalized either in law (energy, transport equipment) or in fact (steel). It appears that the more monopolistic the nationalized sector (e. g. energy), the higher the rate of concentration.

Even though only recently published, all these figures are hopelessly old and are probably out of date. Moreover, they do not take into account the prodigious concentration in the agricultural sector or the spectacular concentration in the commercial field which occurred in the 1970's.

B. Changing Attitudes towards Concentration

It appears certain, however, that during this period industrial concentration must have made considerable progress as a result of the burgeoning of the E.E.C. and the notably increasing participation of French undertakings in international trade. Notwithstanding this, it can be noted that in France this period was also marked by major setbacks in the field, especially in certain sectors of big industry, while in contrast small- and medium-sized enterprises (S.M.E.) came off favourably, using their advantages, talents, and above all their greater pugnacity to good effect. Salaried staff who had previously prized the large factory now discovered the discreet charm of the smaller unit, and a number of unions went along with them, despite the fact that they appreciated this might be to their own disadvantage. Nevertheless, by virtue of cultural tradition, philosophy, and sometimes as a result of poverty of ideas or economic training, the aristo-technocracy which governs France still strongly believes in the virtue of industrial concentration, because in its (sometimes erroneous) opinion it repre-

---

[3] F. Jenny & A. Weber, *L'évolution de la concentration industrielle en France de 1961 à 1969*, 60 ECONOMIE ET STATISTIQUE (Nov. 1974).

[4] F. JENNY & A. WEBER, CONCENTRATION ET POLITIQUE DES STRUCTURES INDUSTRIELLES (Paris, 1974).

[5] *Cf.* 95 ECONOMIE ET STATISTIQUE (Dec. 1977).

sents a private form of the administrative centralization which constitutes its bible. This explains why under the heading of *"industrial restructuring"* the French political administration continues to press for concentration, sometimes even sinking enormous amounts of public funds into this, and even more often objectively abetting the major capitalist powers, which it nevertheless detests.

It is not, however, certain that concentration is the only, or even the best, way of achieving efficiency of economic productivity and profitability. Detailed studies give rise to considerable doubts in this connection,[6] calling attention to the fact that the comparative advantages of large groups and small units depend largely, firstly, on the sector and, then, on the management methods and the capability of the individuals involved. This explains why for some five years now the advocates of "concentration at any price" have adopted a low profile, whereas over the same period voices have been heard pointing out that even the Americans themselves are saying "small is beautiful". With a Prime Minister who is an Economics Professor, an expert on problems of competition and a convinced liberal, and a Minister for the Economy who is the head of a S.M.E.[6a], the technocratic belief that "God is on the side of the big battalions" has undeniably lost its power of conviction to a certain degree. The Law of 1977 was drawn up under the auspices of this new political orientation which is reflected in its provisions, although, as we shall see later, the political circumstances which surrounded the Law's adoption had a less than favourable influence on its content.

This legislation nevertheless constitutes an important step in the history of French economic law. For the first time, a general and direct form of control of concentration, independent of any social, moral, or ideological motivation is set up, and the first and most detailed part of this paper will be devoted to examining this. There had, admittedly, been legislation in this field even prior to 1977, but in the form of indirect controls on individual operations, any intervention being justified by disparate and not exclusively economic considerations, if there was any economic analysis at all. The 1977 Law did not abolish these measures, and since they have undoubtedly been applied much more often than have been the provisions of the 1977 Law during the last three years, they cannot be regarded as having been over-taken. These measures will, therefore, be dealt with as succinctly as possible in the second part of this paper.

II The Direct Control of Concentration under Law No. 77.806 of 19 July 1977[7]

A. The Circumstances in which the 1977 Law was adopted

The Law of 19 July 1977 was adopted in a legal and factual context which has to be borne in mind in order to appreciate the underlying reasons for its

---

[6] *Ibidem.*
[6a] Before the election of 1981.
[7] For the text of the Law *see infra* this volume Annex II 3., pp. 245 *et seq. Cf. also* Application Decree n° 77-1189, 25 October 1977, J.O. 26 October p. 5223, 1977 J.C.P. III.

shortcomings and ambiguities. As other authors have already pointed out,[8] and as we shall see, this Law is not characterised by that vigour of design nor by that firmness and clarity of style for which French legal draftsmen are famous.

The circumstances which surrounded the birth of the legislation explain its legal imperfections without, however, excusing them.

In the first place, there was the element of speed. The need for a "law of concentration" had been felt for a long time, with one section of legal opinion[9] pressing for its introduction whilst another cast doubts on its utility,[10] whereas the public authorities responsible for legal reform did not seem to be considering any action in this connection. In 1973 the E.E.C. Commission presented a proposal for a Regulation, but the procedure for its adoption was dragged out. This draft measure was to provide the inspiration for the French Legislature. It was internal political circumstances rather than any awareness of the outdatedness of French law or any desire to prove a model of Community propriety that appear to have given an additional impetus to a movement that had lost its momentum.

The first factor is to be found in the "liberal bent" that the Prime Minister, Mr Barre (a noted economist) hoped the French economy and its enterprises would take, with the aim of using international competition as a means to meet the economic disturbances due to the dollar crisis, the energy crisis, and redistributions of power on a world-wide scale. It cannot be over-emphasized in this connection that the control of concentration forms only a part of the Law of 19 July 1977, which essentially relates to the reform of the procedure for controlling concerted agreements.

The second factor is linked to the bitter campaign which preceded the legislative elections of March 1978. The socialist-communist opposition, who felt

46349, and circular, 14 February 1978. *See* on this Law, for example, F. C. Jeantet, *La loi sur le contrôle des concentrations économiques en France*, 1977 J.C.P. I. 2879; R. Plaisant, J. Lassier and J. Epstein, *Le contrôle des concentrations en France: La loi n° 77-806 du 19 juillet 1977*, 1978 D.S. chr. 99; A. Lyon-Caen, *Le contrôle des concentrations: étude de la loi française et de la proposition européenne*, 1979 Rev. tr. dr. eur. 1, 440; *cf. also* R. Dumey, *De la notion de concurrence »suffisante«*, Gaz. Pal. 9-10 Nov. 1977, p. 4; C. Gavalda, *Le contrôle des concentrations d'entreprises selon la loi française n° 77-806 du 19 juillet 1977*, 1979 Rev. Soc. 473; X. de Roux, D. Voillemot, Le Droit de la concurrence des Communautés Européennes (Joly, 4ème éd., 1979); Azéma, Le Droit français de la concurrence (Paris, 1981) p. 355-361; J.-J. Burst & R. Kovar Droit de la concurrence (Paris, 1981) pp. 309-326, with the first decisions of the Commission de la Concurrence, especially the cases *Segma, Vallourée, Grange.* In German *cf.* A. Grauel, *Das französische Kartellgesetz vom 19. Juli 1977*, 1978 WuW 751; D. Hoffmann, *Einführung einer Fusionskontrolle in Frankreich*, 1978 RIW/AWD 566; H.-J. Sonnenberger, *Die Konzentrationskontrolle nach der französischen Kartellrechtsnovelle 1977*, 142 ZHR 367 (1978); R. Plaisant, J. Lassier and J. Epstein, *Die Zusammenschlußkontrolle in Frankreich*, 1979 WuW 551.

[8] F. C. Jeantet, *supra* note 7.

[9] J. Paillusseau, *Faut-il un droit des groupes de sociétés en France?* 25 Rev. trim. dr. com. 813 (1972).

[10] Jaudel, *Les tribunaux condamnent-ils le capitalisme?* LE MONDE, 30 December 1969.

they were near to grasping power, relied heavily on attacks on the abuses of concentration, not only as regards their effects on small traders and industrialists, but also as regards their effects on consumers and wage-earners. They accused the majority party of having joined hands with "trusts and large monopolies", and used the absence of any system for the control of concentration in France as a ready argument to support the electoral polemic and to justify the nationalization plans of the "Common Programme". It is scarcely surprising if in these circumstances the Parliamentary work associated with the drafting of the text provides more food for thought for political science than for economic law.

Only an activist policy on the part of the machinery set up to administer the system for the control of concentration could overcome the manifold problems, the lack of precision and the ambiguities of the 1977 Law. But on this point also the lawyer is likely to be disappointed. As far as is known, to date only one single case of this type has given rise to a published decision.[11] The reasons for this "lull in the case-law" which followed "the legislative vacuum" and the disadvantages which it entails will become clearer in the course of the following discussion which will examine, firstly, the main characteristics of the control procedure set up by the 1977 Law, and, secondly, the basic characteristics of the substantive provisions of the rules applicable in this field.

B. The Main Characteristics of the Control Procedure

1. Characteristics linked to the Nature of the Control System Set up

a) "A Priori" or "A Posteriori" Control
In the field of concerted practices and abuses of dominant positions, a formal distinction is traditionally made between systems of "*a priori control*" and "*a posteriori control*". The French system, for example, belongs to the second category, while the European system supposedly belongs to the first, even though Regulation 17 sets up a hybrid system. There is a fundamental difference between these two types of system for the public control of the lawfulness of private economic activities, which relates to the economico-political principles of organization of the company in question. The "a priori" theory is based on the premise that all such activity is *per se* forbidden but allows exemptions to be granted in an individual case, to be judged by an expert body set up for the purpose. The "a posteriori" systems do not, as a matter of principle, condemn such activity per se but require each case to be examined by experts who separate the wheat from the chaff and decide on a case by case basis whether the transaction in question should be allowed to stand.

The system set up by the Law of 19 July 1977 reflects an "a posteriori" approach mitigated by "a priori" elements, whereas that set up by E.E.C. Regulation 17 is the inverse — an "a priori" system mitigated by "a posteriori" elements. Concentrations are not condemned on principle, but can be declared illegal in view of their economic effects. However, in order to reduce the harmful

[11] B.O.S.P. 19 May 1979.

impact on business of the uncertainty resulting from this type of system, companies can voluntarily submit their agreements and even their proposals to the examination of the control authorities which may either declare them to be legal or illegal, or impose conditions whereby they can be legally carried out.

b) The Control Procedure

The Law of 19 July 1977 sets up a procedure which is administrative in nature and reliant on expert assessments. The public economic administrative authorities are given the permanent and driving role whilst, following the recommendation of the Rapporteur on the draft law before the Senate,[12] a quasi-judicial body is set up to assess the economic effects. This body, called the *"Commission de la concurrence et de la concentration"* (C.C.C.) (Competition and Concentration Commission) replaces the *"Commission technique des ententes"* (C.T.E.) (Technical Commission for Concerted Agreements) and its main competence and activities will continue to be the control of concerted agreements. The power of the C.C.C. is limited to giving an expert opinion, but in fact its authority is such that its opinions are as effective in practice as many judicial decisions.

Unlawful concentration, unlike entering into prohibited concerted agreements, is not a criminal offence; therefore, the procedure which is used in respect of the most serious cases of concerted agreements (and which paradoxically constitutes the best form of defence in such proceedings) of referring the case to a second court instance is not available in respect of unlawful concentration. The sanctions are purely administrative, implying a not entirely liberal economy, but the Legislature has nevertheless provided undertakings with a right of appeal, by stipulating that decisions taken by the Minister following a concentration control procedure can be referred to the *Conseil d'État,* the highest administrative law court, which will hear the appeal *en pleine juridiction,* which means that the appellant can challenge both the form and the substance of the Minister's decision before the Court. Although commentators acknowledge that the high standing of this Supreme Court provides certain guarantees, a number of authors have nevertheless raised the question as to whether its members, the traditional guardians of the legality of the acts of public authorities, are qualified to take on the role of expert assessors of the economic desirability of the concentration of private undertakings; and also whether the reasons for decisions taken in this connection could really be set out in a judgment of the *Conseil d'État,* given the laconic, not to mention the esoteric, style which characterises the decrees of the *Conseil.*[13]

c) Purely Administrative Sanctions

Sanctions for abusive concentrations are purely administrative in nature. The absence of criminal penalties has already been mentioned, which distinguishes this system from that relating to detrimental concerted practices and abuses of dominant positions.

---

[12] Cf. J. O. Deb. Sen., 28. 6. 1977, p. 1856. The Reporter was Mr. G. Petit.
[13] F. C. Jeantet, *loc. cit., supra* note 7.

The 1977 Law does not explicitly define what is meant by an unlawful, or rather abusive, concentration. It can, however, be inferred from the provisions that the unlawfulness will always in fact be established in an opinion of the C.C.C., consulted either a priori or a posteriori. This opinion may make it clear that in the light of the basic criteria (which will be examined below), the concentration in question is not acceptable. Where this is the case, the Minister for the Economy, in conjunction with whichever of his colleagues is responsible for the sector of which the undertakings in question form a part, must adopt a decree containing one of the following five "injunctions":

(1) an injunction not to proceed with the project;
(2) an injunction to re-establish the previous legal position;
(3) an injunction to change or to add to the operation;
(4) an injunction to take any measure necessary to assure or re-establish a sufficient degree of competition;
(5) an injunction to conform to requirements aimed at making a sufficient contribution to economic and social progress, in order to compensate for damage done to competition.

The Law lays down that such injunctions are binding in nature.[14] As it is not possible to make a reference to the criminal judge, the secular arm of power, the legislature has had to rely on a system of quasi-penal pecuniary sanctions, in essence borrowed from the system of fiscal fines. The method of recovering such fines, as in the field of direct taxation, is set out in Sections 53 et seq. of Ordinance 45-1483 of 30 June 1945 which applies equally to concentrations, concerted agreements and abuses of dominant positions and which Section 9 of the 1977 Law incorporates by reference. The upper limit laid down for fines in this connection is high: for undertakings, 5% of the pre-tax turnover in France in the sector in question; and 5 million francs for natural persons and legal persons not being undertakings. This penalty can be accompanied by publicity measures.

These provisions are noteworthy in principle and for the future because they mark an important step in French economic law towards achieving autonomy vis-à-vis the criminal law in the only area in which it was still subject to it, i. e. in respect of sanctions, on which the law's practical efficacity depends. No value judgment on this fresh attack on the principle of separation of powers is intended: it is not possible to tell at the moment what direction the control exercised by the Conseil d'État will take and how effective it will be; nor is it possible to predict whether it can effectively safeguard the private interests concerned. Everything will depend on the actual way in which the system will operate.

2. The Operation of the System

One of the original features of the system introduced by the 1977 Law is the coexistence of a priori and a posteriori means of control. It is appropriate to study first the "a priori" system and thereafter the "a posteriori" means of control.

---

[14] Law of 19 July 1977, Section 8.

a) The Notification Procedure ("A Priori" Control)
Undertakings which wish to engage in a concentration operation may choose to
say nothing about it to the economic administration; or, on the other hand, they
may notify the public economic administrative authority of their plans or of the
measures already taken to implement an operation. A circular dated 14 February
1978[15] specifies in detail the administrative, material and legal conditions to be
complied with in connection with this notification. This is yet another example
of the techno-bureaucratic law which is the hall-mark of the current evolution of
our legal system. The file to be submitted must set out all the information which
may be needed by the experts responsible for deciding whether the concentration
in question is injurious, according to the negative criteria which will be examined
below. The Minister has a period of three months within which to decide upon
the lawfulness of the operation in question. In this period, he can either indicate
that he has no objection to it, or that he has decided to refer the case to the
C.C.C. for advice. If he does nothing within the three months, this amounts to
an acceptance. In the event of a reference to the C.C.C., the procedure continues
as in the case of an "a posteriori" control, but the Minister must take a decision
on the basis of the Commission's opinion within eight months of the notification, whereas where the procedure is initated by the administration this time
limit does not apply. It appears that the legislator intended to encourage
undertakings to resort to notification. Is this "incentive" a real one? It does not
appear to be very attractive because to date only a single notification has given
rise to a published decision.

b) Procedure Opened by the Administration Itself ("A Posteriori" Control)
This arises from the watch-dog function which is one of the most important
activities of the public economic authorities. In view of this, and in view of the
powers of enquiry that are available to these authorities, they are sometimes
called the "economic police".

The Law of 19 July 1977 is limited to mentioning that the C.C.C. can be
apprised of a case of concentration at the sole initiative of the Minister for the
Economy or at the request of the Minister responsible for the sector in question
(Section 6). Under the euphemistic terminology of our politico-administrative
system, in these circumstances "the Minister" means the manifold, anonymous,
powerful, cohesive and perennial civil service. The Law's silence gives rise to a
line of reasoning by analogy with the practice relating to competition and price
regulation. Suffice it to say that the enquiries which may lead to an expert
examination and then to control measures will, depending on the circumstances,
either be "ad hoc" enquiries or "enquiries of observation". The former
enquiries, which relate to specific operation, are commenced at the request of a
ministerial authority or of the C.C.C., or as a result of complaints made by third
parties (e. g. competitors, distributors or consumers). The latter enquiries are
carried out on a continuous basis in the sectors where concentration rates are
high or competitive conditions unstable. As will be seen, in France there are

[15] B.O.S.P., 17 February 1978.

numerous statistics, data of various kinds and economic studies which are available concerning both undertakings and markets. The links between the bodies which are in possession of such information and the offices of the Ministry of Economic Affairs are frequently very close, except so far as concerns the Bank of France, which furthermore has privileged information available to it. These data are given a wide circulation and the economic press, whether "gossipy" or not, gives wide publication to rumours. It can be said that the permanent monitoring role of the administration is hindered to a greater extent by the mass of information available than by professional secrecy.

The real obstacle to administrative action appears to be the very conditions which the Law lays down for its success. A number of these require a subjective assessment of the negative impact on competition and of the beneficial economic and social effects of the concentration in question. As the administration is acting as prosecutor and not judge, it cannot be called to account for having made an error in its evaluation of the facts when applying the subjective criteria for determining the acceptibility of the concentration. On the other hand, control is linked objectively to quantitative criteria (which will also be examined below under the heading of "concentration thresholds") in respect of which the administration has no right to make mistakes, even though such criteria involve elements of uncertainty, such as whether one product can be substituted for another (e. g. electric vehicles and automobiles).

The Law of 19 July 1977 has endeavoured to resolve one of the most serious problems of economic law. This is the problem of the rights of the complainant in confrontations with the administration. Essentially administrative in nature, the procedure of expert appraisal in French law remains inquisitorial, marked by the dogma of the absolute pre-eminence of the Public Interest, or even by *"raison d'État"*. Occasionally certain documents, which could call the administration itself or the authority of the State into question, remain secret or are systematically suppressed. It is quite common in practice to find that the declarations of interested parties which contradict the affirmations of sworn agents are not included in the record of proceedings which are drawn up by the latter and which are binding on the former. This is why the two most common approaches adopted by persons subject to the jurisdiction are either to make vigorous denials in the absence of evidence to the contrary; or to show a humility and an acquiescence which ensure the magnanimity of the bureaucratic apparatus whose power is flattered and thus the whole affair is made much easier.

Commentators had called the Legislature's attention to this fundamental point,[16] and the Parliamentary proceedings show that the latter did take note of it.[17] The 1977 Law contains provisions in this connection which operate at two

---

[16] F. C. Jeantet, *Les droits de la défense devant la C.E.E. dans le contentieux de la concurrence*, 1963 J.C.P. – C.I., 1758; *id., Un projet de contrôle des concentrations économiques en France*, 1976, J.C.P. II. 12 238.

[17] Cf. the *Le Theule Report*, J. O. DEB. ASS. NAT., No. 2954 p. 128; and the *Bajeux Report*, J. O. DEB. SEN., No. 459 p. 9.

levels. In the first place, a certain number of Articles[18] provide for the transmission of the documents in the file to private parties and for their comments to be given. Given the nature and the quasi-cultural character of the previous practice in France, it can be asked whether the Legislature should not have been even more precise than it has been in this connection. In the second place, the judicial control exercised by the *Conseil d'État* (mentioned above) represents a second level of guarantee of the rights of undertakings and individuals challenging the acts of the administration in the field of concentration.

Indeed, the fact that the lawfulness or unlawfulness of a concentration is determined upon the basis of the evaluation of economic facts and socio-political determinants — which are the criteria which dominate in the substantive control of concentrations — means that the participation of all possible parties in the procedure is all the more necessary, since the evaluation of such matters inevitably gives rise to disputes among the experts and the airing of all views is essential.

C. The Substantive Characteristics of the Control Set Up by the Law of 19 July 1977

These are certainly the most interesting and innovative aspects from the point of view of the evolution of French economic law. It is not, however, possible to say that they are entirely new, to the extent that notions such as the economic balance sheet or extenuating excuses found in individual economic and social circumstances have been given a considerable trial over a long period in the field of, e. g., competition law. The new element is the recourse by the Legislature itself to quantitative criteria and the audacity with which it admits that socio-political considerations can justify the abrogation of a rule laid down by it. It is rare for a legislature to have opted in such a clear way for a functional law (*"droit structurant"*) to the detriment of provisions of a normative nature (*"droit normatif"*).

This impression is increased by the imprecision of the terms employed. This regrettable shortcoming spoils the numerous positive aspects of this innovative attempt of the Legislature; clearly on this occasion it has not managed to find a style adequate to distinguish "economic law" from "economism without law". The draftsmen have made too much use of evasive formulae such as "likely to . . .", "to the extent that . . ." and "provided that . . ." etc. The fact that the language used leaves much to be desired no doubt betrays the uncertainty of the design, the lack of experience in the field and the incompatibility of the divergent objectives pursued. Unfortunately all four of the substantive criteria laid down in the Law of 19 July 1977 suffer from these defects, as we shall see from the following examination of the criteria.

---

[18] Law of 19 July 1977, Section 7, Para. 2; Section 8, last para.; Ordinance of 30 June 1945, Section 55 (as amended by the Law of 19 July 1977).

1. Legal Nature of the Operations Covered and Type of Persons Concerned

Section 4 of the Law of 19 July 1977 refers to

> any legal act or operation, in whatever form, relating to the transfer of ownership or enjoyment of the whole or part of the assets, rights and obligations of an undertaking, or whose objective or effect is to allow an undertaking or a group of undertakings to exercise directly or indirectly over one or several other undertakings an influence of such a nature as to direct or even to guide the management or the functioning of the latter.

By way of example of the kinds of activity covered, the circular of 14 February 1978 quotes the following types of operation: merger, acquisition of a participating interest, a contribution of assets, the creation of common subsidiaries and also, in more general terms, the various forms of permanent financial links, such as the relationship between a parent company and its subsidiary, inter-locking directorates, formation of undertakings into groups, reciprocal financial engagements, supply and sub-contracting contracts, agreements of cooperation or dependence. This list is far from exhaustive; it can be extended by adding management contracts, commercial licences and exclusive rights, economic interest groupings, etc.

In reality, the legislature wanted to cover any acquisition of control over any industrial asset whenever such acquisition resulted in any increase in the absolute size and the relative weight of the strategic unit, made possible by the unification of control. As one commentator on the Law, Mr. Jeantet, has pointed out,[19] a fundamental weakness has been introduced into the text by the Legislature's decision to expunge from it all reference to the term "control" which in legal practice, in economic reality and in everyday speech expresses in a simple and generally recognized way everything that instead has been very badly expressed in circumlocutions which are contained one within the other like Russian dolls.[20] Why the Legislature should stumble on this obstacle, in view of the fact that it had already used the term "control" in the sense of "domination" on several occasions in earlier texts, it is difficult to say. No doubt it objected to saying "to control control"; it was accordingly left with the choice of substituting the word "maîtrise" (power of command) for "control" in those places where the latter term would have appeared twice. It is the Legislature's task to determine new legal language; it has missed a golden opportunity for doing so.

The persons concerned are primarily "enterprises" (undertakings). The uninhibited use of this term is to be welcomed particularly in view of the fact that many French jurists refuse to recognize it since they never learned it in their faculties, although they encounter the entity that it describes in their daily lives. But the Law also covers "groups of undertakings", whereas the Legislature obstinately and absurdly refuses to give legislative recognition to this notion in France. In the absence of a clearer definition but having regard to the deliberately wide tendency of the Law of 19 July 1977 and its implementing circular, and also

[19] F. C. Jeantet, *loc. cit., supra* note 7, No. 23 *et seq.*
[20] For a discussion on the nature of control, the meaning and the legal scope of this economic and financial concept, *see* C. Champaud, *op. cit., supra* note 1.

to the underlying reasons for this attitude, the author considers that the notion of group is used here in the widest sense, which is the one he himself advocated a number of years ago.[21]

However, although the flexible character of a notion may be fine in theory, it can prove difficult to implement in practice. Let us suppose, for example, that two groups of companies manufacturing every-day products become part of multiple and diversified groups operating in a concentrated market. Let us also suppose that one of the companies possesses a network of integrated distributors selling complementary products. In order to assess the rate of concentration, should one base oneself exclusively on the turnover of the two groups in question, or should one also include the turnover of the integrated distributors? Or the proportion of this variable attributable to the partner concerned? This gives only a brief idea of the questions that can be raised in this connection.

In addition to the undertakings already discussed, and to those dependent or associated with them, the sanctions arising under the Law of 19 July 1977 can apply to other legal and natural persons who do not fall within these categories. As has been seen, (supra paragraph II B.1.(c)), the Ordinance of 1945 to which the 1977 Law refers for the particular sanctions to be applied in the case of perseverance in unlawful concentration, provides for a different fine for undertakings and for "other persons". These could be, for example, a professional employers' association, a company specializing in giving advice in connection with economic "rapprochements" and "marriages", a merchant bank or a public or para-public body which is the initiator of the concentration which is subject to criticism. Experience acquired in the field of concerted agreements or in the treatment of undertakings in difficulty shows that none of these cases is a purely academic hypothesis, the last-mentioned one no more than the others. The day is awaited with interest when this text will be used against an official guilty of initiating a harmful concentration.

2. The Concentration Rate Resulting from the Operation

In order for an operation to be submitted to the consideration of the expert body and to the Minister, the concentration to which it has given or would give rise has to exceed a certain threshold or rate of concentration. The significance of these quantitative criteria and the theoretical implications of their transmutation into legal criteria was examined in the introduction.

In purely legal terms, this constitutes a presumption of economic danger which the concentration in question is deemed to embody for the maintenance of a real and effective degree of competition. This explains why this presumption can be rebutted by proof to the contrary (see point 3 below). This also explains why the risk can be run if the danger which the concentration presents to the economic and social development of the country is less than other evils of the same nature which it makes possible to avoid (see point 4 below).

The measurable variable adopted by the 1977 Law is the turnover. Section 4,

---

[21] C. Champaud, *Les méthodes de groupement des sociétés*, 20 Rev. trim. dr. com. 1003 *et seq.* (1967).

paragraph 7 of the Law defines this element as "the total amount of sales . . . made in France" during the year. The implementing circular of 14 February 1978 provides a number of useful clarifications of an accountancy nature, referring to the methods of calculating these elements and the accounting periods to be employed.

The law provides for two thresholds, corresponding to two economic types of concentration.

In the case of "heterogenous concentration", sometimes called "conglomorate growth", an operation comes within the control once the entities concerned therefore are competitors, the tolerance threshold is crossed when the concentration in question affects more than 40% of the market, i. e., of the turnover realized in France by the overall number of undertakings producing the same goods or services.

In the case of "heterogenous concentration", sometimes called "conglomorate growth", an operation comes within the control once the entities concerned (which the Law uselessly prescribes must be at least two in number) each realize individually at least 25% of the turnover of the national market in the different and non-interchangeable goods and services which they produce.

The first hypothesis is clear, subject to what will be said in a moment. The second hypothesis is less clear. It is of such a nature as to open the door to numerous and interminable discussions of a complicated nature. If one refers to the Parliamentary proceedings it could be thought that a heterogenous concentration is subjected to control where it allows a strategic conglomerate entity to dominate more than 25% of two different markets. In addition to the objections which can be made concerning the real danger of this situation from the economic and competitive point of view, another reason can be found for not attaching too much weight to the guidance of the Parliamentary proceedings on this point. They were in fact marked by a major economic miscomprehension because homogenous concentrations (the first case) and heterogenous ones (the second case) were respectively referred to as "horizontal" and "vertical", which terms have a completely different meaning in this context. This error is all the more regrettable because it has subsequently been adopted in a number of manuals and text-books and threatens to cause long-lasting confusion among jurists in an area with which they are often unfamiliar and in which the legislature has not fulfilled its didactic, semantic and clarifiying role.

The existence of these thresholds or rates of concentration, set out in Section 4 of the Law of 19 July 1977, gives rise to other problems of interpretation.

In the first place, the question could be asked as to whether concentrations which took place a number of years ago are not also capable of being attacked on the basis of this text, by virtue of the administration's right to exercise control "a posteriori", in particular where the relevant thresholds are exceeded after the coming into force of the Law. Such an application would have no retroactive effect at all. In the second place, difficulties of interpretation will certainly arise as a result of the notion of "interchangeable products". Marketing studies show that substitutions in the consumer field take place very frequently and in an unexpected and even disconcerting fashion. In this way the purchase of household equipment goes down markedly during the winter sports season. More typical is the well-known substitution of "red fruit" (cherries and strawberries) for cold meats and canned hors d'œuvres when they appear in April and May. In the third place, there is the problem of obtaining information on measurable and comparable values both at the national level and at the level of the undertakings concerned. In this connection, a recent O.E.C.D. study shows that France is one of the countries possessing the widest range of sources enabling the relevant economic data to be gathered together, processed and compared.[22] France possesses five major sources of systematic and centralized information:

- those relating to the commercial identification of undertakings (R.C.S., BALO and BODAC);
- statistical breakdowns (SIRENE-SIRET) linked to the activity of INSEE, and to the latter's studies;
- fiscal sources;
- the central registry of balance sheets of the Bank of France, of the *Crédit National* and of the *Caisse des Dépôts et Consignations;*
- the social security bodies.

Such an abundance of sources, which reveals the hybrid, not exclusively liberal, character of the French society and economy, favours the implementation of legislation of this nature.

3. Operations of Such a Nature as to Be Harmful to Competition

The concentration thresholds set out in the Law are only presumptions of danger. In order for a transaction to be subject to control, Section 4 (2) requires in addition that it be "of such a nature as to be harmful to sufficient competition in a market". The imprecision of these terms has been justly criticized. It can be asked in particular what is meant by "sufficient competition". The reply resides in the case-law of the C.T.E. which is acknowledged to be a case-law source for the C.C.C.. Without entering into a detailed analysis of the opinions given by that expert body, quasi-judicial in nature, a synthetic reply can be given by stating that competition is sufficient when it is carried out effectively in such a way that the market forces which it produces lead undertakings to innovate, invest and export, while endeavouring to sell their products at the best quality/price ratio.

It is the task of the C.C.C. to clarify the interpretation to be given to the provisions as soon as possible. The first, and only, opinion which it has delivered (concerning a concentration in the welded tube industry) does not resolve this point in a definitive way, the Commission contenting itself with a statement that the operation had as much chance of reviving competition as of making it disappear.[23]

On the other hand, it can be asked whether this precondition for control is really useful. Firstly, it gives the impression that a concentration having a rate

[22] OECD, *op. cit., supra* note 2, p. 29.
[23] *Cf. supra* note 10.

lower than those laid down by the Law is acceptable even where it effectively eliminates all competition in the market. There is, therefore, a contradiction between this eminently subjective, qualitative assessment and the objective, quantitative and precise approach which has given rise to the definition of concentration rates. This represents an internal intellectual conflict which points to the poor quality of the legislative preparation and which underlines the fundamental ambiguity and the formal imperfection of the text.

Further, if the legislature, as was obvious, was anxious to avoid the arbitrariness and inflexibility inherent in quantitative definitions, it would have sufficed for it to make an "escape clause" available (which will be examined next) in order to arrive at this result. The reference to "sufficient competition" is not merely harmful to the clarity of the Law, but is also superfluous within the economy of the system. It can only be a source of confusion.

4. The Absence of Economic and Social Justification

In the field of concerted agreements, French law provides for the possibility of exemptions. A concerted agreement, even one which is fiercely anti-competitive, may be declared immune from attack where it contributes in a substantial way to economic and social progress.[24] In the field of concentration, an operation which attains a concentration rate which is higher than the legal threshold, and which is of such a nature as to be harmful to competition, can nevertheless be exempted if its other effects result in "a sufficient contribution to economic and social progress."[25] The formula is vague and the vocabulary is imprecise, but the intention is clear: a concentration which is economically harmful is politically justified if it allows national undertakings in a particular sector to engage in a "restructuring", resulting in increased productivity and competitiveness so that national industry may, as a result, reconquer the internal French market, take "its place" in the European market, or become successfully implanted in foreign markets. The legislature has made this aspect more precise by providing that the assessment of the evaluation of the operation's contribution to economic and social progress should be made having regard to the "competitiveness of the undertakings concerned in relation to international competition". The French legislature cannot be criticized for having clearly stated the generally accepted conclusion that competition is a medicine to be taken only internally. This is, after all, the basis for the *"rule of reason"*.

III. Indirect Control of Certain Operations Capable of Giving Rise to an Economic Concentration

The general orientation of the conference and the exact title which has been assigned to this report, in the context of this orientation, resulted in Part II, devoted to an analysis of the 1977 Law, being given deliberate, and perhaps excessive, pride of place. However, as has been pointed out, a form of control of

[24] Ordinance 45-1483 of 30 June 1945, Section 51.
[25] Law of 19 July 1977, Section 4, last para.

concentration existed even prior to this Law, as a result of scattered, disoriented and unconnected texts, which were the product of very varied circumstances and intentions, generally marked to a significant extent by political considerations.

Not only did the Law of 19 July 1977 not make these texts obsolete, but it also remains true that the type of activity which calls for their application has since 1977 been ten to a hundred times greater than the kind of activity which led to the enactment of the Law. This explains why it is difficult to say nothing about this aspect of French law in this field. However, because of space limitations, these provisions will be given a simple descriptive enumeration, which is not, however, exhaustive.

Despite the disparity which has just been referred to, it appears possible to classify the provisions in question into two categories depending on whether the control pursues a goal of economic organization, or whether it is inspired by ethical and political, and therefore extra-economic, considerations.

A. Controls Based on the Organization of Competition by the Public Authorities

Three preliminary remarks need to be made in this connection. In the first place, the instances cited are foreign to "industry" in the strict sense of the word (probably outdated) which is the meaning which economists give to it in making it the "second sector" of the economy. In the second place, although having an economic content, these State interventions are strongly characterised by socio-political or even electoral considerations. In the third place, these political overtones, and the fact that these controls apparently work against the development of competition, can result in an optical illusion for the jurist, which can cloud his judgment if he does not go to the root of the problem. For example, the provisions analysed below, considered to be Malthusian in nature, appear in the light of experience to have had anti-monopolistic and competitive effects which are more substantial than the obstacles to competition which they were designed to cover. This is an important point which should be argued and developed, which would require an enormous preliminary study and . . . a second report.

1. The Control of Concentrations in Agriculture

Whereas it is true to say that the public authorities have encouraged co-operative concentration for the transformation and commercialization of agricultural production, and also a certain concentration of exploitation, they have, on the other hand, blocked two other types of concentration that the industrial revolution in agriculture would have normally given rise to.

A regulation prohibits activities to be combined in such a way that, for example, an industrialist in the food sector can directly exploit his sources of supply.[26] Another text regulates agrarian concentration by means of accumulating agricultural holdings.[27] A third regulation restricts the size of intensive

---

[26] C. Rur. Section 188-1 *et seq.*
[27] C. Rur. Section 188-8.

livestock production units. Now this form of livestock farming is purely industrial; there is no longer any link with agriculture in its primary sector form. It can even be considered a heavy industry, with the proportion of capital invested for each job created being greater today than is the case in the steel industry. This sector is therefore particularly well suited to capitalist concentration. This has had to take place by means of "integration contracts" which are themselves subject to judicial control.[28]

2. The Control of Commercial Concentration

Having once been the kingdom of small traders, France has in ten years become the empire of hypermarkets. The destructive effects of this concentration in the tertiary sector in social and political terms are quite clear. The public authorities have nevertheless encouraged this development under the guise of the advantages accruing to consumers from a competitive point of view. Although there are considerable theoretical reasons for doubting the purely beneficial effects of commercial concentration, they constitute a dogma for the French aristo-technocracy. Under the anodyne cover of commercial urbanism, the "Royer" Law[29] has set up a system for the control of such commercial concentrations based partly on the cooperation of the parties and partly administrative (or rather, half-corporate, half-political). Commissions at the level of the *"départements"* and a national Commission are to act as expert assessors and give opinions to the Minister for Trade, who decides on the setting up of new hypermarkets. Activity in this area of economic law is intense and the Royer Law has had, and will have in the long term, a significant impact which will be different to that expected, both as regards concentration of distribution and as regards the previous concentration pattern of industrial undertakings.

B. Controls Based on Extra-Economic Considerations

1. Rules of Proper Conduct in the Exercise of the Supervision of Companies

Concentration operations are a part of the strategy of undertakings and of groups. They therefore fall within the domain reserved to the power of the private economy which is responsible for their control. The French legislature does not prohibit the enjoyment and the organization of this legal control of the assets and policies of companies. It even refuses to impose a general restriction on its exercise. On the other hand, on the occasion of the reform of company law, and since then, by means of various measures and by creating new bodies, it has set up a system for the supervision of the proper conduct of controllers and to ensure that operations of concentration by merger or by acquisition of control are carried out in an ethical way. This complex and disparate system is a result, in the first instance, of the Law of 24 July 1966 and of its implementing Decree of 23 March 1967. However, the most important provisions in this connection are contained in the constituent texts of the "Commission des Opérations de

[28] Law 84.678 of 6 July 1964, Section 17 (1).
[29] Law 73–1133 of 27 December 1973.

Bourse" (Stock Exchange Control Commission)[30], laying down the provisions which regulate "public offers of purchase, sale or exchange", or the "transfer of blocks of shares conferring control".[31] This sector of business law is the object of an intense legal activity which cannot be described here, even briefly, although it constitutes an indirect but real control over concentration operations affecting the corporate structures of the undertakings concerned.

2. The Fiscal Interests of the State

A partial contribution of assets constitutes one of the legal means of carrying out a concentration. These are "mini-divisions-mergers" which can, therefore, fall under a favourable tax regime whose object is to facilitate concentrations. However, the tax authorities reserve the right to supervise the reality of the operation in terms of concentration and also its economic desirability. The operation has to be accorded their prior authorization in order to escape a preventive level of taxation.[32]

3. The Country's Strategic Interests

In France, as in all countries, concentration operations carried out by foreign (non-Community) groups of undertakings or undertakings are subject to a Ministerial authorization, which relates both to the politico-economic desirability of the foreign investment in question and to its financial consequences from the point of view of exchange control in the wide sense of the term, i. e. in so far as the balance of France's external economic relations is concerned.[33]

4. Political Considerations

A number of concentrations are controlled for purely political reasons. This is, for example, true of concentrations in the newspaper field. Since the considerable shakeout which took place in this sector, when France was liberated in 1944, a regulation — although rarely applied and possibly inapplicable — exists to ensure that the multiplicity of political opinions can find expression in a variety of newspapers, which a priori excludes any major concentration.[34] In this field, the control of concentration which rests on legal bases which are clear in their intention, but imprecise in their formulation, is conferred on judicial tribunals. It is not very effective.

---

[30] Ordinance No. 67-883 of 28 September 1967.
[31] Decree of 7 April 1978; Regulation of the Compagnie des Agents de Change of 8 August 1973; D.G.—C.O.B. 25 July 1978.
[32] C.G.I. Section 817.A and Section 301.E; Annex II of C.G.I.
[33] Decree No. 67-78 of 27 January 1967 modifying Decree 69-264 of 21 March 1969 and 71-143 of 22 February 1971; Decree 68-1021 of 24 November 1968; Decree 71-144 of 22 February 1971; Decree 74-721 of 26 July 1974.
[34] Ordinance of 26 August 1944.

Summary

Until quite recently, the French public authorities appeared more anxious to favour the concentration of undertakings than to control it. Only concerted practices were really the object of control, carried out a posteriori and dominated by considerations of political economy and by what appeared appropriate in the circumstances. Despite the social weight and number of small and medium undertakings, the employers' associations requested that there should not be too many obstacles to the concentration of undertakings. For ideological reasons, workers' unions did not object to this. Because of their initial training and philosophy, the powerful aristo-technocracy which controls France's political and administrative apparatus believes in the virtue of a centralizing concentration, in which it sees the reflection of its own structures, thought and rituals.

In the first instance, a judicial or quasi-judicial control of concentration came into French law by the side door. Regulations in the field of agricultural holdings in 1964 and in the field of retail trade in 1973, reflected socio-political considerations rather than trends in economic law. The same was true for piecemeal provisions designed to protect the fiscal or strategic interests of the State endangered by concentration operations, and also for the regulation of newspaper publishers.

It was only the creation of the Commission des Operations de Bourse and the control of a number of concentration operations involving the capital of large corporations that represented the real commencement of a genuine law of economic concentration, in 1967.

It is, therefore, only with the Law of 19 July 1977 that French antitrust law received its second impetus. This statute introduces a general control of the concentration of undertakings. Inspired by draft European regulations, and through them, foreign legislation, the provisions of this Law relate to all forms of concentration and particularly to those in the industrial sector, which is the main object of this debate. Commentators have called attention to a number of technical imperfections in the text, which is certainly no masterpiece of legal drafting. It contains repetitions, is imprecise, and sometimes even incoherent. Finally, the bodies set up in order to exercise such control do not appear to have shown much sign of activity. This lack of activity contrasts with the renewal of the fight against restrictive agreements and practices made possible by this same 1977 Law, introduced at the initiative of a Prime Minister (Mr Barre, an Economics Professor) and a Minister for the Economy (Mr Monory, the head of an enterprise) both convinced of the superiority of the market economy and the virtues of competition and economic freedom. It is a result of their wish that control of concentration has existed in France since 1977. The Law was not sufficient to overthrow the existing mentality and behaviour, which explain the shortcomings of the text and the timidity of its application. The construction of a French antitrust law is a long-term task in a society in which worker socialism and bourgeois Colbertism are working hand in hand in this connection, and in which heads of industry retain feelings of nostalgia for corporatism.

The Swiss Act on Cartels

AND

The Practice of the Swiss Cartel Commission Concerning Economic Concentration

Walter R. Schluep[*]

Zürich

I. Constitutional and Policy Foundations of Swiss Antitrust Law

A. Constitutional Foundations

Like most Western Constitutions, the Swiss Federal Constitution[1] assures the freedom of trade (economic freedom) throughout Swiss territory.[2] However, the principle does not apply without limitations: the Federal Government is empowered by Art. 31 bis 3 to make rules, even in contravention of the principle of freedom of trade, if it considers it necessary to do so, for example, for the protection of agriculture of economically jeopardized areas or for safeguarding the supply of food in times of war.[3] Among the exceptions to the freedom of

---

[*] The author wishes to acknowledge the valuable help provided by his assistant, Felix Zulliger, lic. jur., University of Zürich.

[1] Cf., for the text of the Constitution, SR 101.

[2] Art. 31. 1 of the Constitution. Cf. F. Fleiner & Z. Giacometti, Schweizerisches Bundesstaatsrecht, p. 281 et seq. (Zürich, 1949); J.-F. Aubert, Traité de droit constitutionnel suisse, Vol. 2, p. 669 et seq. (Neuchâtel/Paris, 1967); F. Gygi, Wirtschaftspolitik als Begriff des Verfassungsrechts, in Schweizerische Wirtschaftspolitik zwischen gestern und morgen, Festgabe zum 65. Geburtstag von Hugo Sieber, p. 76 et seq. (Bern/Stuttgart, 1976); id., Die schweizerische Wirtschaftsverfassung, p. 61 et seq. (Bern/Stuttgart, 2nd ed. 1978); H. Marti, Die Handels- und Gewerbefreiheit nach den neuen Wirtschaftsartikeln (Bern, 1950); id., Die Wirtschaftsfreiheit der schweizerischen Bundesverfassung (Basel/Stuttgart, 1976); M. Widmer, Die Gewerbefreiheit nach schweizerischem und die Berufsfreiheit nach deutschem Recht, Abhandlungen zum schweizerischen Recht, Vol. 379 (Bern, 1967); W. Klinkmann, Die Wirtschaftsfreiheit im Staatsrecht der Bundesrepublik Deutschland und der Schweizerischen Eidgenossenschaft (Diss., St. Gall, 1963); U. P. Frey, Das Verhältnis der Handels- und Gewerbefreiheit zu den andern Freiheitsrechten, (Diss., Zürich, 1965); F. Gygi and W. R. Schluep, Schweizerisches Wirtschaftsrecht, in Begriff und Prinzipien des Wirtschaftsrechts, p. 87 et seq. (Frankfurt a. M./Berlin, 1971).

[3] Cf., on the constitutionally permitted deviations from the principle of freedom of trade, Fleiner & Giacometti, supra note 2, at p. 287 et seq.; Aubert, supra note 2, at p. 684 et

trade principle is to be found the basis of the legislation governing cartels and similar organizations. The Constitution[4] authorizes the Legislator to enact regulations against the economically or socially harmful effects of cartels and similar organizations if the general interest[5] calls for them. The present Federal Act on Cartels and Similar Organizations was enacted under this power in 1962.[6] The foreign reader not familiar with Swiss law must here be informed that the constitutional provision is not designed to support legislation which prohibits cartels and similar organizations as such. Rather, the law is designed to combat the economically or socially harmful effects of cartels and similar organizations.[7]

seq.; MARTI, DIE HANDELS- UND GEWERBEFREIHEIT, *supra* note 2, at p. 164 *et seq.; id.,* DIE WIRTSCHAFTSFREIHEIT, *supra* note 2, at p. 138 *et seq.;* and Klinkmann, *supra* note 2, at p. 81 *et seq.*

[4] *Cf.* Art. 31[bis].3.d of the Constitution. On the events leading to the promulgation of the so-called Economic Articles, *see* AUBERT, *supra* note 2, at p. 668 *et seq.;* F. Imboden, Die Handels- und Gewerbefreiheit und die schweizerische Wirtschaftsordnung, p. 90 (Diss., Bern, 1948); MARTI, DIE HANDELS- UND GEWERBEFREIHEIT, *supra* note 2, at p. 24; *id.,* DIE WIRTSCHAFTSFREIHEIT, *supra* note 2, at p. 5 *et seq.;* W. R. Schluep, *Schweizerische Wettbewerbspolitik zwischen gestern und morgen,* in ZUM WIRTSCHAFTSRECHT, p. 145 *et seq.* (Bern, 1978); BOTSCHAFT DES BUNDESRATES AN DIE BUNDESVERSAMMLUNG ÜBER EINE PARTIALREVISION DER WIRTSCHAFTSARTIKEL DER BUNDESVERFASSUNG, VOM 10. SEPTEMBER 1937, 1937 Bbl. II, 833 *et seq.;* ERGÄNZUNGSBOTSCHAFT DES BUNDESRATES AN DIE BUNDESVERSAMMLUNG ÜBER DIE REVISION DER WIRTSCHAFTSARTIKEL DER BUNDESVERFASSUNG, vom 3. August 1945, 1945 Bbl. I, 905 *et seq.;* on the cartel article (31bis.3.d of the Constitution) in particular, *see* H. Huber, *Das Kartellproblem auf der Verfassungsstufe,* 1955 WuR 165; W. Hug, *Zur gesetzgeberischen Ausführung des Kartellartikels der BV,* 1958 WuR 89; L. Schürmann, *Der Kartellartikel der Bundesverfassung,* 1958 WuR 181.

[5] *Cf.,* on the term "general interest", G. von Castelberg, *Das "Gesamtinteresse" der Wirtschaftsartikel,* 1953 WuR 8.

[6] *Cf.,* for the text of the Act, SR 251. Debates in Parliament concluded with the vote of 20 December, 1962. After the expiration of the period allowed for a referendum (19 April, 1963) the new Act came into force on 15 February, 1964. *Cf. also* VORARBEITEN FÜR EIN BUNDESGESETZ ÜBER KARTELLE UND ÄHNLICHE ORGANISATIONEN, BERICHT UND TEXT DES ENTWURFS DER EXPERTENKOMMISSION (Bern, 1959); BOTSCHAFT DES BUNDESRATES AN DIE BUNDESVERSAMMLUNG ZUM ENTWURF EINES BUNDESGESETZES ÜBER KARTELLE UND ÄHNLICHE ORGANISATIONEN, VOM 18. SEPTEMBER 1961, 1961 Bbl. II, 553 *et seq.; also* H. Merz, *Der schweizerische Entwurf zu einem Bundesgesetz über Kartelle und ähnliche Organisationen,* 25 RABELSZ 1 (1960); H. Sieber, *Kritische Würdigung des Entwurfs zu einem schweizerischen Kartellgesetz,* 1959 WuR 245; H. G. Giger, *Eine rechtliche Würdigung des Kartellgesetzentwurfes,* 1959 WuR 163; H. Kronstein, *Gedanken zum schweizerischen Entwurf eines Kartellgesetzes,* 26 RABELSZ 40 (1961); H. von Beringe, *Der schweizerische Kartellgesetzentwurf,* 1960 WuR 328; W. Fikentscher, *Bemerkungen zu den schweizerischen Entwürfen eines Kartellgesetzes,* 26 RABELSZ 467 (1961).

[7] *Cf.* W. R. Schluep, *Die Rule of Reason des amerikanischen Antitrustrechts und das schweizerische Kartellgesetz,* 1966 WuR 64; *id., supra* note 4, at p. 127; *id., Grundzüge des Entwurfs der Expertenkommission zur Revision des BG über Kartelle und ähnliche Organisationen,* 115 ZBJV 66 (1979); *cf. also* O. FISCHER, BUNDESGESETZ ÜBER KARTELLE UND ÄHNLICHE ORGANISATIONEN, p. 9 (Bern, 1963); H. Deschenaux, *L'esprit de la loi*

This suggests that the existence of cartels and similar organizations in Switzerland is constitutionally assured to the extent that their effects are economically and socially harmless. However, it should immediately be added that the Legislator is given a great deal of scope, as the Constitution entirely fails to define the effects of cartels and similar organizations which are to be considered economically or socially harmful, and, as will be obvious to any specialist in cartel law, this state of affairs leaves the definition of economically or socially harmful effects to the Legislator.

At all events, two constitutional barriers have been erected which the Legislator must respect: (1) The law may not result in qualifying the mere existence of a cartel or similar organization as economically or socially harmful; (2) on the other hand, the legislator must not go so far as to simply guarantee the existence of cartels and similar organizations and to qualify all effects as economically or socially harmless. The art of legislation thus resides in admitting cartels and similiar organizations in principle. At the same time, however, the effects of such organizations must be so differentiated that harmless effects are unaffected and harmful ones prohibited. The scope that this leaves to the Legislator quite obviously presupposes that certain criteria exist on the strength of which a concrete decision can be given in the individual case as to whether or not an effect is harmless. However, it is not possible to establish such criteria except on the basis of a fairly clear philosophy.

B. The Underlying Philosophy

As previously stated, competition philosophy is Constitutionally predetermined by the acknowledgment that cartels and similar powerful organizations can have not only negative but also positive effects when considered in the light of the

fédérale sur les cartels et organisations analogues, in MÉMOIRES PUBLIÉS PAR LA FACULTÉ DE DROIT DE GENÈVE, No. 18, p. 207 (Geneva, 1964); *id., La notion d'effets nuisibles des cartels et organisations analogues*, in MÉMOIRES PUBLIÉS PAR LA FACULTÉ DE DROIT DE GENÈVE, No. 24, p. 82 *et seq.* (Geneva, 1969); *id., Aspects d'une révision de la loi sur les cartels et organisations analogues*, 111 ZBJV 130 (1974); H. Kundert, Die Befugnisse des Bundes auf dem Gebiet des Kartellwesens (BV 31bis III d), p. 87 *et seq.* (Diss., Zürich, 1954); KARTELL UND WETTBEWERB IN DER SCHWEIZ, 31. VERÖFFENTLICHUNG DER PREISBILDUNGSKOMMISSION DES EIDGENÖSSISCHEN VOLKSWIRTSCHAFTSDEPARTEMENTES, p. 43 (Bern, 1957); Huber, *supra* note 4, at p. 165 *et seq.*, esp. at p. 169; E. Homburger, *Rechtsgrundlagen der Interessenabwägung bei Anwendung des Kartellgesetzes*, 1970 ZSR Part II, 37 *et seq.;* BOTSCHAFT DES BUNDESRATES . . . VOM 10. SEPTEMBER 1937, *supra* note 4, at p. 889; BOTSCHAFT DES BUNDESRATES . . . *supra* note 6, at p. 555; R. BÄR, KARTELLRECHT UND INTERNATIONALES PRIVATRECHT, ABHANDLUNGEN ZUM SCHWEIZERISCHEN RECHT, VOL. 369, p. 284, note 35 (Bern, 1965) seems to disagree. On the relationship between prohibitory and abuse prevention legislation, see L. Schürmann, *Mißbrauchsprinzip oder Verbotsprinzip*, in KARTELL- UND MONOPOLRECHT, p. 36 *et seq.* (Rüschlikon/Zürich, 1973); KARTELL UND WETTBEWERB IN DER SCHWEIZ, *supra* note 7, at p. 145 et seq.; H. Merz, *Kartellrecht – Instrument der Wirtschaftspolitik oder Schutz der persönlichen Freiheit*, 1966 WuR 31; Schluep, *Grundzüge des Entwurfs*, *supra* note 7, at p. 67 *et seq.*

general interest.[8] However, if it is assumed that action in restraint of competition may have both positive and negative economic and non-economic effects, the Legislator is faced with a dilemma: One alternative is to leave it to the law enforcement agencies to determine in each individual case which effects are useful and which are harmful. These agencies would then ensure that the harmless or useful effects were protected to the full extent possible, while eliminating the harmful ones. However this is not feasible since every cartel provision and every individual course of conduct of a powerful organization may have both useful and harmful effects, and a restraint of competition cannot be dissected in such a way as to be partly prohibited and partly allowed. This leaves only one other avenue: the Legislator itself must effect a general evaluation and prohibits as generally harmful or admits as generally useful certain cartel clauses or behavioural patterns of similar organizations.[9] But this method involves the danger that the Legislator might overshoot the mark, by prohibiting also positive effects by general bans; or that it might fall short by protecting undesirable harmful effects with a general admission.

Swiss competition policy seeks a way out of this dilemma through the concept of protecting such a minimal level of competition as is necessary just barely to protect the favourable possibilities expected from competition.[10] In the communication relating to the present law and jurisdiction, it was graphically explained that restraint of competition was harmful whenever it failed to ensure the "physical subsistence level of competition."[11] The philosophy behind limiting protection to a certain minimal level of competition is to avoid prematurely rendering the positive effects of cartels and similar organizations impossible — in brief, a wish to avoid "throwing out the baby with the bathwater".

To sum up, it can be said that the competition philosophy forming the basis of the 1962 Act rests on two pillars:

(1) On the one hand, on the intention to ensure the positive effects of restraints of competition by not banning restraint as such;

(2) on the other, to guarantee a minimum physical subsistence level for competition so that the negative effects of restraints of competition will not go too far.

Technically speaking, this end should be achieved by means of a combination of civil and administrative law. In terms of civil law, it was intended to avoid having outsiders and newcomers squeezed out of the market by cartels and similar organizations[12]: this could be done simply by protecting the private right

---

[8] *Cf.* Schluep, *Grundzüge des Entwurfs, supra* note 7, at pp. 67 and 74.

[9] Although the Constitution does not support strictly prohibitory legislation, such per se offences would be permissible. *See* on this, L. Schürmann, Wirtschaftsverwaltungs-recht, p. 279 (Bern, 1978); Schluep, *Grundzüge des Entwurfs, supra* note 7, at p. 67.

[10] *Cf.* Kartell und Wettbewerb in der Schweiz, *supra* note 7, at pp. 145 and 203 *et seq.*; Schluep, *Grundzüge des Entwurfs, supra* note 7, at p. 74 *et seq.*

[11] *Cf.* Kartell und Wettbewerb in der Schweiz, *supra* note 7, at p. 160.

[12] *Cf.* Art. 4 of the Cartel Act; Schluep, *Grundzüge des Entwurfs, supra* note 7, at p. 75; id., *Allgemeines Wirtschaftsrecht und schweizerisches Kartellgesetz*, in Zum Wirt-schaftsrecht, p. 109 (Bern, 1978).

of free economic activity.[13] In terms of administrative law, it was felt that a Committee on Cartels appointed by the Government would have to become active, in case the outsiders and newcomers to be protected by the private law provisions should decide voluntarily to dispense with their legal protection with the result that in the final analysis the "minimum subsistence level of competition" would no longer be ensured. The committee would in such cases be authorized to take measures to restore the necessary minimum level of competition.[14]

Attractive as this philosophy may be in theory, however, in practice it has been watered down by the Legislator in favour of cartels and similar organizations,[15] and weakened by the practice of both the courts[16] and the Cartel Commission.[17]

---

[13] *Cf.* Botschaft des Bundesrates, *supra* note 6, at p. 561; A. Koller, *Die Konzeption des möglichen Wettbewerbes, Auslegungshilfe des Kartellgesetzes*, 1970 WuR 151 *et seq.; id., Die Rechtsprechung zum Kartellgesetz*, in Festschrift für W. Hug zum 70. Geburtstag, p. 97 *et seq.* (Bern, 1968); M. Kummer, *Die "Erheblichkeit" der Wettbewerbsbehinderung (KG 4) nach der Praxis des Bundesgerichts*, in Festgabe für H. Deschenaux, p. 560 (Freiburg, 1977); Schürmann, *supra* note 4, p. 185; D. Syz, Die verwaltungsrechtlichen Bestimmungen des Bundesgesetzes über Kartelle und ähnliche Organisationen, p. 4 *et seq.* (Diss., Zürich, 1972); H. Sattler, *Zu den Begriffen des Kartells und der kartellähnlichen Organisation*, Zürcher Beiträge zur Rechtswissenschaft, Issue 348, p. 19 (Zürich, 1970); U. Wältermann, Die rechtliche Behandlung der Exportkartelle im KG, p. 100 (Cologne, 1969); Bär, *supra* note 7, at p. 278 et seq.; Deschenaux, *La notion, supra* note 7, at p. 79; H. Merz, Das schweizerische Kartellgesetz, Abhandlungen zum Schweizerischen Recht, Vol. 376, p. 95 (Bern, 1967); *id., supra* note 7, at p. 1 *et seq.*, esp. p. 13 *et seq.;* W. R. Schluep, *Markenschutzgesetz und Kartellgesetz*, in Stillstand und Fortentwicklung im schweizerischen Recht, St. Galler Festgabe 1965 zum Schweizerischen Juristentag, p. 394 *et seq.* (Bern, 1965); *id., Von der Kontrahierungspflicht der kartellähnlichen Organisationen*, 1969 WuR 207; *id., Die Rule of Reason, supra* note 7, at p. 69.

[14] *Cf.* Art. 20 *et seq.* of the Cartel Act; Schluep, *Grundzüge des Entwurfs, supra* note 7, at p. 75; *id., supra* note 4, at p. 153. There is universal recognition of the essential need for private cartel law to be supplemented by administrative cartel law. *See* L. Schürmann, Bundesgesetz über Kartelle und ähnliche Organisationen, p. 143 *et seq.* (Zürich, 1964); Deschenaux, *L'esprit, supra* note 7, at p. 213; Merz, *Das schweizerische Kartellgesetz, supra* note 13, at p. 97 *et seq.; id.,supra* note 7, at p. 20 *et seq.;* Syz, *supra* note 13, at p. 7 *et seq.;* H. Allemann, *Kartellgesetz und marktmächtige Unternehmen*, 1965 WuR 222; Hug, *supra* note 4, at p. 116 *et seq.;* Botschaft des Bundesrates . . . vom 18. September 1961, *supra* note 6, at p. 599; and the Cartel Commission in 1976 VSKk 88 *et seq.*

[15] *Cf.* Vorarbeiten für ein Bundesgesetz über Kartelle und ähnliche Organisationen, *supra* note 6, at p. 20 *et seq.;* Schluep, *supra* note 4, at p. 153 *et seq.;* Schürmann, *supra* note 14, at p. 80; H. Merz, *Sicherung oder Abbau der Wettbewerbsfreiheit*, NZZ of 27 September 1962; Sieber, *supra* note 6, at p. 245 *et seq.;* H. Allemann, *Die Verwirklichung der Konzeption des "Möglichen Wettbewerbs" im schweizerischen Kartellgesetzentwurf*, 1959 WuR 149 *et seq.;* Giger, *supra* note 6, at p. 163 *et seq.*

[16] First, the Federal Supreme Court required that "private interests must positively favour the public interest, that is to say, they must promote the successful development of the

II. The Swiss Act on Cartels: Present Practice and Pending Reform Plans

A. The Present Law and the Practice of Enforcement Agencies

1. The Protection of Outsiders and Newcomers under Private Law

According to the competition philosophy just discussed, the civil Law portion of the Cartel Act would have had to protect, without compromise, the right of outsiders and newcomers not to be excluded from, or substantially hampered in competition.[18] This would have been possible by a strict interdiction on impeding outsiders and newcomers in competition. While the Legislator has laid down such a prohibition, it has perforated it by providing a fair number of excuses, such as that contained in Art. 5.1 of the present Act[19] which provides:

> Interference with competition is lawful when it is warranted on grounds of overriding legitimate interests,[20] and does not prevent free competition to a degree that is excessive either in terms of its aims, or by its very nature or the manner of its operation.

national economy . . ." (BGE 94 II 339). Subsequently however, in BGE 98 II 376 *et seq.*, it reversed this view, only to return to its original finding shortly afterwards in BGE 99 II 235. In its latest ruling, however, it changed its mind once more, and states: "Apart from the public interest . . . the existence of private interests, provided that they are not contrary to the public interest, can suffice to render this provision effective" (BGE 102 II 442). *See,* on this, also H. Merz, *Die privatrechtliche Rechtsprechung des Bundesgerichts im Jahre 1972, Obligationenrecht,* 115 ZBJV 50 *et seq.* (1974); Deschenaux, *Aspects, supra* note 7, at p. 138 *et seq.;* Schluep, *Grundzüge des Entwurfs, supra* note 7, at p. 78 *et seq.*

[17] *Cf.* Schluep, *Grundzüge des Entwurfs, supra* note 7, at p. 81 *et seq.; see,* for an overview on the practice of the Cartel Commission, SCHÜRMANN, *supra* note 9, at p. 306 *et seq.; see also* Schluep, *supra* note 4, at p. 160 *et seq.*

[18] *Cf.* Allemann, *supra* note 15, at p. 149 *et seq.;* BOTSCHAFT DES BUNDESRATES . . . VOM 18 SEPTEMBER 1961, *supra* note 6, at p. 581; Schluep, *Grundzüge des Entwurfs, supra* note 7, at p. 75.

[19] *Cf.* Schluep, *Grundzüge des Entwurfs, supra* note 7, at p. 75 *et seq.; see also* J. Micheli, Les exceptions à l'illicité des entraves à la concurrence des tiers, p. 15 *et seq.,* (Diss., Lausanne, 1972); SCHÜRMANN, *supra* note 14, at p. 78 *et seq.*

[20] On the problem of "overriding legitimate interests", *see* Schluep, *Von der Kontrahierungspflicht, supra* note 13, at p. 215 *et seq.; id., Markenschutzgesetz, supra* note 13, at p. 396; *id., Die Rule of Reason, supra* note 7, at p. 70; *id., Allgemeines Wirtschaftsrecht, supra* note 12, at p. 112 *et seq.;* MERZ, DAS SCHWEIZERISCHE KARTELLGESETZ, *supra* note 13, at p. 49; *id., Die kartellistische Durchsetzung von Preisvereinbarungen und Kalkulationsnormen,* in MÉLANGES ROGER SECRÉTAN, p. 200 *et seq.* (Montreux, 1964); *id., Der "Mögliche Wettbewerb" und die zivilrechtlichen Bestimmungen im Kartellgesetzentwurf vom 19. April 1959,* 1959 SZVS 431 *et seq.;* W. GREMINGER, DAS OLIGOPOL IM SCHWEIZERISCHEN KARTELLGESETZ, (EUROPÄISCHE HOSCHSCHULSCHRIFTEN, Series V, Vol. 26) p. 107 (Bern & Frankfurt, 1971); P. MATHYS, DAS VERHÄLTNIS ZWISCHEN KARTELLRECHT UND KOLLEKTIVEM ARBEITSRECHT, BASLER STUDIEN ZUR RECHTSWISSENSCHAFT, Vol. 38, p. 98 (Basel & Stuttgart, 1969); Deschenaux, *L'esprit, supra* note 7, at p. 218 *et seq.;* H. MATTMANN, DIE PREISBINDUNG DER ZWEITEN HAND NACH DEM SCHWEIZE

This, naturally, has decisively weakened the original philosophy,[21] because the legal protection of outsiders and newcomers was from the very outset regarded as the minimum necessary for the protection of competition, and now this minimal protection has itself been weakened by admitting the possibility of activities of cartels and similar organizations which can readily hamper outsiders and newcomers.

However, even this regulation might have been acceptable if at the same time the courts had allowed a cartel or similar organizations which hindered third parties *only* if the cartel or oligopoly had unequivocally been proved to be superior in terms of the general interest than the protection of the possibility of competition.[22] That had been contemplated in the Federal Government's original Bill[23] but got lost in the course of the Parliamentary deliberations.[24] The Federal Supreme Court in early cases under the present legislation demanded, in the spirit of the Federal draft, that activities which threatened the position of third parties must be proved to be positively in the general interest,[25] but in later cases the Court accepted that third parties could be hampered, provided the conduct in question was not clearly against the general interest.[26]

This is the current legal position. It is characterized by the fact that effectively the right of outsiders and newcomers to free economic activity must give way whenever cartels or similar organizations can adduce a reasonable argument in favour of keeping outsiders and newcomers out. And even when a cartel or similar organization clearly hinders third parties in maintaining a market

RISCHEN KARTELLGESETZ, p. 58 *et seq.* (Winterthur, 1970); Micheli, *supra* note 19, at p. 39 *et seq.; cf. also* 1969 VSKk 313 *et seq.,* esp. at 318 *et seq.;* and 1971 VSKk 314.

[21] *Cf.* Sieber, *supra* note 6, at p. 250 *et seq.;* Merz, *Das schweizerische Kartellgesetz, supra* note 13, p. 48; Deschenaux, *L'esprit, supra* note 7, at p. 217; MATTMANN, *supra* note 20, at p. 57; P. Tobler, Selbsthilfe im wirtschaftlichen Wettbewerb, p. 91 (Diss., Basel, 1970); SCHÜRMANN, *supra* note 14, at p. 78 *et seq.;* Koller, *Die Rechtsprechung, supra* note 13, at p. 114.

[22] *I. e.,* cartel practices must be shown to positively favour the public interest; *see* Merz, *Das schweizerische Kartellgesetz, supra* note 13, at p. 50; Deschenaux, *Aspects, supra* note 7, at p. 138 *et seq.; id., L'esprit, supra* note 7, at p. 218 *et seq.;* MATTMANN, *supra* note 20, at p. 60; H. Allemann, *Die Wettbewerbpolitik,* in STRUKTURWANDLUNGEN DER SCHWEIZERISCHEN WIRTSCHAFT UND GESELLSCHAFT, FESTSCHRIFT FÜR F. MARBACH ZUM 70. GEBURTSTAG, p. 380 (Bern, 1962). SCHÜRMANN, *supra* note 14, at p. 83 *et seq.,* WÄLTERMANN, *supra* note 13, at p. 59 *et seq.* and L. GITBUD, DIE RECHTLICHE BEHANDLUNG DER PREISUNTERBIETUNG NACH DEM GESETZ GEGEN DEN UNLAUTEREN WETTBEWERB UND DER KARTELLGESETZGEBUNG IN DER SCHWEIZ UND IN DEUTSCHLAND, p. 106 (München, 1974), disagree and hold that practices interfering with competition are eligible for exemption if they are not contrary to the public interest. On the Federal Supreme Court's practice on this point, *see supra* note 16.

[23] *Cf.* BOTSCHAFT DES BUNDESRATES ... VOM 18 SEPTEMBER 1961, *supra* note 6, at p. 582.

[24] *Cf.* SCHÜRMANN, *supra* note 14, at p. 79 *et seq.;* and Schluep, *supra* note 4, at p. 156.

[25] *Cf.* BGE 94 II 339; Schluep, *Grundzüge des Entwurfs, supra* note 7, at p. 78; *id., supra* note 4, at p. 158; Deschenaux, *L'esprit, supra* note 7, at p. 218.

[26] *Cf.* BGE 98 II 376 *et seq.,* and 102 II 442; *see also* Schluep, *supra* note 4, at p. 158 *et seq.;* and *supra* note 16.

organization it may nevertheless be accepted as reasonable, provided it does not patently violate the public interest. In actual fact outsiders and newcomers can thus quite obviously be excluded from, or hampered in, competition whenever the restrictive market organization in question appears warrantable and the exclusion of third parties is not exclusively a way of "keeping out new competitors" (Art. 5.3. of the Cartel Act).[27] One can see that the basic concept of the civil law section has thus been substantially weakened. However, it cannot be said that judicial control of cartels and similar organizations has therefore become ineffectual. In view of this legal situation the question naturally arises as to the extent to which the law has been able to realize the potential of the Cartel Commission in ensuring the "minimum physical subsistence level of competition."

2. The Protection of a Minimum Level of Competition by Administrative Law

It should here be noted that the Legislator has omitted to say clearly that the Cartel Commission must step in when cartels and similar organizations result in a complete breakdown of competition. Instead the Act includes a mysterious formula which uses a great many words to say nothing (Art. 22.1):[28]

> To safeguard the interests of the public, the Federal Economic Department may, on the authority of a special inquiry, within a year from the date on which the report on the inquiry was submitted, institute proceedings before the Federal Court against a cartel or similar organization which prevents competition or interferes with it appreciably in any one branch of the economy or occupation, in a manner that is incompatible with the public interest, especially one detrimental to consumers.

Accordingly it devolved upon the Cartel Commission to determine the prerequisites "for certain cartels or similar organizations to cause economically or socially harmful effects" (Art. 20.1 of the Cartel Act).[29]

In fact the Cartel Commission has done little to promote the original competition philosophy through its operation of the Act. It is true, that at the beginning of its activities, in its special inquiries it always investigated whether cartels and similar organizations left a minimum functional level of competition.[30]

Later, however, the Commission embraced the so-called balance theory which endeavours to set off the economic and extra-economic advantages and disadvantages of restraints of competition in the form of an economic and social balance

---

[27] Cf. Schluep, *Von der Kontrahierungspflicht, supra* note 13, at p. 215; Schürmann, *supra* note 14, at p. 97 *et seq.*; Gitbud, *supra* note 22, at p. 116 *et seq.*; and Botschaft des Bundesrates . . . vom 18. September 1961, *supra* note 6, at p. 587.

[28] Cf. Schluep, *Markenschutzgesetz, supra* note 13, at p. 399 *et seq.*

[29] This provision represents an extremely vague indication of the duties of the Commission; *see* Schluep, *Markenschutzgesetz, supra* note 13, at p. 397; Merz, Das schweizerische Kartellgesetz, *supra* note 13, at p. 111; Greminger, *supra* note 20, at p. 112; Syz, *supra* note 13, at p. 44 *et seq.*

[30] Cf. K. Fröhlicher, *Die Kartellkommission und der Wettbewerb*, 1968 WuR 240 *et seq.*; Schluep, *supra* note 4, at p. 159; *id., Grundzüge des Entwurfs, supra* note 7, at p. 81; and, *e. g.*, 1968 VSKk 100 *et seq.* and 219 *et seq.*; 1974 VSKk 413.

sheet.[31] It should here be noted that, according to the most recent practice of the Commission, the complete exclusion of operational competition is a negative item on the balance sheet, but only one of a great many possible others. This is why it can be counterbalanced with comparative ease by other economic or extra-economic balance-sheet items. In the final analysis this leads to a policy favourable to cartels and similar organizations.[32]

3. Industrial Concentration in the Light of the Swiss Cartel Act

a) Review of the Swiss Cartel Act

The Act only applies to cartels and similar organizations.[33] Cartels are collective arrangements restricting competition;[34] similar, or quasi-cartel, organizations are market-powerful business organizations, or groups of such, which have arisen either by internal or by external growth.[35] It is important to observe here that the Act basically only applies to industrial concentration insofar as market-powerful organizations are either involved in the concentration process,[36] or arise through the concentration process.[37]

b) Points of the Act Tending Towards Supervision of Concentrations

If a concentration process or a concentration comes within the Act, this will have two important consequences in particular.

In terms of the civil law, quasi-cartel organizations are subject to the rule

---

[31] *Cf.* 1968 VSKk 308 *et seq.;* 1969 VSKk 121; 1971 VSKk 250 *et seq.;* 1972 VSKk 137 *et seq.;* 1974 VSKk 413 *et seq.;* 1975 VSKk 102. See also Schluep, *supra* note 4, at p. 160 *et seq.* For an overview on the practice of the Cartel Commission, *see* SCHÜRMANN, *supra* note 9, at p. 306 *et seq.* On the balance theory in general, *see* H. Sieber, *Aktuelle Probleme der schweizerischen Wettbewerbspolitik,* 1967 WuR 25 *et seq.; id., Über die Kriterien der volkswirtschaftlichen und sozialen Schädlichkeit von Kartellwirkungen,* 1973 WuR 48 *et seq.;* L. Schürmann, *Zur neueren Entwicklung der Kartell- und Wettbewerbspolitik aus schweizerischer Sicht,* 1973 WuR 77 *et seq.;* Deschenaux, *La notion, supra* note 7, at p. 91.

[32] *Cf. e. g.,* the special inquiry into the beer market (1974 VSKk 411 *et seq.,* esp. p. 413). *Cf.* also Schluep, *supra* note 4, at p. 161; *id., Grundzüge des Entwurfs, supra* note 7, at p. 81 *et seq.*

[33] *Cf.* Art. 1 of the Cartel Act; SCHÜRMANN, *supra* note 14, at p. 22.

[34] *Cf.* the legal definition in Art. 2.1 of the Cartel Act; for details *see* MAX KUMMER, DER BEGRIFF DES KARTELLS, ABHANDLUNGEN ZUM SCHWEIZERISCHEN RECHT, Vol. 372, p. 2 *et seq.* (Bern, 1966).

[35] *Cf.* the legal definition in Art. 3 of the Cartel Act; H. Tanner, Die Kartellbestimmung der schweizerischen Bundesverfassung, p. 58 *et seq.* (Diss., Bern, 1950); Schürmann, *supra* note 4, at p. 191 *et seq.;* Sattler, *supra* note 13, at p. 30 *et seq.;* Hug, *supra* note 4, at p. 101 *et seq.;* MERZ, DAS SCHWEIZERISCHE KARTELLGESETZ, *supra* note 13, at p. 28 *et seq.*

[36] *Cf.* W. Schluep, *Privatrechtliche Probleme der Unternehmenskonzentration und -kooperation,* 1973 ZSR, Part II, p. 503 n. 10; *see also* J. DROLSHAMMER, MARKTMÄCHTIGE UNTERNEHMEN IM KARTELLGESETZ (Series HANDELS- UND WIRTSCHAFTSRECHT, Vol. 2) p. 20 *et seq.* (Diessenhofen, 1975).

[37] *Cf.* Schluep, *supra* note 36, at p. 504 *et seq.*

against hindering third parties in competition.[38] This rule will be superseded however, if the hindrance has results which are in the public interest.[39] From the point of view of the concentration, this means that no party (subject to Art. 5 of the Cartel Act) can be compelled to join a concentration.[40]

A further consequence of falling within the Act is that the quasi-cartel organization in question is subject to the supervision of the Cartel Commission. The Cartel Commission may, of its own motion, order general inquiries[41] concerning such cases or, at the instance of the Swiss Federal Economic Department, undertake so-called "special inquiries".[42] The object of such inquiries is to establish whether any effects detrimental to the national economic or social interests are observable.

Under the law affecting concentrations, this means that the Cartel Commission will investigate whether the concentration arising from a quasi-cartel organization or resulting in a quasi-cartel organization must, on balance, be rated positively or negatively.[43] If, in the Cartel Commission's opinion, the overall economic and social effect is negative, the Commission may, even under prevailing laws, formulate the necessary disengagement recommendations,[44] and the Federal Economic Department may apply to the Swiss Federal Court to convert them into an enforceable judgment.[45]

[38] *Cf.* E. Homburger, *Kartellgesetz und Unternehmenszusammenschlüsse,* 1972 SJZ 152; Schluep, *supra* note 36, at p. 518.

[39] *Cf.* Schluep, *supra* note 36, at p. 520; *id., Von der Kontrahierungspflicht, supra* note 13, at p. 216 *et seq.;* KARTELL UND WETTBEWERB IN DER SCHWEIZ, *supra* note 7, at p. 170; Micheli, *supra* note 19, at p. 127 *et seq.,* disagrees and holds that a similar organization (in terms of Art. 3 of the Cartel Act) is not required to furnish proof that its actions promote the public interest. *See also* BGE 91 II, 25 *et seq.,* for justification on grounds of rationalization.

[40] *Cf.* Schluep, *supra* note 36, at p. 519; L. Schürmann and H. Sieber, *Die Konzentration als Problem der schweizerischen Wettbewerbspolitik,* 1972 WuR 85; dissenting, Homburger, *supra* note 38, at p. 152, who denies that the consolidation act as such can be an unlawful measure in terms of Art. 4 of the Cartel Act.

[41] *Cf.* Art. 18 of the Cartel Act; for a definition of the general inquiry, *see* H. GUNZ, DAS ÖFFENTLICHRECHTLICHE INSTRUMENTARIUM DES KARTELLGESETZES, p. 31 (Winterthur, 1969); and SCHÜRMANN, *supra* note 14, at p. 150.

[42] *Cf.* Arts. 20 and 21 of the Cartel Act; for a definition of the special inquiry, *see* B. Schmidhauser, *Parteien und Zeugen in der Sonderuntersuchung gemäß Kartellgesetz,* 1968 WuR 103; GUNZ, *supra* note 41, at p. 62; W. Kuster, *Zur Frage der Parteieigenschaft im Zusammenhang mit den kartellrechtlichen Untersuchungsverfahren,* 1970 WuR 249; and BOTSCHAFT DES BUNDESRATES . . . VOM 18. SEPTEMBER 1961, *supra* note 6, at p. 604.

[43] *Cf.* Schluep, *supra* note 36, at p. 548 *et seq.;* Schürman and Sieber *supra* note 40, at p. 87.

[44] *Cf.* Art. 20.2. second sentence; commentators are of two minds about whether recommendations for decartelization are permissible: *See contra,* Giger, *supra* note 6, at p. 175; GUNZ, *supra* note 41, at p. 45; and BOTSCHAFT DES BUNDESRATES, *supra* note 6, at p. 605. *See pro,* L. Schürmann, *Die Durchführung des Kartellgesetzes,* 1969 WuR 86.

[45] *Cf.* Art. 22 of the Cartel Act, and Schluep, *Allgemeines Wirtschaftsrecht, supra* note 12, at p. 110. *See* for the procedure in general, F. GYGI, VERWALTUNGSRECHTSPFLEGE UND

Under the prevailing law, however, it is not possible to bring a market concentration under control already in the initial stage if no market-powerful business organization is involved in the concentration process. Thus, if two organizations which are not market-powerful decide to merge, the merger will not be subject to supervision by the Cartel Commission, unless, that is, the merger has resulted in the creation of a market-powerful organization.[46] Concentrations, even when they have already taken effect, are not subject to the Act and, accordingly, to the Commission's supervision unless they result in producing a market-powerful organization.

Where link-ups are effected in secret, the Cartel Commission, under the prevailing law, has no information facilities sufficient for it to establish whether the concentration process or the resulting concentration is subject to the Act.

4. Proposals for the Revision of the Cartel Act for More Effective Supervision

a) Parliamentary Motions

Several members of the Swiss Parliament have moved for a revision of the 1962 Cartel Act.[47] The reason given has been throughout that a better supervision of concentration is necessary.[48] This revision of the Cartel Act is at present in progress under the direction of the author (the President of the Cartel Commission).

b) Scope for Improving the Supervision of Concentrations

In the author's opinion, link-ups should in future be reported to the Cartel Commission.[49] This duty to report would give the Cartel Commission a clearer insight into concentration processes. This, however, would not alter Switzerland's basic position regarding the assessment of the concentration problem. So the situation will remain that concentrations only come within the Act insofar as they involve or result in market-powerful organizations.

Even so, it will have to be considered whether provision should not be made, at least under the civil law, for generally prohibiting quasi-cartel organizations

VERWALTUNGSVERFAHREN IM BUND, p. 20 *et seq.* (Bern, 2d. ed., 1974). In spite of the difference in the wording (*cf.* Arts. 20 and 22.1 of the Cartel Act), the subjects for investigation and assessment of the special inquiry and the administrative action are identical, *cf.* Schluep, *Allgemeines Wirtschaftsrecht, supra* note 12, at p. 115 *et seq.;* and *id., Über den Begriff der Nachfragemacht,* in FESTGABE FÜR H DESCHENAUX, p. 589 (Freiburg, 1977); MERZ, DAS SCHWEIZERISCHE KARTELLGESETZ, *supra* note 13, at p. 116; Syz, *supra* note 13, at p. 83 *et seq.*

[46] *Cf.* Schluep, *supra* note 36, at p. 501 *et seq.*

[47] *Cf.* Schluep, *Grundzüge des Entwurfs, supra* note 7, at p. 82.

[48] *Cf. Begleitbericht zum Entwurf betreffend die Revision des Kartellgesetzes (November, 1978),* 1979 WuR 101; L. Schürmann, *Materialien zu einer Revision des Kartellgesetzes,* 1972 WuR 302 *et seq.*

[49] *Cf.* Schluep, *Grundzüge des Entwurfs, supra* note 7, at p. 98; Art. 35.1 E (*see* for the text of the bill, 1979 WuR 83 *et seq.*). On the conformity with the Constitution of such a duty to report link-ups, *see* Schluep, *Grundzüge des Entwurfs, supra* note 7, at p. 73 *et seq.;* and *Begleitbericht, supra* note 48, at p. 163.

(and thus, indirectly, also the market-powerful concentrations) from abusing their market power, notably to the detriment of the consumer.[50] Such a tighter civil-law check could be combined with an actionable right of the consumer associations, which, in view of the pattern of interests involved, would keep the Cartel Commission at the gallop even when it would rather proceed at the trot. Whether these suggestions can be implemented will be decided within the forthcoming months.

B. Draft Revision of the Act on Cartels

The draft constitutes a reorientation which must not be overlooked in terms of its practical significance. It is important in that it emphasizes that the conservation of a functional level of competition is the main purpose of the Cartel Act in both the private-law and, more particularly, the administrative-law sections.[51] This reflects the competition policy realization that operational competition is as a rule both an economically and a socially useful instrument.[52]

1. The Private Law Portion of the Draft

A number of innovations are to be mentioned which do not touch on the fundamentals but are designed to operate in the direction of the actualization of the competition concept.

The present Act is applicable to "cartels and similar organizations" (Art. 1). Conversely, it is not applicable to "agreements, decisions and measures relating solely to labour relations" (Art. 1). This is to remain unchanged,[53] although a minority would like to subject the labour market to the scope of the Act.[54] Even if the applicability of the Act is to remain limited to cartels and cartel-type organizations, it should be noted that the connotation of the two terms "cartel" and "similar organization" is broadened by the draft. In the first place, the draft

---

[50] Cf. Art. 6.3 E, *Begleitbericht, supra* note 48, at p. 126 *et seq.;* and Schluep, *Grundzüge des Entwurfs, supra* note 7, at p. 90 *et seq.*

[51] Cf. Schluep, *Grundzüge des Entwurfs, supra* note 7, at pp. 84 and 101 *et seq.*

[52] Cf. Schluep, *supra* note 4, at p. 124 *et seq.;* E. Hoppmann, *Wettbewerb als Norm der Wettbewerbspolitik,* XVIII ORDO 79 *et seq.* (1967); *id., Workable Competition,* 1966 ZBJV 252 *et seq.; id.* FUSIONSKONTROLLE, p. 18 *et seq.* (Tübingen, 1972); *id., Problem einer praktikablen Definition des Wettbewerbs,* in GRUNDLAGEN DER WETTBEWERBSPOLITIK, SCHRIFTEN DES VEREINS FÜR SOCIALPOLITIK, NF 48, p. 13 (Berlin, 1968); O. SCHLECHT, WETTBEWERB ALS STÄNDIGE AUFGABE, p. 10 *et seq.* (Tübingen, 1975); F.-U. WILLEKE, GRUNDSÄTZE WETTBEWERBSPOLITISCHER KONZEPTIONEN, p. 37 *et seq.* (Tübingen, 1973).

[53] Cf. Art. 1.2 E; *Begleitbericht, supra* note 48, at p. 104; Schluep, *Grundzüge des Entwurfs, supra* note 7, at p. 69.

[54] Cf. *Begleitbericht, supra* note 48, at p. 122. A subjection of the labour market, however, would not be covered by the Constitution (*see,* W. R. Schluep, *Überbordungsverfahren von Arbeitskonflikten in unserer Zeit,* in ZUM WIRTSCHAFTSRECHT, p. 177 *et seq.* (Bern, 1978); *id., Grundzüge des Entwurfs, supra* note 7, at pp. 70 and 88; *see also* ERGÄNZUNGSBOTSCHAFT DES BUNDESRATES, *supra* note 4, at p. 921 *et seq.;* and BOTSCHAFT DES BUNDESRATES, *supra* note 6, at p. 571.

provides that not only the fixing of second-hand prices (either collectively or by oligopolies), but also corresponding vertical recommendations to limit competition, are to be considered as tantamount to cartels,[55] which are defined as horizontal restraints of competition. This, however, signifies only that such restraints of competition are subject to the Act, not that they are directly banned. In addition, vertical exclusivity and sales obligations, if they substantially influence the market, are newly created equal in status to the powerful organizations.[56] This is designed to cover cases where parties to a contract who hold no position of power in the market operate in the domain of branded articles (e. g. TV sets) on the strength of a sheaf of similarly worded vertical contracts. The manufacturer of a branded TV set who makes similar contracts with all his customers is a case in point. This equal status is justified since exclusivity and sales obligations are frequently substitutes for vertical integration.[57]

Public ventures are also newly expressly subjected to the Cartel Act, if they operate as cartels or similar organizations.[58] Those cases are excluded in which public ventures are to be withdrawn from competition in view of their performing public services (e. g. agricultural market organizations).[59]

Besides this clearer definition of the Act's scope, the draft is designed to facilitate for the court (and the Cartel Commission) the diagnosis of the market power demanded for the inclusion of cartel-type organizations.[60] What is important above all is that not only the share in the market but also the financial power and the dependence of organizations on the opposite side of the market be considered.[61] This will make it easy to cover the cases of the so-called demand power.[62] The draft not only forbids cartels and similar organizations to

---

[55] *Cf.* Art. 3.2 E; *Begleitbericht, supra* note 48, at p. 125.

[56] *Cf.* Art. 5. E; *Begleitbericht, supra* note 48, at p. 125 *et seq.*; Schluep, *Grundzüge des Entwurfs, supra* note 7, at p. 90; *cf. also* 1978 VSKk 197.

[57] *Cf.* Schluep, *Grundzüge des Entwurfs, supra* note 7, at p. 90.

[58] *Cf.* Art. 1.1 E; *Begleitbericht, supra* note 48, at p. 123 *et seq.*; *cf. also* BOTSCHAFT DES BUNDESRATES, *supra* note 6, at p. 569 *et seq.* On the conformity with the Constitution of the subjection of public ventures, *see* Schluep, *Grundzüge des Entwurfs, supra* note 7, at p. 71 *et seq.*; *Begleitbericht, supra* note 48, at p. 161 *et seq.*

[59] *Cf.* Schluep, *Grundzüge des Entwurfs, supra* note 7, at p. 72 *et seq.*; *Begleitbericht, supra* note 48, at p. 123 *et seq.*; *cf. also* Art. 50.2.b E.

[60] *Cf.* Art. 4.2.E; Schluep, *Grundzüge des Entwurfs, supra* note 7, at p. 89. For the difficulties connected with the task of ascertaining market influence, *see* Schluep, *supra* note 45, at p. 576 *et seq.*; for the intensitiy of market influence of similar organizations that is required under prevailing laws, *see* Sattler, *supra* note 13, at p. 73 *et seq.*; MERZ, DAS SCHWEIZERISCHE KARTELLGESETZ, *supra* note 13, at p. 31 *et seq.*; Schluep, *Die Rule of Reason, supra* note 7, at p. 66 *et seq.*; KUMMER, *supra* note 34, at p. 16 *et seq.*; BOTSCHAFT DES BUNDESRATES, *supra* note 6, at p. 574; *cf. also*, DROLSHAMMER, *supra* note 36, at p. 127; Homburger, *supra* note 7, at p. 30.

[61] *Cf.* Art. 4.2 E; Schluep, *Grundzüge des Entwurfs, supra* note 7, at p. 89.

[62] *Cf.* Schluep, *Grundzüge des Entwurfs, supra* note 7, at p. 89; on demand power in general, *see* Schluep, *supra* note 45, p. 563 *et seq.* O. Angehrn, *Nachfragemacht von Handelsunternehmungen als Problem der Wettbewerbsgestaltung,* 1973 WuR 227 *et*

discriminate against outsiders and newcomers, but also to exploit them.[63] Legal action will, therefore, in the future also be taken against equal (i. e. non-discriminatory) mistreatment of others, as exemplified by tying contracts.[64]

The most important innovation of the bill is the restriction placed on the justifications previously put forward (contrary to the original competition philosophy) by cartels and similar organizations to justify their attacks upon outsiders and newcomers.[65] In the future, no such justification will be possible as soon as the cartel or similar organization has ousted a third party from the market so as to realize legitimate private interests.[66] Rather, the exclusion of third parties from competition will in the future be possible only if it can be shown that the cartelist or oligopolistic market organizations will serve the general interest better than a system of outsiders and newcomers protected by the law. According to the bill, the cartelist or oligopolistic organization can thus supplant freedom of competition only by way of exception and if it proves to be superior in the light of the general interest criteria.[67]

It may in conclusion be said that the draft is intended to get the private-law portion back into line with the Federal Government's original intention for the present Act,[68] and with the position which the Supreme Court actually had adopted at the outset in interpreting the Act.[69]

2. The Administrative Law Portion of the Draft

The first innovation resides in the fact that the draft calls for a specification of the criteria against which the economic or social harmfulness of cartels or similar organizations will in the future be considered.[70] Art. 30.2 of the draft in the version approved by the majority of the Commission contemplates the following rule for the diagnosis of harmfulness: "Effects are economically or socially harmful if competition is excluded or substantially hampered, reduced or falsified". This constitutes the legal establishment of the original concept behind the competition philosophy, namely, that – at least in normal cases – cartels and similar organizations are harmful if they completely eradicate competition in a

---

seq.; G.-R. Marx, Marketing and Marktmacht (Diss., Zürich, 1976); cf. also, 1976 VSKk 53 et seq.

[63] Cf. Art. 6.3 E; Begleitbericht, supra note 48, at p. 126 et seq.; for the differentiation between discriminating and exploiting abuse of market power, see J. Freiin von Friesen, Probleme der Nachfragemacht und Möglichkeiten einer effektiven Kontrolle, SUPPLE-MENT No. 6/1978, 1978 DER BETRIEB 6.

[64] Cf. Schluep, Grundzüge des Entwurfs, supra note 7, at p. 90 et seq.

[65] Cf. Art. 7.1 E; Schluep, Grundzüge des Entwurfs, supra note 7, at p. 91 et seq.; Begleitbericht, supra note 48, at p. 128 et seq.

[66] Cf. supra notes 16 and 26.

[67] Cf. Art. 7.1.E; Begleitbericht, supra note 48, at p. 129 et seq.; Schluep, Grundzüge des Entwurfs, supra note 7, at p. 91 et seq.

[68] Cf. BOTSCHAFT DES BUNDESRATES, supra note 6, at p. 582; and supra note 23.

[69] Cf. BGE 94 II 339 and supra note 16.

[70] Cf. Schluep, Grundzüge des Entwurfs, supra note 7, at p. 96 et seq.; Begleitbericht, supra note 48, at p. 132 et seq.

given market.[71] It is true that the darft does not go beyond stating that elimination of competition in a given market is *as a rule* harmful. It is not overlooked that cartels and similar organizations may *by way of exception* be harmless, under the criteria of general interest, even if they admit of no operational competition whatsoever.

The Commission of Experts thus proves that it proposes to legislate with an eye to reality and not dogmatically. Indeed, one cannot close one's eyes to the fact that, under certain cirumstances, cartelist and oligopolistic organizations may be harmless even when totally eliminating competition. Crises and war situations are cases in point, as are also the trends towards cut-throat competition noticed more and more frequently of late.[72]

This basic competition situation is flanked by two new measures: The obligation to disclose combines of firms;[73] and the obligation to announce price increases which is imposed on cartels and similar organizations.[74]

The obligation to disclose combines of firms is designed to enable the Cartel Commission to investigate in good time whether adequate competition in the market involved is ensured despite such combine. In this context, and with an eye to international competitiveness, sight must not be lost of the fact that even the elimination of competition at home may be necessary to strengthen competitiveness abroad. This is a good example of how, according to the draft, the complete elimination of competition must be tolerated if it is in the general interest. The second supporting measure is that cartels or similar organizations must announce to the Cartel Commission price increases. This provision means in practice that the Cartel Commission can subject price increases to a closer scrutiny (as in the event of price maintenance when costs drop) if adequate competition is lacking. If the price increases (or maintenance) prove to be improper, the Cartel Commission may enact price orders within 30 days.[75] It goes without saying that this provision is more than problematical because nobody, not even the Cartel Commission, is in a position to adduce the scientific proof regarding the circumstances under which a price is adequate or not in the absence of competition.

In so far as legal form and procedure is concerned, according to the version of the draft adopted by the majority, of the Commission of Experts, the Cartel Commission is to be authorized in the future not only to recommend[76] but also

---

[71] *Cf.* Schluep, *Grundzüge des Entwurfs, supra* note 7, at p. 96 *et seq.*

[72] *Cf.* Art. 30.3 E; *Begleitbericht, supra* note 48, at pp. 132 *et seq.* and 135; Schluep, *Grundzüge des Entwurfs, supra* note 7, at p. 97.

[73] *Cf.* Art. 35.1 E; *Begleitbericht, supra* note 48, at p. 135 *et seq.*; Schluep, *Grundzüge des Entwurfs, supra* note 7, at p. 98.

[74] *Cf.* Art. 38.1; *Begleitbericht, supra* note 48, at p. 139 *et seq.*; Schluep, *Grundzüge des Entwurfs, supra* note 7, at p. 98 *et seq.*

[75] *Cf.* Art. 42.2 E; *Begleitbericht, supra* note 48, at p. 143.

[76] *Cf.* Arts. 32 E and 39.3 E; on recommendations under present legislation, *see* Arts. 20.2 of the Cartel Act; SCHÜRMANN, *supra* note 14, at p. 159 *et seq.*; *id., supra* note 44, at p. 86; GUNZ, *supra* note 41, at p. 42 *et seq.*; Syz, *supra* note 13, at p. 120 *et seq.*

to decree[77] measures against harmful effects of cartels and similar organizations
— naturally with provision for subsequent examination by the Supreme Court.[78]
Under present legislation this innovation was apparently not necessary because
all the Commission's recommendations have in fact so far been followed.[79]
However, since the draft is designed actually to enhance the protection of a
minimal level of competition, it must be expected that, if the draft is passed,
cartels and similar organizations will no longer smoothly accept recommendations. This is why the Commision's right to issue decrees is justified.

3. The Subordinate Items of the Draft Revision

The draft is also directed at the establishment of a procedure for the discharge of
Switzerland's international cartel obligations.[80] Art. 15 of the European Free
Trade Association Treaty[81] and Art. 23 of the Agreement with the European
Communities[82] on a European Free Trade Area naturally come to the fore.
However, the draft does not contemplate anything of a revolutionary nature, and
for the following reasons: On the one hand, it is clear that the international
competition rules are not self-executing;[83] and in the second place, it is expressly

---

[77] Cf. Art. 42 E; Begleitbericht, supra note 48, at p. 143 et seq.

[78] Cf. Art. 43.1 E.

[79] Cf., for example, 1968 VSKk 5 and 1973 VSKk 123. Herewith the hopes that were
entertained when the Act was passed (cf. BOTSCHAFT DES BUNDESRATES, supra note 6, at p.
605; FISCHER, supra note 7, at p. 33; Deschenaux, L'esprit, supra note 7, at p. 222; Merz,
supra note 6, p. 20), have been completely fulfilled.

[80] Cf. Arts. 48 and 49 E.

[81] Cf. SR 0.632.31.

[82] Cf. SR 0.632.401.

[83] Cf., for the EFTA rules of competition, WALTERMANN, supra note 13, at p. 144 et seq.;
A. SZOKOLÓCZY-SYLLABA, EFTA: RESTRICTIVE BUSINESS PRACTICES, SCHWEIZERISCHE BEI-
TRÄGE ZUM EUROPARECHT, Vol. 13, p. 199 et seq. (Bern, 1973); R. Mori, Rechtsetzung
und Vollzug in der Europäischen Freihandelsassoziation EFTA, p. 129 et seq. (Diss.,
Bern, 1965). As regards Art. 23 of the Free Trade Agreement with the EC, opinions are
divided. Self-execution in terms of administrative law is approved by most commenta-
tors, cf. Schluep, supra note 36, at p. 556 et seq.; S. Arioli, Die Wettbewerbsregeln des
Freihandelsabkommens, in WETTBEWERB UND KARTELLRECHT IM FREIHANDELSABKOMMEN
SCHWEIZ-EWG, p. 21 et seq. (Zürich, 1974); Schürmann, supra note 31, at p. 106; R.
KÜCHLER, LIZENZVERTRÄGE IM EWG-RECHT, SCHWEIZERISCHE BEITRÄGE ZUM EUROPA-
RECHT, Vol. 19, p. 204 et seq. (Bern, 1976); M. Waelbroeck, L'effet direct de l'accord
relatif aux échanges commerciaux, du 22 juillet 1972, entre la Communauté économique
européenne et la Conféderation Suisse, 1973 SCHWEIZERISCHES JAHRBUCH FÜR INTERNATIO-
NALES RECHT 127 et seq. In favour of self-execution, as regards private law, are
Waelbroeck, loc. cit., p. 127 et seq.; Küchler, loc. cit., p. 207 et seq.; R. Zäch,
Zivilrechtliche Folgen von Verstößen gegen Art. 85 EWGV, 1974 SJZ 264; contra, see
K. Staub, Schadenersatzansprüche aufgrund von Art. 85 EWGV, 1975 SJZ 42 et seq.;
E. Homburger, Zur Tragweite von Art. 23 des Freihandelsabkommens zwischen der
Schweiz und den Europäischen Gemeinschaften, 1975 SJZ 42; A. Koller, Zur Frage der
unmittelbaren Anwendbarkeit von Art. 23 des Freihandelsabkommens Schweiz-EWG,
in FESTGABE FÜR H. DESCHENAUX, p. 600 et seq. (Freiburg, 1977); M. Steiner, Exportkar-
telle und das Freihandelsabkommen Schweiz-EWG, p. 85 et seq. (Diss., Zürich, 1977);

ordered that the Cartel Commission may become active in international affairs only following instructions from the Federal Economic Department.[84]

The second item may be of particular interest to foreigners. The present Act states in Art. 19 that the Government is obliged to consult the Cartel Commission prior to enacting laws that restrain freedom of competition. The Commission may also submit recommendations relating to competition policy to the Government on its own initiative (Art. 19.1).[85] This provision of the present Act balances many of its weaknesses, for it takes account of the fact that in operation competition is much too frequently prejudiced not so much by cartels and similar organizations, as by the disproportionate Government regulation of the regulated sectors. The draft goes still further and authorizes the Cartel Commission *currently* to monitor the Government's competition policy and to submit recommendations to the Government in that context.[86] This peculiarity of the Swiss Cartel Act adequately takes into account the fact that competition must be protected not only against private conspiracies but also against Government slips.[87]

4. Concluding Remarks

As one has gathered from the foregoing, the Swiss competition policy starts from the assumption that a minimum of operational competition is worthy of legal protection owing to the favourable effects it entails for the economy and society. At the same time it recognizes expressly what the Constitution does tacitly: that cartels and similar organizations are not as such harmful. Present legislation as well as court and Cartel Commission practice, however, have so watered down this basic insight in favour of cartels and similar organizations and to the detriment of an operational competition level that a return to the genuinely Swiss competition philosophy became necessary. This (and nothing else) is the object of the draft. In particular, it is out of the question that the draft aims at banning cartels or similar organizations.

Schluep, *supra* note 36, at p. 557; *cf. also* the judgments cited in Schluep, *Grundzüge des Entwurfs, supra* note 7, at p. 100, note 81.

[84] *Cf.* Arts. 48 and 49.2 E; Schluep, *Grundzüge des Entwurfs, supra* note 7, at p. 100.
[85] *Cf.* SCHÜRMANN, *supra* note 14, at p. 153 *et seq.*
[86] *Cf.* Art. 25 E; Schluep, *Grundzüge des Entwurfs, supra* note 7, at p. 95.
[87] Most of the commentaries recognize that free competition can be restricted or distorted through governmental measures as well as through private practices, *cf.* GUNZ, *supra* note 41, at p. 68 *et seq.;* H. Sieber, *Die bisherige Tätigkeit der Schweizerischen Kartellkommission – eine kritische Bestandsaufnahme*, in WETTBEWERBSPOLITIK IN DER SCHWEIZ, FESTGABE ZUM 80. GEBURTSTAG VON FRITZ MARBACH, p. 22 (Bern and Stuttgart, 1972); *id., Aktuelle Probleme, supra* note 31, p. 20; B. Schmidhauser, *Über das Verhältnis zwischen schweizerischem Landwirtschaftsrecht und Kartellrecht,* 1976 BLÄTTER FÜR AGRARRECHT 39; Merz, *Das schweizerische Kartellgesetz, supra* note 13, at p. 117; SCHÜRMANN, *supra* note 14, at p. 153 *et seq.; id., supra* note 31, at p. 88; BOTSCHAFT DES BUNDESRATES, *supra* note 6, at p. 603.

III. The Practice of the Cartel Commission in Concentration Matters Under Prevailing Law

A. The Cartel Act and Industrial Concentration

1. Review

Although the Cartel Act does not provide for intervention against industrial concentrations and, in particular, does not contain any express provisions on mergers, such concentrations do influence the application of the Act, notably with respect to the exceptions from the rule against interference with outside competition,[88] and with respect to the appraisal of the harmful effects of cartels and similar organizations.[89] The Cartel Commission, therefore, carefully observes concentration developments within the scope of its possibilites, and for this purpose has made a number of general inquiries under Art. 18 of the Cartel Act.[90] In particular, it monitors those lines of industry in which concentration processes may result in market-powerful organizations (quasi-cartel organizations as defined by Art. 3 of the Act). It should be remembered, however, that the control or material influencing of a market alone is not sufficient under prevailing law to justify intervention. On this point, the Cartel Commission, conducting a preliminary inquiry, has stated the following:

> The Act does not regard economic size *per se* as undesirable. Thus, in the Government's Message on the Cartel Act it is declared that industrial power as such is permissible, for which reason intervention must be confined to the abuse of such power.
>
> Once an organization succeeds in controlling or materially influencing the market for specific commodities or services, it becomes subject to the Cartel Act (Art. 3 of the Act). This becoming subject, however, does not entail any legal consequences under the Act. For such consequences to arise, there must be an interference with outside competition under private law as defined by Article 4 of the Act which cannot be justified under Article 5 of the Act, or, from the angle of public law, the cartel of similar organization must involve economically or socially harmful effects (Art. 20 of the Act). Yet even under Article 20 of the Act, size as such cannot be considered detrimental, unless the cartel of similar organization adopts arrangements restricting competition.[91]

In effect, the foregoing implies that the Cartel Act in force does not affect internal growth and link-ups resulting from the free intentions of the parties

---

[88] *Cf.* Art. 5.2 c of the Cartel Act (exemption on grounds of structural policy); structural policy as a bulwark against excessive concentration is also approved by SCHÜRMANN, *supra* note 14, at p. 91 *et seq.;* BOTSCHAFT DES BUNDESRATES, *supra* note 6, at p. 586; and the Cartel Commission in 1971 VSKk 44 *et seq.; see also* 1972 VSKk 69. In BGE 91 II 25 *et seq.,* the Federal Supreme Court found that one of the advantages in terms of structural policy of the cigarette cartel's marketing arrangements was the prevention of oligopolistic and monopolistic market structures.

[89] *Cf.* Schürmann and Sieber, *supra* note 40, at p. 87; *see also* Sieber, *Über die Kriterien,* *supra* note 31, at p. 61 *et seq.;* Syz, *supra* note 13, at p. 49; 1974 VSKk 413 *et seq.* and 415 *et seq.*

[90] *Cf.* 1974 VSKk 219 *et seq.;* 1974 VSKk 251 *et seq.;* 1974 VSKk 361 *et seq.;* 1975 VSKk 153 *et seq.;* 1979 VSKk 273 *et seq.*

[91] *Cf.* 1975 VSKk 5.

concerned, and that such processes are beyond the Cartel Commission's powers of intervention. The situation is different where a merger is brought about by a similar organization (as defined in Art. 3 of the Act) abusing its power for the purpose.[92] In such a case, recourse could be had to the civil-law court under Arts. 4 and 5 of the Act. Then the Cartel Commission, making a special inquiry (Arts. 20/21 of the Act), could recommend an injunction against the link-up or a disengagement,[93] if the process were found to be detrimental to the national economic or social interests.

2. On the Individual Provisions of the Act

a) The Private Law Provisions (Arts. 4/5 of the Act)

The degree of cartelization and competition policy have a strong influence on the structural development of the country. In this light, it should be remembered that the Legislator in formulating the Constitutional article (Art. 31 [bis] .3.d of the Constitution), has rejected the principle of an absolute ban on cartels and has instead advocated suppression of abuse,[94] on the consideration that this policy is more likely to encourage the existence of a large number of industrial units and the continuance of small and medium-size business organizations. This comes through clearly in the Act, which makes an exception to the rule against restriction of competition where it is a case of "promoting a structure desirable in the general interest" (Art. 5.2.c of the Act),[95] and it also comes through by implication in the interpretation of the other exceptions in Art. 5.2 of the Act. Thus, the Federal Court, in the *Denner* case[96], held that the preservation of decentralized distribution structures was in the general public interest and could justify a boycott for the purpose of enforcing second-level price ties.

b) The General Inquiry (Art. 18.1 of the Act)[97]

Competition policy does not remain unaffected by the more or less profound structural changes which the concentration trend in industry may cause.[98] The resultant distortion of the competition pattern and the prospect fo so-called

---

[92] *Cf.* Schluep, *supra* note 36, at p. 501 *et seq.;* and esp. at p. 503, note 10; and *supra* note 36.

[93] *Cf. supra* note 44.

[94] *Cf.* the references given in note 7 *supra.* For advantages put forward in favour of the principle of abuse prevention, *see also* H.-W. Roetzel, Das Verbots- und Mißbrauchs-prinzip für Kartelle in der Praxis der Behörden — ein Vergleich zwischen der Bundesrepublik Deutschland und Österreich, p. 150 *et seq.* (Diss., Braunschweig, 1968); MATHYS, *supra* note 20, at p. 12 *et seq.;* Schürmann, *supra* note 7, at pp. 39 and 42; KARTELL UND WETTBEWERB IN DER SCHWEIZ, *supra* note 7, at p. 145 *et seq.*

[95] On the legislative purpose of Art. 5.2.c of the Cartel Act, *see* SCHÜRMANN, *supra* note 14, at p. 91; Micheli, *supra* note 19, at p. 85 *et seq.;* FISCHER, *supra* note 7, at p. 20 *et seq.;* BOTSCHAFT DES BUNDESRATES, *supra* note 6, at p. 586; as well as the Cartel Commission in 1971 VSKk 44 *et seq.; see also supra* note 88.

[96] *Cf.* BGE 98 II 365.

[97] *See generally* on the general inquiry, *supra* note 41.

[98] *Cf.* Schluep, *supra* note 36, at p. 224 *et seq.*

"similar" organizations arising in certain industries could have economically or socially harmful effects.[99] To counter such a development and furnish political and industrial circles with the necessary data for examining the expediency of legislative intervention, it is imperative to know and follow up the development of concentration.

For this purpose, the Legislator, in Art. 18.1, has authorized the Cartel Commission to carry out "inquiries into the situation, evolution and effects of cartels and similar organizations in Switzerland".[100] Under this authorization, the Cartel Commission has so far carried out six concentration inquiries, which will be briefly reviewed in some detail.

c) The Special Inquiries (Art. 20/21 of the Act)

The Swiss Federal Economic Department may instruct the Cartel Commission to make a special inquiry[101] to establish whether certain cartels or similar organizations have economically or socially harmful effects.[102] In concentration matters, the said Department has so far not resorted to this possibility, and so a few theoretical considerations on the economically or socially harmful effects of concentration will have to suffice.

Increasing concentration may involve a variety of *socially harmful effects*.[103] Thus, the change of the social structures may mean a drifting-away from the democratic system based on pluralism. As the number of independent business organizations declines, increasing numbers of citizens become economically dependent on a few employers with whom personal contacts become rarer and must increasingly take the form of representation (company and personnel committees, etc).[104]

---

[99] *Cf.*, on the effects of industrial concentration, Schluep, *supra* note 36, at p. 219 *et seq.*; *see also* E. KANTZENBACH, DIE FUNKTIONSFÄHIGKEIT DES WETTBEWERBS, p. 139 *et seq.* (Göttingen, 1966); *id.*, *Konzentration als Problem der Konkurrenzwirtschaft*, in DIE KONZENTRATION IN DER WIRTSCHAFT, Vol. I, p. 159 *et seq.* (2d ed., Berlin, 1971). For the ambivalent effects on competition *see* H. K. Schneider, *Beeinflussung der Konzentration als Ziel und Mittel der Wirtschaftspolitik*, in DIE KONZENTRATION IN DER WIRTSCHAFT, Vol I, p. 439 *et seq.*, (2d ed., Berlin, 1971).

[100] General inquiries are designed to supply the cartel authorities with information (*cf.* GUNZ, *supra* note 41, at p. 7 *et seq.*; Syz, *supra* note 13 at p. 125; Sieber, *Die bisherige Tätigkeit, supra* note 87, at p. 21; SCHÜRMANN, *supra* note 14, at p. 150). Furthermore, as a rule, the findings of inquiries are published (*cf.* Art. 18.1 of the Cartel Act).

[101] *Cf. supra* note 42.

[102] *Cf.*, for the criteria for appraisal of the effects of cartels and similar organizations, Sieber, *Über die Kriterien, supra* note 31, at p. 53 *et seq.*; *id.*, *Aktuelle Probleme, supra* note 31, at p. 25 *et seq.*; *cf. also* W. Krelle, *Volkswirtschaftliche Kriterien zur Beurteilung von Kartellen*, 1968 SZVS 241 *et seq.* Apart from economic factors, extra-economic considerations must also be taken into account (cf. Deschenaux, *La notion, supra* note 7, at p. 89; Syz, *supra* note 13, at p. 56; Fröhlicher, *supra* note 30, at p. 256; Krelle, *loc. cit.*, p. 243 *et seq.*; Homburger, *supra* note 7, at p. 79 *et seq.*; *cf. also supra* note 31.

[103] *Cf.* Schluep, *supra* note 36, at p. 224 *et seq.*

[104] *Cf.* W. A. Jöhr, *Das Problem der Wirtschaftsordnung*, in INDIVIDUUM UND GEMEIN-

Along with this we find a de facto institutionalization of the big companies. Once a company exceeds a certain magnitude, its dissolution becomes less and less acceptable on account of its importance for the national or regional economy and the large number of people employed. In extreme cases, the Government may even be compelled to intervene for the purpose of preventing bankruptcy and rescuing jobs.[105]

In the private sphere, the consequences of concentration differ from one sector to another. Excessive concentration in the press or in book distribution may result in political and cultural impoverishment, while concentration in food distribution may be detrimental to the elderly, to persons without a car and to the handicapped, because of the difficulties which long distances to the supply centres present to them. Such effects of concentration are carefully analysed in the inquiries into specific industries.

Finally, there is the problem of regional equilibrium. But an examination of this aspect of concentration would go beyond the scope of the Cartel Commission's inquiries.

While it is generally accepted that concentration may have socially harmful effects, these are often contrasted with the *general economic advantages* which warrant certain sacrifices in other spheres. In any case a careful weighing of both advantages and drawbacks is imperative. The advantages of concentration cannot be doubted. Up to a certain degree, concentration means the elimination of inefficient companies or plants and enables efficient organizations to increase their market share without necessarily reducing competition, which on oligopolistic markets may be very brisk indeed.[106] The free-market system naturally implies that business organizations seek to attain a size permitting them to tender their products at favourable prices, while making a profit sufficient to ensure the investments necessary for long-term market supply.

SCHAFT, FESTSCHRIFT ZUR FÜNFZIGJAHRFEIER DER HANDELS-HOCHSCHULE ST.GALLEN, p. 236 (St. Gallen, 1949); *cf. also* E. Salin, *Soziologische Aspekte der Konzentration*, extract from VERHANDLUNGEN AUF DER TAGUNG IN BAD KISSINGEN VOM 18. BIS ZUM 21. SEPTEMBER 1960, INSTITUT FÜR SOZIALWISSENSCHAFTEN DER UNIVERSITÄT BASEL, Vol. 1, p. 18 *et seq.* (Basel, 1966). On the danger of increased influence in the political area, see E. Salin, *Stichwort "Konzentration"*, in WÖRTERBUCH DER SOZIOLOGIE, p. 593 (2d ed., Stuttgart, 1969). *Cf.*, in addition, H. Arndt, *Macht, Konkurrenz und Demokratie*, in KONZENTRATION OHNE KONTROLLE, p. 40 (D. Grosser, ed., Cologne/Opladen, 1969); and E. Kogon, *Wirkungen der Konzentration auf die Demokratie*, in DIE KONZENTRATION IN DER WIRTSCHAFT, Vol. II, p. 591 *et seq.* (2d ed., Berlin, 1971).

[105] *Cf.* Schluep, *supra* note 36, at p. 228; cf. also H. Schmidt, *Die Zeche zahlt der Staat, Sozialisierung der Verluste im deutschen Ruhrkohle-Bergbau*, in SOZIALISIERUNG DER VERLUSTE, DIE SOZIALEN KOSTEN EINES PRIVATWIRTSCHAFTLICHEN SYSTEMS, p. 146 *et seq.* (Munich, 1972); H. Sieber, *Die Zerstörung der Wirtschaft durch ihre Anhänger*, 1972 WuR 186. It is obvious that concentration facilitates in this way the system change towards a socialist economy. On this *see also* J. A. SCHUMPETER, KAPITALISMUS, SOZIALISMUS UND DEMOKRATIE, p. 351 (Bern, 1946); Sieber, *loc.* cit., p. 186; and Salin, *Soziologische Aspekte der Konzentration*, *supra* note 104, at p. 4.

[106] *Cf.* KANTZENBACH, DIE FUNKTIONSFÄHIGKEIT, *supra* note 99, at p. 138 *et seq.; id., Konzentration*, *supra* note 99, at p. 159 *et seq.*, esp. p. 182.

However, it would be mistaken to believe that the objective of optimizing size justifies any concentration process, and that size alone ensures an absolute performance guarantee. The optimal size[107] differs from one case to another, notably when we consider the scope for specialization, which permits small and medium-size organizations to cater for marginal demand. On the other hand, in terms of the economy over all, it is necessary to examine whether the superiority of the mammoth companies is in some cases not due to factors which are not directly connected with the idea of efficiency in the conventional meaning.[108]

The reasons why concentration results in organizations whose size often exceeds the optimal size of the plants, must be sought in cost advantages at the top management level. These are due in particular to the centralization of certain overhead functions, such as sales promotion, research, executive training, and administration. So long as such cost-savings are the objective, centralization is justified in national economic terms, yet the question remains whether such economic advantages cannot be achieved otherwise, notably through co-operation between companies. To this may be added the further question whether it would not be appropriate generally to encourage co-operation with a view to preventing certain harmful effects of concentration in the social and political spheres.

Among the cost-savings which big companies can achieve, special importance attaches to the more favourable purchasing[109] or sales[110] conditions for the products. Such advantages are justified when they arise through savings in purchasing large quantities or when they correspond to the costs of certain services provided by the particular company. It should be noted that big companies are often vital markets for their suppliers; this situation may occasionally be used to demand exceptionally favourable terms or discounts which are not justified by corresponding return services. The distortion of the competition pattern will be further increased where manufacturers and distributors seek to make good their profit shortfalls by increasing the prices or margins with respect to small and medium-size companies.

It is often difficult to distinguish such abuses of economic power – not permitted under the Cartel Act – from acceptable commercial practice, especially as the party suffering the disadvantage hesitates, for fear of reprisals, to institute

---

[107] *Cf.* on optimum size of undertakings, Schluep, *supra* note 36, at p. 192 *et seq.* (with further references).

[108] *E. g.,* to increased freedom of action connected with increased economic power. *See*, H. Arndt, *Oekonomische Theorie der Macht*, in Die Konzentration, *supra* note 99, at p. 120 *et seq.; cf. also* Schluep, *supra* note 36, at p. 202 *et seq.;* and J.-H. von Brunn, *Zur Frage der sogenannten "geplanten Obsoleszenz"*, 1972 WuW 615 *et seq.*

[109] *Cf.* E. Heinen, *Konzentration und Kosten*, in Die Konzentration, *supra* note 99, at p. 392 *et seq.;* K. Hax, *Unternehmenswachstum und Unternehmenskonzentration in der Industrie*, 1961 Zeitschrift für handelswissenschaftliche Forschung 12 *et seq.;* J. S. Bain, Industrial Organisation, p. 177 *et seq.* (2d ed., New York/London/Sydney, 1968); Schluep, *supra* note 36, at p. 196.

[110] *Cf.* Hax, *supra* note 109, at p. 15; Heinen, *supra* note 109, at p. 399 *et seq.;* Schluep, *supra* note 36, at p. 196 *et seq.*

proceedings. Yet if we are to prevent concentration form proliferating,[111] it will be essential to keep abuses in check. The concentration of economic power arising from advanced industrial concentration, and the attendant danger of abuse, present difficult problems for the application of the statutory provisions and for the carrying-out of inquiries.[112]

B. The Concentration Inquiries of the Swiss Cartel Commission

At the beginning of the 1970's, the Cartel Commission decided to investigate systematically the concentration trends in Switzerland's industry. For this purpose, as a first phase, it planned to gain a general view of the development of concentration in the country. As a second phase, it planned to examine individual industries showing marked concentration movements; this second phase is not yet completed, but so far has covered the following fields: press, brewing industry, shoe industry, food retail trade, banking. Briefly, the inquiries showed the following results:

1. State and Development of Plant and Company Concentration in Switzerland (VSKk 1974, p. 219 et seq.)

Jointly with the Swiss Federal Statistics Bureau, the Cartel Commission used the statistical material available (national industrial censuses of 1955 and 1965; industrial statistics of 1966 and 1971) to represent the development of concentration in tabulated form. As a result, it was found that the development had not caused any fundamental structural changes in Swiss industry, although the large and medium-size companies and plants had registered a greater growth than the small units. Despite the increase in the relative quotas of the large and, notably, of the medium-sized units, the small units have not lost their supremacy. As regards the plants, the very small ones, employing 1 to 3 persons, showed the greatest decline (-5%). The concentration trend was generally more marked at the company level than at the plant level. Among the manufacturing plants, plant concentration showed no acceleration between 1966 and 1971.

2. The Inquiries into Individual Industries

a) The Press (VSKk 1974, p. 251 et seq)

In connection with the preliminary studies for the revision of Article 55 of the Swiss Constitution (freedom of the press), the Cartel Commission was instructed to bring up to date the press survey which it had made in 1969. On that occasion it found that the trends indicated in the first report had continued, in that the number of newspapers had further declined and the growth of existing press groups had persisted.

As regards the causes of this concentration, the Cartel Commission pointed to

---

[111] Cf. W. Niederer, *Volkswirtschaftliche Konsequenzen der Unternehmenskonzentration*, 1969 INDUSTRIELLE ORGANISATION 127; W. A. Jöhr, *Die Konzentration als Problem der Theorie der Wirtschaftspolitik*, in DIE KONZENTRATION, *supra* note 99, at p. 472; Schluep, *supra* note 36, at p. 209.

[112] Cf. Schluep, *supra* note 36, at p. 248 *et seq.*

the high cost of new investments and the difficulties in the printing trade (unused capacities): the limited scope for increasing subscription and advertisement prices with a view to offsetting the rising costs; and, finally, the withdrawal of advertisers' patronage from the political newspapers, and the desire of readers for more comprehensive information than formerly.

The report found that the decline in the number of newspapers had weakened the political press and resulted in the formation of several regional press monopolies. Generally, the relations between the political parties and the press had weakened. In the large papers there was a tendency towards extending the spectrum of opinion. Where papers commanded a regional press monopoly, however, they were at least to some extent in competition with the large dailies and with other information media.

To make it easier to decide to what extent market-powerful positions within the meaning of the Cartel Act are forming in the field of the press, it should be possible, in the Cartel Commission's opinion, at any time to identifiy the owners of the various press companies. The report finally points to the deterioration in the economic situation of the press since 1974 and sees the causes in the exceptional rises in paper prices and in the decline of the volume of advertising. But it thought it impossible for the moment to estimate precisely the effects of those developments.

b) Brewing Industry (VSKk 1974, p. 361 et seq.)

While the supplementary report on the press did not reveal any specifically concentration-related pattern, in the brewing industry the Commission did for the first time meet with all aspects of concentration, including capital participation and diversification. In particular, the following findings emerged:

Development of horizontal concentration: In 1963, there were 60 brewing plants in Switzerland, and as many brewery companies. Since then, concentration, notably at the company level, has made great progress. By the end of 1973, the number of plants had dropped to 52, that of companies being separate legal entities to 51. Yet the number of economically independent companies had in fact dropped to 37; and when the co-operation arrangements are taken into account, there were only 27 groups or single companies.

Vertical concentration on the adjacent level is little developed, if at all. On the other hand, there is a marked concentration on the wholesale level: two thirds of the wholesale trade are controlled by the breweries. Yet the widely held opinion that the breweries also control a large number of dispensing establishments on the retail level, was not confirmed. Only 6.7% of the retail and retail dispensing trade (including 4.8% of restaurants, etc.) is controlled by the breweries.

Diversification: The quota of mineral water production directly or indirectly controlled by breweries has risen over the past ten years from about 1% to 10%; on the market for sweet beverages, the increase was over 20%, and the output now controlled by the breweries amounts to 30% of the total national production.

After a close investigation of the causes governing the concentration trend, the Cartel Commission came to the conclusion that concentration has not reached a degree that could adversely affect the beer market. However, if concentration continues at the same pace as in recent years, the appearance of harmful effects is not to be ruled out.

c) Shoe Industry (VSKk 1975, p. 153 et seq.)

This survey, covering the years 1968-1973, showed that – despite the closing-down of 18 companies – there was no ground for speaking of a concentration trend endangering or excluding competition, either on the horizontal or on the vertical plane. The calculations based on the three factors "number employed", "sales in francs" and "production in pairs" did not reveal any – or at the most a minimal – concentration trend. On the other hand, competition has grown considerably keener through a tremendous increase in imports.

The recessive trend in the Swiss shoe industry in the period surveyed (drop in production in pairs from 14.39 million to 10.22; drop in number employed form 10,695 to 6,362; drop in sales in francs from 394 million to 374) is due to the following chief reasons: the importation boom, the changing consumer require-ments, and the difficulties of the Swiss shoe industry in adjusting to the demands of a larger market.

In its summing-up, the Cartel Commission came to the conclusion that the development in the Swiss shoe industry was not negative. The development had eliminated certain companies with outdated structures and inadequate manage-ment, and had resulted in the restructuring of some companies and plants, yet without creating conditions that would no longer ensure properly functioning competition. Indeed, the situation in the Swiss shoe industry had reached the point where it might be worth considering improving the competitive standing of the industry in the international context by closer co-operation or by a certain closer association of companies.

d) Food Retail Trade (VSKk 1979, p. 273 et seq.)

The Cartel Commission's report observes important concentration events in the food retail trade, notably since 1968. This applied especially to plant concentra-tion in small business (closing of local food shops). Many co-operation arrangements indicated the trend towards centralizing certain company-level functions. Less marked was the vertical concentration. On the other hand, the Commission observed a strong trend towards diversification into non-food products.

The causes of concentration are found both outside and inside the sphere of influence of the food retail trade. External causes include the demographic concentration process, the resultant diversion of purchasing power, changes in shopping habits, and various circumstances of public law. Internal causes include financing and plant management problems, industry-specific aspects such as the advent of new forms of operation, the trend towards larger shop units, and the relations of small companies to the large distribution organizations.

On the supply side, with competition functioning, the Cartel Commission at present sees no signs of economically or socially harmful effects due to market-powerful companies. It intimates, however, that it will watch with special attention the behaviour of the large distributors on the demand side. As the forces in the sphere of small retail business are badly split up, the Commission takes the view that further centralization here would improve the competitive standing against the large distributors and might promote the security of continued existence.

e) Banking (VSKk 1979, p. 1 et seq.)

The Cartel Commission's report draws a comprehensive picture of concentration in banking. The survey covers horizontal, vertical and conglomeratic or diagonal concentration.

The facts may be summed up as follows:

As regards *horizontal* concentration, it is only possible, in view of the variety of banking services, to make a representative statement if a number of concentration criteria are adopted. The Cartel Commission applied 24 criteria, including the balance sheet sum, broken down by domestic and foreign business, the number employed, interest and commission. In the survey period (1955 to 1976), on almost all concentration criteria the large banks registered quota gains, some very large indeed (branch offices 9.43%; number employed 8.27%; balance sheet sum 20.07%; domestic balance sheet sum 11.25%). In the category of other banks substantial advances were also made. A decline in the market share was registered by Cantonal banks, regional banks and savings institutes as well as by the "Raiffeisen" institutes. The aggregate decline here exceeds 25% on some criteria (domestic balance sheet sum, etc.).

Apart from the gold refineries of the large banks, the banking industry shows no vertical concentration comparable for instance, to the forward and backward integration of manufacturing companies. Even so, certain banking-related services are operated through special companies, for organizational and other reasons. In this respect, we may speak of *vertical* concentration. Here may be mentioned companies active in financing, leasing and factoring.

In *conglomeratic* concentration, the Cartel Commission first seeks to identify the instruments of concentration. These are to be found in direct and indirect holdings, general powers of representation for shares held in custody, and directorships in companies of the non-banking sector. Long-term loans cannot be considered an instrument of concentration, though the Commission concedes that small companies in particular may become largely dependent in fact on loan-granting banks. The Commission further sets out what interests, custody-shares, general powers of representation and directorships are held in *public companies* by the five large banks and the five largest each of the Cantonal banks, regional banks and savings institutes, foreign-controlled institutes and private banks as at 1 January 1977. This selection of banks in the aggregate holds 50 direct and 17 indirect interests in such companies, though the aggregate interest quota only exceeds 50% in the case of three financing companies; 48 packets of custody-shares with general powers of representation covering 20.1% to 50% of the shares, and 3 packets covering more than 50%; and directorships in 89 companies.

Summing up, the Cartel Commission arrives at the following conclusions:

In *horizontal* concentration, the rise of the large banks is chiefly due to a number of factors which concurrently constitute institutional competitive advantages over the institutes of other categories. The most prominent of these factors are the nation-wide presence; the higher financial power; the universality of the service range offered; greater scope for rationalizing; a centralized supply of bank branch offices, with the latest banking know-how; quality of management; and, finally, size in itself. A reduction of the number of large banks would considerably weaken the competitive structures. A link-up of two of the three really large banks would be wholly undesirable. The Commission takes the view that the large banks should not be allowed to further increase their market shares in any substantial degree. In this light, it formulates guidelines for the large banks and for the institutes of other categories. The large banks should restrain their competition in opening new branches; observe restraint in taking over regional banks and savings institutes; and not unduly compete with the endangered bank categories in their traditional fields of business, notably on the market for small mortgages. Conversely, the endangered institutes are invited to develop their co-operation arrangements and, if necessary, to consider the possibilities of link-ups.

For the present, at any rate, *vertical* concentration gives no cause for critical comment.

As regards *conglomeratic* concentration, the Cartel Commission finds that minority holdings in the share capital of non-banks do not as a rule involve any exclusive business relations for the banks, but merely ensure a certain favourable consideration. The number and the amount of conglomeratic holdings are kept within limits. Yet the Commission would consider any systematic expansion of such holdings undesirable. On the Commission's findings, the custody voting-rights are handled with care, which may be due in no small measure to the relevant guidelines issued by the Bankers Association. There are good reasons, in the Commission's view, for the directorships of bank representatives in non-banks. At present, at any rate, there is unlikely to be any considerable competitive distortion to the detriment of banks having no such representation, or to the detriment of companies having no bank representatives. The Cartel Commission recommends that the banks should disclose holdings from 20% upwards and directorships in public companies.

In conclusion, the Commission states that market imbalances in the banking sector, i. e. buyer and seller markets, tend, in the case of conglomeratic linkages, to distort competition among banks and among companies of the non-banking sector. In these circumstances, there is an interest in terms of competition policy in keeping conglomeratic concentration to a minimum.

Summary

The present Federal Act on Cartels and Similiar Organizations (enacted in 1962) is based on Art. 31bis.3.d of the Swiss Constitution, an exception to the constitutionally guaranteed principle of freedom of trade which permits restrictions on the freedom of trade whenever necessary in the public interest for the avoidance of economically or socially harmful effects.

While not banning cartels as such, the private law portion of the 1962 Act basically prohibits any appreciable interference with outside competition (Art. 4) thus aiming at the protection of outsiders and newcomers and, thereby, the preservvation of the possibility of competition. Exemptions are permissible, however, if interference "is warranted on grounds of overriding legitimate interests" (Art. 5.1). By interpreting the legal requirements for exemption in a way favourable to cartels, the Federal Supreme Court has decisively weakened the effectiveness of the Act.

In its administrative law portion, the Act entrusts the Cartel Commission (a body appointed by the Federal Council and consisting of representatives from the sciences, business and of consumers) with the task of carrying out general inquiries in order to ascertain the competitive situation in Switzerland (Art. 18.1) and to undertake special inquiries, i. e. to assess the effects of a particular cartel or similar organization in terms of its potential economic or social harmfulness (Arts. 20/21). Depending on the results of its special inquiries, the Commission may recommend the cartel to take measures appropriate to eliminate the undesired harmful effects (Art. 20.2). In the last resort, the Federal Economic Department may institute proceedings before the Federal Supreme Court against a cartel not willing to accept the Commission's recommendations (Art. 22).

Concentrations are subject to the Act (and thus to the rule against interference with outside competition and to supervision by the Cartel Commission) only in so far as a market-powerful organization (as defined by Art. 3) is involved in or arises through the concentration process. Up to now there have been six concentration inquiries by the Cartel Commission. There has been one general inquiry (in 1974, on the state and development of plant and company concentration in Switzerland) and five inquiries into individual industries (the Press, 1974; the brewing industry, 1974; the shoe industry, 1975; the food retail trade, 1979; and Banking, 1979).

Current draft proposals for the revision of the Cartel Act are intended to reinforce the protection of outsiders and newcomers and thus the preservation of a minimum functional competition. In future restraints of competition shall be eligible for exemption only if they might prove to produce better results in terms of the general interest than free competition. Furthermore the Cartel Commis-

sion's position shall be reinforced by giving it the power to issue not only recommendations but also binding orders with respect to cartels producing economically or socially harmful effects. Finally it should be noted that the draft reform Bill stipulates the obligation to disclose combines of firms in order to facilitate the Commission's investigations.

Chapter III

Merger Control in the European Communities

Concentration and Mergers in the E.E.C.: Towards a System of Control

Alexis Jacquemin
Louvain

I. Merger Activity and Concentration in Europe

A. Concentration In European Countries

Although it is not easy to obtain comparable data concerning mergers at the European level, the available information indicates that there has been a substantial progression since 1960.[1] Whether one looks at the number of mergers or at their importance in terms of the assets or employment involved, a substantial increase can be seen as from that date.

Such growth has been accompanied by an increase in concentration in the majority of European countries.

1. Overall Concentration

As far as aggregate concentration is concerned, the share of the largest undertakings in overall manufacturing activity has increased markedly. Thus, from 1953 to 1970 the share of the 100 largest British undertakings in terms of net manufacturing product went from 27% to 40%.[2] The sales of the 50 largest European companies expressed as a percentage of the gross industrial output in the Community increased from 15.4% in 1965 to 24.5% in 1976.[3] It is more or

---

[1] *See* generally, for the *United Kingdom:* L. Hannah & J. A. Kay, Concentration in Modern Industry: Theory, Measurement and the U.K. Experience (London, 1977); R. Opie, *Merger Policy in the United Kingdom, supra* this volume pp. 25 *et seq.*, esp. at § I.B.4; for *France:* F. Jenny & A. Weber, Concentration et politique des structures industrielles, (Paris, 1974); C. Champaud, *Merger Control in France: Direct and Indirect Ways of Control, supra* this volume at pp. 101 *et seq.*, esp. at § I; for the *Netherlands:* H. de Jong, *Theory and Evidence Concerning Mergers,* in A. Jacquemin & H. de Jong, eds., Markets, Corporate Behaviour and the State (The Hague, 1976); for *Sweden:* B. Ryden, Mergers in Swedish Industry (Stockholm, 1972); and for *Germany:* the Annual Reports of the Federal Cartel Office (Berichte des Bundeskartellamtes über seine Tätigkeit im Jahre . . ., published in the Bundestags-Drucksachen); and K. Hopt, *Merger Control in Germany: Philosophies, Experiences, Reforms, supra,* this volume at pp. 71 *et seq.*, esp. at § I.A.1. *See also* E. Kaufer, Konzentration und Fusionskontrolle (Tübingen, 1977).
[2] S. J. Prais, The Evolution of Giant Firms in Britain (London, 1976).
[3] G. Locksley and T. Ward, *Note: Concentration in Manufacturing in the E.E.C.,* 3 Cambridge Journal of Economics 91-97 (1979).

Table 1

Number and Share of National and International Operations in the Overall Number of Operations within the Community

Year	Take-overs and mergers		Acquisition of Participating Interests		Creation of Joint Ventures		Total	
	N	I	N	I	N	I	N	I
1973	138	0	384(40)	568(60)	119(22)	429(78)	641(39)	997(61)
1974	165	0	607(60)	411(40)	151(27)	401(73)	923(53)	812(47)
1975	231	0	1118(75)	382(25)	237(52)	313(48)	1586(69)	695(31)
1976	136	0	977(73)	369(27)	213(37)	362(63)	1326(64)	731(36)
1977	146	0	1279(76)	413(24)	194(40)	288(60)	1619(69)	701(31)
1978	137	0	1328(77)	399(23)	162(35)	278(65)	1627(70)	677(30)

N = national operation; I = international operation.
The figures in brackets indicate the percentages.
SOURCE: COMMISSION OF THE EUROPEAN COMMUNITIES, SEVENTH AND EIGTH ANNUAL REPORTS ON COMPETITION POLICY (Brussels, 1978 and 1979)

less generally accepted that it is mergers primarily carried out by the largest companies which are the main cause of this increase.[4]

2. Sectoral Concentration

In terms of sectoral or industrial concentration, it is recognized in the first place, that the majority of mergers in Europe are of a horizontal type, unlike the case in the United States, where conglomerate mergers are more significant. Moreover, the few studies which exist, carried out in a rather piecemeal fashion, show that changes in degrees of industrial concentration are dominated more by mergers than by differentiated internal growth or resulting from random processes.[5]

B. International Trade and Concentration in Europe

The international dimension of the phenomena of concentration and mergers however makes it risky to come to any hasty conclusion concerning their impact on European competition.

Firstly, it should be borne in mind that the frequency of international operations within the E.E.C. is less than that of purely national operations. This is clearly the case for mergers and take-overs in the legal sense of the term, because the existing company laws of the Member States do not authorize inter-country operations; as is shown by Table 1, this is also the case for the acquisition of participating interests (including minority interests) which represent the major form of concentration in Europe. As far as concerns the creation of joint ventures, national operations are clearly catching up. According to statistics, the total for 1978 was 70% for national operations as against 30% for international operations.[6]

In a limited number of cases, undertakings have, in order to by-pass legal and institutional obstacles to transnational mergers, set up complex formulae in order to allow the desired grouping to be achieved:[7] this is the case with Agfa-Gevaert, now controlled by Bayer; with Glaverbel-Mecaniver; with Royal Dutch-Shell; with Siemens-Philips; with Unilever ... which are constituted in the form of international groups having holding or double holding companies or joint contractual groups (horizontal groups). This topic will be reverted to in the following section.

---

[4] International comparisons clearly show that in general the size of the acquiring company is greater than the average size of companies in the same industry and greater than that of the company acquired.

[5] *See*, for the U.K., HANNAH & KAY, *supra* note 1; for *Germany*, J. Muller, *The Impact of Mergers on Concentration: A Study of Eleven West German Industries*, 25 JOURNAL OF INDUSTRIAL ECONOMICS 113-132 (1976).

[6] It is to be noted that these figures give no indication of the volume of activities in question.

[7] A. JACQUEMIN & H. DE JONG, EUROPEAN INDUSTRIAL ORGANIZATION (London, 1977). For further consideration of the practicalities of merger *see* W. Bayer, *Horizontal Groups and Joint Ventures in Europe: Concepts and Reality* in K. HOPT, ed., GROUPS OF COMPANIES IN EUROPEAN LAWS (Volume II of LEGAL AND ECONOMIC ANALYSES ON MULTINATIONAL ENTERPRISES) pp. 3 *et seq.* (Berlin, New York, 1981).

Secondly, the relatively low rate of increase in international concentration operations should be linked to the remarkable increase in the flow of imports and exports within the Common Market: during the last ten years, the percentages of imports and exports compared to available resources have increased in a very substantial way in all European countries, suggesting that during this period, there may have been an intensification rather than a diminution in competitive pressures. Similarly, calculations of the degree of concentration corrected to take account of exports and imports result in levels which are much lower than those generally employed.[8] This has led F. M. Scherer[9] to write that for the Member States of the European Common Market and a number of other countries such as Switzerland, considerably dependent on international trade, the national degrees of concentration are, for many industries, more or less devoid of significance. Thus, the fact that an increase in national concentrations as a result of mergers is recorded still leaves open the question of whether or not competition in Europe is reduced in overall terms.

II. The Determinants and Effects of Concentration and Mergers

A. Improvements in Efficiency or in Market Power?

Traditionally, two main contrasting approaches are used to explain concentration operations: on the one hand, the pursuit of increased efficiency linked to economies of scale, whether the latter be purely technological or related to the fields of research, marketing, financing or management; on the other hand, the wish to acquire or reinforce monopoly power, by reducing the number of independent suppliers and promoting their collusion. The problem is particularly delicate for horizontal mergers. A merger can doubtless be imagined which does not affect production costs nor market power, as can mergers which increase efficiency without affecting monopoly power or which increase mo-

---

[8] In the case of the degree of concentration measured according to the share of the m largest companies, the formula should be as follows:

$$C_m = \sum_{i=1}^{m} \frac{TO_i - X_i}{TOT - X + M}$$

Where TO_i = the total turnover of company i;
  TOT = the total turnover of n companies in the industry;
  X_i = the turnover exported by company i
  X = the turnover exported by the industry;
  M = the turnover represented by competitive imports.

Applying this formula to Belgian industry, it has been shown that the average share of the four largest companies is 25%, compared to 51.5% where there is no correction for exports and imports. *See* A. Jacquemin, E. de Ghellinck and C. Huveneers, *Concentration industrielle en économie ouverte: Le cas de la Belgique*, 5 Bulletin de Statistique 390-416 (1978).

[9] F. Scherer, Industrial Market Structure and Economic Performance 63 (Chicago, 1980).

nopoly power without affecting efficiency. The most difficult case is, however, that where the two effects are present at the same time: at that moment there is a reduction in costs (increase in efficiency), an increase in prices, a quantitative reduction in production and a growth of the rate of profit. This is illustrated in Figure 1.

Figure 1

The Effect of a Simultaneous Increase
in Monopoly Power and Efficiency in a Sector

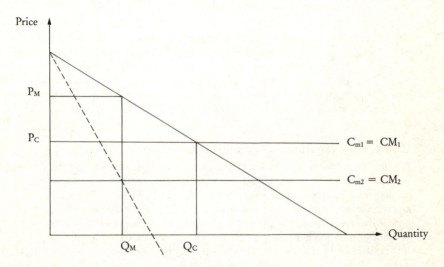

The competitive price P_C is deemed to exist prior to the merger and to be more or less equal to the marginal cost C_{m1}. Following the merger, there is a simultaneous lowering of costs to the level C_{m2} (efficiency) and an increase in price to the level P_M (monopoly power). The consequences from a welfare point of view have been analysed by O. Williamson.[10]

B. Towards a More Realistic Evaluation of Mergers

In the light of this type of model, numerous authors have endeavoured to determine the observable consequences of mergers. The most recent study for Europe has been effected under the direction of D. Mueller.[11] Basing themselves on an international comparison of the results obtained for E.E.C. countries and

[10] *Economies as an Antitrust Defense: the Welfare Trade-offs*, 58 (1) AMERICAN ECONOMIC REVIEW 18-36 (1968).
[11] DETERMINANTS AND EFFECTS OF MERGERS (Cambridge, Ma., 1980).

looking only at mergers in the legal sense of the term, this study came to the conclusion that:

(1) All tests relating to the pursuit of economies of scale turn out to be meaningless. Among other things, the size of acquiring companies is generally larger than the minimum optimum size in the industry concerned.

(2) Tests relating to profitability following mergers suggest that mergers have little or no effect on the profitability of the merging company in the 3 to 5 years following the merger. Similarly, there is no significant difference in the earnings per share 3 years after the merger. This confirms the results obtained in a large number of American studies.[12]

(3) Mergers do not result in price reductions, nor in increased sales.

Thus, these results, largely negative, give reason to believe that it is not possible to find a single explanation for mergers: neither the pursuit of efficiency, nor of monopoly power, appear to provide a universal explanation.[13] The results moreover suggest that the chances of success are fairly small and that the cost of changes in structure (difficulties in "digesting" the operation, cost disadvantages of a large organization) is often greater than the advantages which are claimed by the promoters.

C. Merger by Acquisition of a Controlling Interest

A separate mention should be made of operations involving "concentration without merger" (in the corporate law sense), by the means of the acquisition of participating interests conferring control. As has been seen above, this is the most common form of concentration in Europe. This creation of industrial groups can again reflect the pursuit of efficiency:[14] this amounts to obtaining the advantages of a merger without the disadvantages, due to the maintenance of a sufficiently decentralized structure. From this point of view, it is possible to distinguish between the problem of the coordination of the objectives of the large undertaking, and that of the allocation of resources within the latter.

1. Policy Objectives of the Firms

As regards the determination of objectives, the formula of concentration without merger makes it possible to make a clear distinction between the domain of the overall objectives (the power to determine which is deliberately conferred on a centralized entity), and the aims to be pursued by each component unit. In fact,

---

[12] See SCHERER, supra note 9, at pp. 138-139.

[13] Other explanations, such as the spreading of risk (linked more closely to diversification) or motives of a speculative nature linked to an underestimate of the stock exchange volume of certain companies as compared to their long term prospects are even less general, even though encountered in practice. See SCHERER, supra note 9, at p. 128 et seq.

[14] Concentrations without mergers can of course pursue other aims, especially the desire not to effect an immediate and complete merger between parties which do not know each other very well, or, as has been seen, because it is legally impossible to effect a complete merger.

each member of the group is set up as a semi-autonomous profit making centre, subjected to the need to comply with a number of external constraints laid down by requirements emanating from the centre. Each member will adopt the point of view of an entrepreneur able to deal freely with his assets and responsible for his performance, rather than the bureaucratic approach of an employee. This "management by objectives" already exists in groups organized by subordination (vertical groups). Control, even if it is 100%, is only exercised in connection with certain key elements, especially in the financial sphere. The situation is equally clear in the case of coordinated groups, where agreement only exists for a defined and limited objective: thus, the objective of the French economic "interest grouping" is to attain an efficient dimension in a certain field (research, marketing, or financing), while allowing each member the freedom to pursue its main objectives in the way that it sees fit.

2. Allocation of Resources

As regards the allocation of resources, the basic idea is that this form of concentration ensures a large measure of mobility in human and capital resources as compared to mergers of a legal type, or internal growth. Thus, it is comparatively easy for a member to withdraw or be expelled from a group where market conditions or alternative groups make this preferable. Whether sub-contracts or acquisition of participating interests are concerned, the economic and institutional costs of a change in partners are much less than in the case of the splitting up of an integrated company. Similarly, the penetration or the abandonment of a sector or a geographical market is much easier than in the case of slow economic growth or a rigid merger. The mobility of assets and their efficient allocation are encouraged as a result. In the same way, the fact that legally the enterprises are separate reduces the risk by limiting the size of the amount contributed, making it possible to undertake operations which would have been considered too uncertain but for that protection. Such dissociation also provides a better adaptation to the natural or institutional needs of the local or national market.

Besides the freedom in respect of becoming and ceasing to be a member, which protects the group against the dangers of rigid bureaucracy, "concentration without merger" has consequences relating to internal organization. Rather than a meddlesome hierarchy based on personal relations, the system is one in which management decisions are clearly left to the discretion of the component units and in which control is exercised at the level of results: internal competition is moreover frequent and makes it possible to avoid the sclerosis due to gigantism.

However, it is equally true that the grouping of undertakings is in its turn capable of giving rise to abuse. On the one hand, the interests of minority shareholders (also called "free" or "external" shareholders) can be prejudiced, as can those of creditors and workers. It is in view of this that in the proposal for a Council regulation on the Statute for European Companies,[15] the Commission of

---

[15] Commission Proposal for a Council Regulation on the Statute for European Compa-

the European Communities has proposed a law of groups capable of reconciling the guarantees to be given to individual interests with respect for the right of the dominant undertaking to give instructions to dependent undertakings, this being the linch-pin for the success of the formula.[16] On the other hand, it is equally clear that concentration without a formal merger is as capable of substantially reducing competition as merger, but is less easy to detect and to subject to supervision. Practices such as subsidising sales in a highly competitive market in order to cause the bankruptcy of competitors or to force them to be taken-over; conditional sales which transfer monopoly power from one sector to another; reciprocal agreements; patent monopolies; recourse to internal transfer pricing, are all the more dangerous when they emanate from bodies whose legal form often makes it possible to escape external analysis and even a simple calculation of market share. A number of recent studies nevertheless show that the degree of concentration when calculated on a basis which takes into account all of the companies the majority of whose shares are held by a group, is much higher than when based solely on companies which are legally autonomous. Thus, in France, a substantial increase can be seen in 119 sectors out of 295.[17] Empirical studies concerning the effects of industrial groups are also rare. Existing data suggest, however, that the performance of the largest companies characterized by the control of subsidiaries is not superior to that of smaller companies, whether this is in terms of profitability, growth or research.[18] A recent study of French industrial groups shows in a more precise way that the performance of such groups is not systematically better.[19]

Thus, whatever the legal form taken by the concentration operation, merger or acquisition of a controlling interest, two aspects clearly emerge: (1) these phenomena are linked to the reinforcement of industrial and global concentration; (2) they do not, in general, result in directly measurable advantages in terms of economies of cost or increase in profit.

III. In Favour of a Control of Concentration Operations in the E.E.C.

Since the publication of the famous work of J. J. Servan-Schreiber,[20] the myth of size, and the brilliant performance associated with it, has not ceased to haunt the imagination of the political powers and of public opinion. For Servan-Schreiber,

nies under Art. 149(2) EEC Treaty: Original Proposal, June 1970, O.J.E.C., Vol. 13, C 124 (1970), and Supplement to EC Bulletin 8/1970; amended proposal, 1975, Supplement to EC Bulletin 4/1975.

[16] For a general analysis, *see* the Reports of R. Houin, P. van Ommeslaghe, A. Jacquemin and B. Michaux in COMMISSION DROIT ET VIE DES AFFAIRES, LES GROUPES DE SOCIÉTÉS (The Hague, 1973).

[17] INSEE, LES GROUPES DE SOCIÉTÉS DANS LE SYSTÈME PRODUCTIF FRANÇAIS (Series E, No. 7, March 1980).

[18] A. JACQUEMIN, ECONOMIE INDUSTRIELLE EUROPÉENNE (Paris, 1979).

[19] D. Encaoua and B. Franck, *Performances sectorielles et groupes de sociétés,* 31 REVUE ECONOMIQUE 397-429 (1980).

[20] LE DÉFI AMÉRICAIN (Paris, 1967).

the essential step to be taken is "the setting up of large industrial groups capable of a world-wide strategy." Quoting P. Uri, he writes: No other policy than that which consists in reinforcing the strong points – which demagogy condemns with the global and vague term of "monopolies" – will enable us to escape from relative underdevelopment.[21]

The European Commission had already started along this road with its memorandum of April 1966 concerning concentrations, which affirmed that concentrations improved profitability, lowered production costs and speeded up technical progress. As for the current President of the Court of Justice of the European Communities, he advocated the setting up of "a framework allowing European undertakings to acquire the size and the means to confront what J. Houssiaux referred to as industrial dinosaurs."[22]

In the present crisis situation, this approach is starting to change in a remarkable way: empirical studies have scarcely born out the presumption in favour of size and of concentration operations, the largest undertakings appear to be those which have least well stood up to the crisis, and the socio-political viewpoint highlights the dangers of private economic power in the face of governments which are increasingly subject to pressure groups and are unable to cope with them.

In this climate, it is useful to emphasize certain aspects of industrial and competition policy, in order to assess to what extent antagonism really exists.

A. "European" Industrial Policies

As regards industrial policy, recent trends suggest that the role of reinforcing industrial size by means of external growth has been relegated to a secondary position. The questions which have now come to the fore are those such as:
– the extent to which production involves the work of qualified labour;
– policies of intra-industrial specialisation and differentiation of products;
– "non-pricing" policies (commercial policy, after-sales service, quality standards etc.);

---

[21] "Aucune autre politique que celle qui consiste à renforcer les points forts - que la démagogie condamne sous le terme global et vague de 'monopoles' - ne nous permettra d'échapper au sous-développement relatif". *Ibid.*, p. 177.

[22] R. Lecourt, *Concentrations et fusions, facteurs d'intégration*, 1968 Revue du Marché Commun 6-24. In the same issue A. Marchal stated that "the aim to be achieved is to make the EEC into an oligopolistic market. This is because it is concentration and the struggle between concentrated firms that at the end of the day result in the advantages that are expected from the restructuring of European industry . . .. Intra-Community concerted practices and concentrations are powerful factors of integration, even if this is primarily due to the fact that cooperation at a distance can only be carried out between groups that are themselves organized". A. Marchal, *Nécessité économique des concentrations et fusions*, 1968 Revue du Marché Commun 25, 30 and 45. The whole of the January-February issue of 1968 Revue du Marché Commun (pp. 1-552) is dedicated to the subject "Cooperations, concentrations, fusions d'enterprises dans la CEE" (Reporting the proceedings of a Colloquium held in Paris in 1967).

– penetration of third country markets;
– the role of small and medium-sized enterprises.[23]

However, in a context of crisis and of an increasing development of international trade,[24] a grouping of undertakings is still considered to be a useful defence against world-wide competition and as a means of safeguarding a sufficient market share. Unlike periods of regular growth, the rate of concentration speeds up in a period of rapid structural change. The recent agreements between the leading European car manufacturers (Fiat, Mercedes, Renault, Peugeot-Citroën, British Leyland and Volvo), or the acquisition of participating interests by Saint-Gobain-Pont-à-Mousson in Honeywell-Bull and Olivetti, are seen to be normal reactions to meet the technological challenge presented by American and Japanese companies. It would be risky to maintain that such alliances, formed between multinationals coming from the E.E.C., do not have positive consequences as far as concerns the adoption of new techniques and the diffusion of innovations.

There is accordingly a major temptation to permit greater concentration between the principal European companies as a response to increases in the pressures of international competition, and to rely on such pressures to prevent the setting up of excessively powerful monopolies.

B. "European" Competition Policy

Despite the international competitive advantages, this approach is open to criticism. In the first place, we have seen that available statistics do not make it possible to discover systematic advantages linked to existing merger operations, so that the onus of proof appears now to rest on the shoulders of those who hold the contrary opinion. In the second place, it can be asked whether operations of external growth are not simply substitutes for an internal growth which would have given rise to fresh investment linked to a more advanced technology and to a greater dynamism, and also whether they do not stand in the way of the entry of new undertakings. In the third place, groupings formed by means of acquisition of participating interests and the exchange of directors can easily not result in a genuine technical and economic integration, linked to the advantages of scale, and can be limited to more or less speculative financial advantages, or even to a suppression of competition within the group. Finally, a completely lax attitude risks giving rise to an asymmetric oligopolistic structure for the principal markets, which once established would be irreversible: in the light of the American experience, it appears illusory to allow the current developments to have their head and then to hope to control abusive exploitation once the dominant positions have already been acquired.[25]

---

[23] P. COFFEY, ed., ECONOMIC POLICIES OF THE COMMON MARKET (London, 1979).

[24] See § I. B. *supra*.

[25] E. Mason, in his preface to the famous work by C. KAYSER & D. TURNER, ANTITRUST POLICY: AN ECONOMIC AND LEGAL ANALYSIS (Cambridge, Ma., 1965) wrote: "The struggle against size was largely lost in the merger movement of 1897-1901". It was at

C. Implications of a European Merger Control

The implications of the above-mentioned considerations are relatively clear. It would appear to us naïve if, on the basis of the limited amount of information currently available, European authorities were to systematically encourage external concentration operations, having regard to the level already attained.[26]

Inversely, the strict American approach is not satisfactory. According to the decision of the Supreme Court in the case *Ford Motor Co. v. United States*:[27]

> A merger is not saved from illegality under § 7 [of the Clayton Act (15 USC § 18)], we said [in *United States* v. *Philadelphia National Bank*, 374 US 321, 371], "because, on some ultimate reckoning of social or economic debits and credits, it may be deemed beneficial. A value choice of such magnitude is beyond the ordinary limits of judicial competence, and in any event has been made for us already, by Congress when it enacted the amended § 7. Congress determined to preserve our traditionally competitive economy. It therefore proscribed anticompetitive mergers, the benign and the malignant alike, fully aware we must assume, that some price might have to be paid."

The criteria relating to the anticompetitive nature of horizontal mergers are remarkably restrictive, since in a concentrated market (in which the share of the four largest undertakings amounts to 75% or more) the Department of Justice has indicated that it will take action against a merger if the acquiring undertaking possesses 4% of the market and the undertaking being absorbed 4% or more of the same market.[28]

Following the uncertainties which continue to affect the consequences of concentration in the present economic and social context, and in the light of the European approach to competition – a privileged instrument, but not an end in itself – such a degree of severity seems inappropriate. On the contrary, the competent authorities should be in a position to assess the possible beneficial effects of the operation in question.

D. Institutional Set-Up of European Merger Control

The choice of institutional level at which this assessment should be made is, however, essential. In our view, the role of an effective anti-trust authority is to determine whether a restriction on competition exists, and if so, whether this is substantial in quantitative terms. It should not be necessary to have regard at one and the same time to criteria relating to industrial policy, to the effects on international trade, to employment, or to technical progress. If the two

---

that moment that the main asymmetric oligopolistic structures were set up, in the absence of effective public control. Once they were established, it became more or less impossible to change the position. For an analysis of the stability of dominant positions, *see* J. VAN DAMME, ed., LA RÉGLEMENTATION DU COMPORTEMENT DES MONOPOLES ET ENTREPRISES DOMINANTES EN DROIT COMMUNAUTAIRE (Bruges, 1977).

[26] *See* § I.A. *supra*.

[27] 405 U.S. 562, at 570 (1972), *per* Douglas J. delivering the opinion of the Court.

[28] The "incipiency" doctrine goes even further. *See* United States v. Von's Grocery Company, 384 U.S. 270 (1966).

approaches are mixed up, this results in criteria being brought in which are not easily comparable, in surreptitious compromises being arrived at, in value judgments being made which belong to the political powers: a confusion of objectives and tasks is created, and also it becomes practically impossible to exercise a democratic control over the options adopted.

On the contrary, it appears preferable to distinguish two levels. On the one hand, the body in charge of competition rules should assess whether in technical terms, on the basis of criteria which are more or less quantifiable, the concentration operation results in an appreciable restriction of competition. On the other hand, a distinct authority of the ministerial type, could intervene once the antitrust authority had established the existence of a substantial quantitative restriction. Basing itself on motives of economic policy, this ministerial authority would not override this decision, but could take the view, on the basis of a reasoned decision, that current socio-economic circumstances made the operation a desirable one. This is more or less the German system, in which the assessment of the cost-benefit of a merger is undertaken by the Minister of Economic Affairs. Thus on the Federal Cartel Office level it is possible to avoid interminable confrontations based on allegations which are not easily verified and quantified, in terms of the economic and social effects of a concentration operation,[29] and it is left to the executive power to make the final political choice.[30]

E. Evaluation of the Draft Regulation of the E.E.C.

Turning to a draft regulation to be adopted by the Council of Ministers of the European Communities relating to economic concentration (modified version in 1976 and once more under discussion),[31] several aspects appear to be valid to us, in particular:

- the creation of a system of prior notification (Article 4), insofar as concentration operations are not reversible or can only be reversed at a generally prohibitive economic and social cost;
- the adoption of quantitative criteria making it possible to limit the control to European operations of considerable size (Articles 1 and 4 (2)), leaving undertakings of the second rank the freedom to form groups, so as to combat larger undertakings on equal terms.[32]

The question is more delicate concerning the criterion of general economic

---

[29] For an example of false statements and information provided by persons taking part in a merger project in the U.S. see SCHERER *supra* note 9.

[30] For further consideration of the German system *see* Hopt, *Merger Control in Germany: Philosophies, Experiences, Reforms, supra* this volume at pp. 71 *et seq.*, esp. at § III.

[31] O.J.E.C., Vol. 16, C 92 p. 11 (1973). The text of the draft is reproduced *infra* this volume at pp. 253 *et seq.*, Annex II.4.c. The draft is discussed in detail in P. Schmitt, *Multinational Corporations and Merger Control in Community Antitrust Law, infra* this volume at pp. 169 *et seq.*

[32] Moreover, this preserves a sphere of autonomy for the national authorities.

policy (Article 3), i. e., to determine the concentration operations which are to be exempted because they are deemed to be indispensable to the realization of an objective which is considered to have priority in the general interest of the Community (imperatives of common policies, or failing these, national policies which are consistent with the Community's general interest. This criterion certainly involves an analysis of the socio-economic costs and benefits of such an operation. Having regard to the considerations examined earlier, it therefore appears dangerous to mix together preoccupations of competition policy and those of industrial policy in negotiations between the various Directorates-General. It is not the role of competition policy to ensure a better regional allocation of activities or to safeguard employment. Its aim is to attack market practices and structures which limit existing, or potential competition in a substantial way. The task of judging the desirability of a great reduction in competition should therefore be conferred on an authority which is sufficiently distinct and specialized, so that the alternative objectives, the respective costs, and the necessary choices, can be clearly cast into relief. If this distinction is not made, and if, in accordance with Article 3 para. 4 of the Draft Regulation, the Commission is to resolve within itself the confrontation between the costs and the benefits of the transaction, the technocratic arbitrage to which this would give rise would dilute the efficacy of competition policy and lead to the democratic processes being set aside in favour of internal compromises involving politicians, senior officials and representatives of the private sector. Without laying down the ideal formula at this stage, it can be envisaged that, within the context of the Treaty, it would be possible to give a greater degree of autonomy to Directorate General IV, responsible for competition policy. In the absence of any favourable presumption in respect of major concentration operations, this Directorate General would in particular be permitted to publish its analyses, opinions and decisions in its annual report, without having to assess the "objectives considered to have priority in the general interest of the Community". The latter assessment would be left either to the Directorate responsible for industrial policy, or to the Council of Ministers, with the possibility of debates in the European Parliament. In the absence of a total separation of this nature, it would in any event be indispensable that in the decisions of the Commission a clear distinction be made between, on the one hand, the conclusions relating to the competitive effects of the concentration operation; and, on the other hand, the aspects relating to industrial policy and the general interest.

Summary

In the first section of this paper, the evolution of concentration and mergers in Europe is analyzed. Aggregate concentration — the proportion of economic activity controlled by the largest firms in the economy – has increased appreciably during the last ten years in European countries. In 1977, the share in percentage of the sales of the 50 largest EEC firms in industrial output reached 24.5%. There has also been a significant increase in market concentration during the same period in most countries. These increases in concentration can be largely ascribed to mergers. This does not, however, imply a decline in competition. During the last two decades, the liberalization and expansion of international trade in industrial production has been such that it could be argued that there has been an increase in, rather than less, competition in Europe.

The second section reviews the results of, and conclusions to be drawn from, recent studies on the determinants and effects of mergers in European countries. Two possible consequences of a horizontal merger are usually underlined: an increase of market power (making the demand more inelastic and raising the profit maximizing prices) and/or an increase in efficiency (driving down costs and prices). However, the existing data suggest no merger effects on profitability, growth of sales and price-levels.

The third section develops some implications for public policies. A more critical policy towards mergers should be adopted. It is necessary to shift from a positive or a neutral approach to a stricter system. The Antitrust Authority should have the power to decide that the only basis for escaping the prohibition of the law is that mergers do not significantly reduce competition. If, on the contrary, it has to judge cases on the basis of their social, regional and industrial benefits, this Authority is led to make competition policy part of its overall economic and industrial policy. This could create a dangerous discretionary power and a most inefficient confusion of functions. It would be better to delimit clearly the function of each public goal. The premise of an antitrust policy is that competition is the best way to serve the public interest and that the legality of market-conduct depends on the extent of its anti-competitive effects. It must of course be possible to question such a premise, but this should be done at a different level of public policy. This calls for a separation of functions similar to that applied in West Germany, where the Minister of Economics can reverse a decision of the Federal Cartel Office in the "overriding interest of the public". At this stage, the onus of proof should be placed firmly on the firms to show that a proposed merger would result in net benefits. From this point of view the EEC proposal for a system of merger control is not satisfactory.

Multinational Corporations and Merger Control in Community Antitrust Law

Paul M. Schmitt*

Brussels

I. European Community Competition Policy and Multinationals

Since Community law on competition is fully and uniformly applicable without discrimination throughout the entire "Common Market" to all restrictive or abusive practices by firms wherever their head office may be situated,[1] this paper will begin with a general introduction outlining the aims of the competition policy of the Commission of the European Communities and some of the cases in which this policy has been applied to multinational corporations.

A. The Aims of the E. C. Commission's Competition Policy

The Community system for ensuring that competition is not distorted, provided for in general terms by Article 3(f) of the European Economic Community (EEC) Treaty and spelled out in the rules applying to undertakings in Article 85 (prohibition of restrictive practices) and Article 86 (prohibition of abuse of dominant positions), which constitute an integral part of the Community's public economic order, has three main objectives.

First, competition policy in a system designed to ensure that competition in the Common Market is not distorted must first and foremost contribute to the smooth working of the common market which was set up as the basis for economic integration, and ensure the unity and openness of this market. It must, therefore, be geared to detecting and preventing restrictive trade practices which re-establish territorial market divisions in order to enable artificially different prices to be charged or unfair terms of sale to be imposed.

Second, any competitive system contains the seeds of its own destruction. Any excessive concentration of economic, financial and business power leads to structural changes that make it impossible for competitive forces to regulate economic activity as they ought. And so, as the common market develops, the degree of competition that is needed if the EEC Treaty's demands and objectives

---

* The views expressed in this paper are those of the author and not necessarily those of the Community Institution by which he is employed.

[1] Commission of the E.C., Third Report on Competition Policy, Doc. 118/74 (Brussels, May 1974).

are to be met must be guaranteed at all times. The Commission must keep a close eye not only on the possibility that dominant firms might abuse their power but also on the mergers that such firms use as a means of suddenly – and substantially – expanding their market shares. In 1973, with this point in mind, the Commission put forward a proposal for a Council Regulation providing for more efficient Community control as regards large mergers.[2]

Third, an open and unified common market where undistorted competition is a reality is basically a market governed by the general principle of economic fair play, the paramount objective being to assure that all firms enjoy equal access to the common market. In particular, firms outside the Community which do business either directly or through subsidiaries in the common market must be subject to the same rules as European firms. Secondly, fair account must be taken of the different situations in which firms may find themselves, and among other things this means applying the rules of competition in a way that is favourable to small and medium sized firms.

Lastly, the principle of economic fair play involves giving the fullest consideration possible to the legitimate interests of workers, users and consumers. For example, the Commission's proposed merger-control regulation includes provisions enabling Community authorities to take account of the industrial, social or regional aspects of mergers caught by the regulation.

B. Competition Policy Applied to Multinational Corporations

To date, the Commission has taken 138 decisions of substance (i. e., not including procedural decisions); 56 of these involved multinational companies – 56 European companies and 38 companies with headquarters outside the Community. As territorially Community competition law applies to Community-based multinationals in exactly the same way as to exclusively Community firms, this paper concentrates, principally, on the specific problems arising in connection with the Commission's authority over non-Community multinationals.

Decisions of all four main types provided for under Articles 85 and 86 of the EEC Treaty have been addressed to non-Community multinationals.

Negative clearance — which means a declaration that the prohibition on restrictive practices in Article 85 (1) does not apply in the relevant case — was given, for example, to *Burroughs*[3] and *Nagoya*,[4] controlled by Toyota-Mitsui, where the restrictions on competition were not considered appreciable; to *Kodak*,[5] for standard general conditions of sale applying throughout the

---

[2] Commission Proposal for a Regulation (EEC) of the Council on the Control of Concentrations between Undertakings, O.J.E.C., Vol. 16, C 92 p. 1 (1973). The text of this proposal is reproduced, *infra* this volume, Annex II 4c at pp. 253 *et seq.*
[3] Decision of 22 December 1971, O.J.E.C., Vol. 15, L 13 p. 50 and 62 (1972).
[4] Decision of 9 June 1972, O.J.E.C., Vol. 15, L 143 p. 39 (1972).
[5] Decision of 30 June 1970, O.J.E.C., Vol. 13, L 147 p. 24 (1970).

common market; and to *Tate and Lyle Refineries Limited* [6] for long-term raw cane sugar supply agreements.

Article 85 (3) exemption from the prohibition on restrictive practices has been given to foreign-based multinationals such as *Colgate-Palmolive*,[7] for a joint research and development programme; *Davidson Rubber*,[8] of the McCord Group, for exclusive patent and know-how licensing agreements; *De Laval International*,[9] controlled by the Trans-America Corporation conglomerate, for a joint venture and *Parke Davis* [10] for a joint research and development programme.

Cease-and-desist decisions under Article 85 (1) have been taken against *Ciba, Geigy, Sandoz* and *ICI* [11] for price-fixing; *Pittsburgh Corning Europe* [12] for concerted discriminatory pricing; *WEA-Fillipachi Music SA* [13] (in which Warner Brothers Inc. has a 51% holding and Banque Rothchild 39%) and *Miller International* [14] (an MCA subsidiary) for forbidding wholesale distributors of grammophone records established in France to export to the Federal Republic of Germany, where prices are considerably higher; and *Kawasaki* [15] and *Pioneer* [16] for preventing wholesale distributors in those common market countries in which the products were cheap from supplying countries where they were less so.

Decisions have also been taken under Article 86 against foreign multinationals who abused a dominant position. The *Commercial Solvents Corporation* was one of the first to be caught when its Italian subsidiary stopped supplying an Italian pharmaceutical company with the raw materials required for manufacturing an antitubercular drug in which the American company had a de facto world monopoly.[17] *United Brands Company*, formerly United Fruit, was found to have refused to sell Chiquita branded bananas and to have charged discriminatory prices.[18] Proceedings were taken against *Hoffmann-La Roche* because of exclusive or preferential supply contracts with several important purchasers of vitamins in bulk; most of its customers were themselves multinational groups, so that these contracts covered the entire world-wide demand.[19]

Continental Can,[20] another Article 86 case, deserves special mention in this

---

[6] Decision of 7 December 1979, O.J.E.C., Vol. 23, L. 39 p. 64 (1980).
[7] Decision of 23 December 1971, O.J.E.C., Vol. 15, L 14 p. 14 (1972).
[8] Decision of 9 June 1972, O.J.E.C., Vol. 15, L 143 p. 31 (1972).
[9] Decision of 25 July 1977, O.J.E.C., Vol. 20, L 215 p. 11 (1977).
[10] Decision of 17 January 1979, O.J.E.C., Vol. 22, L 70 p. 11 (1979).
[11] Decision of 24 July 1969, O.J.E.C., Vol. 12, L. 195 p. 11 (1969).
[12] Decision of 23 November 1972, O.J.E.C., Vol. 15, L 272 p. 35 (1972).
[13] Decision of 22 December 1972, O.J.E.C., Vol. 15, L 303 p. 52 (1972).
[14] Decision of 1 December 1976, O.J.E.C., Vol. 19, L 357 p. 40 (1976).
[15] Decision of 12 December 1978, O.J.E.C., Vol. 21, L 16 p. 9 (1978).
[16] Decision of 14 December 1979, O.J.E.C., Vol. 23, L 60 p. 21 (1980).
[17] Decision of 14 December 1972, O.J.E.C., Vol. 15, L 299 p. 51 (1972).
[18] Decision of 17 December 1975, O.J.E.C., Vol. 19, L 95 p. 1 (1976).
[19] Decision of 9 June 1976, O.J.E.C., Vol. 19, L. 223 p. 27 (1976).
[20] Decision of the Commission of 9 December 1971, O.J.E.C., Vol. 15, L 7 p. 25 (1972);

paper because it provided the starting point for the establishment of merger control under the competition rules of the EEC Treaty. We shall be considering this case in more detail further on.

This paper does not attempt to define multinational corporations; yet there is no doubt that the corporations or groups mentioned in the above examples are multinationals. All these firms constitute, with the foreign-based parent company, economic entities whose decisions are taken at a single centre that controls several manufacturing and distributing firms established in different countries both within the common market and elsewhere.

Following this general introduction, the paper will deal in three parts with the specific problems faced by the Community in controlling cross-frontier mergers involving multinationals, in particular where the multinationals concerned have a decision-making centre outside the Community. We shall deal first with what is known as the extra-territorial application of Community competition law, then go on to consider the application of this body of law as a means of controlling undesirable mergers involving multinationals, and conclude with some ideas on the consequences for multinationals of a new merger control system on the lines proposed by the Commission.

II. The Application of Community Competition Rules to Foreign Multinational Corporations

The Commission of the European Communities is one of the first antitrust authorities in the western world to have effectively applied the effects doctrine; it has done so to preserve the internal market of the Community from the restrictive or abusive practices of, among others, firms established outside the Community.

A. Application of the Effects Doctrine

The extreme application of the effects doctrine gives legislative bodies full territorial jurisdiction over restrictive trade practices as soon as a direct, appreciable and foreseeable effect is felt on the internal market, irrespective of the place in which the acts causing the effect have been committed or decided, and irrespective of the place where the firm concerned is situated.[21]

The Court of Justice of the European Communities to some extent upheld this doctrine in *Béguelin*,[22] where there was an exclusive dealing agreement between a Japanese firm and a distributor established in the common market:

Judgment of the Court of Justice of the E.C. of 21 February 1973, Case 6/72 Europemballage Corporation and Continental Can Company Inc. v. Commission [1973] E.C.R. 215.

[21] O.E.C.D., Restrictive Business Practices of Multinational Companies: Report by the Committee of Experts on Restrictive Business Practices, para. 119 *et seq.* (Paris, 1977).

[22] Judgment of 25 November 1971, Case 22/71, Béguelin Import Co. *et al.* v. S.A.G.L. Import Export *et al.* [1971] E.C.R. 949.

The fact that one of the undertakings which are parties to the agreement is situated in a third country does not prevent the application of [Article 85 of the EEC Treaty] since the agreement is operative on the territory of the common market.[23]

It is true that in *Béguelin* the effects doctrine was not applied in its extreme form, since one of the parties to the agreement was established in the common market thus providing a connecting factor to the Community. The most interesting aspect of the doctrine is that it provides the basis in international law for jurisdiction to legislate so as to ensure that the internal public order is respected within the territory by firms acting from outside. But it cannot, of itself, solve the problem of enforcement, since foreign firms are protected in public international law by the fact that non-member countries enjoy full sovereignty.

But there are usually no insurmountable barriers to the application of Community competition rules to foreign-based multinationals, in particular the merger rules, for they generally have one or more subsidiaries somewhere in the Community, and these subsidiaries may act on the instructions and on behalf of the foreign parent company to bring about mergers caught by Article 86 of the EEC Treaty.

B. Attributing the Behaviour of a Subsidiary to its Parent Company: The Principle of Internal Behaviour and the Notion of an Economic Unit

In *ICI v. Commission,* the Court did not have to ratify the effects doctrine when dealing with the relations between what was then a foreign parent company and its European subsidiary, because it found that the producers in non-member countries had required their Community subsidiaries to choose prices and operate other terms of business that had been agreed in concert with competitors in the common market (contrary to Article 85 of the Treaty). It found that " in the circumstances the formal separation between these companies, resulting from their separate legal personality, cannot outweigh the unity of their conduct on the market for the purposes of applying the rules on competition."[24] The actions of the subsidiaries can, therefore, be attributed to the parent company when the subsidiaries do not enjoy genuine autonomy in determining their business policy. Since the responsibility of the foreign parent companies had thus been established, the fines were rightly imposed upon them.

The judgment of the Court in *Europemballage Corporation and Continental Can Company Inc. v. Commission*[25] includes the following remark about attributing the behaviour of a subsidiary to the parent company:

It is certain that Continental caused Europemballage to make a take-over bid to the shareholders of TDV in the Netherlands and made the necessary means available for this. On 8 April 1970 Europemballage took up the shares and debentures in TDV offered up to

---

[23] *Id.* at 959.
[24] Judgment of the Court of Justice of the E.C. of 14 July 1972, Case 48/69, I.C.I. Ltd. v. Commission [1972] E.C.R. 619. For the Commission's decision *see supra* note 11.
[25] *Supra* note 20.

that point. Thus this transaction, on the basis of which the Commission made the contested decision, is to be attributed not only to Europemballage, but also and first and foremost to Continental. Community law is applicable to such an acquisition, which influences market conditions within the Community.[26]

Having first considered the principle of internal behaviour, the Court went on to analyse the concept of the economic entity consisting of the parent company and its subsidiaries, as a legal basis for the Commission's authority over parent companies situated in non-member countries. This concept is basically depend- ent on the fact that the parent company has controlling power, and can be considered responsible for the offending conduct.[27]

In view of the cases decided by the Court of Justice on which the Commission bases its administrative practice, there should be no insurmountable difficulties in applying Community rules of competition, and in particular the Commis- sion's powers over mergers, to multinationals, even when they are foreign-based. The Commission can, for instance, gather the information required by means of checks carried out at the subsidiaries established in the common market or by sending them requests for information; notify documents, such as the statement of objections or a formal decision to the subsidiaries; and enforce a decision within the Community without exceeding its authority.

III. The Application of Community Law as a Means of Controlling Unacceptable Large Mergers Under EEC Treaty Article 86

The Commission examines all the transactions announced or carried out in the Community for compatibility with Article 86 of the Treaty, which prohibits the abuse of a dominant position. It acts either at the request of the firms merging or on its own initiative, particularly when large market shares are involved or complaints are filed by firms which consider that they have suffered damage as a result of mergers between their competitors or their suppliers.

The judgment of the Court of Justice in *Continental Can*[28] establishes the principle of Community law that Article 86 applies where a dominant firm abuses its dominant position in order to strengthen it yet further.

The Commission had already said as much in its 1966 memorandum on concentration,[29] where it also expressed the opinion that Article 85 should not apply to this type of transaction. It applied the principle for the first time in its decision of 9 December 1971 concerning the US multinational Continental Can.[30]

---

[26] *Id.* at p. 242, para. 16.
[27] Judgment of the Court of Justice of the E.C. of 6 March 1974, Cases 6 and 7/73, Istituto Chemioterapico Italiano SpA and Commercial Solvents Corporation v. Commission [1974] E.C.R. 223.
[28] *Supra* note 20.
[29] Le Problème de la Concentration dans le Marché commun (Competition Study No. 3, Brussels, 1966).
[30] O.J.E.C., Vol. 15, L 7 p. 25 (1972).

In 1969 Continental Can Company Inc., New York, which manufactured (among other things) metal containers and machines for manufacturing and using them, acquired control of Schmalbach-Lubeca-Werke, easily the largest German manufacturer of metal containers. In 1970, through its Delaware subsidiary Europemballage Corporation, which has an office in Brussels, Continental Can acquired a controlling interest in the Dutch company Thomassen Drijver-Verblifa, the largest manufacturer of metal containers in Benelux.

In its decision, the Commission considered that through its subsidiary SLW Continental Can held a dominant position on the German market, which was a substantial part of the common market. It found that Continental Can had abused this dominant position by buying up its competitor TDV, which held a strong position on a neighbouring market.

Although the Court set the Commission's Decision aside because it had not, as a matter of law, sufficiently established the existence of a relevant product market, it confirmed the Commission's interpretation of Article 86 as being applicable to mergers.

A merger is contrary to Article 86 if two conditions are fulfilled: there must be a dominant position and the strengthening of this position must constitute an abuse.

A. The Dominant Position

The Commission bases its assessment of dominance on the guidelines laid down in the recent judgments in *United Brands*[31] and *Hoffmann-La Roche*.[32] The Court gave a precise definition of what constitutes a dominant position, in line with the Commission's idea: "a position of economic strength enjoyed by an undertaking which enables it to prevent effective competition being maintained on the relevant market by affording it the power to behave to an appreciable extent independently of its competitors, its customers and ultimately of the consumers."[33]

There are a number of components that make up a dominant position.

1. The Market Share

a) Extremely large market shares generally of themselves constitute evidence of dominance. Such was the case of the 80% or more market shares held by Roche for certain classes of vitamins.

b) Where the market share is smaller, additional yardsticks have to be used, and particularly the relationship between the market share held by the relevant firm and the share held by its competitors; this means looking at the structure of

---

[31] Judgment of the Court of Justice of the E.C. of 14 February 1978, Case 27/76, United Brands Company and United Brands Continental B.V. v. Commission [1978] E.C.R. 207 ("Chiquita Bananas").

[32] Judgment of the Court of Justice of the E.C. of 13 February 1979, Case 85/76, Hoffmann-La Roche & Co. AG v. Commission [1979] E.C.R. 461.

[33] [1979] E.C.R. 461, 520 at para. 38.

the relevant market. In the *Chiquita bananas* case,[34] the Court held that United Brands dominated a substantial part of the common market in bananas with a share of 40 to 45%, considering other aspects of the structure both of the firm itself (in particular its high degree of vertical integration, its technical know-how and its control over all stages of distribution) and of the relevant markets (in particular the fact that UBC's market share was several times as large as that of its nearest competitor and that there were substantial barriers to entry).

In the *Hoffmann-La Roche* case, the Court also found that Hoffmann-La Roche had a dominant position on the market for vitamins, where it held a market share of between 45% and 80%, and noted that these shares were much larger than those of its nearest competitors. Valid indicia of a dominant position are also, according to the Court, supplied by a firm's technical advance over its competitors, and the absence of potential competition. What is interesting is that the Court denied the relevance of certain indicia used in the Commission's decision,[35] notably the fact that Roche is the world's largest vitamin manufacturer and largest pharmaceutical group, that it manufactures a wider range of vitamins than any of its competitors and that its sales exceed the sales of all other vitamin manufacturers combined. Having regard to the peculiar features of the relevant industry, and particularly to the fact that each group of vitamins constitutes a separate market, these factors, all of which relate to the size of the firm, are not such as to give it a competitive advantage over other vitamin suppliers.

c) Can a firm with a market share of less than 40% be in a dominant position?

Although in Hoffmann-La Roche the Court felt that there was inadequate evidence of dominance on the market for one group of vitamins where Roche's market share had varied during the material period between 20% and 40%, it reached this conclusion because a major competitor was also working that market and the Commission had provided no additional evidence.

Obviously, as the relevant market shares decline, so the additional factors gain in importance: there must be more of them, and they must be more conclusive.

2. The Product Market

The concept of the relevant market implies that there can be effective competition between the products which form part of it and this presupposes that there is a sufficient degree of interchangeability between all the products forming part of the same market.[36]

In *Continental Can,* the Court annulled the Commission's decision precisely because it found that the Commission had not properly distinguished the relevant market. The decision referred to three separate markets:
– the market for light containers for canned meat products;

[34] The United Brands case, *supra* note 31.
[35] O.J.E.C., Vol. 19, L 223 p. 27 (1976).
[36] *See* the Hoffmann/La Roche case *supra* note 32.

– the market for light containers for canned seafood;
– the market for metal closures for the food packing industry other than crown corks.

The Court felt that the Commission had not given any details of how these three markets differed from each other, or said anything about how they differed from the general market for light metal containers.

However, in *United Brands*, the Court confirmed that the relevant market was indeed the market for bananas, as the Commission held, and not the fruit market in general, as United Brands claimed, because bananas are only to a limited extent interchangeable with other fruits. Similarly, in *Hoffmann-La Roche*, each group of vitamins was considered to constitute a separate market because each has specific metabolizing functions. When a merger is scrutinized in terms of Article 86, it is important to define the relevant market. The applicability of this article to a merger will clearly depend on whether the market considered relevant is large or small.

3. The Geographic Market

Articles 86 applies to the abuse of a dominant position in the common market or in a substantial part thereof. When the dominant position extends over the entire territory of the Community, allowing for imports and even for potential competition from outside the Community, the definition of the geographic market raises no problems. Such was the case in *Commercial Solvents*, where a multinational had a world-wide monopoly for the production of the relevant raw materials, and in *Hoffmann-La Roche*.

It is more difficult to define the geographic market when the relevant market does not cover the entire Community. What test should be used to define a distinct submarket within the Community? In *United Brands*, the Court defined a single geographic market as an area where the objective conditions of competition applying to the product in question must be the same for all traders. Applying this test the Court agreed with the Commission in excluding the French, Italian and British markets as there were national market organizations there. But it agreed with the Commission that the six other States constituted a single geographic market, even though the applicable tariff provisions and carriage costs were different (but not discriminatory). It also considered the "factors which go to make the relevant market a single market", i. e. the firm's strategy of marketing its products in the whole of the relevant part of the Community from a single sales centre.

The market as thus defined must, however, constitute "a substantial part of the common market". The Court has held that each of the large and medium-sized countries of the Community, and even a part of a large country, may constitute a substantial part of the common market. However, the geographical extent of the territory considered is not the only factor: others include the structure and the volume of production and consumption in the region compared with those in the Community as a whole.

Does Article 86 apply when a firm occupying a dominant position in a given area that constitutes a substantial part of the common market strengthens this position by extending it to neighbouring markets by means of merger? To put it another way, can a dominant position already occupied in one territory be abused in another? In *Continental Can,* the Commission said that it could, and the Court of Justice concurred. Continental Can was blamed for having extended to the Benelux market the dominant position it held through a subsidiary in the German market. Before they were brought together under the control of Europemballage, SLW and TDV were potential competitors in a wide area straddling the frontiers between Germany and the Benelux. In view of the siting of these firms' factories and of the break-even points for transport costs, it was found that the area to which both had access covered virtually the whole of the territory formed by the Netherlands, Belgium and Luxembourg and Northern and Central Germany. When Continental Can acquired a majority share in TDV, this effectively eliminated all competition between TDV and SLW in this area, which represented a substantial part of the common market.

B. Strengthening a Dominant Position as a Form of Abuse and the Effects on Trade between Member States

1. Strengthening a Dominant Position as a Form of Abuse

According to the principle laid down by the Court of Justice in *Continental Can:*

> abuse may . . . occur if an undertaking in a dominant position strengthens such position in such a way that the degree of dominance reached substantially fetters competition, i. e. that only undertakings remain in the market whose behaviour depends on the dominant one.[37]

The possibility of applying Article 86 to mergers thus depends on how the merger changes the structure of the market, and in particular on how it affects the relationship between competing firms and the new unit.

There is no need for competition to be completely eliminated: the market does not have to become a quasi-monopoly. But the change in the structure of supply must be so substantial that the competitors which are left no longer constitute an adequate countervailing force and consumers have only very limited freedom of choice.

It would seem that when the original dominant position is based on very large market shares and on a significant difference between these shares and those of competing firms, external expansion by the dominant firm is much more likely to constitute an abuse. This is because the aggregate market share accounted for by competitors is reduced when one of their number is taken over, and the ability of the competitors to counterbalance the new unit is correspondingly reduced. The competitive role of the firm taken over also has to be considered on the basis of both structural tests (market shares and so on) and behavioural tests (pricing, tendency to innovate and the like).

---

[37] *Supra* note 20 at 245 para. 26.

2. Trade between the Member States

Like restrictive practices and abuse of dominance, the strengthening of a dominant position is prohibited under Article 86 only if it is liable to affect trade between the Member States. It follows from cases decided by the Court of Justice regarding the application of Article 86 to an existing dominant position that this condition is fulfilled when dominance is so exploited as to compromise the achievement of the aims of a single market, notably by changing the structure of competition in the common market. A merger of any size will generally have this effect.

Since the purpose of the effect-on-trade condition is to demarcate the field of Community competition law from the field of the Member States' competition laws, mergers taking place wholly within a single Member State are subject solely to national rules. In practice, however, it rarely happens that the effects of a relatively large merger will be felt on the market of only one Member State. Consequently, wherever the Member States have merger control facilities, national and Community rules are likely to be applied at the same time. Until a new Council Regulation under Article 87 (2) (e) provides otherwise, national and Community competition law may clearly be applied simultaneously to the same economic phenomenon, so that two parallel procedures are possible. Even if the Commission found that a given merger was compatible with Article 86, it could not prevent a national authority from prohibiting it on the basis of stricter national legislation, since the EEC Treaty does not provide for the kind of premerger control that is to be found in the European Coal and Steel (ECSC) Treaty. Thus in *GKN-Sachs,* the fact that the Commission decided to take no action under Article 86 did not prevent the German Cartel Office from prohibiting the merger under its national legislation.[38] But if the Commission prohibits the merger by virtue of Article 86, the merger cannot be authorized by virtue of national law.

C. Specific Consequences for Multinational Corporations

From these remarks we can draw a series of conclusions regarding external growth policies of multinational corporations in relation to Article 86.

(1) The typical features of multinationals, (a large number of production and distribution centres, a highly integrated structure and a technological lead over their competitors) may, when combined with a market share which although substantial does not in itself dominate, provide conclusive evidence of a dominant position.

(2) Bearing in mind the scope of Community rules, the position of a multinational on the world market is taken into consideration only if the firm accounts for a large share of production and sales on the Community market.

(3) Multinationals do business throughout the relevant geographic market from

---

[38] See K. Hopt, *Merger Control in Germany: Philosophies, Experiences, Reforms,* supra this volume pp. 71 *et seq.,* esp. at p. 81 and pp. 98-99.

a single decision-making centre; competing firms working part of this market do not necessarily constitute an effective countervailing power.

(4) A strategy of gradually spreading to different parts of the Community from a strong base in one specific area may, in some cases, constitute abuse of a dominant position through expansion.

(5) When a multinational conglomerate uses its dominant position on one product market as a basis for achieving a dominant position on the market for an allied product, this may also constitute abuse of a dominant position through expansion.

(6) Although there can be no question of a blanket prohibition on vertical integration by firms that already dominate this or that stage of a given market, such integration might also constitute abuse, depending on the extent to which the dominant firm's market power is enhanced as a result of the merger.

(7) Although it is difficult to define general quantitative tests for determining whether a merger constitutes abuse, it is likely that a market leader that takes its nearest competitor over is guilty of abuse, though obviously the position of other competitors must also be considered; in other types of merger further factors relating to the countervailing power of the remaining competitors in the relevant geographic and product markets must also be brought into the equation.

IV. Towards more Systematic Control of Large-Scale Mergers

In its judgment of 21 February 1973,[39] the Court of Justice established a rule of law to the effect that Article 86 of the EEC Treaty applies to mergers that constitute abuse of a dominant position; on 20 July 1973 the Commission therefore presented the Council with a proposal for a Council Regulation on the control of concentrations (the merger-control Regulation).[40] Before going into the basic reasons for this proposal and describing its features it is worth giving a brief summary of the earlier merger-control in Article 66 of the Treaty establishing the European Coal and Steel Community.[41] Finally, we shall consider the probable effects of more systematic merger control on multinationals, particularly foreign multinationals.

A. Article 66 of the ECSC Treaty

Since 1954, some 350 mergers have been authorized unter Article 66 originally by the High Authority of the ECSC and later by the Commission of the

---

[39] *Supra* note 20.

[40] *Supra* note 2.

[41] For the text of Art. 66 ECSC *see* Annex II 4 (a) *infra* this volume at pp. 249 *et seq.* The text of ECSC High Authority Decision No. 24-54 of 6 May 1954 laying down in implementation of Article 66 (1) of the Treaty a regulation on what constitutes control of an undertaking, O.J.E.C.S.C. of 11 May 1954 p. 345, is also annexed. *See* infra Annex II 4 (b) pp. 252 *et seq.*

European Communities, which succeeded it in 1967.[42] Article 66, together with Article 65 (prohibition of restrictive practices), was the subject of lively political discussions until the very last moment during the negotiation of the ECSC Treaty. These Articles subjecting the entire coal and steel industry of the six member countries to lasting supranational control, were intended to replace the unilateral control introduced by the allied powers over German heavy industry after the Second World War. Not only was political discrimination against German industry removed, but in the second paragraph of Article 66 (2) the principle of non-discrimination for industrial structures was affirmed, so that the deconcentration of German industry imposed by the Allies could be reversed up to the point at which concentration in Germany was comparable to that among their Community competitors.

The administrative practice has broadly been to encourage a harmonious pattern of concentration leading towards an admittedly increasingly narrow oligopoly; the harmony was almost broken by the highly acquisitive strategy operated, between 1959 and 1964, by the German group *August-Thyssen-Hütte*. But Article 66 was used to restore balance. Another important aspect of administrative practice has been the systematic attempt to eliminate links between the major steel groups in the form of minority holdings, however small (in many cases cross-holdings), and interlocking directorates; such links involve no sharing of the industrial risks but are liable to hamper the normal competitive behaviour of the resulting exchange of information.

The most important provision of Article 66 and the regulations implementing it are the principle of prior notification and authorization for mergers (Article 66 (1)); the fact that authorization must be granted if it is found that the proposed transaction will not, among other things, "hinder effective competition" (Article 66 (2));[43] the power to order divestiture (Article 66 (5), second and subsequent subparagraphs); and, the imposition of fines (Article 66 (6)). The definition of what constitutes control in Article 66 (1) is also interesting, if only because the provisions came into force so long ago; the elements of control of an undertaking include mergers, the acquisition of shares or interests in the assets, loans and contracts, and these elements are specifically defined in decision No. 24-54 of May 1954 on what constitutes control of an undertaking.[44] This decision defines the control exercised by one firm over another in economic terms by reference to the extent to which the controlling firm can determine the behaviour of the controlled firm.

Article 66 has always been taken to mean that authorization may not be granted for mergers that would generate a dominant position – what we call external growth. Even so the grouping of large firms with a wide range of products under single control has sometimes given the new group a substantial

---

[42] These authorizations include various types of decision, including for example the authorization of joint ventures and interlocking directorates.

[43] This idea can be found in the Continental Can Case, *supra* note 20, at p. 244 para. 25; and in Article 1 (1) of the Proposed Regulation, *supra* note 2.

[44] *See supra* note 41.

share in the output[45] of some products; for example, the *Arbed-Röchling* merger accounted for 30% of the Community output of girders.

Coal production (which is largely nationalized or controlled by public corporations) and steel production have developed essentially within national frontiers. There are some groups with multinational features, such as the Luxembourg-based steel company Arbed, which would be somewhat hemmed in within its small territory, or the medium-sized groups controlled by Franco-Belgian holding companies. The only really important transnational concentration occurred in 1976 when the German firm *Hoesch* and the Dutch firm *Hoogovens* were brought together under the management of *Estel*. At the time, the new group was the second largest Community producer of cast iron, with 9.3% of output, and of crude steel, with 9.9%.[46]

There are very few non-Community firms with interests in European heavy industry that come under the ECSC Treaty. The application of Article 66 to multinational firms has never yet caused problems. Indeed, it may have encouraged mergers, as in the case of Estel, which in the absence of specific provisions covering mergers in broad terms might have been caught by Article 65's rules on restrictive practices, because the initial relations between firms planning to merge will tend to be cautious rather than bold. In particular, relations between firms in different countries are usually established by a slow process. The merger itself may be preceded by structured cooperation.

B. The Proposed Merger Control Regulation

1. The Proposal of 1973[47]

The proposal is based on Article 87 (empowering the Council to adopt measures giving effect to Article 85 and 86) and on Article 235 (by which the Community may give itself the powers of action necessary for the attainment of its objectives) of the EEC Treaty. Article 235 had to be invoked because of the first three of the following provisions that are not covered by the Court of Justice decision in *Continental Can:*

(1) A merger that creates a dominant position is incompatible with the common market in the same way as a merger which consolidates a pre-existing dominant position (Article 1 (1) of the proposal).

(2) A merger that is indispensable to the attainment of an objective which is given priority treatment in the common interests of the Community may be declared compatible with the common market (Article 1 (3)).

(3) Mergers must be notified in advance (Article 4), and fines may be imposed (Article 13 (2)). Unlike Article 66 of the ECSC Treaty, the proposed Regulation does not apply the prior authorization principle, nor even the principle of prohibition. Neither of these two principles is realistic, since

---

[45] Community output, disregarding exports from the Community and imports from non-member countries.

[46] 15TH GENERAL REPORT OF THE E.C.S.C., p. 189 (Luxemburg, March 1977).

[47] *Supra* note 2.

they would have to apply to structural measures in the field of general economic activity. The principle of prohibition might also, in the legal systems of some of the Member States, mean that acts carried out in the framework of an unauthorized merger were void.

(4) Mergers involving firms with an aggregate turnover of less than 200 million units of account and a volume of business of less than 25% of the turnover in each member country are not covered (Article 1 (2)).

(5) Mergers are defined in the same way as in decision No. 24-54 ECSC (Article 2).[48]

(6) The only formal decisions provided for are decisions declaring the merger to be incompatible with the common market, decisions ordering divestiture and decisions declaring Article 1 (1) to be inapplicable (Article 3 (1), (3), (4)).

(7) Prior notification is required when the aggregate turnover of the firms concerned exceeds 1,000 million units of account (Article 4 (1)).

(8) Prior notification is not required if the firm to be taken over has a turnover of less than 30 million units of account.

(9) The procedure is rapid: the Commission has three months to commence proceedings (Article 6), and decisions must be taken within nine months of the date of commencement (Article 17).

These are the main provisions of the Commission's proposal, which was approved by the European Parliament on 12 February 1974[49] and by the Economic and Social Committee on 28 February 1974.[50] When these two bodies were discussing the proposal, the Commission accepted some amendments so that plans by independent firms or groups to set up joint ventures would no longer be exempt from prior notification.

2. The Progress of the Proposal to Date

Since 1974 the Council has met several times to discuss the proposal; there is *broad consensus on* four basic points:

First, the field of application should be defined in relation to two tests taken together, with thresholds of between 500 million and 1,000 million units of account as regards the aggregate annual total turnover of the firms concerned and between 20% and 25% of the common market as regards their aggregate product market share;

Second, public undertakings, banks and insurance companies come under the Regulation, but there will have to be specific rules for implementation to banking and insurance;

Third, derogations from the principle of incompatibility with the common market should also be given for the purposes of national industrial, technological, social or regional policies, particularly when the policy is in the general interests of the Community, or when there is no common policy;

---

[48] *See supra* note 41 and accompanying text.
[49] O.J.E.C., Vol. 17, C 23 p. 19 (1974).
[50] O.J.E.C., Vol. 17, C 88 p. 19 (1974).

Fourth, the principle of compulsory prior notification is accepted for example when the total turnover involved in the transaction is more than 1,000 units of account.

Discussions are still going on in the Council about liaison with the authorities of the Member States (Article 19) and their involvement in the decision-making process. Although the proposed procedure, which corresponds to Article 10 of Regulation 17 of 1962 implementing Articles 85 and 86 of the EEC Treaty,[51] is probably inadequate to ensure closer involvement of national authorities, provisions involving the Council as such in procedures to deal with individual cases must be avoided.

C. The Outlook for the Proposed Merger Control

Further lengthy discussions will be necessary before the Regulation can be adopted. Once the political problems and basic points have been dealt with, procedural provisions will have to be decided upon, and mergers defined. The Commission's work on groups of companies in preparation for the Ninth Directive on the coordination of national laws on links between undertakings could be of help here. If the original proposal is substantially amended by the Council, as seems very likely, Parliament and the Economic and Social Committee will have to be consulted again. For the moment it is by no means certain that the Regulation will actually be adopted, although most of the Member States are in favour of a regulation applying in particular to cross-frontier mergers that are so difficult to deal with under national law.

If a regulation introducing more systematic merger-control is passed, the probable outcome can be summarized under eight points:

1. The Applicable Law

(1) The new Regulation ought to have precedence over Article 86 as implemented by Regulation No. 17 because of the procedural advantages, the derogations provided for and the fact that the Member States are more closely
involved in decision-making;
(2) The Regulation should define clearly the respective powers of national
authorities applying their own law and Community authorities applying
Community law.
(3) When two sets of laws apply, the principle that the stricter provisions prevail
could be introduced.

2. Multinational Corporations, Including Non-Community Multinationals

(4) Where non-Community parent companies with subsidiaries in the Community merge and thereby acquire or strengthen a dominant position within
the common market, they would be subject to the Regulation as it applies to
internal structural effects: Article 1 of the proposal refers specifically to "a
concentration between undertakings or groups of undertakings, at least one
of which is established in the common market".

[51] J. O. 1962, 204.

(5) The total turnover of about 1,000 million units of account to be taken into consideration is the worldwide turnover, and thus affects multinationals in particular.

(6) Multinationals with a wide range of products are more likely to acquire a market share of 20 to 25% of the common market in a particular product through merger.

(7) Since the maximum turnover and market share are at present regarded as cumulative tests, i. e. both must be satisfied if the merger is to be caught by the Regulation, multinationals will be the firms most often involved.

(8) Lastly, in view of the increasingly stringent attitude taken by anti-trust authorities, the provisions granting dispensation from compulsory prior notification or exempting the acquisition of small firms (at present those with a turnover of less than 30 million units of account) may end up by applying to mergers with an even lower turnover threshold; this could affect multinational conglomerates.

The specific problems of applying Community competition law to multinationals are not insoluble, particularly those of controlling mergers in the common market. The problems noted do not affect the principle that competition rules within the Community apply without discrimination to all firms doing business there. Although multinationals are more likely than other firms to be affected by these rules, this is not because they are multinationals, but because of their market position and their market power; indeed when these are assessed they are treated in exactly the same way as any other firm.

Summary

This paper deals with various questions of Community competition law concerning the control of cross-frontier mergers involving multinational corporations, in particular where they have a decision-making centre outside the Community.

In the first part, the general principles governing the application of Community competition rules to foreign multinational corporations are described, notably the "effects doctrine" and the principle of enterprise unity concerning affiliated corporations.

The second part deals more specifically with the use of Article 86 of the Treaty of Rome as a means of controlling unacceptable large mergers. Here, emphasis is placed on the interpretation of the notion of dominant position of market power by the European Court of Justice in recent cases and on the so-called "Continental Can doctrine" concerning the strengthening of a dominant position as a form of abuse.

The third part considers the possibilities for a more systematic Community control of large-scale mergers. The starting point is Article 66 of the ECSC Treaty governing mergers in the coal and steel sectors. A description of the main features of the 1973 Commission proposal for a merger-control Regulation and an assessment of the current status of this proposal after some discussion in the Council of Ministers follows.

The paper concludes with an attempt to forecast the probable outcome of these discussions. On the whole, the paper stresses that the specific problems of applying Community competition law to multinational corporations, particularly to mergers involving multinationals, are not insoluble. Although multinational corporations because of their size and market power are more likely than other firms to be affected by these rules, solutions can be found respecting the principle of equal treatment without regard to the multinational character or the location of the decision-making centre of the enterprise involved.

Annex I

Discussion Report

Colloquium on Multinational Corporations
in European Corporate and Antitrust Laws,
28-31 May 1980
at the European University Institute in Florence*
(Volume I: European Merger Control)

JOSEPH H. H. WEILER
Florence

Chapter I:
Economic Considerations

I. Multinational Enterprises in the 1970's: An Economist's Overview of Trends, Theories and Policies

REPORTER: PROFESSOR J. H. DUNNING

The Report indicated a changing pattern in the activities of multinationals, the economic theories associated with these activities and governmental policies towards multinationals. The following issues were raised in discussion.

A. Growth

The analysis revealed that even if there had been a measure of growth in international direct investment (foreign direct investment being taken as the operative definition of the multinational enterprise (M.N.E.)) the rate of growth has now slowed down quite considerably: the policy-maker is thus dealing with a phenomenon which seems to have outgrown its phase of rapid growth and to have more or less stabilised. This regularization of activities would indicate perhaps an easier climate within which to deal with the M.N.E. At the same time it was recorded that the general recession and decline in economic growth have created a situation in which economic stimuli are needed and in which the M.N.E. may be seen anew as providing such stimuli.

---

* This Discussion Report is prepared as a supplement to the National and European Community Reports published in this volume. Utilizing the wealth of comment offered at the Colloquium it tries to highlight those features which seemed most interesting and enlightening in relation to the different reports.

B. Type and Location of Activities

In present world market conditions an important share of multinational activity may be seen to be shifting into high technology investment. In addition U.S. dominance seems to be declining even if it remains sizeable. Significantly, Japan has increased its share in foreign direct investment by eighteen times and Germany by ten. These data coupled with the geographical distribution of foreign direct investment highlight another potential change in policy concern, namely the significant shift of investment from developing to developed countries which is interlinked with the shift into high technology industries. The U.K. and Germany (along with Canada and the U.S.) are now the leading host countries to foreign direct investment.

European countries are thus coming to the fore at both the giving and receiving end of M.N.E. activity. The multinational "défi" may now be Japanese (or South Korean) rather than American, but in Europe the policy conundrums remain, involving a delicate excercise of balancing the conflicting interests implicit in these data. Thus, e. g., as was pointed out in discussion, European measures aimed at *foreign* M.N.E.'s would have to be considered in the light of possible retaliation against European M.N.E.'s operating abroad. Equally, policies originally designed to encourage the evolution of the European M.N.E.'s as a vehicle for foreign direct investment abroad would have to be reconsidered when these, in view of the shift to high technology investment, turn their attention to their own home ground.

C. Control by Multinationals – Merger or Contract?

A further aspect highlighted by the Reporter concerned the pattern of internal organization of multinationals. Two trends were apparent here. In the first place there has been a move away from the 100% owned subsidiary towards greater local participation. Secondly, increasingly, a contractual ("externalized") mode of technology and management transfer is replacing the direct ("internalized") route.

Here as well the policy and legal implications are acute. Do these changes indicate that the multinationals are not merely "quantitatively" in decline (point A above) but also "qualitatively" at bay, or even in retreat, as some of the observers cited by the Reporter would suggest? And if this is so, what legal implications would follow from this trend? This issue served as a focus for several comments:

1. The changing pattern of external and internal practices was attributed to several factors, including the greater control excercised by states through say, their fiscal measures; the volatility of exchange rates which facilitated European foreign direct investment in the 70's especially in America; and last, but not least, the relatively reduced efficiency of U.S. enterprises when compared to their German and South East Asian competitors.

2. As regards internal organization – does the trend towards contractual "externalized" operations signal a trend towards less or more control by the parent company? This issue was to be a theme throughout the Colloquium. A

complementary question was whether one could work out a framework by which the issue of centralization or decentralization of decision-making in the multinational corporation could be assessed in relation to the advantages and disadvantages to the home and host country respectively, as well as to the multinational enterprise itself.

If this question could be answered, many of the policy problems associated with the new external trend of activities of multinationals could be solved. The policy-maker would have a guideline as to the model of activity which a new generation of laws should encourage or discourage. And yet, as expected, the issues of control and benefits in relation to centralization or decentralization did not lend themselves to clear cut evaluation. On its face "internal" equity control would suggest a higher degree of domination by the parent company than would the contractual — external — method. Yet, as the Reporter pointed out, by devices such as long term supply contracts in, say, the hotel industry, it can be shown that formal independence of the subsidiary need not imply lesser control by the parent. The crucial question becomes that of examining the terms of the contracts in any given transaction. There can thus be no *a priori* preference for one system or another in terms of potential benefits to the organization of the enterprise and industry, nor to the issue of control by the host (and home) countries.

The decentralized model would seem, on its face, to offer greater advantages to the host country — at least in terms of allowing more independence to the subsidiary, which, in turn, could facilitate a smoother integration of the subsidiary within the local economy. To that extent policies which would discourage 100% ownership may seem promising to the host country.

The evolution of the external method throws this above assumption into doubt. For, as was seen, it would be possible for the parent company to allow a large measure of constitutional independence — which in itself may be useful to the parent by limiting its financial risk in the event of failure and minimizing its actual commitments of investment funds — but to maintain tight control through the externalized contractual method.

The classic definitions of control and centralization, therefore, break down; the evaluation of costs and benefits to the home and host countries become at best a matter of ad hoc examination and at worst impossible. Equally, the classic distinction between corporate law expressed through equity control and anti-trust law expressed through concerted (contractual) practices also loses some force if enterprises aim to achieve the same result by using one device or the other.

D. Changing Governmental Policies Towards the M.N.E and Its Interpretation

The Reporter suggested, in terms of Governmental policies, that there has recently been a change towards a conciliatory and more mutually rewarding relationship compared to the antagonism of the 60's.

The reasons for this change, in the eyes of the Reporter, are a general global trend towards political and economic conservatism; the decline in economic growth which has given multinationals a very saleable commodity, namely, investment; the evolution of competition among multinational corporations; a less paranoid attitude to multinationals now that the phenomenon is somewhat better known and better understood; a less aggressive attitude on the part of multinationals themselves; a reappraisal of direct investment in which multinationals have equity control which does mean — in a less healthy economic climate — that the multinational has a real stake in the success or otherwise of its subsidiaries; and, finally, better international control such as Article 86 of the European Economic Community Treaty, the OECD guidelines, etc.

That the field and its interpretations are in a state of flux was apparent from the discussion which followed this analysis. Whereas the actual prediction of a more relaxed relationship between governments and multinationals was not disputed, different explanations were suggested for this new trend. Thus it was suggested that the relaxed attitude derived simply from the will of countries to protect their own multinationals abroad and their fear of retaliatory action, should foreign multinationals be constrained. In other words, we may be seeing here the evolution of a system of international and reciprocal comity in respect of multinational activity. A second suggestion went even further. Multinationals, it was submitted, had simply out-manoeuvred the governments by playing one government against another. The decline in economic growth had given the multinationals more power and leverage over governments. The Rhodesian oil sanction busting was cited as one illustration as well as Ford Motor Cars' European investment negotiations and strategy. In other words, the leopard had not changed its spots: Multinationals remained masters of their employees and, except marginally, not responsible to their governments. The relaxation, therefore, was an indication of rejuvenation of M.N.E. strength.

II. Merger Policy in the United Kingdom

REPORTER: MR. R. G. OPIE

In this paper the Reporter analyzed some of the economic and policy considerations which affected the work of the British Monopolies Commission. As this Report was discussed together with the national Report on Merger Control in the U.K., reference should be made also to the discussion comments thereon, (below, Chapter II.I).

A. The Problem of Economic Assessment

It was clear from the speakers' presentation that the assessment of the economic and commercial impact of the merger remains extremely difficult. This is true both as regards the phenomenon of merger itself, as well as the utility of the control tools. The Colloquium heard that it was not uncommon for the British Monopolies Commission to receive evidence which indicated that mergers were contemplated by company executives on the flimsiest of economic and commercial evidence as to the likely result. In some cases the motivating force was the general trend which pervaded the 60's and 70's, namely that "bigger is better"; in other cases the motivation could be a businessman's "whim". Likewise the task of the Monopolies Commission and the Merger Panels of the Office of Fair Trading in its preliminary screening is problematical: Gazing into the economic and commercial crystal ball, and assessing the impact of a proposed merger with any measure of confidence is extremely difficult. Indeed it is doubtful whether economic analysis can always be a substitute for business acumen and entrepreneurial intuition. In predicting the future, the control authorities would inevitably get involved in hypothetical permutations. In a post hoc analysis, it was pointed out, it was very difficult to gauge the success or otherwise of decisions taken in relation to proposed mergers, given that it is all but impossible to tell with any measure of confidence what the results would have been had a different decision been taken. One Reporter indicated that the Monopolies Commission has made a brave attempt in its effort to arrive at a defensible economic position regarding the narrow issues of the reductions in competition resulting from mergers as opposed to potential increase in efficiency. In this, the British Monopolies Commission, in contrast to the Commission of the European Communities, has perhaps — as pointed out by the Reporter — adopted a more sophisticated approach in defining the relevant market and making allowances for potential competition from other close markets in the situation where the barriers to entry are rather low. At the same time there are inherent limits to an exercise which has to take place in a short period of four to six months, although the task is facilitated when the merger is contested and evidence is submitted by the adversaries (in the U.K., merger also includes the case of an involuntary stockmarket takeover which is often strenuously resisted by the "target" company). One tactic of resistance is to request that a reference be made to the Monopolies Commission. In these situations the "target" company will, naturally, try to built up as strong a case as possible against the merger — a situation which offers a useful analysis of the issues; in uncontested mergers where both parties are agreeable to the merger, no such evidence would be voluntarily forthcoming, thereby increasing the difficulties of the Commission.

B. The Composition and Choice of Members of the Monopolies Commission

One feature of the U.K. regime which was regarded with particular interest was the part-time nature of the Commission working with only a full-time chairman. One direct result of this was the very low cost of the operation, estimated by the Reporters at one hundred thousand pounds per annum. The question was then raised as to the composition of this body. This would seem an extremely acute problem, given the task of the Monopolies Commission of sizing up the "public interest". It was pointed out that a balance between economists, trade unionists, merchant bankers, businessmen and lawyers was always aimed at. The lawyer would invariably be the chairman. This same composition was also maintained in respect of each panel considering a specific merger. It should be noted that this wide composition of the various bodies was important for more than one reason. In the first place it ensured that decisions reflected more than narrow sectorial interests. Only a wide body could consider the public interest as it is defined in the legislation. In addition, it was noted that decisions of the Monopolies Commission were subject to a measure of judicial review. Administrative bodies so subject are charged by the courts when reviewing their decisions with the duty of acting according to the canons of "natural justice", one aspect of which is that there should be a fair hearing. Achieving a fair hearing is facilitated by the interests represented on the Commission and its panels. (It was recorded that *Hoffmann-La Roche* sued the Commission for substantial damages in respect of certain proceedings, which indicates that these requirements are not purely academic.)

C. Coordination between Policy-Making Bodies

In their presentation the Reporters noted proliferation of British governmental or quasi-governmental bodies dealing with the issue of concentration. Thus the two main examples already discussed were on the one hand the Monopolies Commission and on the other hand institutions such as the Industrial Reorganization Corporation and its progeny. With different bodies dealing with the same phenomenon — often with immediately diverging interests — the question was raised whether there was a measure of coordination between these bodies exercising public functions. Could there ever be an overt conflict between say the National Enterprise Board promoting a merger and the Monopolies Commission turning it down? In reply it was apparent that the solution in the United Kingdom was very "English". On its face there was no overt coordination and theoretically there could be conflicts. But, given the well-known influence of civil servants in policy-making, there would necessarily be a covert process of "underground" coordination in the corridors of Whitehall. In effect no real clashes or conflicts have ever come to the surface although it is possible that these were avoided by this indirect coordination process.

Chapter II:
Merger Control Systems in European Countries

I. Control of Mergers in the U.K. on Grounds of Competition: Legislation, Practice and Experience

REPORTER: DR. V. KORAH

The British experience was discussed also in the context of the economic and policy considerations of merger control (Chapter I.II) and the following comments represent that part of the Colloquium discussion which related more specifically to Dr. Korah's Report.

A. Defining the Public Interest

Defining the public interest was one of the most intriguing aspects of the British regime and one which surfaced in the discussion throughout the Colloquium. As may be seen in the legislation, the general public interest is as important as a criterion for approval or disapproval of a merger as is the narrow economic consideration. In the U.K. the two factors form part and parcel of the same test and are not, unlike other systems, separated either substantively or procedurally. Given the acknowledged difficulty of arriving at economically foolproof decisions regarding mergers, and given that the question of deciding the public interest was inherently unquantifiable, did not the combined test become extremely elusive? How then was the Commission to decide upon this issue. The Reporters agreed that in practice the statutory guidelines were never considered strictly and members of the Commission in the final analysis would utilize a large measure of intuition. This did not necessarily negate the utility of the exercise: it may still reveal many weak points in the merger proposals. In addition, the hearings coerce the merging undertakings to rethink and defend their positions – an exercise which, one Reporter suggested, had a *per se* value given the summary manner in which some mergers are conceived.

B. Onus of Proof

A potential weakness which was highlighted in the British procedure concerned the onus of proof and the nature of the decision of the Monopolies Commission. The current critical test is whether a merger is *against* the public interest. Further, the onus is to prove that the merger is against the public interest. Yet it is clear that whereas a merger may not be against the public interest, it may have no great positive advantages, either for the merging companies themselves, or for the economy at large. In addition, the Commission may feel that a different type of merger with, say, other partners – or one other partner – would be much more beneficial, but this of course would be outside its brief. Here then was the manifestation in this field of the classic clash between a libertarian tradition of commercial freedom with the tradition of a public stake in the affairs of undertakings capable of influencing large sectors of the economy. In the existing U.K. regime, the onus of proof marginally favours the former tradition. It was suggested that in the light of practice and changing economic perceptions a shift of presumption may be called for.

C. The Duty to Refer

In the British system there is no duty on the parties to a contemplated merger to inform the competent authorities of their intention. In theory the various authorities and particularly the Office of Fair Trading are charged with advising the Minister of potentially harmful mergers by gleaning information from the press and other public or private sources. This, on its face, and to several Colloquium members, seemed a rather inefficient method to have been adopted by British policy-makers in this legislation. The Reporters however pointed out that the possibility which existed in the United Kingdom law of a post hoc reference by the Office of Fair Trading with a recommendation to the minister for an investigation of a merger was sufficient to create a de facto duty on behalf of undertakings contemplating merger to inform the authorities in order to get a preliminary reaction. The prospect of an investigation and a possible instruction to dismantle and demerge seemed a sufficiently strong incentive to make all companies contemplating mergers and coming within the qualifying circumstances for investigation interested in making their intentions known to the competent authorities.

D. Assurances

Another feature of the U.K. experience which intrigued participants was the informal nature of parts of that procedure. In certain cases the minister, in whose hands lies the final decision-making power (subject to Parliamentary control), would rely on promises and assurances given by the merging companies. In relation to queries on this point the Reporters emphasized two points: As regards substance, *Dr. Korah* indicated that in certain instances the assurances given by an undertaking (case of BICC/Pyrotenax) did not make much economic sense, as a profounder economic analysis revealed. As regards procedure, speakers emphasized that whereas these assurances were legally meaningless and unenforceable in the courts, the minister would be following a tradition of British life, relying on the notion of good faith in British economic practice.

E. The Problem of Time and Confidentiality

These were issues raised by several participants. The dilemma is many-sided. Commercial considerations will at times make an early indication of the authorities' attitude to a merger imperative. This may be the case when there are possibilities of merging with different undertakings or when, e. g., unhealthy stock market speculation is expected. For their part, the authorities in merger control offices will be interested in as long a period as possible with the objective of gathering sufficient evidence for arriving at an informed economic and public policy decision. A similiar conflict arises in relation to the issue of confidentiality. The prospective parties to a merger will often wish that the transaction or proposed transaction remain confidential until a definite decision is taken. Public authorities may wish, in certain circumstances, to receive public evidence on the desirability or otherwise of a proposed merger. The two interests may come into conflict. In addition mergers are at times conducted on non-par conditions, where the competitive position of one merging company vis-à-vis the other is held out in an effort to improve the merger terms. In the course of an investigation into the desirability of the merger, evidence may be revealed which will erode the competitiveness of one of the merger parties such as its marketing schemes, discount practices etc. These points were put to the speakers, who outlined the United Kingdom position in relation to them. As regards time the three tier system with a preliminary investigation by a Merger Panel of the Office of Fair Trading, was a useful device in relation to the time problem. For the decisions of the Merger Panel were usually fairly speedy (a matter of weeks rather than months) and companies could know with a high measure of confidence whether the proposed merger would *not* be referred to the Monopolies Commission. It was also pointed out that there have been no complaints of a breach of confidentiality by the various organs dealing with the matter. The Monopolies Commission enquiries may last for several months, although six months is the usual limit – which is a relatively short period. It was, however, pointed out that many companies proposed a merger on condition that there should not be a reference to the Monopolies Commission. This could be not only a result of the time factor, but also of the general repercussions of a public investigation. In this sense the system did seem "loaded" against the merger. Companies willing to undergo the procedure were in some cases concerned in a merger which took the nature of a takeover rather than a jointly agreed venture.

F. Externalised Mergers

A further issue that was raised in discussion concerned the case of a merger between a United Kingdom undertaking with foreign based firms, namely an externalised merger.

The competent bodies such as the Monopolies Commission would presumably, it was put to the Reporter, have to consider a different range of policy considerations. The Reporter first noted that there had been no cases where a reference was made in respect of a British firm taking over an overseas firm. As regards take-over of firms in Britain by overseas undertakings it was pointed out that the type of consideration which the Monopolies Commission would weigh would be, for example, the advantage of introducing superior technology against disadvantages such as the escape of research out of Britain. As regards balance of payments considerations, the Monopolies Commission would probably follow the advice of the Bank of England.

II. Merger Control in Germany: Philosophies, Experiences, Reforms

REPORTER: PROFESSOR K. J. HOPT

A. The Problem of Economic Assessment

Whatever measure of precision German antitrust law has managed to attain in the initial "competition examination" by the Federal Cartel Office, the German, like the British, system faces the intractable problem of assessing the efficacy of the policies and criteria. Thus the Reporter emphasised that figures drawn from the overall measure of increase of economic concentration would be misleading since "German merger control is not directed against economic concentration as such, but rather against certain aspects of external growth while leaving internal growth untouched".

Equally misleading would be the figures relating to the rate of prohibitions on mergers notified by the Cartel Office (24 prohibitions out of 2,849 notifications in the period 1973-1979). For here we are faced with the perennial problem affecting assessment of legal measures, namely gauging the deterrent effect of the measure in question. The Reporter estimated that, especially among the larger German enterprises, there would be awareness of the difficulties and burdens of merger control which prima facie would infringe the substantive "no-go" provisions of the law and that thus many potential abusive mergers would be voluntarily avoided. In general, whereas there was no complacency, the impression at the Colloquium was that the procedural and substantive precision aimed at by the German regime and particularly the differentiation between the economic "take-up" and "no-go" criteria, as opposed to the political "let-off" criteria, made companies more sharply conscious of the legal regime and more able to base their policies in consideration of the law.

B. The Contrast with the British System

The German experience of merger control contrasted sharply with that of the U.K. In relation to the latter, the Conference noted on the one hand some of the subtle methods employed in Britain both in the selection of the merger control bodies, the definition of their competences and the exercise of their powers. On the one hand it was felt that the British experience and the British machinery was characterized by a certain measure of vagueness in, say, defining the criteria for control of mergers. There was, for example, a mixture of economic and non-economic factors to be considered by the Monopolies Commission. Although in considering the competition aspects of mergers the British Mono-polies Commission achieved a measure of sophistication, the overall picture was one of decisions influenced to some extent by sheer intuition. There was also a measure of duplicity in the decision-making process; the Monopolies Commission was charged in its enabling Act with examining the overall public interest as a criterion for control. The minister, as a higher instance, was also to refer to that criterion although he would, perhaps, be influenced more overtly by political considerations. Reliance on fair play, public assurances by undertakings and gentlemanly agreements also had a part to play in the British procedure. Some continental commentators felt as a result that the British machinery would make the task of predicting the likely reaction to a merger by the authorities extremely difficult for undertakings and their legal and economic advisers.

C. Economic Considerations vs. Wider Public Interest

One major difference between the British and the German systems which was noted was the attempt in Germany to separate commercial-economic considerations of competition, efficiency and the like on the one hand, to be entrusted to the Federal Cartel Office, and, on the other hand, to leave questions of the public interest defined in its wider terms to the Ministry of Economic Affairs – squarely and fairly in the political domain. Certain consequences flow from this sharp division in the German system. The Cartel Office can use its resources, focus its attention and build up its experience with the sole concentration on commercial and economic considerations. Whether, or not, the economic criteria (the "no-go" criteria) evolved by these bodies are meaningful and adequate in the general policy of merger control is one question; but they will certainly have a large measure of precision and consequently a high predictability potential. In addition, judicial review of decisions of the Cartel Office may be improved. For the courts will be confronted in reviewing these decisions with economic and commercial data, certain guidelines and more technical justiciable issues. The courts would not have to embroil themselves at that stage with the far less justiciable issues of the public interest in its wider sense. Indeed, in relation to the latter, the Reporter indicated in reply to a question that judicial review of this second tier political decision by the minister (which takes place on extremely rare occasions) is confined to findings of facts and to logical mistakes and excludes a substantive evaluation of the political issues.

At the same time, it was pointed out that in certain instances it was difficult to maintain this strict separation. The Reporter alluded to the case of the "reorganization merger" in which a failing company is taken over by another sound enterprise. Allowing the merger to go through will save a failing company, will prevent destruction of resources and will, arguably, save jobs. On the other hand, as has been pointed out, often the only candidate to take over the failing company will be a market leader which thereby would increase its level of concentration. Under the German system the Cartel Office must theoretically confine itself to the effect on competition of the proposed reorganization merger. It could take into consideration factors such as the competitiveness of the failing enterprise in a particular market and so forth; it cannot – in sharp contrast to the British Monopolies Commission – consider such factors as the effect on jobs, the disadvantages to the region and so forth. Yet the line in practice between these two aspects is at times artificial and blurred, and the strict separation is not easy to maintain.

D. Ministerial Discretion

The sharp separation between the economic commercial decision and the wide public policy decision has an additional dimension. Both in relation to the British experience and the German experience, the issue of the impartiality of ministerial discretion was raised. The possibility of a decision being based not so much on a general public consideration, but rather on partisan party politics (jobs in a minister's constituency etc.) was an issue which was raised by participants. It was suggested by the reporter for Germany that the strict division between the two ranges of consideration increased the potential for ministerial impartiality. Although the grounds on which the minister exempts merging companies from a Cartel Office prohibition are in the German system fairly wide, it becomes difficult for the minister, after the long proceedings before the Federal Cartel Office and possible review by the courts, and taking into account all the economic damage which in the eyes of the Cartel Office would result from the merger, to approve it without weighty justification. The public interest considerations must be clearly spelt out and cannot be enmeshed with vague economic generalities.

E. Substantive Criteria for Prohibitions on Mergers

Two main criteria are employed by the German legislation. The first one is that of the strengthening or creation of a position of market domination. Market domination in turn is decided according to the existence or otherwise of substantial competition. This in turn can only be defined in relation to the relevant market of the product. Whereas within the category of the relevant market the German system has moved away from the traditional break-down according to branches of industry and substituted in its stead a "functional-interchangeability-of-different-products-for-the-user" test with a measure of examination of cross-elasticity of prices, the market share still remains "the single most important criterion for evaluating the existence of substantial competition". Both economists and jurists from other legal systems doubted this heavy reliance by the German system on the criterion of market shares and relevant markets. It was pointed out in the first place that a low market share could still be compatible with a dominant position and the more sophisticated British approach of looking at barriers to entry was recorded. The Reporter pointed out that the 1973 reform introduced the notion, as a second criterion, of "the superior market position". This new concept would take account of the general strength of the undertaking, its reliance on one single product (which would reduce its market position considerably), the ability to resist periods of depression etc. The law gives illustrative but not exhaustive examples for determining superior market position, such as relative market share, financial strength, access to supply and sales markets etc. Whereas this latter approach does offer a higher measure of sophistication, it of course reduces one of the other aims of the German legislature, namely, its precision, certainty and predictability.

At this stage the issue which the conference left open was the degree to which the aims of achieving clear, justiciable and predictable juridico-economic criteria for merger control was dependent on adopting fairly simple and perhaps not sufficiently sophisticated substantive tests. Was the complexity of the merger issue today such as to create an either/or dichotomy on this issue and was it legitimate to exclude at the initial phases considerations of employment and the like when – as was pointed out – accepting justification criteria became more difficult in the wake of an adverse economic decision? The choice between these approaches is perhaps as much a question of policy as it is of technique and no clear cut solution seemed inherently "correct".

F. Notification

Although in Germany there is only a qualified duty to notify, there is, as in Britain, a de facto total obligation. For without notification, whether compulsory or voluntary, the sanctions against an offensive merger may be exercized at any point in time. This is too large a risk for sizeable companies to take and, therefore, it is in their interest to notify even if the proposed merger does not come within the obligatory guidelines.

G. The Question of Time and Confidentiality

In relation to queries the Reporter noted that to his knowledge there has never been a breach of confidentiality in the preliminary investigatory stages. By law the Cartel Office is obliged to give its decision within four months. Failure to give a decision is tantamount to a positive clearance. Whereas the British Reporter commented on the possible superficiality of analysis that resulted from the time limit, the German Reporter indicated that in Germany the main problem was the drain on resources which the time limit imposed. Half the personnel of the Cartel Office were engaged in merger investigation because of the short time limit. At the same time it was strongly felt that extension of the allotted time would severely impede the commercial viability of many potentially beneficial mergers.

H. Judicial Review

A noticeable distinction between the British and German system emerged in relation to judicial review. Germany seemed to be characterized by a greater measure of judicial review of Cartel Office decisions. This is partly explicable in terms of the greater precision in the guidelines of the German Cartel Office, which makes these decisions more susceptible to judicial review; in part by the special judicial machinery designed to deal with this type of case as well as, perhaps, by a tradition according to which courts will more readily be involved in economic decision-making. Whereas judicial review on the whole is a welcome phenomenon, one of the participants, a member of the German cartel bench, commented on this phenomenon. It is true that the more precise economic-commercial considerations to which the Cartel Office has to confine itself make judicial review more easy in Germany than in Britain, but this of course has certain disadvantages. A single merger, it was pointed out, might involve four legal proceedings, each one going through all instances of appeal. Thus there may be legal proceedings going up to the Supreme Court on the issue of notification; legal proceedings concerning a prohibition by the Cartel Office, which again may go as far as the Supreme Court; a third round of legal proceedings may concern the dissolution of a merger which had gone ahead during previous legal proceedings contesting a prohibition. And, albeit in rare cases, there may be legal proceedings concerning the discretional decision of the minister to whom an application was made for exemption on grounds of general economic policy and public interest. Whether this is preferable to the U.K. system characterized by a lower measure of judicial review and whether finding a via media is possible, was an issue left open at the Colloquium.

III. Merger Control in France: Direct and Indirect Ways of Control

REPORTER: PROFESSOR C. CHAMPAUD

In his Report Professor Champaud emphasized that there was very little practical experience with the new legislation which in turn made assessment of its impact difficult to gauge. Colloquium participants focussed thus on theoretical points which the French legislation seemed to throw up. The following issues seemed of greatest interest.

A. The Economic Phenomenon

In his Report Professor Champaud noted the unimpressive economic and commercial record of French concentration. As a preliminary question the Reporter was asked if any explanation could be found for this apparent failure of French mergers. In response, several reasons were mentioned. In certain cases concentrations were artificial: Failing companies merging with others in an attempt at survival, a case of the blind leading the blind or "the blind leading the paralytic". In other cases French concentration could not emulate the American formula characterized by fusion in terms of turnover coupled with simplification in the direction of the joined enterprises. In France, by contrast, fusion often resulted in a very top heavy direction which made the company cumbersome and inefficient in responding to market conditions. Further, concentrations in France often led to higher costs, more difficult communications and so forth; the advantages of concentrations, such as the ability to engage in research, to undertake tasks which would not immediately be profitable, greater information and market control, were not balanced against these other factors and so the chemistry was not always successful. The reasons for the relatively high rate of merger failure in France were thus linked to an inability to grasp the concentration techniques rather than deep-seated economic reasons.

B. The Effectiveness of the System: Economic Assessment

As the Colloquium noted in relation to other systems of control, paucity of judicial or administrative decisions did not necessarily indicate the ineffectiveness of the legal regime. Merger control could be simply effective by means of its deterrent effect. Could any conclusion be drawn as regards the situation in France?

The Reporter replied that he would wish to reserve judgement at this point. Indeed, the most worrying aspect of the French Law was the fact that since 1977 the Law although legally in force had simply not been used. This necessarily indicated a certain lack of confidence in the machinery which had been set up, rather than a lack of consciousness. In theory, the advantage of the 1977 Law is that it introduces in its substantive provision economic criteria where economic criteria should be introduced. The main deficiency of the Law is that in addition to these criteria it introduces a further mélange of other non-juridical and political criteria which make it vague and imprecise and difficult to apply. This perhaps contributed to the non-confidence.

C. Legal vs. Fiscal Measures

In discussing extra-legal controls of concentrations, the French Reporter noted that certain fiscal measures existed whereby the authorities could favour or restrict mergers in a given sector. The question was thus put whether by perfecting these fiscal mechanisms one could arrive at a system of control as efficient as that specified in the 1977 Law whilst avoiding its deficiencies?

The Reporter acknowledged the efficacy of fiscal measures. At the same time a juridical system which sets up institutions has advantages, such as being able to tackle specific operations on an individual basis; in addition operations which do not result in complete juridical fusion but which effectively amount to concentration would not be susceptible to fiscal measures. Fiscal measures can thus be applied only at the grand economic level whereas the juridical legal measures can be applied "surgically" to concentrations which operate at a lower level but are nonetheless destructive. A further question would be whether the fiscal authorities were in the best position to make the type of decision relevant to concentration.

D. Judicial Review and the Value of Adjudicatory Fora

Doubts were expressed about the utility of the *Conseil d'État* as a forum for judicial review of merger control. Participants were mindful of the pitfalls that excessive recourse to courts could engender. The note of caution introduced by a German judge regarding the excessive litigation in Germany concerning mergers was recorded. On this view the British and French systems which discouraged litigation whilst maintaining a final judicial review instance had much to commend themselves. At the same time it was queried whether the *Conseil d'État* was the best organ to be charged with this task. Both its general — not specialized — jurisdiction, as well as the laconic style of its decisions did not seem conducive of the type of exercise judicial review of economic law decisions entailed.

At the same time the fusion of economic and non-economic criteria in the ultimate decision of the minister would appear to favour a body which would be competent to deal with that type of mixed issue. Once again, in the absence of empirical data it seemed difficult to reach final conclusions on this question. It was to be raised again in relation to the jurisdiction of the European Communities.

IV. The Swiss Act on Cartels and the Practice of the Swiss Cartel Commission Concerning Economic Concentration

REPORTER: PROFESSOR P. FORSTMOSER (in the absence of Professor W. R. Schluep)

A. Sectoral and General Enquiries as a Subsidiary Method of Control

Despite the lack of specific formal control, the Swiss experience is characterized by fully fledged enquiries into sectoral and general concentration in Switzerland. A feature of these enquiries is that they are not limited to a mere measurement of concentration, but include specific evaluation of its impact and its desirability. The enquiries go so far as to make recommendations as to possible future concentration in various sectors.

Despite the possibility of introducing a merger control regime in Switzerland, it was suggested that perhaps in a country of Swiss size and given its peculiar social and political characteristics, such informal measures and unofficial policy indications are sufficient as an elastic and flexible method of control.

B. Pragmatism vs. Theory

It was noted in relation to the Swiss concentration reports that no rigid theory of concentration was applied. Rather, the reports try to isolate in relation to each sector the specific features and results which concentration would yield. The evaluation of concentration also depended on the sector in question, in some giving emphasis to the direct effects on consumers, in others the state of the industry etc.

This pragmatism when contrasted with attempts to construe strict formal legal regimes in other countries commanded some appeal.

C. The Need for Merger Control?

The final questionmark left as a result of the Swiss Report was whether in general formal merger control was needed – and whether it could not be tackled on an ad hoc basis in a pragmatic fashion. Perhaps such an extreme solution would not be suitable for the very different conditions in other countries, but in the analysis of merger control options this was certainly one possibility.

Chapter III:
Merger Control in the European Communities

I. Concentration and Mergers in the E.E.C.: Towards a System of Control

Reporter: Professor A. Jacquemin

II. Multinational Corporations and Merger Control in Community Antitrust Law

Reporter: Mr. P. M. Schmitt

The Colloquium concluded its discussions on the merger control systems in European antitrust law by examining the situation in the European Communities. Merger control at the transnational level and particularly within a system aiming at the establishment of a Common Market adds several problematic dimensions to the issues discussed above. Two of these problems should perhaps be mentioned. Transnational control of mergers implies not only the traditional problems as to "take-up", "no-go" and "let-off" criteria, but also complex decisions as to the position and competence of the decision-making body and the effects of the decision which can touch upon vital national interests. In this context the problem becomes one of international economic politics. In the second place one must record that there is an in-built tension in the attitude of the EEC towards transnational mergers. On the one hand they would, to the extent that European Community competition policy adopts the traditional doctrines of antitrust law, be subject to the same considerations as mergers in national legal systems, albeit on a larger scale. On the other hand, in some respects, the merger between undertakings from different countries is precisely the type of transnational activity which the Communities are eager to promote, illustrating most forcefully the breaking down of national economic boundaries. (Obviously transnational mergers can be used as a vehicle for creating other artificial barriers to Community trade.)

Finally, it was noted that results derived from recent studies on the effects of mergers and their determinants in European countries suggest that there has been no significant effect on profitability, growth of sales and price level. The need, thus, for policy control at the transnational level as well was evident.

Being the last of the merger control sessions, the discussion on the European Community regime was expanded to include comparative remarks which covered many of the issues raised in relation to all the national Reports.

A. The Choice of Adjudicatory Fora for Decisions on Mergers

As will be recalled, the suitability of the *Conseil d'État* to review decisions based on the 1977 French Law had been raised, given the mixture of economic and political criteria and the non-expert character of that judicial forum. By contrast the European Community Reporter indicated satisfaction with the European Court of Justice in its dealings with the application of competition rules in the European Communities. Article 86 was certainly no more precise than the 1977 French Law – especially in relation to the question of concentration. Why then should not the *Conseil d'État* be able to do what the Court of Justice had done? In reply the European Reporter recorded that there were differences in the composition of the courts, as well as in their judicial style and jurisdiction. Thus, for example, the first French judge in the European Court of Justice who served for ten years, was a distinguished economist who had a profound influence on the development of the Court's jurisprudence on antitrust law. There were other economists as well. This was a very healthy combination in this sphere of the law.

Secondly the European Court of Justice has jurisdiction to examine questions of fact, whereas the *Conseil d'État* is restricted on the whole to questions of law. The European Court of Justice can re-evaluate the factual economic appreciation of the situation and not merely the legal consequences that follow from a given factual set up. Finally, on the whole, the European Court of Justice is seized much more often with questions of economic law and thus builds up a certain expertise in this matter. The French Reporter, dealing with the same issue, added that there is a difference in style: whereas the *Conseil d'État's* decisions are much more minute and precise, (a lawyer's delight!) the European Court of Justice's decisions are much more expansive. He further acknowledged that France was in need of judges with an economic orientation to give decisions in economic law. In other words, it is a problem of the *corps de juges,* the creation of a *magistrat spécial.* Indeed if the *Conseil d'État* had wished to play a role similar to that of the European Court of Justice it would represent a completely new direction in its jurisprudence. At the same time it was pointed out that the 1977 French Law stipulates review by the *Conseil d'État* sitting *en plein juridiction* and not the usual *recours pour excès de pouvoir.* In this type of procedure the decisions are somewhat more long and expansive.

B. Courts, Extra-Judicial Panels, and Judicial Review

The difference between the approaches of the two Courts led to the related subject of Courts v. extra-judicial panels. Would the complex aims of antitrust law be served better by one or the other? This tied in with the substantial point raised in the European Report on the question of substitutability in relation, say, to the *United Brands case.* Why was the Court's opinion to be preferred to that of the Commission; how is a judge — not always versed in economic and commercial life — able to decide the substitutability of different products? Is a decision taken by an inexpert judge on the basis of expert advice, as happens in many other branches of law, a satisfactory solution?

The issue of extra judicial bodies and judicial review was raised also in relation to decisions of the Monopolies Commission in Great Britain. In reply to a question, one of the British reporters suggested that the review of decisions on grounds of public interest was extremely difficult. The concept of the public interest is so broad that everything which the Monopolies Commission would *think* relevant would in fact *be* relevant. Thus in substance it is almost taken out of the realms of justiciable issue. The attempt to produce a different means of assessment of the public interest which was much more precise and with which judges could more easily cope hardly worked. When judges decided that a price fixing agreement was not contrary to the public interest they were submitted to considerable professional criticism. On the other hand those judgments which condemned agreements were in general very vague and unspecific. It is probable therefore that the Monopolies Commission which is not a judicial body can by virtue of its wide and varied composition perform the task of assessing the public interest in a manner which is preferable to that of professional judges.

It was suggested on the question of justiciability that the British system which discouraged judicial review of decisions on the public interest was influenced by considerations related to the period of enactment when mergers were, on the whole, considered a favourable and beneficial phenomenon. Now, with the changing perception of the impact of mergers, the British system may move closer towards the German system.

In contrast to the British position, it was pointed out that in Germany 70% of the prohibiting orders came to court and were decided by the courts. Justiciability, therefore, in the German system was less of a problem. Here one records, of course, that the clear division between the economic and non-economic criteria in Germany made the review by the court far easier.

The issue of decisions on the public interest and the question of the appropriate forum to determine it was also discussed by the Swiss participants, who pointed out that in Switzerland there would be no difficulty in conferring this type of policy discretion on the judiciary – accustomed to it from other fields.

C. The Role of the "Market Share" as a Determining Factor in Establishing a Dominant Position or a Position of Concentration

It was pointed out that over-reliance on this criterion, even if the threshold is put at a very high level of say 80%, does not give a sufficiently sophisticated tool. In the first place the ascertainment of the market share will depend on the definition of the relevant market, which is an ambiguous and not easily determinable concept, depending in turn on questions of substitutability. In the second place, it was hypothesised that an undertaking might have a market share of 80% and yet economically not be in a dominant position. Other factors must be taken into account such as barriers to entry; the strategic and economic potence of the undertaking in question; its ability to resist competition from other undertakings should it emerge; the fluidity of the product market in question, in terms of changing demand (an undertaking might have a high market in a product but demand for that product might be ephemeral in nature) and the rate of cross-over in the industry concerned.

This question of market shares and relevant markets, and the difficulties in their application was reinforced by one of the participants. In the *Hoffmann-La Roche* case, it was pointed out that whereas the European Court started off with the right approach by considering the market of vitamins as a whole and (accepting the barriers to entry test as a criterion for determining dominance) by enumerating certain barriers to entry (whether high or not it was difficult to say), it then shifted position and apparently disregarding the earlier analysis of barriers to entry considered that the large market share of 80% and over solely for vitamins was in itself sufficient as an indication of a dominant position. The Court was not explicit on how one should relate the two different criteria, if indeed one is related to the other.

At the same time, the *Commission* did take into account the world trade in vitamins in the case of *Hoffmann-La Roche* and in particular the possibility of imports from other non-Community sources such as Yugoslavia and Japan, but established that these imports were often sporadic and did not really affect the *Hoffman-La Roche* operation. In effect, it could be said that indirectly the Community legal system was engaging slowly in a "barriers to entry" evaluation. There was a slow movement away from the rigid market share analysis.

On the question of market shares it was intimated that in Germany a market share of, say, 80% would be conclusive for establishing a dominant position and/or a measure of concentration. The issue of barriers to entry in the German view would be too speculative, being based in addition to economic considerations on an entrepreneurial decision. This would make the decision-making of the tribunal too speculative and in principle the German position preferred a clear-cut criterion. As regards a separation of competition and economic and commercial considerations on the one hand, and judgments largely linked to the public interest on the other, the German regime, as we have seen, adopts this position, but several consequences follow from it. One consequence is the time issue. In the first place there is the procedure before the Federal Cartel Office which takes a certain measure of time which can be, and often is, prolonged. This in itself is already somewhat hostile to the merger: an almost built-in procedural presumption against it. Subsequently there might be a further period of waiting if the decision is to be contested at the second, ministerial level. As already pointed out by a member of the German judiciary, the procedure can be further prolonged by an intervention of the Courts at every stage of the process. The separation between economic legal considerations on the one hand, and the public interest decision on the other hand, makes the issue far more justiciable than, say, the British counterpart. This might result in up to three or four trials in relation to one merger decision. The advantages of the separation would be that a measure of transparency is achieved in the decision-making process. The Court's decision and reasoning on the one hand, and the ministerial political decision on the other hand, are far more transparent when the political and legal-economic issues are so clearly distinguished.

D. Extra-Territorial Application of Antitrust (Merger) Law

It was suggested that there existed a divergence in attitude between the E.C. Commission and Court whereby the Commission was aiming at an all-out application of the effects theory whereas the Court — despite certain statements — always insisted or implied that one of the partners be present in the Common Market or invoked the "economic entity doctrine". Indeed from an economic political point of view a fully fledged adoption of the effects theory would be extremely doubtful, perhaps dangerous: should for example, the existence of a cartel of major Japanese exporters to the Common Market really be tackled on a strict legal antitrust basis, or is it not rather a question of Japanese commercial policy which should be and can only effectively be tackled at the political level? It is perhaps with this in mind that in the Community's proposed merger Regulation a point of contact with the Community is always insisted upon.

E. Separation of the "Economic" and "Political" Decision in Matters of Merger

It was recorded that the French and other reporters drew a distinction between that which was "political" in relation to competition and that which was a matter of industrial policy; would that distinction be applicable and useful at the level of the Community and its Commission? Is the Commission really the best body to take the "non-economic" decisions, especially as regards exemptions to the prohibitive regime?

In the Community this was one of the major obstacles preventing the application of the new proposed Regulation on the control of concentration at the European level. Some Member States are very keen to be associated more closely in the process of this type of decision-making. The desire for involvement is not merely in relation to the prohibitory measures, but also in relation to the justification regime. On the other hand, it was pointed out that it would be damaging if individual decisions would come, as has been suggested in certain quarters, to the table of the Council of Ministers. The Council of Ministers is not geared towards that type of decision-making and it would be wrong from the point of view of individual enterprises that mergers should be subject to the usual type of horsetrading and package deals which now characterize the Council of Ministers' work. The Council, however, could play a role in defining sectoral policies in relation to different markets and different industries which could provide guidelines for decisions of competent Commission authorities. There is a per se value in this approach in a separated system which provides for decisions in the first instance purely on competition grounds and eventually a judgment pertaining to elements other than competition. In the eyes of the Reporter there was no reason why the Commission could not assume this task of double decision. Further, the Court of Justice could maintain that separation and could pronounce very clearly on the authorization of mergers in relation to the different bases.

The European Community Reporter, however, raised objections to tendencies which would try to separate *institutionally* the decision-making between pure competition considerations and wider socio-political issues, a system which would also introduce judicial review of each type of decision. A possible compromise would be to introduce closer Member State participation in the process of decision-making in defining the policy of transnational concentration; to define more clearly the relative competences of the Member States and of the Commission in the matter of concentration; and finally to make sure that the economic considerations in a judgment and all other non-economic considerations in the judgment are clearly explained and distinct for purpose of transparency and eventual judicial review.

F. Non-Competition Barriers to Entry

Another dimension in the control of concentration was raised by referring to the indirect protection of concentrated industries created by high entry barriers resulting from other aspects of the legal order. It was pointed out that barriers to entry are created by a variety of consumer protection regulations, product liability laws and the like which increased significantly the difficulty of new enterprises entering into a market or switching from one product to similar products which might break down concentration. Complying with safety regulations and consumer protection regulations caused increased costs to penetration. Various municipal agencies have to be satisfied before products can be put on the market. Two issues result from this observation. In the first place one has a conflict of policies whereby the wish to discourage inefficient concentration must be squared with the goals of consumer protection in terms of product liability and health and safety rules of products. In addition and of particular importance in the European Community, the jurisdiction of the EEC in the field of consumer protection can indirectly bear fruit in dismantling barriers to entry. By harmonizing the different national rules of consumer protection, the barriers inherent in the need to adapt products from market to market would disappear. (This naturally benefits non-Community competitors as well). It was also recorded that antitrust law in all its variants, including merger control, was indirectly but significantly concerned with protecting the consumer. Thus to the extent that the above conflict of policies exists, it could be regarded partially as a conflict of methods as to how to protect the consumer.

G. The Measurement of Concentration

A different question concerned the measurement of concentration where groups of companies were concerned. The issue is particularly potent in that it illustrates another link between antitrust law and corporation law. At what stage in the centralization of enterprises, it was asked, can we start talking about concentration by that enterprise? This becomes a matter of micro-economic analysis of macro-economic phenomena. To the lawyer, the question presents itself in a situation where an undertaking reaching a "legally dangerous" level of concentration decentralizes so as to avoid the rigours of control measures. In discussion the economists conceded that probably this issue would have to be treated on a case by case basis and, even if certain categorizations could be achieved, the exact allocation of individual enterprises into categories would be an extremely difficult operation. In any event it is possible to engage in high powered legal and economic analysis of undertakings to reach concrete evaluations in terms of administration of enterprises and the location of decision-making power, so as to arrive at a considered decision as to the level of centralization which would in turn affect any measurement of concentration.

Analysis is complicated by the developments in business sciences in which the organizational form of a company is not perceived to be the critical factor in its efficiency. It would, therefore, become difficult to assess to what extent changes in the centralization of an undertaking were due to bona fide economic reasons or to reasons of legal avoidance. From the legal point of view it was pointed out that this problem illustrated different facets of antitrust law on the one hand and merger control law as a branch of it on the other hand. In antitrust law one is often concerned with intra-enterprise doctrine, examining the internal structure of groups and determining the freedom of subsidiaries in relation to each other. Developed merger control systems need not be influenced by this, because it is then a factor which could be changed by the enterprises themselves so as to avoid control. The area of concern therefore, is rather the potential effects on the market structure and less the internal organization of the enterprises concerned.

Annex II

Relevant Legal Provisions

1. The Federal Republic of Germany

1.a. Law Against Restraints of Competition (as of 1980): Sections 22-24b*

Chapter 3
Market Dominating Enterprises
Section 22
*[Market Dominating Enterprises, Powers of Cartel Authority]***

(1) An enterprise is market dominating within the meaning of this Act insofar as, in its capacity as a supplier or buyer of a certain type of goods or commercial services,

1. it has no competitor or is not exposed to any substantial competition, or
2. it has a paramount market position in relation to its competitors; for this purpose in addition to its share of the market its financial strength, its access to the supply or sales markets for goods and services, its links with other enterprises and the legal or actual barriers to the market entry of other enterprises shall in particular be taken into account.

(2) Two or more enterprises shall also be deemed market dominating insofar as, in regard to a certain type of goods or commercial services, no substantial competition exists between them, for factual reasons, either in general, or in specific markets, and they jointly meet the requirements of subsection (1).

(3) It shall be presumed that

1. an enterprise is market dominating within the meaning of subsection (1), if it has a market share of at least one-third for a certain type of goods or commercial services; this presumption shall not apply when the enterprise recorded a turnover of less than DM 250 million in the last completed business year;
2. the conditions specified in subsection (2) are met if, in regard to a certain type of goods or commercial services,
   (a) three or less enterprises have a combined market share of 50% or over, or

---

* With the kind permission of the Federal Cartel Office, Berlin. There are also two other excellent translations: R. MUELLER, M. HEIDENHAIN & H. SCHNEIDER, GERMAN ANTI-TRUST LAW. AN INTRODUCTION TO THE GERMAN ANTITRUST LAW (with German text and synoptic English translation of the Act Against Restraints of Competition) (Frankfurt am Main, Fritz Knapp Verlag, 2d ed., 1981); A. RIESENKAMPFF & J. GRES, LAW AGAINST RESTRAINTS OF COMPETITION, TEXT AND COMMENTARY IN GERMAN AND ENGLISH (Cologne, Verlag Otto Schmidt KG, 2d ed., 1981).
** The section titles [. . .] are unofficial.

(b) five or less enterprises have a combined market share of two-thirds or
   over;
this presumption shall not apply, insofar as enterprises are concerned which
recorded turnovers of less than DM 100 million in the last completed business
year.
As regards the calculation of the market share and turnover, Section 23 (1)
sentences 2 to 10 shall apply, as appropriate.

(4) In regard to market dominating enterprises, the cartel authority shall have
the powers set out in subsection (5), insofar as these enterprises abuse their
dominating position in the market for these or any other goods or commercial
services. An abuse within the meaning of sentence 1 is present, in particular, if a
market-dominating enterprise as a supplier or buyer of a certain type of goods or
commercial services

1. impairs the competitive possibilities of other enterprises in a manner relevant
   to competition on the market in the absence of facts justifying such
   behaviour;
2. demands considerations or other business terms which deviate from those
   which would result in all probability if effective competition existed; in this
   context in particular the practices of enterprises on comparable markets
   characterised by effective competition have to be taken into account;
3. demands less favourable considerations or other business terms than are
   demanded from similar buyers on comparable markets by the market-
   dominating enterprise, unless there is a factual justification for such differentiation.

(5) If the conditions laid down in subsection (1) are satisfied the cartel
authority may prohibit abusive practices by market dominating enterprises and
declare agreements to be of no effect; Section 19 shall apply as appropriate. Prior
to such action, the cartel authority shall request the parties involved to
discontinue the abuse to which objection was raised.

(6) Insofar as the conditions laid down in subsection (1) are satisfied in regard
to an affiliated company (Konzernunternehmen) within the meaning of Section
18 of the Joint Stock Companies Act, the cartel authority may use its powers
under subsection (5) in relation to each affiliated company (Konzernunternehmen).

Section 23

[Duty to Notify Mergers of Enterprises]

(1) The merging of enterprises shall immediately be notified to the Federal
Cartel Office, if

1. within the total area of application of this Act or in a substantial part thereof a
   market share of at least 20% is obtained or increased by the merger or if a
   participating enterprise has a share of at least 20% in another market, or
2. the participating enterprises together at some date during the completed
   business year preceding the merger had at least 10,000 employees or recorded a
   turnover of at least 500 million in this period.

If one of the participating enterprises is a controlled or controlling enterprise within the meaning of Section 17 of the Joint Stock Companies Act or an affiliated company (Konzernunternehmen) within the meaning of Section 18 of that Act, the enterprises linked in this manner shall be regarded as a single enterprise for the calculation of market shares, number of employees and turnovers; if several enterprises as a result of an agreement or otherwise act together in such a way that they jointly are able to exercise a controlling influence on a participating enterprise, each of them shall be regarded as a controlling enterprise. Section 158 (1) and (2) of the Joint Stock Companies Act shall apply as regards the calculation of the turnovers; revenues from supply of goods and services between enterprises which are linked within the meaning of sentence 2 (intra-group revenues), value added tax as well as consumption taxes shall be left out of account; turnovers in a foreign currency shall be converted into Deutsche Mark at the official exchange rate. In the case of credit institutions and building and loan associations, there shall be substituted for turnover one tenth of the total assets, and as regards insurance companies, the premium income of the last completed business year. Amounts recorded as investments in affiliated enterprises as defined in sentence 2 shall be deducted from the balance sheet total; premium income shall mean income from insurance and reinsurance business including amounts ceded to reinsurers. As regards enterprises whose operations wholly or partially consist of trade in goods, only three-fourths of the turnover shall be taken into account. As regards enterprises whose operations wholly or partially consist of publishing, producing or distributing newspapers or magazines or parts of them, twenty times the amount of the turnover shall be taken into account; sentence 6 remains unaffected. Where all or a substantial part of the assets of another enterprise are acquired, the calculation of the market share, number of employees and turnover of the selling enterprise shall take account of the sold assets only. Sentence 8 shall apply, as appropriate, to the acquisition of shares, insofar as less than 25 per cent of the shares are retained by the seller and the merger does not satisfy the conditions set out in subsection (2) No. 2 sentence 3 and No. 5. If a person or an association of persons not being an enterprise is entitled to the majority interest in an enterprise, he, she or it shall be deemed to be an enterprise for the purposes of this Act.

(2) The following transactions shall be deemed mergers within the meaning of this Act:

1. acquisition of all or of a substantial part of the assets of another enterprise by amalgamation, reconstruction or in any other way;
2. acquisition of shares in another enterprise, provided the shares alone or together with other shares already held by the acquiring enterprise
   (a) amount to 25% of the voting capital of the other enterprise, or
   (b) amount to 50% of the voting capital of the other enterprise, or
   (c) secure the enterprise a majority interest within the meaning of Section 16 (1) of the Joint Stock Companies Act.

The shares held by the acquiring enterprise shall include also the shares belonging to a linked enterprise within the meaning of subsection (1), sentence 2, or held by another enterprise for the account of one of these enterprises, and, if the owner of the enterprise is a sole proprietor, any other shares belonging to the owner. If several enterprises simultaneously or successively acquire shares in another enterprise to the extent above mentioned, this shall also be deemed a merger of the participating enterprises (joint venture) (Gemeinschaftsunternehmen) as regards the markets in which the other enterprise operates. The acquisition of shares shall also be deemed a merger, insofar as the acquirer obtains, by means of an agreement, by laws, articles of association, or a resolution, the legal position held in a joint stock company by a shareholder owning more than 25 per cent of the voting capital. Shares in an enterprise shall be equal to voting rights.

3. Agreements with another enterprise by which:
   (a) a Konzern within the meaning of Section 18 of the Joint Stock Companies Act is formed or the group of affiliated companies (Konzernunternehmen) is enlarged, or
   (b) the other enterprise undertakes to carry on its operations for the account of the enterprise or to transfer its profit wholly or partially to the enterprise, or
   (c) the plant of the other enterprise or a substantial part thereof is leased or otherwise transferred to the enterprise.

4. Bringing into existence a situation where at least half the members of the supervisory boards, the boards of management, or any other managing bodies of enterprises consist of the same persons.

5. Any other combination of enterprises as a result of which one or several enterprises are able directly or indirectly to exercise a controlling influence on another enterprise.

   (3) A merger shall also be presumed to occur if the participating enterprises are already combined as defined in subsection (2), except when such merger does not result in a substantial strengthening of the existing relationship. If a credit institution acquires shares in another enterprise, on its formation or when its capital is increased, or otherwise within the context of its business operations, for the purpose of selling them on the market, this shall not be deemed a merger so long as the credit institution does not exercise the voting rights attaching to the shares and provided the sale is effected within one year; when an enterprise is established, exercise of voting rights at the first general meeting following the establishment shall not constitute a merger. If an enterprise participating in a merger is an affiliated company within the meaning of subsection (1), sentence 2, then the controlling enterprise as well as the enterprises by which the controlling enterprise is itself controlled shall be considered participants in the merger. If two or more enterprises merge, this shall also be deemed a merger of the enterprises controlled by them.

   (4) Notification shall be required:

1. in the case of amalgamation or reconstruction, by the owners of the acquiring or newly formed enterprise or their representatives, or, in the case of legal persons and partnerships, by the persons designated as their representatives by law or by the articles of association;

2. in other cases
   (a) by the owners of enterprises participating in the merger, and
   (b) where subsection (2), Nos. 1 und 2, applies, also by the sellers or their
   representatives, or, in the case of legal persons and partnerships, by the
   persons designated as their representatives by law or by the articles of
   association; where letter b) applies, subsection (3), sentence 3, shall apply as
   appropriate.
   (5) The notification shall indicate the form taken by the merger. Furthermore
it shall include the following data regarding each participating enterprise:
1. firm name or other designation and location of establishment or registered
   office;
2. type of business;
3. insofar as the conditions of subsection (1), sentence 1, are satisfied, the market
   share including the basis of its calculation or estimate, the number of
   employees and the turnovers; as regards credit institutions and building and
   loan associations, the total assets shall be stated instead of the turnover and, as
   regards insurance companies, the premium income;
4. when shares in another enterprise are acquired (subsection (2) No. 2), the
   amount of the shareholding acquired and of the total shareholding owned in
   it.
If a participating enterprise is an affiliated company within the meaning of
subsection (1), sentence 2, the particulars required in sentence 2, Nos. 1 to 3 shall
also be given for such affiliated companies, and the Konzern relationships,
degrees of dependency and percentages of holdings of the affiliated companies
shall be included in such particulars.
   (6) The Federal Cartel Office may request each of the participating enterprises
to supply information on market shares including the basis for their calculation
or estimate as well as the turnover for a specific type of goods or commercial
services which the enterprise recorded in the last business year ending before the
merger. If a participating enterprise is an affiliated company within the meaning
of subsection (1), sentence 2, the Federal Cartel Office may also request such
information regarding the affiliated companies; it may also request the information from the affiliated companies. Section 46 (2), (5) and (9) shall apply, as
appropriate. The Federal Cartel Office shall set a reasonable time-limit for the
furnishing of the information. The powers of the Federal Cartel Office under
Section 46 shall remain unaffected.

Section 23a
[Presumption of Vertical and Conglomerate Mergers]

   (1) Notwithstanding Section 22 (1) to (3), for merger control purposes a
paramount market position shall be presumed to be created or strengthened as a
result of a merger, if
1. an enterprise which recorded a turnover of at least DM 2,000 million in the last
   completed business year preceding the merger merges with another enterprise
   which
   (a) operates in a market in which small and medium-sized enterprises have a

combined market share of at least two-thirds and the enterprises participating in the merger have a combined market share of at least 5 per cent,
or

(b) is market-dominating in one or several markets which in the last completed calendar year had a total turnover of at least DM 150 million, or

2. the enterprises participating in the merger recorded a combined turnover of at
least DM 12,000 million in the last completed business year preceding the
merger and at least two of the participating enterprises recorded individual
turnovers of at least DM 1,000 million; this presumption shall not apply,
insofar as the merger also satisfies the conditions of Section 23 (2) No. 2
sentence 3 and the joint venture does not operate in a market with a turnover
of at least DM 750 million in the last calendar year.

(2) For merger control purposes a totality of enterprises shall also be deemed
market-dominating, if

1. it consists of three or less enterprises which in one market hold the highest
market shares and a combined market share of 50 per cent, or

2. it consists of five or less enterprises which in one market hold the highest
market shares and a combined market share of two-thirds,

unless the enterprises prove that the conditions of competition may be expected
to leave substantial competition between them also following the merger or the
totality of enterprises have no paramount market position in relation to the other
competitors. Sentence 1 shall not apply if enterprises are involved which
recorded turnovers of less than DM 150 million in the last completed business
year or if the enterprises participating in the merger hold a combined market
share not exceeding 15 per cent. Section 22 (2) and (3) sentence 1 No. 2 shall
remain unaffected.

(3) Section 23 (1) sentences 2 to 6 and 8 to 10 shall be applied regarding the
calculation of the turnovers and market shares.

Section 24
[Merger Control]

(1) If it is likely that a market dominating position will be created or
strengthened as a result of a merger, the cartel authority shall have the powers
specified in the following provisions, unless the participating enterprises prove
that the merger will also lead to improvements in the conditions of competition
and that these improvements will outweigh the disadvantages of market
domination.

(2) If the conditions of subsection (1) are present, the Federal Cartel Office
shall prohibit the merger. The Federal Cartel Office may prohibit a merger as
soon as the merger project has come to its knowledge; completed mergers may
be prohibited by the Federal Cartel Office only within a one-year period from
the receipt of the full notification under Section 23; Section 24a (2), sentence 2,
Nos. 1 and 5 to 6 shall apply as appropriate. Prior to prohibition the supreme
Land authorities in whose territory the participating enterprises are located shall
be given an opportunity to present their views. If the Federal Cartel Office has
taken the decision mentioned in sentence 1, it shall be unlawful to complete the

merger without the authorisation of the Federal Minister for Economic Affairs, or to participate in the completion of the merger; legal transactions in violation of this prohibition shall be of no effect; this shall not apply to agreements covering the amalgamation, reconstruction, integration or establishment of an enterprise and to agreements among enterprises within the meaning of Sections 291 and 292 of the Joint Stock Companies Act, once they have become enforceable by entry in the Commercial Register or the Co-operative Societies Register. A completed merger which has been prohibited by the Federal Cartel Office shall be dissolved, unless the Federal Minister for Economic Affairs authorises its continuation.

(3) Upon application, the Federal Minister for Economic Affairs shall authorise the merger if, in the case involved, the restraint of competition is outweighed by advantages to the whole economy resulting from the merger or if the merger is justified by a predominating public interest; in this respect the competitiveness of the participating enterprises in markets outside the area of application of this Act shall also be taken into account. The authorisation may only be given if the extent of the restraint of competition does not endanger the market economy system. The authorisation may contain restrictions and conditions. However, these must not aim at subjecting the actions of the participating enterprises to a continued control. Section 22 shall remain unaffected.

(4) The application for an authorisation for the merger shall be filed with the Federal Minister for Economic Affairs in writing within a one-month period. The period shall commence with the service of the decision taken by the Federal Cartel Office as described in subsection (2), sentence 1; if the decision is contested within the period of time provided in Section 65 (1), sentences 1 and 2, the period for the application for authorisation shall run from the date when the decision taken by the Federal Cartel Office becomes final. The Federal Minister for Economic Affairs shall decide on the application within four months from the expiry of the period specified in sentences 1 and 2 for the application for authorisation. Prior to the decision, the supreme Land authorities in whose territory the participating enterprises are located shall be given an opportunity to present their views.

(5) The Federal Minister for Economic Affairs may revoke the authorisation, or amend it by ordering restrictions, or include conditions, if the participating enterprises violate a condition attached to the authorisation. The Federal Minister for Economic Affairs may withdraw the authorisation, if the participating enterprises have obtained it by fraud, threats, bribery or by supplying information which was false or incomplete to a material extent.

(6) The dissolution of a completed merger may also consist in the restraint of competition being eliminated by means other than a return to the former situation. The Federal Cartel Office shall order the measures necessary to dissolve the merger, if

1. its decision defined in subsection (2), sentence 1, has become final; and
2. the participating enterprises had filed an application for authorisation for the merger with the Federal Minister for Economic Affairs and the rejection of

this application or, where subsection (5) applies, the revocation or withdrawal has become final.

In so doing, and while safeguarding the interests of third parties, it shall order such measures as will attain the desired goal with a minimum of expense and burden for those involved.

(7) To enforce its order the Federal Cartel Office may in particular:

1. by imposing a non-recurring or recurring penalty payment of DM 10,000 to DM 1,000,000 cause those under a duty to dissolve the merger to take the measures ordered immediately;

2. prohibit the exercise of voting rights attaching to shares in one of the participating enterprises held by another participating enterprise or attributed to it, or make the exercise of the voting rights or the manner in which they are exercised conditional upon the authorisation of the Federal Cartel Office;

3. declare agreements bringing about the merger of the nature specified in Section 23 (2) Nos. 1 and 3 to be of no effect; this shall not apply to agreements covering the amalgamation, reconstruction, integration or establishment of an enterprise and to agreements among enterprises within the meaning of Sections 291 and 292 of the Joint Stock Companies Act, once they have become enforceable by entry in the Commercial Register or in the Co-operative Societies Register;

4. appoint a trustee who shall execute the necessary legal documents on behalf of the enterprise obliged to dissolve the merger and take all necessary measures; in this respect it shall have to be determined to what extent the rights of those involved will be suspended so long as the trusteeship is in effect; as regards the legal relationship between the trustee and the enterprise involved, Sections 664, 666 to 670 of the Civil Code shall apply as appropriate; the trustee may demand reasonable compensation from the enterprise involved.

(8) Subsections (1) to (7) shall not apply

1. if the participating enterprises recorded a combined turnover of less than DM 500 million in the last completed business year, or

2. if an enterprise which is not a controlled enterprise and in the last completed business year recorded a turnover of less than DM 50 million affiliates itself to another enterprise; except when one enterprise recorded a turnover of at least DM 4 million and the other a turnover of at least DM 1,000 million, or

3. insofar as a market is affected in which goods or commercial services have been supplied for at least five years and which in the last calendar year had a turnover of less than DM 10 million.

Section 23 (1) sentences 2 to 10 shall be applied regarding the calculation of the turnovers.

(9) Subsection (8) sentence 1 No. 2 shall not apply insofar as competition in the publication, production or distribution of newspapers or periodicals or parts of them is restricted within the meaning of subsection (1) as a result of the merger.

Section 24a
[Notification of Merger Projects]

(1) A merger project may be notified to the Federal Cartel Office. The project shall be notified to the Federal Cartel Office, if

1. one of the enterprises participating in the merger recorded a turnover of at least DM 2,000 million in the last completed business year, or

2. at least two of the enterprises participating in the merger recorded individual turnovers of DM 1,000 million or over in the last completed business year, or

3. the merger is to be effected under the law of a Land by legislation or any other governmental act.

As regards the notification, Section 23 shall apply as appropriate, save that when Section 23 (1), sentence 1, No. 2 and subsection (6) is applied, for the date of the merger there shall be substituted the date of the notification, and that in the case of an amalgamation or reconstruction the owners, representatives, or persons appointed as representatives of the parties to the merger shall be obliged to file notification. The notification shall only be considered effective when the particulars specified in Section 23 (5) are included. Section 46 (9) shall apply, as appropriate, to the information and documents obtained in connection with the notification.

(2) If the merger project has been notified to it, the Federal Cartel Office may prohibit the merger only if it informs the person who has effected the notification within a period of one month from receipt of the notification that it has begun an examination of the merger project and if the decision under Section 24 (2), sentence 1, is taken within a period of four months from receipt of the notification. The Federal Cartel Office may also prohibit the merger after the expiry of the four-month period, if

1. the enterprises participating in the merger have agreed to an extension of time, or

2. the merger is completed, although the one-month period specified in sentence 1 or, if the Federal Cartel Office has sent the communication referred to in sentence 1, the specified four-month period has not yet expired, or

3. the merger is completed other than as notified, or

4. the merger has not yet been completed and the conditions which caused the Federal Cartel Office to refrain from sending the communication referred to in sentence 1 or from prohibiting the merger under Section 24 (2), sentence 1, have materially changed, or

5. the Federal Cartel Office has sent the communication referred to in sentence 1 or not prohibited the merger under Section 24 (2), sentence 1, by reason of false or incomplete particulars having been supplied by the enterprises participating in the merger or by any other person, or

6. information under Section 23 (6) or Section 46 was not supplied or not supplied in due time and this has caused the Federal Cartel Office to act as described in No. 5.

(3) The notification of the merger project shall not affect the obligation to notify the merger under Section 23; when notification under Section 23 is filed,

reference may be made to the material submitted for the notification of the merger project.

(4) If a merger project has to be notified under subsection (1) sentence 2, it shall be unlawful either to complete the merger prior to the expiry of the one-month period specified in subsection (2) sentence 1, and, if the Federal Cartel Office has given the information referred to in subsection (2) sentence 1 prior to the expiry of the specified four-month period or the extension of time agreed upon, or to participate in the completion of the merger, except when the Federal Cartel Office, prior to the expiry of the periods mentioned in subsection (2) sentence 1 has given written information to the person who has effected the notification that the merger project does not meet the conditions of prohibition set out in Section 24 (1); legal transactions violating this prohibition shall be of no effect; this shall not apply to agreements covering the amalgamation, reconstruction, integration or establishment of an enterprise and to agreements among enterprises within the meaning of Sections 291 and 292 of the Joint Stock Companies Act, once they have become enforceable by entry in the Commercial Register or in the Co-operative Societies Register.

Section 24b
[Monopolies Commission]

(1) A Monopolies Commission shall be established to issue regular opinions on the trend of business concentration in the Federal Republic of Germany and the application of Sections 22 to 24a. It shall consist of five members who must have special knowledge and expertise in the fields of economics, business administration, social policy, technology, or commercial law.

(2) The members of the Monopolies Commission must not be members either of the government or any legislative body of the Federal Republic or a Land or of the public service of the Federal Republic, a Land or any other public body, except as university teachers or staff members of a scientific institution. Furthermore, they must not be representatives of an economic association or of an employers' or employees' organisation, or be employed with one of them under a regular employment contract or special service contract. Nor must they have held such a position during the year preceding their appointment to the Monopolies Commission.

(3) In its opinion, the Monopolies Commission shall assess the current state of business concentration and its foreseeable trends from the standpoint of economic policy, and in particular competition policy, and shall evaluate the application of Sections 22 to 24a. It shall also indicate such amendments to the relevant provisions of this Act as it may deem necessary.

(4) The Monopolies Commission shall only be bound by the terms of this Act and shall carry on its activity independently. If a minority holds dissenting views when an opinion is drafted, it may express them in the opinion.

(5) The Monopolies Commission shall issue every two years, by June 30, an opinion covering the situation which prevailed during the last two completed calendar years and submit it immediately to the Federal Government, the first opinion being due on June 30, 1976. The opinions pursuant to sentence 1 shall

immediately be submitted to the legislative bodies by the Federal Government and at the same time be published by the Monopolies Commission. Within a reasonable period the Federal Government shall present its views and comments on the opinions to the legislative bodies. The Monopolies Commission may give additional opinions as it deems appropriate. The Federal Government may instruct it to give additional opinions. The Monopolies Commission shall submit opinions pursuant to sentences 4 and 5 to the Federal Government and publish them. The Federal Minister for Economic Affairs has to request an opinion from the Monopolies Commission in particular cases which are submitted to him for decision under Section 24 (3).

(6) The members of the Monopolies Commission shall be appointed by the President of the Federal Republic of Germany on a proposal by the Federal Government. One member shall retire from the Commission on July 1 of each year in which an opinion is to be issued under subsection (5), sentence 1. The sequence of retirement shall be determined by lot at the first meeting of the Monopolies Commission. On a proposal by the Federal Government, the President of the Federal Republic shall on each such occasion appoint one new member for a term of four years. Re-appointment shall be permissible. The Federal Government shall hear the members of the Monopolies Commission before proposing new members. The members shall be entitled to resign their office by notice to the President of the Federal Republic. If a member retires prematurely, a new member shall be appointed for the term of office of the retiring member; sentences 4 to 6 shall apply as appropriate.

(7) Decisions of the Monopolies Commission shall require agreement of at least three members. The Monopolies Commission shall elect its chairman from among its members. The Monopolies Commission shall establish its own rules of procedure.

(8) The Monopolies Commission shall have its own secretariat. The work of the secretariat shall comprise passing on and compiling source material, making technical preparations for meetings of the Monopolies Commission, printing and publishing the opinions as well as handling other administrative duties.

(9) The members of the Monopolies Commission and the staff of the secretariat shall be bound to secrecy as regards its discussions and discussion documents labelled as confidential by the Monopolies Commission. The secrecy requirement shall also cover information supplied to the Monopolies Commission and marked confidential. Section 46 (8) and (9) as well as Section 47 shall remain unaffected.

(10) The members of the Monopolies Commission shall receive a lump-sum compensation and they shall be reimbursed their travelling expenses. These shall be determined by the Federal Minister for Economic Affairs in agreement with the Federal Minister of the Interior. The costs of the Monopolies Commission shall be borne by the Federal Republic.

1.b. Federal Cartel Office, Information in Respect of Merger Control Under Section 23 et seq. of the Act Against Restraints of Competition (ARC) (as of 1980)*

Merger control introduced by the Second Act to Amend the Act Against Restraints of Competition (Section 24 of the ARC) covers completed mergers – which must immediately be notified to the Federal Cartel Office – as well as merger projects. The latter may be notified to the Federal Cartel Office by the participating enterprises prior to the completion of the merger; in specified cases they must be notified in advance. By the Fourth Act to Amend the ARC the duty to notify merger projects has been substantially extended. They now have to be notified to the Federal Cartel Office, if

1. one of the enterprises participating in the merger recorded a turnover of at least DM 2,000 million in the last completed business year; or

2. at least two of the enterprises participating in the merger each recorded a turnover of DM 1,000 million or over in the last completed business year; or

3. the merger is to be brought about under state law by legislation or other governmental act.

The duty of notification as described above does not arise if a merger is exempted from merger control under Section 24 (8). This is the case in particular if an enterprise which is not controlled by another and which recorded a turnover not exceeding DM 50 million in the last completed business year merges with another enterprise, unless the acquired enterprise had a turnover of at least DM 4 million and the acquiring enterprise a turnover of at least DM 1,000 million. However, also in such cases the merger has to be notified to the Federal Cartel Office after it has been completed. Unlike the notification of completed mergers, the prenotification of merger projects is subject to a fee. The notification, which must be effected also in the case of prenotified merger projects after they have been completed, is published in the Federal Gazette (Bundesanzeiger) in respect of such data as firm name, registered office and type of business as well as form of the merger (Section 10 (1) No. 5 of the ARC).

If the conditions of Section 24 (1) are satisfied the Federal Cartel Office has to prohibit mergers. In doing so, it has to observe certain time-limits, i. e. one year for notified mergers and four months for notified merger projects. The periods can be extended in agreement with the enterprises involved, and they begin to run upon receipt of the *complete* notification of the merger or the merger project at the Federal Cartel office.

---

* With the kind permission of the Federal Cartel Office. Act Against Restraints of Competition in the version of the Pronouncement of 4 April 1974 (Bundesgesetzblatt I, p. 869) as last amended by the Fourth Act to Amend the Act Against Restraints of Competition of 26 April 1980 (Bundesgesetzblatt I, p. 458).

A. Required Particulars

In order to be complete the notifications under Section 23 (1) sentence 1 (completed mergers) and Section 24 a (1) sentence 1 and 2 (merger projects) of the ARC must contain the data listed in Section 23 (5), in particular:

1. Data Concerning the Merger

The notification must identify the enterprises that have been merged or are intended to be merged. Furthermore the form of the merger must be indicated (Section 23 (5) sentence 1 of the ARC); insofar as the merger is based on contracts it is expedient to enclose certified copies or photostats of such contracts.

When shares are acquired under Section 23 (2) No. 2 of the ARC the amount of the shareholding acquired and of the total shareholding owned must be indicated (as regards the calculation of the total shareholding, see Section 23 (2) No. 2 sentence 2 of the ARC).

If the merger has already been completed the date of completion (e. g. the date of a required entry in the Commercial Register) must be indicated.

2. Data Regarding the Enterprises

The information given below must be supplied not only in respect of domestic but also of foreign participating or linked enterprises.

2.1. Regarding *each* participating enterprise and *regarding each enterprise linked to* a participating enterprise the firm name (or other designation), the registered office (or location of establishment) and the type of business must be indicated. To characterise the business at least the stage of the economy (e. g. production, wholesale trade) and the line of industry must be shown accurately (a general entry such as "metalworking" is not sufficient but a more specific designation such as "manufacture of builders' hardware" is required); in any case it is expedient to give a summary account of the range of products or services supplied by the enterprise concerned.

2.2. Regarding *each* participating enterprise (or acquired assets) *including linked enterprises* the following particulars must be supplied under Section 23 (5) No. 3 of the ARC:

2.2.1. the highest number of employees at some date during the last completed business year preceding the merger (when notifying completed mergers under Section 23 (1) sentence 1) or during the last business year ending before the notification (when notifying merger projects under Section 24 a (1) sentences 1 and 2);

2.2.2. the turnover achieved during the last completed business year preceding the merger (when notifying completed mergers under Section 23 (1) sentence 1) or during the last business year ending before the notification (when notifying merger projects under Section 24 a (1) sentences 1 and 2);

2.2.3. the domestic market shares including the basis of their calculation or estimate.

Thus, *the number of employees, turnover and market shares* must be indicated only regarding each enterprise participating in the merger including enterprises linked to it but not for each linked enterprise separately. It will, however, be expedient to show the data of the enterprises directly involved in the merger separately.

If all participating enterprises *together* including enterprises linked to them do not satisfy one of the criteria mentioned in Section 23 (1) sentence 1 Nos. 1 and 2 of the ARC (10,000 employees, turnover of DM 500 million, 20% market share), the data regarding the pertinent criterion may be dropped for all enterprises. As regards the calculation of the market shares, there may be uncertainty in a particular case as to the market definition as well as to the domestic market shares of the other participants (see No. 5 below). For the sake of completeness of the notifications it is therefore advisable to supply details on market shares and market definitions also where the 20% threshold is not reached.

2.3. If a participating enterprise is linked to another participating enterprise or to a third enterprise, then the Konzern relationships and the degrees of dependency and percentages of holdings of the affiliated companies must be reported.

B. Explanation of Individual Terms

The provisions governing notifications use individual terms in a strictly defined sense which is not always identical with the meaning in which they are used in other fields of law. This applies, in particular, to the following terms:

1. Participating Enterprises

What enterprises are deemed to participate in a merger depends on how the merger is brought about.

Participating enterprises are, e. g.,

1.1. in the case of acquisition of assets

(a) by amalgamation and by amalgamating reconstruction, the enterprises that are amalgamated;

(b) in any other way, the acquirer and the selling enterprise, the latter, however, only as regards the assets transferred;

1.2. in the case of acquisition of shares in another enterprise

– the acquirer

– the other enterprise

– further enterprises only if the selling enterprise keeps at least 25% of the shares in the other enterprise or if the merger satisfies the conditions of Section 23 (2) No. 2 sentence 3 or of Section 23 (2) No. 5;

1.3. in the case of agreements within the meaning of Section 23 (2) No. 3 of the ARC, the parties to the agreement;

1.4. when situations are brought into existence in bodies of enterprises as defined by Section 23 (2) No. 4 of the ARC, the enterprises whose bodies consist of the same persons;

1.5. in the case of any other combination of enterprises within the meaning of

Section 23 (2) No. 5 of the ARC, the enterprises which are able to exercise a controlling influence and the enterprise subject to that influence.

2. Linked Enterprises

This term is not identical with the corresponding term as defined by the Joint Stock Companies Act (Aktiengesetz). Under Section 23 (1) sentence 2 of the ARC enterprises linked to a participating enterprise are

2.1. enterprises which in relation to a participating enterprise are controlled or controlling enterprises within the meaning of Section 17 of the Joint Stock Companies Act;

2.2. enterprises which are affiliated companies (Konzernunternehmen) of the same group (Konzern) as a participating enterprise (Section 18 of the Joint Stock Companies Act);

2.3. enterprises on which the participating enterprise, as a result of an agreement or otherwise, together with other enterprises is able to exercise a controlling influence; enterprises which, as a result of an agreement or otherwise, together with other enterprises are able to exercise a controlling influence on a participating enterprise.

If an enterprise holds 50% of the shares in another enterprise, the Federal Cartel Office, as a rule, assumes that the enterprise is able to (co-)exercise a controlling influence on the other enterprise.

3. Substantial Part of the Assets

A substantial part of the assets within the meaning of Section 23 (2) No. 1 of the ARC does not only mean a part of the assets which in relation to the seller's total assets is sufficiently large in terms of quantity, a part of assets is considered substantial whenever it has a significance of its own in relation to production, distribution targets and current market conditions and which therefore appears to be a unit separable from the other assets of the selling enterprise.

4. Turnover (Section 23 (1) Sentences 3 to 7)

As regards the calculation of the turnover, Section 158 (1) and (2) of the Joint Stock Companies Act is to be taken as a basis. Value added tax and excise duties are to be left out of account. Turnover recorded abroad is to be included; turnover in a foreign currency is to be converted into Deutsche Mark at the official exchange rate. Where the turnover is given for several linked enterprises together, revenues from the supply of goods and services between those enterprises (intra-group revenues) are to be excluded.

Insofar as the operations of an enterprise consist of *trade in goods,* only three-fourths of the turnover are to be taken into account. No trade turnover in this sense is involved if the goods produced or processed by an enterprise are purchased and resold by another enterprise linked to it.

In the case of *insurance companies* the premium income is substituted for the turnover. Premium income means income from insurance and reinsurance business including amounts ceded to re-insurers.

As regards *credit institutions* and *building and loan associations*, one-tenth of the total assets is substituted for the turnover. If data have to be given for several linked credit institutions or building and loan associations together, amounts recorded as investments in linked enterprises are to be deducted from the balance sheet total. If the total turnover of a group of enterprises which among other enterprises also comprises a credit institution or a building and loan association is stated, the balance sheet total of the credit institution or the building and loan association is to be added to the other turnover, but only to the extent of one-tenth.

As regards enterprises whose operations wholly or partially consist of publishing, producing or distributing *newspapers* or *magazines* or parts of them, twenty times the amount of the pertinent turnover is to be taken into account. One-fourth is then to be deducted from revenues resulting from the distribution of newspapers or magazines, as is done in the case of other trade turnover.

Insofar as the actual turnover is reduced (trade) or multiplied (press) as a result of special cartel law provisions, or total assets (banks and building and loan associations) are to be taken into account instead, this must be expressly indicated.

5. Market Shares

The basis for calculating market shares is the entire area of application of the Act (Federal Republic of Germany including West Berlin). If an enterprise does not operate in the entire territory of the Federal Republic or its market position shows considerable regional differences, it is necessary besides the market shares for the entire area of application also to give data in respect of the shares in the individual regional markets.

For the market share calculation, the most recent statistical information is to be used and the basis of its calculation or estimate stated.

The market share calculation may be based on sales in terms of quantity or value. It is expedient to calculate the market share both ways and present the pertinent calculations.

Only those goods or commercial services are to be attributed to a market which in the buyers' view are substitutable according to nature, use and price. As regards industrial goods, the Goods Classification for the Industry Statistics with its six or seven-digit categories of goods may serve as guidance. However, often those categories of goods comprise products of different kinds so that a more detailed breakdown is necessary. As regards credit institutions, the breakdown of the Bundesbank Statistics by individual types of business may be taken as a basis for defining a market. A detailed breakdown of the markets for the calculation of the market shares to be indicated does not prejudge the enterprises as regards the determination of market-dominating positions.

C. Legal Consequences

1. Any person who wilfully or negligently fails to immediately file a notification under Section 23 (1) to (5) of the ARC or furnishes false or incomplete

information commits an administrative offence under Section 39 (1) No. 2 of the ARC which may be punished by a fine of up to DM 50,000. In addition, the period of prohibition under Section 24 (2), second half of sentences 2, does not begin to run before a complete notification has been filed.

2. A notification of a merger project is not deemed to be effective unless it contains all particulars required (Section 24a (1) sentence 4 of the ARC). The periods provided for in Section 24a (2) of the ARC do not begin to run before a complete notification has been filed.

Any person who furnishes false or incomplete information in a notification under Section 24a (1) sentence 2 of the ARC commits an administrative offence which may be punished by a fine of up to DM 50,000 (Section 39 (1) No. 3 of the ARC). An administrative offence is also committed by any person who contrary to the legal prohibition completes, or participates in the completion of, a notifiable merger project (Section 38 (1) No. 8 in conjunction with Section 24a (4) of the ARC). Pursuant to Section 38 (4) of the ARC, the administrative offence is punishable by a fine of up to DM 1 million. Furthermore, legal transactions contravening the prohibition in Section 24a (4) of the ARC are ineffective.

3. Subject to review by the courts, the pertinent decision division of the Federal Cartel Office decides on whether the data supplied for a notification are complete. The courts are not bound by the considerations spelled out above. In the case of notifications under Section 24a (1) sentences 1 and 2 of the ARC it is expedient before filing the notification to obtain the views of the decision division regarding its completeness. The enterprises involved will thus be sure the merger can be prohibited only within a period of four months at most after the filing of the notification (exceptions: Section 24a (2) sentence 2 of the ARC).

D. Examination Procedure

The Federal Cartel Office endeavours (see also the General Directive of the Federal Minister of Economic Affairs of 30 May 1980, Bundesanzeiger (Federal Gazette) No. 103/80 of 7 June 1980) to carry out examination procedures under Section 24 (1) in conjunction with Section 24a of the ARC which do not lead to a prohibition as quickly as possible. If on the data supplied to or already available at the Office it is foreseeable that a market-dominating position within the meaning of Section 24 (1) of the ARC is unlikely to be created or strengthened, the Federal Cartel Office will inform the notifying enterprises without delay after receipt of the complete notification that the conditions of prohibition are not met. The merger project may be completed immediately after this information has been received (Section 24a (4) of the ARC). If a foreign merger project is notified and the Federal Cartel Office is satisfied that, due to foreign legal provisions applicable to the merger or for other reasons, the enterprises are prevented from supplying all particulars required under Sections 24a (1) sentence 4, 23 (5) prior to the completion, it will not make the statement mentioned above conditional upon the completeness of the notification, provided that it is clear from the furnished or available data that a prohibition of the merger project is unlikely to be considered. Also in this case, however, a complete notification must be made under Section 23 (5) of the ARC upon completion of the merger. The powers of the Federal Cartel Office under Section 24a (2) sentence 2 No. 5 remain unaffected.

1.c. Federal Cartel Office, Memorandum on "Domestic Effects Within the Meaning of Section 98 (2) of the Act Against Restraints of Competition in the Case of Mergers"*

For an interpretation of the term "domestic effect" within the meaning of Section 98 (2) the protective purpose of the relevant provision of the Act to be applied in each case must be considered (Federal Supreme Court decision of July 12, 1973, WuW/E "Ölfeldrohre").

The purpose of Sections 23 et seq. is to cover concentration because it may impair competition. The term "restraints of competition" in Section 98 (2) sums up all restraints of competition regulated in the relevant provisions of the Act. With regard to Sections 23 et seq. the restraint of competition within the meaning of Section 98 (2) is the merger process as such. It is irrelevant whether the intensity of domestic competition is actually reduced by a merger.

A. Domestic effects within the meaning of Section 98 (2) are, therefore, present *whenever* a merger is completed *within the Federal Republic*** (e. g. acquisition of the assets or the shares of a domestic enterprise, formation of a joint venture within the Federal Republic – even where the acquirers or the founders are foreign enterprises). As regards the domestic subsidiaries of the participating enterprises, a merger effected abroad is held to be a merger completed in the Federal Republic (Section 23 (3) sentence 4 of the ARC).

B. *Mergers completed abroad* have domestic effects if the merger affects the structural conditions for domestic competition and if the domestic enterprises (including subsidiaries and other affiliated companies) is a party to the merger.

1. As regards mergers effected abroad *between two directly participating enterprises only* (all merger situations except for the formation of joint ventures – e. g. acquisition of the assets or the shares of a foreign enterprise by a domestic enterprise –)

a) there are domestic effects, if both enterprises were already operating in the Federal Republic before the merger either directly or through subsidiaries, branches or importers;

b) there may be domestic effects, if only one of the enterprises was operating in the Federal Republic before the merger but if, for instance,

   aa) after the merger a foreign party to the merger is likely to deliver goods to the Federal Republic due to production links with the domestic party

---

* With the kind permission of the Federal Cartel Office, Berlin.
** Including West Berlin.

(preceding or subsequent production stages) or of links relating to the range of products. Whether such future deliveries to the Federal Republic are likely usually depends on whether goods of the same or a similar kind are already covered by trade between the countries involved and whether there are no technical and administrative trade barriers to such deliveries;

bb) the know-how of a domestic enterprise is perceptibly enhanced or industrial property rights accrue to it as a result of the merger.

2. As regards the *formation of joint ventures* abroad, the domestic effect primarily depends on the product and geographical markets on which the joint venture operates. The question of when a joint venture's activities have domestic effects is determined on the principles set out under B.1.; in this connection the production links and/or links affecting the range of products have to be judged by the relationship between the joint venture and the domestic party.

Furthermore, the formation of a joint venture abroad may also have domestic effects, if

a) a foreign enterprise participating in the joint venture was already operating in the joint venture's field of activity within the Federal Republic before the merger or if it can be reasonably expected to enter the domestic market without the merger (cf. B.1. aa);

b) the domestic party to the joint venture thereby obtains additional production capacity which perceptibly alters its capacity available for domestic supply (substitution of domestic production destined for exportation by production abroad). In general, it is a prerequisite for a change in capacity being perceptible that the domestic party already enjoyed a strong market position before the merger.

2. The United Kingdom

The Fair Trading Act 1973: Sections 57-77, 84

Part V
Mergers

Newspaper merger references

57. — (1) In this Part of this Act —

(a) "newspaper" means a daily, Sunday or local (other than daily or Sunday) newspaper circulating wholly or mainly in the United Kingdom or in a part of the United Kingdom;

(b) "newspaper proprietor" includes (in addition to an actual proprietor of a newspaper) any person having a controlling interest in a body corporate which is a newspaper proprietor, and any body corporate in which a newspaper proprietor has a controlling interest;

Meaning of "newspaper", "transfer of newspaper or of newspaper assets" and related expressions.

and any reference to the newspapers of a newspaper proprietor includes all newspapers in relation to which he is a newspaper proprietor and, in the case of a body corporate, all newspapers in relation to which a person having a controlling interest in that body corporate is a newspaper proprietor.

(2) In this Part of this Act "transfer of a newspaper or of newspaper assets" means any of the following transactions, that is to say —

(a) any transaction (whether involving a transfer or not) by virtue of which a person would become, or would acquire the right to become, a newspaper proprietor in relation to a newspaper;

(b) any transfer of assets necessary to the continuation of a newspaper as a separate newspaper (including goodwill or the right to use the name of the newspaper);

(c) any transfer of plant or premises used in the publication of a newspaper, other than a transfer made without a view to a change in the ownership or control of the newspaper or to its ceasing publication;

and "the newspaper concerned in the transfer", in relation to any transaction falling within paragraph (a), paragraph (b) or paragraph (c) of this subsection, means the newspaper in relation to which (as mentioned in that paragraph) the transaction is or is to be effected.

(3) In this Part of this Act "average circulation per day of publication", in relation to a newspaper, means its average circulation for the appropriate period, ascertained by dividing the number of copies to which its circulation amounts for that period by the number of days on which the newspaper was published during that period (circulation being calculated on the basis of actual sales in the United Kingdom of the newspaper as published on those days); and for the purposes of this subsection "the appropriate period" —

(a) in a case in which an application is made for consent under the next following section, means the period of six months ending six weeks before the date of the application, or

(b) in a case in which a transfer or purported transfer is made without any such application for consent, means the period of six months ending six weeks before the date of the transfer or purported transfer.

(4) For the purposes of this section a person has a controlling interest in a body corporate if (but only if) he can, directly or indirectly, determine the manner in which one-quarter of the votes which could be cast at a general meeting of the body corporate are to be cast on matters, and in circumstances, not of such a description as to bring into play any special voting rights or restrictions on voting rights.

Prohibition of
certain newspaper
mergers.
58.—(1) Subject to the following provisions of this section, a transfer of a newspaper or of newspaper assets to a newspaper proprietor whose newspapers have an average circulation per day of publication amounting, together with that of the newspaper concerned in the transfer, to 500,000 or more copies shall be unlawful and void, unless the transfer is made with written consent given (conditionally or unconditionally) by the Secretary of State.

(2) Except as provided by subsections (3) and (4) of this section and by

section 60 (3) of this Act, the consent of the Secretary of State under the preceding subsection shall not be given in respect of a transfer until after the Secretary of State has received a report on the matter from the Commission.

(3) Where the Secretary of State is satisfied that the newspaper concerned in the transfer is not economic as a going concern and as a separate newspaper, then —

(a) if he is also satisfied that, if the newspaper is to continue as a separate newspaper, the case is one of urgency, he may give his consent to the transfer without requiring a report from the Commission under this section;

(b) if he is satisfied that the newspaper is not intended to continue as a separate newspaper, he shall give his consent to the transfer, and shall give it unconditionally, without requiring such a report.

(4) If the Secretary of State is satisfied that the newspaper concerned in the transfer has an average circulation per day of publication of not more than 25,000 copies, he may give his consent to the transfer without requiring a report from the Commission under this section.

(5) The Secretary of State may by order made by statutory instrument provide, subject to any transitional provisions contained in the order, that for any number specified in subsection (1) or subsection (4) of this section (whether as originally enacted or as previously varied by an order under this subsection) there shall be substituted such other number as is specified in the order.

(6) In this section "satisfied" means satisfied by such evidence as the Secretary of State may require.

59. — (1) Where an application is made to the Secretary of State for his consent to a transfer of a newspaper or of newspaper assets, the Secretary of State, subject to the next following subsection, shall, within one month after receiving the application, refer the matter to the Commission for investigation and report. *Newspaper merger reference.*

(2) The Secretary of State shall not make a reference to the Commission under the preceding subsection in a case where —

(a) by virtue of subsection (3) of section 58 of this Act he is required to give his consent unconditionally without requiring a report from the Commission under this section, or

(b) by virtue of subsection (3) or subsection (4) of that section he has power to give his consent without requiring such a report from the Commission, and determines to exercise that power,

or where the application is expressed to depend on the operation of subsection (3) or subsection (4) of that section.

(3) On a reference made to them under this section (in this Act referred to as a "newspaper merger reference") the Commission shall report to the Secretary of State whether the transfer in question may be expected to operate against the public interest, taking into account all matters which appear in the circumstances to be relevant and, in particular, the need for accurate presentation of news and free expression of opinion.

60. — (1) A report of the Commission on a newspaper merger reference shall be made before the end of the period of three months beginning with the date of the *Time-limit for report on*

newspaper merger   reference or of such further period (if any) as the Secretary of State may allow for
reference.   the purpose in accordance with the next following subsection.

(2) The Secretary of State shall not allow any further period for a report on
such a reference except, on representations made by the Commission and on
being satisfied that there are special reasons why the report cannot be made
within the original period of three months; and the Secretary of State shall allow
only one such further period on any one reference, and no such further period
shall be longer than three months.

(3) If on such a reference the Commission have not made their report before
the end of the period specified in subsection (1) or of any further period allowed
under subsection (2) of this section, the Secretary of State may, without waiting
for the report, give his consent to the transfer to which the reference relates.

Report on   61.—(1) In making their report on a newspaper merger reference, the Commis-
newspaper merger   sion shall include in it definite conclusions on the questions comprised in the
reference.   reference, together with —

(a) such an account of their reasons for those conclusions, and
(b) such a survey of the general position with respect to the transfer of a
newspaper or of newspaper assets to which the reference relates, and of the
developments which have led to that position,

as in their opinion are expedient for facilitating a proper understanding of those
questions and of their conclusions.

(2) Where on such a reference the Commission find that the transfer of a
newspaper or of newspaper assets in question might operate against the public
interest, the Commission shall consider whether any (and, if so, what) conditions
might be attached to any consent to the transfer in order to prevent the transfer
from so operating, and may, if they think fit, include in their report recommendations as to such conditions.

Enforcement   62.—(1) Any person who is knowingly concerned in, or privy to, a purported
provisions relating   transfer of a newspaper or of newspaper assets which is unlawful by virtue of
to newspaper   section 58 of this Act shall be guilty of an offence.
mergers.
(2) Where under that section the consent of the Secretary of State is given to a
transfer of a newspaper or of newspaper assets, but is given subject to one or
more conditions, any person who is knowingly concerned in, or privy to, a
breach of that condition, or of any of those conditions, as the case may be, shall
be guilty of an offence.

(3) A person guilty of an offence under this section shall be liable, on
conviction on indictment, to imprisonment for a term not exceeding two years or
to a fine or to both.

(4) No proceedings for an offence under this section shall be instituted —

(a) in England or Wales, except by, or with the consent of, the Director of Public
Prosecutions, or
(b) in Northern Ireland, except by, or with the consent of, the Director of Public
Prosecutions for Northern Ireland.

Other merger references

63.—(1) Sections 64 to 75 of this Act shall have effect in relation to merger references other than newspaper merger references; and accordingly in those sections "merger reference" shall be construed — Mergers references to which ss. 64 to 75 apply.

(a) as not including a reference made under section 59 of this Act, but

(b) as including any merger reference relating to a transfer of a newspaper or of newspaper assets, if the reference is made under section 64 or section 75 of this Act in a case falling within section 59 (2) of this Act.

(2) In the following provisions of this Part of this Act "enterprise" means the activities, or part of the activities, of a business.

64.—(1) A merger reference may be made to the Commission by the Secretary of State where it appears to him that it is or may be the fact that two or more enterprises (in this section referred to as "the relevant enterprises"), of which one at least was carried on in the United Kingdom or by or under the control of a body corporate incorporated in the United Kingdom, have, at a time or in circumstances falling within subsection (4) of this section, ceased to be distinct enterprises, and that either — Merger situation qualifying for investigation.

(a) as a result, the condition specified in subsection (2) or in subsection (3) of this section prevails, or does so to a greater extent, with respect to the supply of goods or services of any description, or

(b) the value of the assets taken over exceeds £ 5 million.

(2) The condition referred to in subsection (1)(a) of this section, in relation to the supply of goods of any description, is that at least one-quarter of all the goods of that description which are supplied in the United Kingdom, or in a substantial part of the United Kingdom, either —

(a) are supplied by one and the same person or are supplied to one and the same person, or

(b) are supplied by the persons by whom the relevant enterprises (so far as they continue to be carried on) are carried on, or are supplied to those persons.

(3) The condition referred to in subsection (1)(a) of this section, in relation to the supply of services of any description, is that the supply of services of that description in the United Kingdom, or in a substantial part of the United Kingdom, is, to the extent of at least one-quarter, either —

(a) supply by one and the same person, or supply for one and the same person, or

(b) supply by the persons by whom the relevant enterprises (so far as they continue to be carried on) are carried on, or supply for those persons.

(4) For the purposes of subsection (1) of this section enterprises shall be taken to have ceased to be distinct enterprises at a time or in circumstances falling within this subsection if either —

(a) they did so not earlier than six months before the date on which the merger reference relating to them is to be made, or

(b) they did so under or in consequence of arrangements or transactions which were entered into without prior notice being given to the Secretary of State or to the Director of material facts about the proposed arrangements or transactions and in circumstances in which those facts had not been made public, and notice of those facts was not given to the Secretary of State or to the Director or made public more than six months before the date mentioned in the preceding paragraph.

(5) In determining whether to make a merger reference to the Commission the Secretary of State shall have regard, with a view to the prevention or removal of uncertainty, to the need for making a determination as soon as is reasonably practicable.

(6) On making a merger reference, the Secretary of State shall arrange for it to be published in such manner as he thinks most suitable for bringing it to the attention of persons who in his opinion would be affected by it.

(7) The Secretary of State may by order made by statutory instrument provide, subject to any transitional provisions contained in the order, that for the sum specified in subsection (1)(b) of this section (whether as originally enacted or as previously varied by an order under this subsection) there shall be substituted such other sum (not being less than £ 5 million) as is specified in the order.

(8) The fact that two or more enterprises have ceased to be distinct enterprises in the circumstances described in subsection (1) of this section (including in those circumstances the result specified in paragraph (a), or fulfilment of the condition specified in paragraph (b), of that subsection) shall, for the purposes of this Act, be regarded as creating a merger situation qualifiying for investigation; and in this Act "merger situation qualifying for investigation" and any reference to the creation of such a situation shall be construed accordingly.

(9) In this section "made public" means so publicised as to be generally known or readily ascertainable.

Enterprises ceasing to be distinct enterprises.

65. — (1) For the purposes of this Part of this Act any two enterprises shall be regarded as ceasing to be distinct enterprises if either —

(a) they are brought under common ownership or common control (whether or not the business to which either of them formerly belonged continues to be carried on under the same or different ownership or control), or

(b) either of the enterprises ceases to be carried on at all and does so in consequence of any arrangements or transaction entered into to prevent competition between the enterprises.

(2) For the purposes of the preceding subsection enterprises shall (without prejudice to the generality of the words "common control" in that subsection) be regarded as being under common control if they are —

(a) enterprises of interconnected bodies corporate, or

(b) enterprises carried on by two or more bodies corporate of which one and the same person or group of persons has control, or

(c) an enterprise carried on by a body corporate and an enterprise carried on by a person or group of persons having control of that body corporate.

(3) A person or group of persons able, directly or indirectly, to control or materially to influence the policy of a body corporate, or the policy of any person in carrying on an enterprise, but without having a controlling interest in

that body corporate or in that enterprise, may for the purposes of subsections (1) and (2) of this section be treated as having control of it.

(4) For the purpose of subsection (1)(a) of this section, in so far as it relates to bringing two or more enterprises under common control, a person or group of persons may be treated as bringing an enterprise under his or their control if —

(a) being already able to control or materially to influence the policy of the person carrying on the enterprise, that person or group of persons acquires a controlling interest in the enterprise or, in the case of an enterprise carried on by a body corporate, acquires a controlling interest in that body corporate, or

(b) being already able materially to influence the policy of the person carrying on the enterprise, that person or group of persons becomes able to control that policy.

66.—(1) Where under or in consequence of the same arrangements or transaction, or under or in consequence of successive arrangements or transactions between the same parties or interests, successive events to which this subsection applies occur within a period of two years, then for the purposes of a merger reference those events may, if the Secretary of State thinks fit, be treated as having occurred simultaneously on the date on which the latest of them occured. *Time when enterprises cease to be distinct.*

(2) The preceding subsection applies to any event whereby, under or in consequence of the arrangements or the transaction or transactions in question, any enterprises cease as between themselves to be distinct enterprises.

(3) For the purposes of subsection (1) of this section any arrangements or transactions may be treated by the Secretary of State as arrangements or transactions between the same interests if it appears to him to be appropriate that they should be so treated, having regard to the persons who are substantially concerned in them.

(4) Subject to the preceding provisions of this section, the time at which any two enterprises cease to be distinct enterprises, where they do so under or in consequence of any arrangements or transaction not having immediate effect, or having immediate effect in part only, shall be taken to be the time when the parties to the arrangements or transaction become bound to such extent as will result, on effect being given to their obligations, in the enterprises ceasing to be distinct enterprises.

(5) In accordance with subsection (4) of this section (but without prejudice to the generality of that subsection) for the purpose of determining the time at which any two enterprises cease to be distinct enterprises no account shall be taken of any option or other conditional right until the option is exercised or the condition is satisfied.

67.—(1) The provisions of this section shall have effect for the purposes of section 64(1)(b) of this Act. *Valuation of assets taken over.*

(2) Subject to subsection (4) of this section, the value of the assets taken over —

(a) shall be determined by taking the total value of the assets employed in, or appropriated to, the enterprises which cease to be distinct enterprises, except any enterprise which remains under the same ownership and control, or if none of the enterprises remains under the same ownership and control, then that one of the enterprises having the assets with the highest value, and

(b) shall be so determined by reference to the values at which, on the enterprises ceasing to be distinct enterprises or (if they have not then done so) on the making of the merger reference to the Commission, the assets stand in the books of the relevant business, less any relevant provisions for depreciation, renewals or diminution in value.

(3) For the purposes of subsection (2) of this section any assets of a body corporate which, on a change in the control of the body corporate or of any enterprise of it, are dealt with in the same way as assets appropriated to any such enterprise shall be treated as appropriated to that enterprise.

(4) Where in accordance with subsection (1) of section 66 of this Act events to which that subsection applies are treated as having occurred simultaneously, subsection (2) of this section shall apply with such adjustments as appear to the Secretary of State or to the Commission to be appropriate.

Supplementary provisions as to merger situations qualifying for investigation.
68. — (1) In relation to goods or services of any description which are the subject of different forms of supply —

(a) references in subsection (2) of section 64 of this Act to the supply of goods, or

(b) references in subsection (3) of that section to the supply of services,

shall be construed in whichever of the following ways appears to the Secretary of State or the Commission, as the case may be, to be appropriate in all the circumstances, that is to say, as references to any of those forms of supply taken separately, to all those forms of supply taken together, or to any of those forms of supply taken in groups.

(2) For the purposes of the preceding subsection the Secretary of State or the Commission may treat goods or services as being the subject of different forms of supply whenever the transactions in question differ as to their nature, their parties, their terms or their surrounding circumstances, and the difference is one which, in the opinion of the Secretary of State or of the Commission, as the case may be, ought for the purposes of that subsection to be treated as a material difference.

(3) For the purpose of determining whether the proportion of one-quarter mentioned in subsection (2) or subsection (3) of section 64 of this Act is fulfilled with respect to goods or services of any description, the Secretary of State or the Commission, as the case may be, shall apply such criterion (whether it be value or cost or price or quantity or capacity or number of workers employed or some other criterion, of whatever nature) or such combination of criteria as may appear to the Secretary of State or the Commission to be most suitable in all the circumstances.

(4) The criteria for determining when goods or services can be treated, for the purposes of section 64 of this Act, as goods or services of a separate description

shall be such as in any particular case the Secretary of State thinks most suitable in the circumstances of that case.

69.—(1) Subject to the following provisions of this Part of this Act, on a merger reference the Commission shall investigate and report on the questions — *Different kinds of merger references.*

(a) whether a merger situation qualifying for investigation has been created, and

(b) if so, whether the creation of that situation operates, or may be expected to operate, against the public interest.

(2) A merger reference may be so framed as to require the Commission, in relation to the question whether a merger situation qualifying for investigation has been created, to exclude from consideration paragraph (a) of subsection (1) of section 64 of this Act, or to exclude from consideration paragraph (b) of that subsection, or to exclude one of those paragraphs if the Commission find the other satisfied.

(3) In relation to the question whether any such result as is mentioned in section 64(1)(a) of this Act has arisen, a merger reference may be so framed as to require the Commission to confine their investigation to the supply of goods or services in a specified part of the United Kingdom.

(4) A merger reference may require the Commission, if they find that a merger situation qualifying for investigation has been created, to limit their consideration thereafter to such elements in, or possible consequences of, the creation of that situation as may be specified in the reference, and to consider whether, in respect only of those elements or possible consequences, the situation operates, or may be expected to operate, against the public interest.

70.—(1) Every merger reference shall specify a period (not being longer than six months beginning with the date of the reference) within which a report on the reference is to be made; and a report of the Commission on a merger reference shall not have effect, and no action shall be taken in relation to it under this Act, unless the report is made before the end of that period or of such further period (if any) as may be allowed by the Secretary of State in accordance with the next following subsection. *Time-limit for report on merger reference.*

(2) The Secretary of State shall not allow any further period for a report on a merger reference except on representations made by the Commission and on being satisfied that there are special reasons why the report cannot be made within the period specified in the reference; and the Secretary of State shall allow only one such further period on any one reference, and no such further period shall be longer than three months.

71.—(1) Subject to the following provisions of this section, the Secretary of State may at any time vary a merger reference made under section 69 (4) of this Act. *Variation of certain merger references.*

(2) A merger reference made under section 69 (4) of this Act shall not be so varied that it ceases to be a reference limited in accordance with that subsection.

(3) Without prejudice to the powers of the Secretary of State under section 70

of this Act, a merger reference shall not be varied so as to specify a period within which a report on the reference is to be made which is different from the period specified in the reference in accordance with that section.

Report of
Commission on
merger reference.

72.—(1) In making their report on a merger reference, the Commission shall include in it definite conclusions on the questions comprised in the reference, together with —

(a) such an account of their reasons for those conclusions, and

(b) such a survey of the general position with respect to the subject-matter of the reference, and of the developments which have led to that position,

as in their opinion are expedient for facilitating a proper understanding of those questions and of their conclusions.

(2) Where on a merger reference the Commission find that a merger situation qualifying for investigation has been created and that the creation of that situation operates or may be expected to operate against the public interest (or, in a case falling within subsection (4) of section 69 of this Act, find that one or more elements in or consequences of that situation which were specified in the reference in accordance with that subsection so operate or may be expected so to operate) the Commission shall specify in their report the particular effects, adverse to the public interest, which in their opinion the creation of that situation (or, as the case may be, those elements in or consequences of it) have or may be expected to have; and the Commission —

(a) shall, as part of their investigations, consider what action (if any) should be taken for the purpose of remedying or preventing those adverse effects, and

(b) may, if they think fit, include in their report recommendations as to such action.

(3) In paragraph (a) of subsection (2) of this section the reference to action to be taken for the purpose mentioned in that paragraph is a reference to action to be taken for that purpose either —

(a) by one or more Ministers (including Ministers or departments of the Government of Northern Ireland) or other public authorities, or

(b) by one or more persons specified in the report as being persons carrying on, owning or controlling any of the enterprises which, in accordance with the conclusions of the Commission, have ceased to be distinct enterprises.

Order of
Secretary of State
on report on
merger reference.

73.—(1) The provisions of this section shall have effect where a report of the Commission on a merger reference has been laid before Parliamant in accordance with the provisions of Part VII of this Act, and the conclusions of the Commission set out in the report, as so laid, —

(a) include conclusions to the effect that a merger situation qualifying for investigation has been created and that its creation, or particular elements in or consequences of it specified in the report, operate or may be expected to operate against the public interest, and

(b) specify particular effects, adverse to the public interest, which in the opinion of the Commission the creation of that situation, or (as the case may be) those elements in or consequences of it, have or may be expected to have.

(2) In the circumstances mentioned in the preceding subsection the Secretary of State may by order made by statutory instrument exercise such one or more of the powers specified in Parts I and II of Schedule 8 to this Act as he may consider it requisite to exercise for the purpose of remedying or preventing the adverse effects specified in the report as mentioned in the preceding subsection; and those powers may be so exercised to such extent and in such manner as the Secretary of State considers requisite for that purpose.

(3) In determining whether, or to what extent or in what manner, to exercise any of those powers, the Secretary of State shall take into account any recommendations included in the report of the Commission in pursuance of section 72(2)(b) of this Act and any advice given by the Director under section 88 of this Act.

74.—(1) Where a merger reference has been made to the Commission, and does not impose on the Commission a limitation under section 69 (4) of this Act, then, with a view to preventing action to which this subsection applies, the Secretary of State, subject to subsection (3) of this section, may by order made by statutory instrument —

Interim order in respect of merger reference.

(a) prohibit or restrict the doing of things which in his opinion would constitute action to which this subsection applies, or

(b) impose on any person concerned obligations as to the carrying on of any activities or the safeguarding of any assets, or

(c) provide for the carrying on of any activities or the safeguarding of any assets either by the appointment of a person to conduct or supervise the conduct of any activities (on such terms and with such powers as may be specified or described in the order) or in any other manner, or

(d) exercise any of the powers which, by virtue of paragraph 12 of Schedule 8 to this Act, are exercisable by an order under section 73 of this Act.

(2) In relation to a merger reference the preceding subsection applies to any action which might prejudice the reference or impede the taking of any action under this Act which may be warranted by the Commission's report on the reference.

(3) No order shall be made under this section in respect of a merger reference after whichever of the following events first occurs, that is to say —

(a) the time (including any further period) allowed to the Commission for making a report on the reference expires without their having made such a report;

(b) the period of forty days beginning with the day on which a report of the Commission on the reference is laid before Parliament expires.

(4) An order under this section made in respect of a merger reference (if it has not previously ceased to have effect) shall cease to have effect on the occurrence of whichever of those events first occurs, but without prejudice to anything previously done under the order.

(5) Subsection (4) of this section shall have effect without prejudice —

(a) to the operation, in relation to any such order, of section 134 (1) of this Act, or

(b) to the operation of any order made under sections 73 of this Act which exercises the same or similiar powers to those exercised by the order under this section.

Reference in anticipation of merger.

75.—(1) A merger reference may be made to the Commission by the Secretary of State where it appears to him that it is or may be the fact that arrangements are in progress or in contemplation which, if carried into effect, will result in the creation of a merger situation qualifying for investigation.

(2) Subject to the following provisions of this section, on a merger reference under this section the Commission shall proceed in relation to the prospective and (if events so require) the actual results of the arrangements proposed or made as, in accordance with the preceding provisions of this Part of this Act, they could proceed if the arrangements in question had actually been made, and the results in question had followed immediately before the date of the reference under this section.

(3) A merger reference under this section may require the Commission, if they find that a merger situation qualifying for investigation has been created, or will be created if the arrangements in question are carried into effect, to limit their consideration thereafter to such elements in, or possible consequences of, the creation of that situation as may be specified in the reference, and to consider whether, in respect only of those elements or possible consequences, the situation might be expected to operate against the public interest.

(4) In relation to a merger reference under this section, sections 66, 67, 69, 71, 72, 73 and 74 of this Act shall apply subject to the following modifications, that is to say —

(a) section 66 shall apply with the necessary adaptations in relation to enterprises which will or may cease to be distinct enterprises under or in consequence of arrangements not yet carried into effect or not yet fully carried into effect;

(b) in section 67 (4) the reference to subsection (1) of section 66 shall be construed as a reference to that subsection as modified in accordance with the preceding paragraph;

(c) in section 69, subsection (1) shall be construed as modified by subsection (2) of this section; in subsections (2) and (3) any reference to the question whether a merger situation qualifying for investigation has been created, or whether a result mentioned in section 64 (1) (a) of this Act has arisen, shall be construed as including a reference to the question whether such a situation will be created or such a result will arise if the arrangements in question are carried into effect; and subsection (4) of that section shall not apply;

(d) in section 71, in section 72 (2) and in section 74 (1) the references to section 69 (4) of this Act shall be construed as references to subsection (3) of this section; and

(e) in section 73 (1), the reference to conclusions to the effect that a merger situation qualifying for investigation has been created shall be construed as including a reference to conclusions to the effect that such a situation will be created if the arrangements in question are carried into effect.

(5) If, in the course of their investigations on a merger reference under this

section, it appears to the Commission that the proposal to make arrangements such as are mentioned in the reference has been abandoned, the Commission —

(a) shall, if the Secretary of State consents, lay the reference aside, but

(b) shall in that case furnish to the Secretary of State such information as he may require as to the results until then of the investigations.

Supplementary

76. It shall be the duty of the Director —

(a) to take such steps as are reasonably practicable for keeping himself informed about actual or prospective arrangements or transactions which may constitute or result in the creation of merger situations qualifying for investigation, and

(b) to make recommendations to the Secretary of Sate as to any action under this Part of this Act which in the opinion of the Director it would be expedient for the Secretary of State to take in relation to any such arrangements or transactions.

Functions of Director in relation to merger situations.

77.—(1) For the following purposes, that is to say —

(a) for the purpose of determining under section 57 (1) of this Act whether a person is a newspaper proprietor and, if so, which newspapers are his newspapers;

(b) for the purpose of determining under section 65 of this Act whether any two enterprises have been brought under common ownership or common control; and

(c) for the purpose of determining what activities are carried on by way of business by any one person, in so far as that question arises in the application, by virtue of an order under section 73 of this Act, of paragraph 14 of Schedule 8 to this Act,

Associated persons.

associated persons, and any bodies corporate which they or any of them control, shall (subject to the next following subsection) be treated as one person.

(2) The preceding subsection shall not have effect —

(a) for the purpose mentioned in paragraph (a) of that subsection so as to exclude from section 58 of this Act any case which would otherwise fall within that section, or

(b) for the purpose mentioned in paragraph (b) of the preceding subsection so as to exclude from section 65 of this Act any case which would otherwise fall within that section.

(3) A merger reference other than a newspaper merger reference (whether apart from this section the reference could be made or not) may be so framed as to exclude from consideration, either altogether or for any specified purpose or to any specified extent, any matter which, apart from this section, would not have been taken into account on that reference.

(4) For the purposes of this section the following persons shall be regarded as associated with one another, that is to say —

(a) any individual and that individual's husband or wife and any relative, or husband or wife of a relative, of that individual or of that individual's husband or wife;

(b) any person in his capacity as trustee of a settlement and the settlor or grantor and any person associated with the settlor or grantor;

(c) persons carrying on business in partnership and the husband or wife and relatives of any of them;

(d) any two or more persons acting together to secure or exercise control of a body corporate or other association or to secure control of any enterprise or assets.

(5) The reference in subsection (1) of this section to bodies corporate which associated persons control shall be construed as follows, that is to say —

(a) in its application for the purpose mentioned in paragraph (a) of that subsection, "control" in that reference means having a controlling interest within the meaning of section 57 (4) of this Act, and

(b) in its application for any other purpose mentioned in subsection (1) of this section, "control" in the reference shall be construed in accordance with section 65 (3) and (4) of this Act.

(6) In this section "relative" means a brother, sister, uncle, aunt, nephew, niece, lineal ancestor or descendant (the stepchild or illegitimate child of any person, or anyone adopted by a person, whether legally or otherwise, as his child, being taken into account as a relative or to trace a relationship in the same way as that person's child); and references to a wife or husband shall include a former wife or husband and a reputed wife or husband.

Part VIII
Additional Provisions relating to references to Commission

Public interest.   84. — (1) In determining for any purposes to which this section applies whether any particular matter operates, or may be expected to operate, against the public interest, the Commission shall take into account all matters which appear to them in the particular circumstances to be relevant and, among other things, shall have regard to the desirability —

(a) of maintaining and promoting effective competition between persons supplying goods and services in the United Kingdom;

(b) of promoting the interests of consumers, purchasers and other users of goods and services in the United Kingdom in respect of the prices charged for them and in respect of their quality and the variety of goods and services supplied;

(c) of promoting, through competition, the reduction of costs and the development and use of new techniques and new products, and of facilitating the entry of new competitors into existing markets;

(d) of maintaining and promoting the balanced distribution of industry and employment in the United Kingdom; and

(e) of maintaining and promoting competitive activity in markets outside the United Kingdom on the part of producers of goods, and of suppliers of goods and services, in the United Kingdom.

(2) This section applies to the purposes of any functions of the Commission under this Act other than functions to which section 59 (3) of this Act applies.

3. France

Law No. 77-806 of 19 July 1977 Concerning the Control of Economic Concentration and the Suppression of Illegal Concerted Practices and of Abuses of a Dominant Market Position: Sections 1-11*

Title I
The Commission on Competition

Section 1. – A Commission on Competition shall be established.

This Commission shall decide, in an advisory capacity, all questions concerning competition which have been brought before it by the Government. Furthermore it shall exercise the competences defined by the present Law in the field of the control of concentrations and the suppression of illegal concerted practices and of abuses of a dominant market position.

Section 2. – The Commission on Competition shall be composed of:

A President named by decree for a period of six years; he shall be chosen from amongst the members of the Conseil d'Etat and the members of the administrative or ordinary judicial order.

Ten Commissioners named by decree for a period of four years; they shall be chosen in part from amongst the members of the Conseil d'Etat and the members of the administrative or ordinary judicial order and in part by virtue of their special competence in economic, social or consumer matters.

The appointments of the President and the ten Commissioners may be renewed.

The Commission shall be assisted by a General Reporter and by reporters.

The offices of the President, of the General Reporter and of specific reporters are full-time employments.

Section 3. – The Commission on Competition shall meet either in plenary session or in sections. The sections shall be presided over by the President of the Commission or by a Commissioner.

---

* Translated by Mr. Pierre Maurey, Mont-Saint-Aignan, France (with the kind intervention of Professor Barthélémy Mercadal, University of Rouen, France).

Title II
The Control of Economic Concentration

Chapter I
Transactions Subject to Control

Section 4. — Under this Title, a concentration results from any legal act or transaction in whatever form, relating to the transfer of ownership or enjoyment of the whole or part of the assets, rights and obligations of an undertaking, or whose objective or effect is to allow an undertaking or a group of undertakings to exercise directly or indirectly over one or several other undertakings an influence of such a nature as to direct, or even guide the management or the functioning of the latter.

Any concentration which might restrain sufficient competition in a market can be subject to control.

This control can only be effected if the turnover of the undertakings concerned on the domestic market and for the legal year preceding the concentration has been in excess of:

40 percent of the domestic consumption, for all undertakings concerned taken together, if the goods, products or services are of the same nature or can be substituted for each other;

25 percent of the domestic consumption, for each of at least two of the contracting parties or groups of undertakings concerned, if the goods, products or services are of a different nature and cannot be substituted for each other.

Under this Section, the undertakings concerned are those which are the parties to the legal act or transaction, or which are the objects thereof, or those which have economic links with the undertakings involved in the concentration.

Domestic consumption refers to the total amount of the sales of goods made and services performed in France during the legal year preceding the legal act or transaction mentioned in the first paragraph. Where a project of a legal act or transaction has been notified, pursuant to paragraph one of Section 5 of this Law, the relevant legal year shall be that preceding this notification.

The legal act or transaction shall not give rise to any of the measures stipulated in Section 8 if they bring a contribution to economic and social progress sufficient to offset the restraints of competition they entail. The contribution shall be evaluated taking into account the competitiveness of the undertakings concerned with respect to international competition.

Chapter II
Control Procedure and Sanctions

Section 5. — Notice to the Minister in charge of the Economy of projects of a legal act or transaction as defined in Section 4 is not compulsory. Furthermore, notice may be given within three months after the date when the acts and transactions become final. The undertakings concerned may accompany their notices with commitments.

In the absence of notice, the President of the Commission on Competition, ex officio, may order inquiries to ascertain whether legal acts or transactions under

Section 4 of this Law have been concluded or entered into by undertakings. The findings of the inquiry shall be communicated to him together with the documents in support of these findings.

The same inquiries may be ordered by the Minister in charge of the Economy, either at his own initiative or on request from the Minister in charge of the sector concerned. The Minister in charge of the Economy immediately informs the President of the Commission on Competition that inquiries are under way; he communicates to him the findings of the inquiry together with the documents in support of these findings.

Section 6. − At his own initative or on request from the Minister in charge of the sector concerned, the Minister in charge of the Economy may bring before the Commission on Competition any legal act or transaction as defined in Section 4, whether it has been notified or not.

Where notice has been given, the Minister shall not refer the matter to the Commission after the expiration of a three-month period following notice, unless any commitments which may have accompanied the notice are not carried out.

If no notice has been given, the matter shall not be referred to the Commission before the expiration of the three-month period stipulated in paragraph one of Section 5.

Section 7. − The Commission on Competition examines the legal acts and transactions which are submitted to it by the Minister in charge of the Economy. It ascertains whether the provisions of the last paragraph of Section 4 must be applied. In its opinion, it mentions, as the case may be, the measures that should be taken.

The reports on the basis of which the Commission is called upon to formulate its opinion, as well as the information and the documents or excerpts therefrom on which the reporter bases his opinion, are communicated to the parties concerned; the latter shall be allowed to submit their observations in the course of the procedure, in the manner stipulated in the decree mentioned in Section 20 of this Law [i. e. the decree determining the conditions of applications of the present Law].

Section 8. − The Minister in charge of the Economy and the Minister(s) in charge of the economic sector(s) concerned may, in a reasoned decree, and within the limits set by the advisory opinion of the Commission on Competition, order the undertakings to take within a specified time one of the following measures:

Either not to carry out the project of the legal act or transaction;

Or to restore the legal situation which existed prior to the legal act or transaction;

Or to modify the legal act or transaction, or make additions to it;

Or to take any measure proper to protect or restore sufficient competition.

The Ministers mentioned in the preceding paragraph may also, under the same conditions, make the application of the legal act or transaction subject to compliance with instructions aimed at ensuring a contribution to economic and social progress sufficient to offset the restraints of competition entailed.

However, if the legal act or transaction has been notified, no decision pursuant to the two preceding paragraphs can be taken after the expiration of a period of eight months following receipt of the notice, except if the commitments offered by the undertakings in support to their notification are not carried out, or if the Ministers' injunctions or instructions are not complied with.

The decisions taken pursuant to this Section shall not be enforced until the parties concerned have been given the opportunity to submit their observations.

Section 9. — Injunctions and instructions pursuant to Section 8 have binding force; they shall apply notwithstanding the provisions of the agreement of the parties. If they are not complied with, the Minister in charge of the Economy and the Minister in charge of the economic sector concerned may impose a fine, the amount of which shall be determined after consulting the Commission on Competition, in accordance with the conditions and limits stipulated in Sections 53, 54, 56 and 57 of Ordinance no. 45-1483 (30 June 1945) relating to prices.

Section 10. — The Minister in charge of the Economy and the Minister in charge of the economic sector concerned determine the fines according to the part played by each of the undertakings involved.

Section 11. — The officers specified in Section 13 of Ordinance no. 45-1483 (30 June 1945) relating to prices are empowered to conduct the inquiries mentioned in Section 5 of this Law, and those ordered by the President of the Commission on Competition for the purposes of the cases submitted to the Commission.

These officers are granted the powers stipulated in Book Two of Ordinance no. 45-1484 (30 June 1945) Concerning the Discovery, the Prosecution and the Suppression of Violations against the Economic Law.

The reporters of the Commission on Competition have the same powers, and shall be bound by the same rules of secrecy, as the above mentioned officers.

Title III
The Sanctions to be Applied in Case of Violation of the Legislation on Concerted Illegal Practices and Dominant Market Positions
[*Sections 12-19* omitted]

Title IV
Various and Transitional Provisions
[*Sections 20-23* omitted]

4. European Communities

4.a. European Coal and Steel Community Treaty: Article 66

Article 66

1. Any transaction shall require the prior authorisation of the High Authority, subject to the provisions of paragraph 3 of this Article, if it has in itself the direct or indirect effect of bringing about within the territories referred to in the first paragraph of Article 79, as a result of action by any person or undertaking or group of persons or undertakings, a concentration between undertakings at least one of which is covered by Article 80, whether the transaction concerns a single product or a number of different products, and whether it is effected by merger, acquisition of shares or parts of the undertaking or assets, loan, contract or any other means of control. For the purpose of applying these provisions, the High Authority shall, by regulations made after consulting the Council, define what constitutes control of an undertaking.

2. The High Authority shall grant the authorisation referred to in the preceding paragraph if it finds that the proposed transaction will not give to the persons or undertakings concerned the power, in respect of the product or products within its jurisdiction:

– to determine prices, to control or restrict production or distribution or to hinder effective competition in a substantial part of the market for those products; or

– to evade the rules of competition instituted under this Treaty, in particular by establishing an artificially privileged position involving a substantial advantage in access to supplies or markets.

In assessing whether this is so, the High Authority shall, in accordance with the principle of non-discrimination laid down in Article 4 (b), take account of the size of like undertakings in the Community, to the extent it considers justified in order to avoid or correct disadvantages resulting from unequal competitive conditions.

The High Authority may make its authorisation subject to any conditions which it considers appropriate for the purposes of this paragraph.

Before ruling on a transaction concerning undertakings at least one of which is not subject to Article 80, the High Authority shall obtain the comments of the Governments concerned.

3. The High Authority shall exempt from the requirement of prior authorisation such classes of transactions as it finds should, in view of the size of the assets or undertakings concerned, taken in conjunction with the kind of concentration to be effected, be deemed to meet the requirements of paragraph 2. Regulations made to this effect, with the assent of the Council, shall also lay down the conditions governing such exemption.

4. Without prejudice to the application of Article 47 to undertakings within its jurisdiction, the High Authority may, either by regulations made after consultation with the Council stating the kind of transaction to be communicated to it or by a special request under these regulations to the parties concerned, obtain from the natural or legal persons who have acquired or regrouped or are intending to acquire or regroup the rights or assets in question any information needed for the application of this Article concerning transactions liable to produce the effect referred to in paragraph 1.

5. If a concentration should occur which the High Authority finds has been effected contrary to the provisions of paragraph 1 but which nevertheless meets the requirements of paragraph 2, the High Authority shall make its approval of that concentration subject to payment by the persons who have acquired or regrouped the rights or assets in question of the fine provided for in the second subparagraph of paragraph 6; the amount of the fine shall not be less than half of the maximum determined in that subparagraph should it be clear that authorisation ought to have been applied for. If the fine is not paid, the High Authority shall take the steps hereinafter provided for in respect of concentrations found to be unlawful.

If a concentration should occur which the High Authority finds cannot fulfil the general or specific conditions to which an authorisation under paragraph 2 would be subject, the High Authority shall, by means of a reasoned decision, declare the concentration unlawful and, after giving the parties concerned the opportunity to submit their comments, shall order separation of the undertakings or assets improperly concentrated or cessation of joint control, and any other measures which it considers appropriate to return the undertakings or assets in question to independent operation and restore normal conditions of competition. Any person directly concerned may institute proceedings against such decisions, as provided in Article 33. By way of derogation from Article 33, the Court shall have unlimited jurisdiction to assess whether the transaction effected is a concentration within the maning of paragraph 1 and of regulations made in application thereof. The institution of proceedings shall have suspensory effect. Proceedings may not be instituted until the measures provided for above have been ordered, unless the High Authority agrees to the institution of separate proceedings against the decision declaring the transaction unlawful.

The High Authority may at any time, unless the third paragraph of Article 39 is applied, take or cause to be taken such interim measures of protection as it may consider necessary to safeguard the interests of competing undertakings and of third parties, and to forestall any step which might hinder the implementation of its decisions. Unless the Court decides otherwise, proceedings shall not have suspensory effect in respect of such interim measures.

The High Authority shall allow the parties concerned a reasonable period in which to comply with its decisions, on expiration of which it may impose daily penalty payments not exceeding one tenth of one per cent, of the value of the rights or assets in question.

Furthermore, if the parties concerned do not fulfil their obligations, the High Authority shall itself take steps to implement its decision; it may in particular suspend the exercise, in undertakings within its jurisdiction, of the rights attached to the assets acquired irregularly, obtain the appointment by the judicial authorities of a receiver of such assets, organise the forced sale of such assets subject to the protection of the legitimate interests of their owners, and annul with respect to natural or legal persons who have acquired the rights or assets in question through the unlawful transaction, the acts, decisions, resolutions or proceedings of the supervisory and managing bodies or undertakings over which control has been obtained irregularly.

The High Authority is also empowered to make such recommendations to the Member States concerned as may be necessary to ensure that the measures provided for in the preceding subparagraphs are implemented under their own law.

In the exercise of its powers, the High Authority shall take account of the rights of third parties which have been acquired in good faith.

6. The High Authority may impose fines not exceeding:
- 3 per cent of the value of the assets acquired or regrouped or to be acquired or regrouped, on natural or legal persons who have evaded the obligations laid down in paragraph 4;
- 10 per cent of the value of the assets acquired or regrouped, on natural or legal persons who have evaded the obligations laid down in paragraph 1; this maximum shall be increased by one twenty-fourth for each month which elapses after the end of the twelfth month following completion of the transaction until the High Authority establishes that there has been an infringement;
- 10 per cent of the value of the assets acquired or regrouped or to be acquired or regrouped, on natural or legal persons who have obtained or attempted to obtain authorisation under paragraph 2 by means of false or misleading information;
- 15 per cent of the value of the assets acquired or regrouped, on undertakings within its jurisdiction which have engaged in or been party to transactions contrary to the provisions of this Article.

Persons fined under this paragraph may appeal to the Court as provided in Article 36.

7. If the High Authority finds that public or private undertakings which, in law or in fact, hold or acquire in the market for one of the products within its jurisdiction a dominant position shielding them against effective competition in a substantial part of the common market are using that position for purposes contrary to the objectives of this Treaty, it shall make to them such recommendations as may be appropriate to prevent the position from being so used. If these recommendations are not implemented satisfactorily within a reasonable time, the High Authority shall, by decisions taken in consultation with the Government concerned, determine the prices and conditions of sale to be applied by the undertaking in question or draw up production or delivery programmes with which it must comply, subject to liability to the penalties provided for in Articles 58, 59 and 64.

4.b. Decision No. 24-54 of 6 May 1954 Laying Down in Implementation of Article 66 of the Treaty a Regulation on What Constitutes Control of an Undertaking [ECSC]*

THE HIGH AUTHORITY,

Having regard to Article 66 of the Treaty;

Whereas by virtue of Article 66 (1) the High Authority must by regulation determine what constitutes control of an undertaking;

Whereas control may reside either in persons in whom certain rights are vested or in those who are entitled to exercise such rights with complete freedom;

After consulting the Council of Ministers;

DECIDES:

Article 1

The rights or contracts specified below shall constitute the elements of control of an undertaking, where either separately or jointly, and having regard to the considerations of fact or law involved, they make it possible to determine how an undertaking shall operate as regards production, prices, investments, supplies, sales and appropriation of profits:

(1) Ownership or the right to use all or part of the assets of an undertaking;
(2) Rights or contracts which confer power to influence the composition, voting or decisions of the organs of an undertaking;
(3) Rights or contracts which enable any person, by himself or in association with others, to manage the business of an undertaking;
(4) Contracts made with an undertaking concerning the computation or appropriation of its profits;
(5) Contracts made with an undertaking concerning the whole or an important part of its supplies or outlets, where the duration of these contracts or the quantities to which they relate exceed what is usual in commercial contracts dealing with those matters.

Article 2

There shall be no control of an undertaking within the meaning of Article 1 where, upon formation of an undertaking or increase of its capital, banks or financial institutions acquire shares in that undertaking with a view to selling them on the market but do not exercise voting right in respect of those shares.

Article 3

1. The elements specified in Article 1 shall constitute control of an undertaking by individuals, undertakings or groups of persons or of undertakings who:
(1) are holders of the rights or entitled to rights under the contracts concerned;

* O.J.E.C.S.C., 11. 5. 54, p. 345. For the English text, see O.J.E.C., Special Edition, Vol. I, 1952–1958, p. 16 (1972).

(2) while not being holders of such rights or entitled to rights under such contracts, have power to exercise the rights deriving therefrom;

(3) in a fiduciary capacity own assets of an undertaking or shares in an undertaking, and have power to exercise the rights attaching thereto.

2. If, however, the power to exercise the rights of another person is deprived from a legal act, the provisions contained in subparagraphs (2) and (3) of the preceding paragraph shall not apply where the holder of the power proves:

(1) that his power may be revoked at any time; and

(2) that he is bound by special instructions from the donor; and

(3) that he is authorised to communicate to the High Authority, should it so request, the name and address of the donor.

Article 4

This Decision shall enter into force within the Community on 1 June 1954.

This Decision was considered and adopted by the High Authority at its meeting on 6 May 1954.

4.c. Commission Proposal for a Regulation (EEC) of the Council on the Control of Concentrations between Undertakings*

(Submitted to the Council by the Commission on 20 July 1973)

THE COUNCIL OF THE EUROPEAN COMMUNITIES,

Having regard to the Treaty establishing the European Economic Community and in particular to Articles 87 and 235 thereof;

Having regard to the proposal from the Commission;

Having regard to the Opinion of the European Parliament;

Having regard to the Opinion of the Economic and Social Committee;

Whereas, for the achievement of the objectives of the Treaty establishing the European Economic Community, Article 3 (f) requires the Community to institute 'a system ensuring that competition in the common market is not distorted';

Whereas analysis of market structures in the Community shows that the concentration process is becoming faster and that the degree of concentration is growing in such manner that the preservation of effective competition in the common market and the objective set out in Article 3 (f) could be jeopardized;

Whereas concentration must therefore be made subject to a systematic control arrangement;

Whereas the Treaty already provides some powers of action of the Community to this end;

Whereas Article 86 applies to concentrations effected by undertakings holding

* O.J.E.C., Vol. 16, C 92 p. 1 (31. 10. 73).

a dominant position in the common market or in a substantial part of it which strengthen such position to such an extent that the resulting degree of dominance would substantially restrict competition;

Whereas the power of action aforesaid extends only to such concentrations, as would result in only undertakings remaining in the market whose conduct depended on the undertaking which had effected the concentration; whereas it does not extend to the prevention of such concentrations;

Whereas additional powers of action must be provided for to make it possible to act against other concentrations which may distort competition in the common market and to establish arrangements for controlling them before they are effected;

Whereas under Article 235 of the Treaty the Community may give itself the powers of action necessary for the attainment of its objectives;

Whereas, to institute a system ensuring that competition in the common market is not distorted, it is necessary, in so far as trade between Member States may be affected, to submit to control arrangements such concentrations which give undertakings the power to prevent effective competition in the common market or in a substantial part of it, or which strengthen such a power;

Whereas the power to prevent effective competition must be appraised by reference, in particular, to the scope for choice available to suppliers and consumers, the economic and financial power of the undertakings concerned, the structure of the markets affected and supply and demand trends for the relevant goods or services;

Whereas concentrations which, by reason of the small significance of turnover and market share of the undertakings concerned, are not likely to impede the preservation of effective competition in the common market may be excluded from this Regulation;

Whereas it may be found necessary, for the purpose of reconciling objectives to be attained in the common interest of the Community, especially within the frame of common policies, to exempt certain concentrations from incompatibility, under conditions and obligations to be determined case by case;

Whereas the Commission should be entitled to take decisions to prevent or terminate concentrations which are incompatible with the common market, decisions designed to re-establish conditions of effective competition and decisions declaring that a particular concentration may be considered to be compatible with the common market; whereas the Commission should be given exclusive jurisdiction in this matter, subject to review by the Court of Justice;

Whereas, to ensure effective supervision, prior notification of major concentrations and the suspension of concentrations by undertakings should be made obligatory;

Whereas a time limit within which the Commission must commence proceedings in respect of a concentration notified to it and a time-limit within which it must give a final decision on the incompatibility of a concentration with the common market should be laid down;

Whereas undertakings concerned must be accorded the right to be heard by the Commission as soon as proceedings have commenced, and third parties showing a sufficient interest must be given the opportunity of submitting their comments;

Whereas the Commission must have the assistance of the Member States and must also be empowered to require information to be given and to carry out the necessary investigations in order to examine concentrations in the light of provisions of this Regulation;

Whereas compliance with this Regulation must be enforceable by means of fines and periodic penalty payments; whereas it is desirable to confer upon the Court of Justice, pursuant to Article 172, unlimited jurisdiction to that extent;

Whereas this Regulation should extend both to concentrations which constitute abuses of dominant positions and to concentrations which give the undertakings concerned the power to prevent effective competition in the common market; whereas it should therefore be stipulated that Regulations (EEC) Nos 17 and 1017/68 no longer apply to concentrations from the date of entry into force of the present Regulation.

HAS ADOPTED THIS REGULATION:

Basic provisions
Article 1

1. Any transaction which has the direct or indirect effect of bringing about a concentration between undertakings or groups of undertakings, at least one of which is established in the common market, whereby they acquire or enhance the power to hinder effective competition in the common market or in a substancial part thereof, is incompatible with the common market in so far as the concentration may affect trade between Member States.

The power to hinder effective competition shall be appraised by reference in particular to the extent to which suppliers and consumers have a possibility of choice, to the economic and financial power of the undertakings concerned, to the structure of the markets affected, and to supply and demand trends for the relevant goods or services.

2. Paragraph 1 shall not apply where:
– the aggregate turnover of the undertakings participating in the concentration is less than 200 million units of account and
– the goods or services concerned by the concentration do not account in any Member State for more than 25% of the turnover in identical goods or services or in goods or services which, by reason of their characteristics, their price and the use for which they are intended, may be regarded as similar by the consumer.

3. Paragraph 1 may, however, be declared inapplicable to concentrations which are indispensable to the attainment of an objective which is given priority treatment in the common interest of the Community.

Article 2
Definition of concentration

1. The concentrations referred to in Article 1 are those whereby a person or an undertaking or a group of persons or undertakings, acquires control of one or several undertakings.

2. Control is constituted by rights or contracts which, either separately or jointly, and having regard to the considerations of fact or law involved, make it possible to determine how an undertaking shall operate, and particularly by:

(1) Ownership or the right to use all or part of the assets of an undertaking;

(2) Rights or contracts which confer power to influence the composition, voting or decisions of the organs of an undertaking;

(3) Rights or contracts which make it possible to manage the business of an undertaking;

(4) Contracts made with an undertaking concerning the computation or appropriation of its profits;

(5) Contracts made with an undertaking concerning the whole or an important part of supplies or outlets, where the duration of these contracts or the quantities to which they relate exceed what is usual in commercial contracts dealing with those matters.

3. Control is acquired by persons, undertakings or groups of persons or undertakings who:

(1) Are holders of the rights or entitled to rights under the contracts concerned;

(2) While not being holders of such rights or entitled to rights under such contracts, have power to exercise the rights deriving therefrom;

(3) In a fiduciary capacity own assets of an undertaking or shares in an undertaking, and have power to exercise the rights attaching thereto.

4. Control of an undertaking is not constituted where, upon formation of an undertaking or increase of its capital, banks or financial institutions acquire shares in that undertaking with a view to selling them on the market, provided that they do not exercise voting rights in respect of those shares.

Article 3
Powers of decision of the Commission

1. When the Commission finds that a concentration is caught by Article 1 (1) and that the conditions laid down in Article 1 (3) are not satisfied, it shall issue a decision declaring the concentration to be incompatible with the common market.

2. The decision by which the Commission declares a concentration to be incompatible within the meaning of paragraph 1 shall not automatically render null and void the legal transactions relating to such operation.

3. Where a concentration has already been put into effect, the Commission may require, by decision taken under paragraph 1 or by a separate decision, the undertakings, or assets acquired or concentrated to be separated or the cessation of common control or any other action that may be appropriate in order to restore conditions of effective competition.

4. When the Commission finds that a concentration is caught by Article 1 (1) and that the conditions laid down in Article 1 (3) are satisfied, it shall issue a decision declaring Article 1 (1) to be inapplicable; conditions and obligations may be attached thereto.

5. Subject to review by the Court of Justice, the Commission shall have sole power to take the decisions provided for in this Article.

Article 4
Prior notifications of concentrations

1. Concentrations shall be notified to the Commission before they are put into effect, where the aggregate turnover of the undertakings concerned is not less than one thousand million units of account.

2. Where concentrations proposed by an undertaking or a group of undertakings have already reached or exceeded the amounts referred to in paragraph 1, they shall be exempted from the obligation of prior notification, if the turnover of the undertaking, the control of which they propose to acquire is less than 30 million units of account.

3. The obligation to notify shall be discharged by the person or undertaking or the group of persons or undertakings which proposes to acquire control within the meaning of Article 2.

4. Concentrations which are not caught by paragraph 1 may nevertheless be notified to the Commission before they are put into effect.

Article 5
Detailed rules for calculating turnover and market shares

1. (a) The aggregate turnover specified in Articles 1 (2) and 4 (1) shall be obtained by adding together the turnover for the last financial year for all goods and services of:
   (i)   the undertakings participating in the concentration;
   (ii) the undertakings and groups of undertakings which control the undertakings participating in the concentration within the meaning of Article 2;
   (iii) the undertakings or groups of undertakings controlled within the meaning of Article 2 by the undertakings participating in the concentration.
   (b) The market shares referred to in Article 1 (2) near those held in the last financial year by all the undertakings listed in subparagraph (a) above.

2. In place of turnover as specified in Articles 1 (2) and 4 (1) and in paragraph 1 of this Article, the following shall be used:
– for banking and financial institutions: one tenth of their assets;
– for insurance companies: the value of the premiums received by them.

Article 6
Commencement of proceedings

1. Where the Commission considers that a concentration is likely to become the subject of a decision under Article 1 (1) or (3), it shall commence proceedings and so inform the undertakings in question and the competent authorities in the Member States.

2. As regards concentrations notified to it, the Commission shall commence proceedings within a period not exceeding 3 months unless the relevant undertakings agree to extend that period. The period of 3 months shall commence on the day following receipt of the notification, or if the information to be supplied with the notification is incomplete, on the day following the receipt of the complete information.

3. The Commission may commence proceedings after the expiry of the 3 months period where the information supplied by the undertakings in the notification is false or misleading.

4. Without prejudice to paragraph 3 a concentration notified to the Commission shall be presumed to be compatible with the common market if the Commission does not commence proceedings before expiration of the period specified in paragraph 2.

Article 7
Suspension of the effecting of the concentration

1. Undertakings shall not put into effect a concentration notified to the Commission before the end of the time limit provided for in Article 6 (2) unless the Commission informs them before the end of the time limit that it is not necessary to commence proceedings.

2. Where the Commission commences proceedings it may by decision require the undertakings to suspend the concentration until it has decided whether the concentration is compatible with the common market or has closed the proceedings.

Article 8
Communications of objections and hearings

1. Before taking decisions as provided for in Articles 3, 7, 13 and 14, the Commission shall give the undertakings concerned the opportunity of being heard on the matters to which the Commission has taken objection. The same opportunity shall be given to associations of undertakings concerned before decisions before being taken as provided for in Articles 13 and 14.

2. If the Commission or the competent authorities of the Member States consider it necessary, the Commission may also hear other natural or legal persons. Applications to be heard on the part of such persons shall, where they show a sufficient interest, be granted.

3. Articles 2, 3, 4, 7, 8, 9, 10 and 11 of Regulation No 99/63/EEC shall be applied.

Article 9
Closure of proceedings

If, after having commenced proceedings, the Commission considers that there are no grounds for action against a concentration, it shall close the proceedings and so inform the undertakings concerned and the competent authorities of the Member States.

Article 10
Requests for information

1. In carrying out the duties assigned to it by this Regulation, the Commission may obtain all necessary information from the governments and competent authorities of the Member States and from undertakings and associations of undertakings.

2. When sending a request for information to an undertaking or association of undertakings, the Commission shall at the same time forward a copy of the

request to the competent authority of the Member State in whose territory the seat of the undertaking or association of undertakings is situated.

3. In its request the Commission shall state the legal basis and the purpose of the request and also the penalties provided for in Article 13 (1) (b) for supplying incorrect information.

4. The owners of the undertakings or their representatives and, in the case of legal persons, companies or firms, or of associations having no legal personality, the persons authorized to represent them by law or by their constitution, shall supply the information requested.

5. Where an undertaking or association of undertakings does not supply the information requested within the time limit fixed by the Commission, or supplies incomplete information, the Commission shall by decision require the information to be supplied. The decision shall specify what information is required, fix an appropriate time limit within which it is to be supplied and mention the penalties provided for in Article 13 (1) (b) and Article 14 (1) (a) and the right to have the decision reviewed by the Court of Justice.

6. The Commission shall at the same time forward a copy of its decision to the competent authority of the Member State in whose territory the seat of the undertaking or association of undertakings is situated.

Article 11
Investigations by the authorities of the Member States

1. At the request of the Commission, the competent authorities of the Member States shall undertake the investigations which the Commission considers to be necessary under Article 12 (1), or which it has ordered by decision pursuant to Article 12 (3). The officials of the competent authorities of the Member States responsible for conducting these investigations shall exercise their powers upon production of an authorization in writing issued by the competent authority of the Member Sate in whose territory the investigation is to be made. Such authorization shall specify the subject matter and purpose of the investigation.

2. If so requested by the Commission or by the competent authority of the Member State in whose territory the investigation is to be made, officials of the Commission may assist the officials of such authority in carrying out their duties.

Article 12
Investigating powers of the Commission

1. In carrying out the duties assigned to it by this Regulation, the Commission may undertake all necessary investigations into undertakings and associations of undertakings.

To this end the officials authorized by the Commission are empowered:
(a) to examine the books and other business records;
(b) to take or demand copies of or extracts from the books and business records;
(c) to ask for oral explanations on the spot;
(d) to enter any premises, land and means of transport of undertakings.

2. The officials of the Commission authorized to carry out these investigations

shall exercise their powers upon production of an authorization in writing specifying the subject matter and purpose of the investigation and the penalties provided for in Article 13 (1) (c) in cases where production of the required books or other business records is incomplete. In good time before the investigation, the Commission shall inform the competent authority of the Member State in whose territory the investigation is to be made of the investigation and of the identity of the authorized officials.

3. Undertakings and associations of undertakings shall submit to investigations ordered by decision of the Commission. The decision shall specify the subject matter and purpose of the investigation, appoint the date on which it is to begin and indicate the penalties provided for in Article 13 (1) (c) and Article 14 (1) (b) and the right to have the decision reviewed by the Court of Justice.

4. The Commission shall take decisions referred to in paragraph 3 after consultation with the competent authority of the Member State in whose territory the investigation is to be made.

5. Officials of the competent authority of the Member State in whose territory the investigation is to be made may, at the request of such authority or of the Commission, assist the officials of the Commission in carrying out their duties.

6. Where an undertaking opposes an investigation ordered pursuant to this Article, the Member State concerned shall afford the necessary assistance to the officials authorized by the Commission to enable them to make their investigation. Member States shall, after consultation with the Commission, take the necessary measures to this end before . . .

Article 13
Fines

1. The Commission may by decision impose on undertakings and associations of undertakings fines of from 1 000 to 50 000 units of account where intentionally or negligently:
(a) they supply incorrect or misleading information in a notification pursuant to Article 4
(b) they supply incorrect information in response to a request made pursuant to Article 10 or fail to supply information within the time limit fixed by a decision taken pursuant to Article 10,
(c) they produce the required books or other business records in incomplete form during investigations under Article 11 or 12, or refuse to submit to an investigation ordered by decision taken pursuant to Article 12.

2. The Commission may by decision impose on natural or legal persons fines of from 1 000 to 1 000 000 units of account where, either intentionally or negligently, they commit a breach of the obligation to notify under Article 4.

3. The Commission may by decision impose fines not exceeding 10% of the value of the reorganized assets where undertakings either intentionally or negligently, conclude an unlawful concentration before the end of the time limit provided for in Article 6 (2) or in spite of a decision taken by the Commission under Articles 3 (1) or 7 (2).

Article 14
Periodic penalty payments

1. The Commission may by decision impose on undertakings or associations of undertakings periodic penalty payments up to 25 000 units of account for each day of the delay calculated from the date appointed by the decision, in order to compel them:

(a) to supply complete and correct information which it has requested by decision taken pursuant to Article 10;

(b) to submit to an investigation which it has ordered by decision taken pursuant to Article 12.

2. The Commission may by decision impose on such undertakings periodic penalty payments up to 50 000 units of account for each day of the delay, calculated from the day appointed by the decision, in order to compel them to apply the measures resulting from a decision taken pursuant to Article 3 (3).

Article 15
Review by the Court of Justice

The Court of Justice shall have unlimited jurisdiction within the meaning of Article 17 of the Treaty to review decisions whereby the Commission has fixed a fine or periodic penalty payment; it may cancel, reduce or increase the fine or periodic penalty payment imposed.

Article 16
Professional secrecy

1. Information acquired as a result of the application of Articles 10, 11 and 12 shall be used only for the purpose of the relevant request or investigation.

2. The Commission and the competent authorities of the Member States, their officials and other servants shall not disclose information acquired by them as a result of the application of this Regulation and of the kind covered by the obligation of professional secrecy.

3. The provisions of paragraphs 1 and 2 shall not prevent publication of general information or surveys which do not contain information relating to particular undertakings or associations of undertakings.

Article 17
Time limits and publication of decisions

1. (a) Decisions under Article 3 (1) and (4) shall be taken within 9 months following the date of commencement of proceedings, save where there is agreement with the relevant undertakings to extend that period.

(b) The period of 9 months shall not apply where the Commission is obliged to request information by decision taken pursuant to Article 10 or require an investigation by decision taken pursuant to Article 12.

2. The Commission shall publish the decisions which it takes pursuant to Article 3.

3. The publication shall state the names of the parties and the main content of the decision; it shall have regard to the legitimate interest of undertakings in the protection of their business secrets.

Article 18
Unit of account

For the purpose of this Regulation the unit of account shall be that used in drawing up the budget of the Community in accordance with Articles 207 and 209 of the Treaty.

Article 19
Liaison with the authorities of the Member States

1. The Commission shall forthwith transmit to the competent authorities of the Member States a copy of the notifications together with the most important documents lodged with the Commission pursuant to this Regulation.

2. The Commission shall carry out the procedure set out in this Regulation in close and constant cooperation with the competent authorities of the Member States; such authorities shall have the right to express their views upon that procedure, and in particular to request the Commission to commence proceedings under Article 6.

3. The Advisory Committee on Restrictive Practices and Monopolies shall be consulted prior to the taking of any decision under Articles 3, 13 and 14.

4. The Advisory Committee shall consist of officials having responsibility for restrictive practices and monopolies. Each Member State shall appoint an official to represent it; he may be replaced by another official where he is unable to act.

5. Consultation shall take place, at a meeting convened at the invitation of the Commission, not earlier than fourteen days following dispatch of the invitation. A summary of the facts together with the most important documents and a preliminary draft of the decision to be taken, shall be sent with the invitation.

6. The Committee may deliver an opinion even if certain members are absent and unrepresented. The outcome of the consultation shall be annexed to the draft decision. The minutes shall not be published.

Article 20
Exclusive application of this Regulation

Regulations (EEC) No 17 and 1017/68 shall not apply to the concentrations covered by this Regulation.

Article 21
Implementing provisions

The Commission shall have power to adopt implementing provisions concerning the form, content and other details of notifications pursuant to Article 4 of this Regulation.

Article 22

This Regulation shall enter into force . . .

This Regulation shall be binding in its entirety and directly applicable in all Member States.

List of Abbreviations

AG	Aktiengesellschaft, Die Aktiengesellschaft
Ass. Nat.	Assemblée Nationale
art.	article(s)
BALO	Bulletin des annonces légales obligatoires
BAnz	Bundesanzeiger
BB	Betriebs-Berater
Bbl	Bundesblatt der Schweizerischen Eidgenossenschaft
Betrieb	Der Betrieb
BGE	Entscheidungen des schweizerischen Bundesgerichts, Amtliche Sammlung
BGH	Bundesgerichtshof
BGHZ	Entscheidungen des Bundesgerichtshofes in Zivilsachen
BKartA	Bundeskartellamt
BODAC	Bulletin officiel des annonces civiles et commerciales
B.O.S.P.	Bulletin officiel des services des prix
BR-DrS	Bundesrats-Drucksache
BT-DrS	Bundestags-Drucksache
Bull.	Bulletin
BWM	Bundeswirtschaftsministerium
C.C.C.	Commission de la concurrence et de la concentration
cf.	confer
C.G.I.	Code général des impôts
Cmd, Cmnd	Command Paper (U.K.)
C.M.L.R.	Common Market Law Reports
C. rur.	Code rural
C.T.E.	Commission technique des ententes
C.U.P.	Cambridge University Press
D.	recueil Dalloz
DAC	Development Assistance Committee (OECD)
DB	Der Betrieb
Décr.	décret
Diss.	Dissertation (thesis)
DM	Deutsche Mark
D.S.	Dalloz Sirey
E	Entwurf der Schweizerischen Kartellkommission (als Expertenkommission) vom 25. September 1978 zu einem Bundesgesetz über Kartelle und ähnliche Organisationen samt Erläuterungen vom November 1978
EC	European Communities

ECR	European Court Reports (official reports of the Court of Justice of the EC)
ECSC	European Coal and Steel Community (Treaty)
ed., eds.	editor(s); edition
EEC	European Economic Community (Treaty)
e.g.	for example
esp.	especially
et seq.	following
FAZ	Frankfurter Allgemeine Zeitung
FIW	Forschungsinstitut für Wirtschaftsverfassung und Wettbewerb
Gaz. Pal.	Gazette du Palais
gnp	gross national product
GWB	Gesetz gegen Wettbewerbsbeschränkungen
H.C.P.	House of Commons Papers
INSEE	Institut National de la Statistique et des Etudes Economiques
J.C.P.	Jurisclasseur Périodique
J.C.P.-C.I.	Jurisclasseur Periodique (édition commerce et industrie)
J.O.	Journal officiel
J.O. Déb. Ass. Nat.	Journal officiel des débats de l'Assemblée Nationale
J.O. Déb. Sén.	Journal officiel des débats du Sénat
Kart	Kartellsachen (Aktenzeichen)
Kfz	Kraftfahrzeug
MNE	multinational enterprise
mod.	modified
n.	note
NIC	newly industrialising developing country
NJW	Neue Juristische Wochenschrift
No.	number
NZZ	Neue Zürcher Zeitung
OECD	Organization for Economic Co-operation and Development
O.J. (E.C.)	Official Journal (of the European Communities)
O.J.E.C. C	Official Journal of the E.C., C series
O.J.E.C. L	Official Journal of the E.C., L series
OLG	Oberlandesgericht
Ord.	ordonnance
p., pp.	page(s)
para., paras.,	paragraph(s)

RabelsZ	Rabels Zeitschrift für ausländisches und internationales Privatrecht
R.C.S.	Registre du commerce et des sociétés
Rev. trim. dr. com.	Revue trimestrielle de droit commercial et de droit économique
Rev. tr. dr. eur.	Revue trimestrielle de droit européen
RIW/AWD	Recht der Internationalen Wirtschaft/Außenwirtschaftsdienst des Betriebs-Beraters
Rz	Randziffer
S., sec., secs.	Section(s)
SIRENE-SIRET	Système informatique pour le répertoire des entreprises et des établissements
SJZ	Schweizerische Juristen-Zeitung
SR	Systematische Sammlung des Bundesrechts
SZVS	Schweizerische Zeitschrift für Volkswirtschaft und Statistik
TNC	transnational corporation
TZ	Textziffer
VSKk	Veröffentlichungen der Schweizerischen Kartellkommission
WuR	Wirtschaft und Recht
WuW	Wirtschaft und Wettbewerb
WuW/E	Wirtschaft und Wettbewerb/Entscheidungssammlung zum Kartellrecht
ZBJV	Zeitschrift des Bernischen Juristenvereins
ZGR	Zeitschrift für Unternehmens- und Gesellschaftsrecht
ZgS	Zeitschrift für die gesamte Staatswissenschaft
ZHR	Zeitschrift für das gesamte Handelsrecht und Wirtschaftsrecht
ZSR	Zeitschrift für Schweizerisches Recht

Table of Cases and Enterprises

II. Federal Republic of Germany

V. USA

Index

(Numbers refer to pages, numbers in italics refer to Annex II with the text of relevant legal provisions)